T0298468

# China in the World Economy

As the Chinese economy continues to steam ahead, its consequences for China's society and environment become more visible, and its impact on the world becomes ever more important. Reforms are being undertaken in many areas within China, both to encourage continued economic growth and also to mitigate the adverse effects of growth on society and the environment. This book, based on extensive original research by a wide range of leading experts, examines many key issues connected to China's economic growth and its impact. Subjects covered amongst many others include: structural changes and the transition process; growth and inequality; labour market reforms; employment, unemployment and training; openness and productivity; technological innovations and their impact; and the search for economic development that is ecologically sustainable.

**Zhongmin Wu** is Reader in Economics, Nottingham Business School, Nottingham Trent University. He served as President of the Chinese Economic Association in the UK during 2007–2008. Zhongmin received his PhD in Economics from the University of Southampton. Recent work has appeared in *Regional Studies, Annals of Operations Research, Economics of Planning, Applied Economics*, and *China Economic Review.*

# Routledge Studies on the Chinese Economy

**Series Editor**
Peter Nolan, *University of Cambridge*
**Founding Series Editors**
Peter Nolan, *University of Cambridge* and
Dong Fureng, *Beijing University*

The aim of this series is to publish original, high-quality, research-level work by both new and established scholars in the West and the East, on all aspects of the Chinese economy, including studies of business and economic history.

# China in the World Economy

## Edited by Zhongmin Wu

**Zhongmin Wu** is Reader in Economics, Nottingham Business School,
Nottingham Trent University. He served as President of the Chinese
Economic Association in the UK during 2007–2008. Zhongmin received his
PhD in Economics from the University of Southampton. Recent work has
appeared in *Regional Studies*, *Annals of Operations Research*, *Economics of
Planning*, *Applied Economics*, and *China Economic Review*.

Routledge
Taylor & Francis Group

LONDON AND NEW YORK

First published 2009
by Routledge
2 Park Square, Milton Park, Abingdon, Oxon OX14 4RN

Simultaneously published in the USA and Canada
by Routledge
270 Madison Avenue, New York, NY 10016

*Routledge is an imprint of the Taylor & Francis Group,
an informa business*

© 2009 Zhongmin Wu for selection and editorial matter; the
contributors for individual chapters

Typeset in Times New Roman by
RefineCatch Limited, Bungay, Suffolk

*British Library Cataloguing in Publication Data*
A catalogue record for this book is available from the British Library

*Library of Congress Cataloging in Publication Data*
A catalog record for this book has been requested

ISBN10: 0–415–47002–1 (hbk)
ISBN10: 0–203–87120–0 (ebk)

ISBN13: 978–0–415–47002–5 (hbk)
ISBN13: 978–0–203–87120–1 (ebk)

# Contents

**15  Efficient and equitable compensation for agricultural land
conversion: theory and an application for China**                  296
XIUQING ZOU AND ARIE J. OSKAM

# Figures

# Tables

# Contributors

**Alberto Bagnai** is Associated Professor of Economic Policy, Faculty of Economics, University Gabriele D'Annunzio, Chieti (Italy), and Faculty of Law, University Leonardo Da Vinci, Torrevecchia Teatina (Italy). His research has focused on current account sustainability, especially in China and the US, the twin deficits phenomenon, international capital mobility and export-led growth models. He has a general interest in applied international macroeconomics and macroeconomic modelling, with special attention paid to the issue of structural breaks in economic relations. His work uses mainly time series econometrics, and in particular cointegration methods. Recent work has appeared in *Economic Modelling, International Economics and Economic Policy, Open Economies Review, Applied Economics* and *China Economic Review*.

**Benu Bidani** is Lead Economist at the World Bank, where she is currently part of the Poverty Reduction and Economic Management Network. Her main research interests are within the areas of poverty and inequality. She holds a BA (with Honours) in Economics from the University of Delhi and an MA and PhD in Economics from Vanderbilt University. Her research papers have appeared in the *Journal of Econometrics, World Bank Economic Review* and *Bulletin of Indonesian Economic Studies*.

**Niels-Hugo Blunch** is Assistant Professor of Economics at Washington and Lee University and Research Fellow at IZA (Institute for the Study of Labour). His main research and teaching interests are within the areas of labour and population economics, economics of education, health economics, development economics and applied econometrics. He holds a BA and an MA degree in Economics from the University of Aarhus, an MSc in Economics and Econometrics from the University of Southampton and a PhD in Economics from the George Washington University. His published research has appeared in *World Bank Economic Review, International Labour Review, International Journal of Training and Development, Economic Change and Restructuring* and *African Development Review*.

**Teng Ge** is a research student in the Department of Economics, University of

Essex. He is primarily concerned with applied and theoretical micro-economics, with particular interest in the labour market. Current research focuses on how job agencies, geographic frictions, leisure preferences and wage determination affect the worker–firm matching process. Other areas of interest include the causes, volatility and consequences of equilibrium unemployment; the effects of labour taxation on migration; and equilibrium business cycles theory.

**Chor-ching Goh** is Senior Economist at the World Bank. Currently, she is part of the World Development Report 2009 team. She joined the World Bank as a Young Professional in 1999, working on health, nutrition and education issues in the Independent Evaluation Group. During 2001–07, her work programme in the East Asian region covered poverty, inequality, the labour market and social sector issues. She holds simultaneous BA and MA degrees, summa cum laude, from Yale University, and a PhD in Economics from Harvard University.

**Jiannan Guo** is Associate Professor of Economics at the Research Institute of Economics and Management, South-western University of Finance and Economics (*Xi Nan Cai Da*), China. He completed his undergraduate and Masters education at Peking University, and received a PhD in Economics from the University of Warwick. His research has mainly focused on Development and Industrial Economics, and its applications to the Chinese economy. In 2007, he received the Best PhD Paper Award at the CEA (UK) 18th Annual Conference in Nottingham.

**Maria Jesús Herrerrías** is PhD Student in Economics at the University Jaume I of Castellon (Spain). She has participated in international and national conferences such as CEA (UK) in Nottingham, CCES in Shanghai, CERDI in France and Jornadas de Economía Internacional in Spain in 2007. She published monthly reports on South America in OCEI during 2004–05. Currently, she is working on the Chinese Economy Development Process for her thesis. Her work uses mainly time series econometric analysis such as co-integrated VAR models.

**John Kidd**, Aston Business School, Birmingham, UK. John Kidd's research lies in the overlap of technological and human factors in information and communication systems, especially those that have a global reach. These factors are seen to interact in his studies of knowledge management and organizational learning in strategic alliances of multinational firms, and their supply chains – where there are many cultural influences at work. He has authored many papers for journals, and has written book chapters across several management disciplines. His recent books include *Fighting Corruption in Asia: Causes, Effects and Remedies* (World Scientific Press, 2003), *Trust and Antitrust in Asian Business Alliances* (Palgrave, 2004), *Infrastructure and Productivity in Asia* (Palgrave, 2005) and *Development Models, Globalisation and Economics* (Palgrave, 2006).

**Genia Kostka** is DPhil Candidate in the Department of International Development, the University of Oxford. Her doctoral thesis examines the role of local governments in private sector development in Anhui Province, China. Her research interests mainly concern economic development in China, local governments, regional inequality, and a comparison of the development experience of China and Africa. From January to June 2007, she was a Visiting Fellow at the Chinese Academy of Social Sciences (CASS) in Beijing.

**Jun Li** is Senior Lecturer in Entrepreneurship and Innovation at the School of Entrepreneurship and Business, University of Essex, UK. He previously held posts at the University of Bedfordshire Business School, Birmingham City University Business School, the Chinese Academy of Sciences, and is currently a Visiting Professor at Zhejiang University and Zhongnan University of Economics and Law in China. He teaches and researches in the areas of entrepreneurship and policies, innovation management and Chinese entrepreneurship. His recent publications include *Financing China's Rural Enterprises* (RoutledgeCurzon, 2002), and an edited special issue in entrepreneurship and small business development in China for the *Journal of Small Business and Enterprise Development* (2006).

**Aaron Mehrotra** is an Economist at the Bank of Finland's Institute for Economies in Transition (BOFIT). At BOFIT, his research focuses on the Chinese economy and economic policy, and monetary policy in transition economies. His work has appeared in the *Journal of Comparative Economics & Fiscal Studies*. He holds a PhD in Economics from the European University Institute, Florence, Italy.

**Guangjie Ning** is Associate Professor in Economics, Nankai University, China. He obtained his PhD degree in economics from Nankai University in 1999. He also studied in Ritsumeikan University, Japan (2002) and Regina University, Canada (2006). His research has focused on labour economics and political economy. His current research topics include technological change and employment, wage mechanism, education expansion and income inequality in China. His work uses mainly econometric analysis. Recent published books in Chinese include *Unemployment: A Micro Analysis Framework* (Shaanxi Renmin Press, 2004) and *Labour Economics* (Economy and Management Publishing House, 2007).

**Christopher O'Leary** is Senior Economist at the W. E. Upjohn Institute for Employment Research. His research has focused on the design and evaluation of public employment programmes. He has initiated field experiments, targeting models and decision support systems for employment ministries in North America and Europe. For the US Department of Health and Human Services, he is currently studying the role of unemployment insurance as a safety net for recent leavers from cash social assistance. His research papers have appeared in the *Journal of Human*

*Resources, Journal of Policy Analysis and Management, International Labour Review* and *Economics of Transition.*

**Vicente Orts** is Professor in Economics, Department of Economics and Institute of International Economics in the University Jaume I of Castellon (Spain). His research has focused on the determinants of international trade flows, and the relationship between foreign direct investment and trade, openness and growth and economic development. Recent work has appeared in the *Review of World Economics, Economics Letters, Open Economies Review, Journal of Development Studies, Journal of International Development, Review of Development Economics, Scandinavian Journal of Economics* and *Southern Economic Journal.*

**Arie J. Oskam** is Professor and Head of Agricultural Economics and Rural Policy Group, Wageningen University, the Netherlands. He is a fellow and board member of the Netherlands Network of Economics. His research is oriented on agricultural and food economics and policy, rural economics and policy and environmental and resource economics in relation to agriculture and rural areas. He has edited or authored 12 books and published circa 50 articles in refereed scientific journals and given circa 150 presentations on the basis of written papers.

**Christian A. Mongeau Ospina** is a PhD student in economics, University of Rome 'La Sapienza'. He graduated in economics with a thesis focused on the rise of the Chinese economy in the international scenario and its impact on world growth. His current research interests include development economics, macroeconomic modelling, time series analysis and structural changes.

**Gopal Krishna Pal** is Reader in Economics at P. N. Das College, India. He has presented papers at many national and international conferences and seminars on development economics and was also invited to present his papers on the Chinese economy in Ireland, France and Sweden. He is the Joint Secretary of the Bengal Economic Association, India and member of the Indian Economic Association. His areas of interest are the Chinese economy, political economy, regional economics and development economics. He has published many articles in journals and has also published book on regional economics.

**Xuebing Peng** is Associate Professor in Management, Zhejiang University of Science and Technology. He is currently a doctoral candidate at Zhejiang University. His research focuses on entrepreneurship and innovation, especially on technological entrepreneurship and technology innovation in China. He also has a research interest in governance structure and its selection. His recent work (in Chinese) has appeared in *Studies of Science, Science Research Management, Science and Technology Process and Policy* and *Jiangsu Commercial Forum.*

**Riliang Qu** (PhD) is Lecturer in Marketing at Aston Business School, UK. His research area covers strategic marketing of MNCs and marketing in emerging markets. Recent research contributions include articles in the *Journal of Public Policy and Marketing, Journal of Strategic Marketing* and *Tourism Management*.

**Jouko Rautava** is an Economist at the Bank of Finland's Institute for Economies in Transition (BOFIT). At BOFIT, he has focused on Russia and China's economies and economic policies. His latest work includes a paper on modelling the role of oil prices in Russia's economy (*Journal of Comparative Economics*, 2004) and an article on the significance of the Chinese and Indian economies in the world economy (in Leena Mary Eapen, *Economic Growth in India and China*, 2006).

**Marielle Stumm** is a senior researcher at INRETS, Arcueil, France. Her main focus is on electronic communication and logistics; generally, on the economic impact of advanced systems for freight transport, and, more specifically, on new information systems and telecommunications, which constitute strategic tools in the intermodal transport sector. All studies are grounded within the corporate governance of international organizations. Basically, her activities focus on two directions: (a) integrated advanced logistic systems, and (b) network technology. Having participated in several European Union projects she is also a visiting professor at the Ecole Nationale des Ponts et Chaussées (ENPC), and at the Université de Versailles-Saint Quentin en Yveline. She has published widely in journals and presented at seminars.

**Zhongmin Wu** is Reader in Economics, Nottingham Business School, Nottingham Trent University. He is the President of the Chinese Economic Association in the UK (2007–08). Zhongmin organized the CEA (UK) 18th Annual Conference in Nottingham (April 2007) and co-organized the CEA (UK) and CCES joint international conferences in Shanghai (September 2007). He won the Best Paper Award of the Chinese Economic Association in the UK (2003 and 2002). Zhongmin received his PhD in Economics from the University of Southampton. His research has focused on employment, unemployment and migration, both in the UK and in China. He has a general interest in labour economics, and the Chinese economy and its labour market. His work uses mainly econometric analysis of panel data. Recent work has appeared in *Regional Studies, Annals of Operations Research, Economics of Planning, Applied Economics* and *China Economic Review*.

**Gang Zhang** is Professor in Business Administration, School of Management, Zhejiang University in China. His research has focused on knowledge management, organization theory, innovation and entrepreneurship. He has received grants from the National Nature Science Foundation of China and the National Social Science Foundation of China. His general interest is in organization and knowledge, with specific regard to the organization as an allocating mechanism of knowledge. He has published three books and more than 20 papers on this topic.

**Ru Zhang** is a graduate student in Economics, Nanjing University, China. She presented papers at the 6th, 7th and 8th China Economic Annual Conferences in Wuhan (December 2006), Shenzhen (December 2007) and Chongqing (November 2008), the 1st China Statistics Annual Conference in Tianjin (October 2006), the All China Economics International Conference in Hong Kong (December 2007) and the 4th Asia-Pacific Economic Association International Conference in Beijing (December 2008). Her research interest is economic growth, development and inequity, and open economy macroeconomics. Recent work has appeared in the *Journal of Data Analysis, World Economic Papers* and *Nanjing Social Science*.

**Xiuqing Zou** is Associate Professor in Economics, Jiangxi University of Finance and Economics, Nanchang, China. He is the project leader of farmers' land property rights in China (2005–08), sponsored by the National Social Science Foundation of China. His research has focused on land property rights arrangements in China. He has a general interest in agricultural economics and land economics. Recent work has appeared in *China & World Economy*.

# Introduction

## China in the world economy: an overview

*Zhongmin Wu*

The phenomenal rise of the Chinese economy has generated both admiration and envy. The awakening of this sleeping dragon has created a huge amount of interest in the western press. Books on China and its impact on the world are flying off the shelves of major bookshops. These are generally written by authors with no academic background and authority to speak of. *China in the World Economy* will provide the interested reader with analysis and views from the most senior academics on this topic. It will dispel myths and fear mongering about the Chinese economy. The enormous success of the 18th annual CEA conference gave the editor a vast amount of high quality papers from the most respected academics to choose from in forming this book. As a result, unlike other reference books on China, *China in the World Economy* has a clear focus, with each theme having its own part. The papers are picked from the best and most up-to-date work from the leading scholars. This will give the interested reader who may not be familiar with the academic work on China an instant insight into the views of the most respected academics.

This book is intended to introduce researchers and practitioners who are interested in the development of the Chinese economy to the most resent research results and update the general public about the economic issues and problems faced by China. We have selected 15 papers from 145 submissions to the 18th CEA annual conference. The volume editor and two independent referees have reviewed each of the 15 papers selected here. We are grateful for the help of the following scholars who reviewed manuscripts for this book, including Alberto Bagnai, María Jesús Herrerías, Richard Schiere, Shanshan Wu, Aaron Mehrotra, Matthieu Llorca, John Kidd, Jing Zhang, Gopap Krishna Pal, Yu Song, Niels-Hugo Blunch, Ge Teng, Guangjie Ning, Kelly Labar, Ziping Wu, Genia Kostka, Jiannan Guo, Xiuqing Zou, Yundan Gong, Huan Zou and Maggie Maurer-Fazio. Thanks also go to Xiaming Liu, Shujie Yao, Terry Clague, Stephanie Rogers, Tom Bates, Peter Sowden and Dongxu Wu for their help.

## Part I: Three decades of economic growth

In Chapter 1, Bagnai and Mongeau Ospina present a medium-size structural macroeconometric model of the Chinese economy, consisting of 59 equations estimated with annual data from 1978 to 2006. The estimation methodology accounts for structural breaks of unknown date in the long-run parameters, thus allowing them to include a large span of data, encompassing the different stages of the reform process, in the estimation sample. The resulting equations display good statistical properties and the parameter estimates are in line with their theoretical values. The structural breaks detected by the econometric procedure are related to known major turning points in the transition process. The simulation experiments confirm the crucial role that foreign direct investment plays in the economic growth and competitiveness of China and shed some light on the issue of reducing the Chinese external imbalance.

In Chapter 2, Mehrotra and Rautava evaluate the usefulness of business sentiment indicators for forecasting developments in the Chinese economy. They use data on diffusion indices collected by the People's Bank of China for forecasting industrial production, retail sales and exports. Their bivariate vector autoregressive models, each composed of one diffusion index and one real sector variable, generally outperform univariate AR models in forecasting one to four quarters ahead. Similarly, principal components analysis, combining information from various diffusion indices, leads to enhanced forecasting performance. Their results indicate that Chinese business sentiment indicators convey useful information about current and future developments in the real economy. They also suggest that the official data provide a fairly accurate picture of the Chinese economy.

China has seen exceptional growth in many of its sectors over the last few decades – and this growth is forecasted to continue. However a barrier to progress exists, namely, the lack of mobility of resources from their place of origin to where they are needed in China. To support its huge logistic needs, China has embarked upon extensive development of its ports, rail system and roads. But it is expected that it will fall short of its needs. In Chapter 3, Kidd and Stumm suggest that installing the Maglev transportation systems will go a long way to filling the logistics gap. Maglev systems are cheaper to install and operate than high-speed passenger trains such as the TGV and can carry freight as well as passengers on the same tracks at very high speeds. Therefore, we propose that Maglev be installed on the Eurasian Landbridge route (the New Silk Road) and all other major national rail links, even reaching the newly proposed Russia/Alaska link across the Bering Straits. In addition, we propose that China consults with its neighbours in Russia, Central Asia and the South East Asian states to install Maglev as one coherent fast transportation system. This infrastructure development will act as the bedrock for regional growth and harmony into the future. And it will guarantee that China remains in the forefront of global manufacturing for decades.

In Chapter 4, Ru Zhang uses the empirical analysis of the economic growth disparity in China from 1978 to 2005 to test the hypothesis of convergence in economic growth theory in the regional growth of China. Multiple statistical techniques are applied to analyse some of the stylized facts about regional growth disparity in China over the last 27 years. Then the chapter introduces a model within a framework of human capital and technology development. Panel data of 31 regions of China during the 27 years is applied to verify the conditional convergence in regional economic growth, and some characteristic factors that determine the growth disparity are specified and empirically tested. In conclusion, absolute convergence does not exist in regional growth in China during the time period. Nevertheless, after controlling the investment rate, investment efficiency, human capital and the level of technology, economies that have a higher level of initial output per labour may undergo a lower growth rate, that is, the rate of conditional convergence is approximately 1.4 per cent per year. This rate is a little slower than that in the western industrial countries.

In Chapter 5, Pal attempts to examine how far pre- and post-reform China was successful in achieving the goals of income equality and removal of poverty while gaining economic growth. Eradicating inequality traps and opportunity gaps are the main objectives of economic development of many developing countries at present. In reality, it is hard to find any definite relation between growth and inequality, growth and poverty, and inequality and poverty. For rapid economic development, some countries emphasized growth, while others tried to achieve development by emphasizing socio-economic equality and removal of poverty. China adopted two types of development strategy post-1949. Before reform, it tried to achieve economic equality and social sector development by 'pro-poor' development strategies. During the reform period, a 'growth-orientated' strategy was adopted. The problems with China's development policies are that, before reform, growth was hampered, while, during the reform period, economic inequality increased. China has at present high inequality but low poverty, while India has more poverty and low inequality. The reasons for such opposite features are examined and possible measures to address them are also suggested in this study.

## Part II: Labour market reform

Using the manufacturing industry's data from 1998 to 2004 in transitional China, in Chapter 6 Ning empirically analyses the impact of technology adoption on employment quantity and employment skill structure at the industry level. The econometric results indicate that, basically, technology adoption has a positive impact on employment quantity, and demands the improvement of the employees' skill structure. However, different types of technology create different impacts; contrary to the prediction of traditional theory, the impacts of process innovation on both the employment quantity

and the employment skill structure are positive, whereas the impacts of product innovation are virtually negative or insignificant. The performance of
technology in different ownership enterprises also varies. The coefficient of
technology's impact on employment quantity in state-owned enterprises is
the lowest or is insignificant. Regarding the coefficient of technology's impact
on employment skill structure, that of foreign enterprises is the lowest or
insignificant.

Recent years have seen a surge in the evidence on the impacts of active
labour market programmes for numerous countries. However, little evidence
has been presented on the effectiveness of such programmes in China. Recent
economic reforms associated with massive lay-offs, and accompanying public
retraining programmes make China fertile ground for rigorous impact evaluations. In Chapter 7, Bidani, Blunch, Goh and O'Leary evaluate retraining
programmes for laid-off workers in the cities of Shenyang and Wuhan, using
a comparison group design. The evidence suggests that retraining helped
workers find jobs in Wuhan, but had little effect in Shenyang. The study raises
questions about the overall effectiveness of retraining expenditures, and it
offers some directions for policy-makers about future interventions to help
laid-off workers.

In Chapter 8, Ge adds flows in and out of the labour market to the benchmark searching and matching model of Mortensen and Pissarides, and shows
that the extended model meets most of the stylized facts of the labour
market. Further, it provides determinants of the equilibrium rate of participation and unemployment, and characterizes the participation margin of the
labour force.

In Chapter 9, Wu analyses how rural–urban income inequality in China
has affected urban youth unemployment. The underlying hypothesis is
that, the higher the rural–urban income gap the more incentives rural
people have to migrate to the cities. Rural-to-urban migration increases
the pressure on job seeking, reducing the chances for urban school leavers
to find employment. Employing Okun's law and using a panel data set of
29 provinces over a ten-year period, 1989–98, the empirical results show
that rural–urban income inequality is an important factor in the rise in
urban youth unemployment. Okun's law is also validated in the Chinese
context.

## Part III: Sustainable development and policy

The purpose of Chapter 10 is to explore the main determinants of labour
productivity in China for the period 1962–2004. Herrerías and Orts focus on
two factors that have apparently played a significant role in China, namely,
openness and investment. They examine these effects independently of each
other by employing the co-integrated VAR model with different specifications. Their results provide evidence that trade encourages labour productivity in the long run. In addition, they also found that investment and R&D

expenditure have played a significant role in the process of improving productivity performance.

Since economic reform began in 1978, Chinese private enterprises (*siying qiye*) have developed rapidly. While this growth first centred on the coastal region, private small and medium-sized enterprises (SMEs) in China's interior provinces have also flourished in recent years. Theories on economic geography and the resource-based view of private enterprises offer an explanatory model of how interior coastal provinces adjacent to coastal provinces benefit from their developed neighbours. In Chapter 11, Kostka labels this positive impact 'radiant energy'. In a first level of analysis, financial, human and information resource flows measure radiant energy from the East. In a second step, different types of government policy adopted by interior local governments towards private enterprise development are evaluated in their degree of support for economic growth. Local government policies, such as industrial park policy, relocation policy of coastal enterprises, financial and migration policies, differ depending on local characteristics specific to the selected counties examined.

Public ownership had dominated China's township and village enterprises (TVEs) and made a significant contribution to the TVE growth miracle for many years. However, since the 1990s, TVEs have conducted a series of radical restructuring in their ownership and governance arrangements, and the most striking feature is the fading out of public ownership. In Chapter 12, Guo offers a rationale to explain the dynamics of this change by considering a one-stage non-cooperative game between government officials, private entrepreneurs and workers under different circumstances during economic transition. The theoretical model suggests the optimal ownership arrangement will change within alternative institutional environments, or put another way, ownership arrangement cannot be changed effectively unless the institutional environment has been changed. Hence, reckless privatization regardless of the institutional situation will more likely lead to economic inefficiency. This explains the low performance of TVEs in some provinces: the optimal arrangement cannot be reached because of the intervention of local government in this determination process. A panel dataset dating back to 1986 covering 28 provinces in China is then used to verify the model findings empirically.

Previous research on corporate social responsibility focuses mainly on its nature and impact on business performance. In Chapter 13, Qu reports on a study that contributes to our understanding of the determinants of corporate social responsibility by focusing specifically on the role played by three strategically important variables, namely, government regulation, ownership structure and market orientation. Results of the survey conducted in China suggest that market orientation is the most significant predictor of corporate social responsibility, followed by government regulation. In contrast, the ownership structure is found to have little effect.

In Chapter 14, Zhang, Peng and Li are concerned with regional variations in technological entrepreneurship and impacts of entrepreneurship policies on the spatial disparities. There are two gaps in prior research into technological entrepreneurship. First, research in the field has shown a relatively narrow focus on high-technology entrepreneurship, compared with the broader domain of technological entrepreneurship which can be defined as the 'discovery and exploitation of market opportunity of technology' in all sectors. Second, exploratory case studies appeared as the dominant research method and few used explanatory research designs to test correlations between entrepreneurship policies and technological entrepreneurship. This chapter sets out to redress these two issues in the context of Chinese technological entrepreneurship. On the basis of the literature review, this chapter develops a conceptual framework that accounts for the interrelationships between technological entrepreneurship and entrepreneurship policies. Technological entrepreneurship in this chapter is defined in terms of entrepreneurial constructs and entrepreneurial outcomes, while entrepreneurship policies are defined in terms of public policies in technologies, human resources, investment and market development. Cross-sectional data from 30 regions over 2003–04 in China were collected to conduct factor analysis and hierarchical cluster analysis. It was found that considerable regional variations in technological entrepreneurship existed in China, with technological entrepreneurship most active in Shanghai and Beijing. There was also evidence to suggest that policies to support the development of markets for technology transfer and the capital market had a positive impact on technological entrepreneurship.

In Chapter 15, Zou and Oskam explore the value development mechanism of agricultural land conversion during the land-taking process. Assuming bargaining power is equal, efficient and equitable compensation is obtained under the hypothesis of perfect market conditions. The value of transferable agricultural land's development rights is measured. From the state-of-the-art view of land appraisal, practical approximation of the theoretical optimal compensation will provide an effective solution if land markets are lacking. An example for China – where considerable problems are observed in land taking – reveals significant practical and policy implications.

As the Chinese economy continues to steam ahead, its consequences for China's society and environment becomes more visible; and its impact on the world becomes ever more important. Reforms are being undertaken in many areas within China, both to encourage continued economic growth and also to mitigate the adverse effects of growth on society and the environment. This book, based on extensive original research by a wide range of leading experts, examines many key issues connected to China's economic growth and its impact. Subjects covered, amongst many others, include: structural changes and the transition process; growth and inequality; labour market reforms; employment, unemployment and training; openness and productivity; technological innovations and their impact; and the search for economic development that is ecologically sustainable.

# Part I

# Three decades of economic growth

# 1 China's structural changes and transition process

*Alberto Bagnai and Christian A. Mongeau Ospina*

## Introduction

Since the beginning of economic reform in 1978, with the adoption of the 'open door policy', the performance of the Chinese economy has been impressive: from 1978 to 2005 GDP per capita increased almost nine-fold (in constant US dollars at purchasing power parity), with an average growth rate of 8.4 per cent per year (World Bank 2007). At the same time, life expectancy at birth increased from 66 to 72 years, the mortality rate under five years more than halved, the poverty rate (measured by the proportion of people living with less than one USD a day) dropped from 64 per cent in 1981 to 10 per cent in 2005 (ibid.), and the percentage of urban dwellers within the total population has more than doubled (NBS 2006). As a result, China is constantly increasing its ranking in the Human Development Index: in 2005, China ranked eighty-first (UNDP 2006), gaining four places over previous years and heading towards the high human development countries.

The increased relevance of China in the global economy, together with its geopolitical pre-eminence in East Asia, and with the increased availability of data, has provided great momentum to macroeconometric modelling of the Chinese economy. Interpreting and forecasting its recent trends is crucial to every economic scenario analysis, both at a global and single-country level. Consider, for instance, that from 1978 to 2004 the share of imports from China over total imports has increased from 0.2 per cent to 9 per cent in the euro area and from 0.2 per cent to 13.4 per cent in the United States (OECD 2005). The increasing commercial penetration of China is seen from time to time as a threat or as an opportunity. To reach a sound judgement on this point, one needs reliable estimates of the future developments of Chinese macroeconomic fundamentals. Of course, the more the underlying model is able to capture the true long-run features of the economy, the more reliable the forecast scenarios will be.

This leads naturally to the adoption of cointegration (Engle and Granger 1987) as the most appropriate tool of analysis. In fact, cointegration analysis is more and more applied to the study of the Chinese economy. Among the topics considered, we recall the investment function (Sun 1998), the long-run money demand function (Chen 1997), the dynamics of prices (Kojima *et al.* 2005) and of public expenditure (Li 2001), and the long-run relation between the main economic sectors (Yao 1996). Cointegration estimates feature also in a number of full structural models of the Chinese economy, for example those of Tsang and Ma (1997), Dées (2001) and Qin *et al.* (2006).

However, the recent economic history of China, as that of most transition countries, is characterized by a number of structural breaks in macro-economic relations. These breaks, or regime changes, result from a number of causes: institutional and political changes, increased openness to other market economies, changes in the system of national accounts, and so on. The presence of structural breaks has at least two direct consequences, as far as econometric modelling is concerned: first, it prevents the application of most widely used cointegration estimators (e.g. the Johansen (1988) maximum likelihood estimator), as they usually require a long span of data generated by stable data generating process (DGP). Second, even in the more familiar ordinary least square (OLS) setting, ignoring the presence of struc-tural breaks in the sample means omitting one or more significant shift variables from the regression: this specification error leads to biased and inconsistent estimates and worsens the out-of-sample performance of the model.

The increasing awareness of these problems has led a number of authors to take into account the existence of structural breaks in their analyses (e.g. Smyth and Inder 2004; Sun and Ma 2004; Yao 1996). However, in the estima-tion of full macroeconometric models the issue of structural changes is mostly coped with in a pragmatic way, by including shift dummies without resorting to formal econometric testing. The most interesting and extensive development in this respect is probably that of Dées (2001): using quarterly data from 1984 to 1995, Dées estimates a structural econometric model of China where the behavioural relations are specified as error correction models conditional on a structural break in the third quarter of 1988. How-ever, the hypothesis that a major structural change affects most of the behavioural equations in the same date, besides being questionable, is not tested. Moreover, since the power of cointegration tests depends on the sample span, rather than on the frequency of observations (for a recent assessment, see Otero and Smith 2000), the use of quarterly data, while increasing the number of sample observations, does not ensure that the sample span is large enough to warrant the use of cointegration techniques and to detect structural shifts in the long-run parameters.

In our view, this leaves some scope for a more rigorous and systematic analysis of structural changes in the Chinese economy. This chapter aims to fill this gap by performing a systematic structural break analysis on the long-run equations of a medium-sized model of the Chinese economy. The model specification follows the standard aggregate supply/aggregate demand (AS/AD) framework and its equations are estimated on annual data from 1978 through 2006, using the Gregory and Hansen (1996) cointegration estimator that allows for the presence of a regime change in an *a priori* unspecified point of the estimation sample. The model consists of 58 equations, of which 24 are stochastic equations, specified as error correction models.

The empirical results are promising: the structural breaks detected in the long-run parameters are consistent with the recent economic history of China; moreover, the dynamic equations estimated conditional on these structural breaks show good statistical properties, both in terms of fit and of diagnostic tests. The model properties are investigated through a set of simulations that analyse the impact on Chinese macroeconomic performance of an increase in government consumption, an increase in the foreign direct investment (FDI) flow, and a revaluation of the CNY/US$ exchange rate.

## The model's specification and database

### Integrating China in a model of the world economy

Specifying an appropriate model structure for an economy undergoing a transition process is obviously a difficult task. Our attempt was framed by two basic requirements. First, the model was designed to be added to an existing model of the world economy, described in Bagnai (2004). Therefore, it had to share with the existing model some basic features, among which were level of disaggregation, structure of trade linkages among country sub-models and specification of trade competitiveness equations. Second, the model was designed to perform *ex ante* medium- to long-run scenario analysis. In this respect, its structure had in some way to anticipate some likely features of the future structure of the Chinese economy. Therefore, it seemed more appropriate to us to adopt tentatively a structure relatively close to that of a market economy, and to let the data tell us to what extent this structure proved inappropriate when extending the sample back to 1978.

Keeping these requirements in mind, we took as a reference framework the specification of the country/area sub-models of Bagnai (ibid.). These follow the standard AS/AD model, where output is demand constrained in the short run, while its long-run path depends on the supply side. This, in turn, is specified in terms of the wage and price equations, following the approach described by Wallis (2000), where the unemployment rate plays a crucial role as a measure of disequilibrium between aggregate supply and demand. Labour demand follows from cost minimization under neoclassical technology; the real wage long-run behaviour is determined by productivity and the unemployment rate, while prices are specified by a set of mark-up equations. In the linked simulations, real-world GDP is endogenous and affects, together with competitiveness, the demand for exports of each sub-model, while imports depend on real domestic GDP and competitiveness. There are two separate competitiveness measures for exports and imports, that depend both on prices and bilateral exchange rates, weighted with different sets of weights.

This common framework was modified in order to take into account some important characteristics of the Chinese economy. In our view, three major features called for some modification of the standard structure outlined above: the absence of reliable data on the unemployment rate, the rapidly changing sectoral distribution of output, and the process of urbanization.

As is well known, in China the official unemployment figures are widely believed to understate the phenomenon and show little or no variance over the last 30 years (Knight and Xue 2006). This prevents the utilization of unemployment as the main measure of labour market slack, as in the standard AS/AD approach outlined above. As a consequence, most authors utilize output gap measures in the Chinese wage and price equations. Scheibe and Vines (2005) provide a recent survey of this literature. Following their conclusions, we substituted the output gap for the unemployment rate in the wage equation; moreover, we decided to measure the output gap as the estimated residual of a long-run production function.

As for the sectoral composition of output, the transition process has been associated with deep changes in the relative weight of the economic sectors. In order to take into account this phenomenon, we disaggregated the supply side into the three main economic sectors. Therefore, we estimated three sectoral production functions (for the primary, secondary and tertiary sector), and three labour demand functions. Following the approach of Inada (2000), the investment function is specified at the aggregated level, and the sectoral distribution of the aggregate flow is taken as exogenous. As a consequence, the output gap is endogenized at the aggregate economy level as the deviation of (log) aggregate demand from (log) potential output, the latter defined as the sum of the estimated sectoral outputs.

The last feature that called for modifications in the model structure was the process of urbanization. The urbanization of the Chinese population has been widely recognized as an important phenomenon, both for its dimensions and for its repercussions on economic growth (Knight and Song 1999; Zhang and Song 2003; Zhao 2005). As the labour market segregation determined by the Chinese household registration (*hukou*) system has become less severe, the share of urban over total population has kept increasing, going from about 26 per cent at the beginning of the 1990s to an estimated 45 per cent in 2006. This massive labour force reallocation has taken place in the presence of a rising urban–rural household income differential, going from 120 per cent in 1990 (when the per capita annual income of a rural household was 686 yuan, and that of an urban household 1510 yuan) to 220 per cent in 2004. As the rural–urban income gap is the most important 'pull factor' of the urbanization process, this process is likely to continue in the medium run, with a number of consequences at the macroeconomic level, mostly through the channel of aggregate demand. Building on previous macroeconometric modelling studies, and in particular on Inada (2000), we decided therefore to take it into account in a number of ways: first, the rural and urban per capita incomes are modelled separately, thus endogenizing the rural–urban income gap; this, in turn, affects the share of urban over total population, thus explaining the urbanization dynamics; the consequences on aggregate demand are dealt with by specifying two separate consumption functions for rural and urban households.

### Data issues

The model equations were estimated on annual data from 1978 to 2006. The main data sources were the 2006 CD-Rom edition of the World Development Indicators (WDI; World Bank 2006) and the 2005 China Statistical Yearbook online (CSY; NBS 2006).[1] These sources were supplemented with the database in Inada (2000) and the Economist Intelligence Unit online database (EIU 2006).[2]

Starting from the supply side, the data on output in the primary, secondary and tertiary sectors, as well as the investment data, come from WDI.[3] WDI does not report the sectoral distribution of investment; that was drawn from the database of Inada (2000), supplemented with several issues of CSY for the years following 1996. The sectoral capital stock series were obtained by a permanent inventory relation:

$$K_{j,t} = (1 - \delta) K_{j,t-1} + I_{j,t}$$

where $j = 1, 2, 3$ indicates the sector (primary, secondary, tertiary). The permanent inventory relation was applied starting from the initial conditions on the sectoral capital/output ratio provided by Inada (2000), according to which in 1978 this ratio was equal to 0.41 in the primary, 2.85 in the secondary and 2.34 in the tertiary sectors. This gives a capital/output ratio equal to 1.79 for the whole economy. By way of comparison, the updated estimates provided by Holz (2006) fall in a range between 1.69 and 2.29. By multiplying the sectoral capital/output ratio for sectoral output, we obtained the initial condition of the sectoral capital stocks. Following previous studies (Wang and Yao 2003), the depreciation rate was set equal to 5 per cent. The application of the permanent inventory at the sectoral level results in an aggregate time series the pattern of which is very close to the preferred estimates in Holz (2006): for instance, the average growth rate of aggregate capital from 1978 to 1999 is equal to 10.9 per cent in our database, and to 10.1 per cent in Holz (2006, series B–C.4 in Table 6). The data on population, labour force and employment (total and sectoral) come from NBS (2006, Tables 4–1 and 5–2).[4]

On the demand side, the national accounts data, both on real and nominal terms, come from WDI. The data on foreign direct investment come from NBS (2006, Table 18–13), as well as the rural–urban disaggregation of private consumption and disposable income (Tables 3–18 and 10–2). The import price competitiveness, *PMREL*, is measured by the ratio of the import price index, *PM*, to the GDP deflator, *PGDP*, while the export price competitiveness, *REER*, is measured as the ratio of export prices, *PXGS*, to the export price of competitor countries, *PXF*, the latter constructed as a weighted average of the competitors' export prices (for a similar approach, see Laxton *et al.*

1998: 60). The unit wage was measured as the 'average wage of staff and workers', reported in Table 5–21 of NBS (2006).

As for the financial variables, the stock of money was calculated as the sum of money and quasi money, extracted from the IMF (2006), while the data on government revenues, expenditures and debt are drawn from NBS (2006, Tables 8–1 and 8–19). The stock of financial wealth was proxied by the sum of the stocks of money, public debt and net foreign assets, the latter constructed as the cumulated sum of the current account balances.

All the flow and stocks data were expressed in CNY billions. The real data were calculated using 2001 as the base year for price deflators.

The time series of the variables involved in the estimation of stochastic equations were first tested for the presence of unit roots using the *ADF* test of Dickey and Fuller (1979). The order of lags in the *ADF* regression was selected by a model reduction procedure (Enders 2004), and the structure of the deterministic component of the underlying process was specified following the general-to-specific approach suggested by Dolado *et al.* (1990), starting from an auxiliary regression with trend and drift. The results are summarized in Table 1.1. The hypothesis of the presence of a unit root in the level of the series is not rejected for almost all the variables in the model dataset, with the possible exception of urban consumption and primary GDP, that appear to be generated by a trend stationary process, and of the competitiveness measures, *PMREL* and *REER*, that are $I(0)$.[5]

## The structural breaks: estimation methodology and empirical results

### *Methodology*

The model equations were estimated separately in two stages. In the first stage, the long-run cointegrating relations were estimated conditional on the structural breaks detected by the Gregory and Hansen (1996) test. In the second stage, the lagged cointegrating residuals were included as error correction terms in the short-run adjustment equations, as in the usual Engle and Granger (1987) two-stage procedure.

The Gregory and Hansen (1996) test evaluates the null of no cointegration against the alternative of cointegration with a single structural break of unknown date in the long-run parameters of the equations. We adopted this test whenever the customary Cointegrating Regression Augmented Dickey Fuller (CRADF) statistic proposed by Engle and Granger (1987) failed to reject the null of no cointegration. In other words, we verified whether the non-rejection of the null could be determined by the substantial loss in power experienced by the standard CRADF statistic in the presence of structural breaks, documented by the Monte Carlo simulations in Table 3 of Gregory and Hansen's paper.[6]

The breaks are modelled using the shift dummy variable $\varphi_{\tau t} = I(t > [T\tau])$,

*Table 1.1* Unit roots tests on the model variables

| Series | $\tau_\tau$ | $\Phi_3$ | $\tau_\mu$ | $\Phi_1$ | $\tau$ | $p$ |
|---|---|---|---|---|---|---|
| logCPRV | −1.77 | 3.62 | −2.21 | 7.61* | | 1 |
| logCPUV | −4.58* | | | | | 3 |
| logET1 | −2.15 | 2.61 | −1.85 | 2.36 | 1.04 | 1 |
| logET2 | 0.31 | 9.09* | | | | 0 |
| logET3 | −0.07 | 3.15 | −2.59 | 10.25* | | 1 |
| logGDEV | −2.39 | 3.05 | 0.47 | 6.73* | | 4 |
| logGDP1V | −4.92* | | | | | 3 |
| logGDP2V | −1.91 | 2.27 | −0.97 | 6.41* | | 3 |
| logGDP3V | −3.53 | 8.13* | | | | 5 |
| logGDPV | −1.24 | 2.94 | −2.08 | 9.81* | | 5 |
| logIDV | −1.09 | 0.94 | 0.71 | 7.32* | | 3 |
| logIFV | −0.28 | 3.45 | −2.61 | 4.42 | 0.17 | 3 |
| IRL | −1.81 | 2.32 | −1.78 | 1.60 | −0.31 | 1 |
| IRLR | −2.44 | 2.99 | −2.43 | 2.69 | −1.67 | 2 |
| logK1V | −0.70 | 1.57 | 1.42 | 2.86 | 2.04 | 2 |
| logK2V | −2.39 | 3.10 | 0.56 | 6.49* | | 5 |
| logK3V | −1.60 | 1.30 | 0.11 | 4.09 | 1.94 | 3 |
| logMGSV | −1.30 | 2.24 | 1.43 | 5.64* | | 3 |
| logMONEYS | −0.36 | 2.21 | −2.14 | 4.97 | 0.83 | 3 |
| logPCPR | −2.39 | 3.00 | −1.03 | 1.37 | −1.63 | 1 |
| logPCPU | −1.29 | 1.68 | −1.52 | 2.39 | −1.41 | 1 |
| logPGDP | −1.79 | 2.21 | −1.37 | 1.90 | −1.92 | 3 |
| logPGDP1 | −2.06 | 2.24 | −0.88 | 1.69 | −1.59 | 1 |
| logPI | −1.64 | 1.71 | −1.21 | 2.02 | −1.89 | 2 |
| logPM | −0.56 | 1.93 | −2.00 | 8.83* | | 0 |
| logPMREL | −1.27 | 3.92 | −2.54 | 4.07 | −2.41* | 3 |
| logPOP | −0.74 | 1.57 | −1.76 | 1.55 | 0.02 | 4 |
| logPOPR | −0.72 | 2.07 | −1.56 | 2.44 | −1.52 | 2 |
| logPOPU | −1.60 | 1.31 | −0.34 | 7.86* | | 1 |
| logPPI | −1.84 | 1.89 | −0.95 | 1.99 | −1.81 | 3 |
| logPXF | −0.58 | 1.82 | −1.94 | 8.95* | | 0 |
| logPXGS | −0.25 | 4.41 | −2.87 | 14.18* | | 0 |
| logREER | 0.76 | 3.19 | −1.69 | 2.41 | −2.21* | 2 |
| logULC | −0.49 | 1.03 | −1.44 | 5.38* | | 2 |
| logUWB | −2.55 | 3.54 | 0.50 | 7.48* | | 3 |
| logXGSV | −0.13 | 3.35 | 2.28 | 3.89 | 1.72 | 4 |
| logYDHR | 0.10 | 2.43 | −2.20 | 4.58 | 1.43 | 3 |
| logYDHU | −0.31 | 1.52 | −1.77 | 8.07* | | 3 |
| logYQDHR | −0.67 | 0.85 | −1.21 | 1.68 | 1.04 | 4 |
| logYQDHU | −0.63 | 1.33 | −1.58 | 6.20* | | 3 |
| logYROW | −2.26 | 2.66 | −0.48 | 5.45* | | 3 |
| 5% critical values | −3.60 | 7.24 | −3.00 | 5.18 | −1.95 | |

*Notes:* Results of the integration tests; $\tau_\tau$, $\tau_\mu$ and $\tau$ are the Dickey–Fuller statistics for the hypothesis of integration in processes with trend and drift, with drift, and without trend and drift, respectively (Fuller 1976: Table 8.5.2); $\Phi_1$ and $\Phi_3$ are the Dickey–Fuller statistics for the hypothesis that the drift (respectively, the trend) is not statistically significant, conditional on the series being I(1) (Dickey and Fuller 1981, Tables IV and VI); an asterisk indicates a 5% significant statistic; $p$ is the number of lags in the auxiliary regression; the meaning of the variables is explained in the Appendix.

where $I$ is the indicator function, $T$ is the sample size, $\tau$ the relative timing of the change point and $[.]$ the integer part function. Three kinds of break are considered:

Model C-level shift: $\qquad\qquad\qquad y_t = \mu_1 + \mu_2\varphi_{\tau t} + \boldsymbol{a}'\boldsymbol{x}_t + z_t$

Model C/T-level shift with trend: $\quad y_t = \mu_1 + \mu_2\varphi_{\tau t} + \beta t + \boldsymbol{a}'\boldsymbol{x}_t + z_t$

Model C/S-regime shift: $\qquad\qquad y_t = \mu_1 + \mu_2\varphi_{\tau t} + \boldsymbol{a}_1'\boldsymbol{x}_t + \boldsymbol{a}_2'\boldsymbol{x}_t\varphi_{\tau t} + z_t$

where $y_t$ is the dependent variable, $x_t$ a vector of $k$ explanatory variables, $\boldsymbol{a}$, $\beta$ and the $\mu_j$ are parameters, $\varphi_{\tau t}$ is the shift dummy variable and $z_t$ is the cointegrating residual. Models C and C/T allow the equilibrium relation to shift, while model C/S allows it to rotate as well.

The test statistic is evaluated as $ADF_i^* = \inf_\tau ADF_i(\tau)$, where $ADF_i(\tau)$ is the CRADF statistic calculated using the OLS residuals in model $i$ ($i$ = C, C/T, C/S). In other words, $ADF_i^*$ is the smallest among the CRADF statistics that can be evaluated in model $i$ across all possible dates of structural break. The point in the sample where the smallest statistic is obtained gives an estimate of the change point. It is useful to recall that these estimates are subject to statistical error, and that, according to the simulations in Gregory and Hansen (1996, Table 4), the change points occurring in the second half of the sample (i.e. in our study, after 1992) are estimated more precisely.

As we generally had no *a priori* information on the shape of the relevant alternative, we calculated the $ADF_i^*$ statistics for each of the three models C, C/T and C/S. Where the null of no cointegration was rejected in favour of more than one alternative, we chose the model with the more meaningful parameters from the point of view of economic theory (considering also the plausibility of the break date).[7]

### A summary of the structural break test statistics

The scope of the present work prevents us from discussing the estimation results in full. We focus instead on the structural changes detected in the long-run equations, whose estimates are listed in the Appendix, while Table 1.2 reports a summary of the cointegration-with-structural-break tests.[8] The ordinary cointegration test generally fails to reject the null of non-cointegration, the only exception being the import function (Equation (7) in the Appendix), where non-cointegration is rejected at the 10 per cent level. At this stage of the analysis, the evidence of non-cointegration could reflect equally well the pervasiveness of the reform process (that could have induced structural changes in the long-run equations), as well as other forms of mis-specification of the long-run equations (e.g. the omission of relevant variables, the adoption of incorrect functional forms, etc.).[9]

However, once the existence of a structural break is taken into account, a meaningful long-run relation emerges in 11 out of the remaining 22 cases,

Table 1.2 Co-integration tests on the model equations

| Number | Dependent variable | CRADF | $ADF^*_C$ | $ADF^*_{CIT}$ | $ADF^*_{CIS}$ | BDM |
|---|---|---|---|---|---|---|
| [1] | LogGDP1V | −1.77 | −2.77 [2002] | −3.14 [1983] | −5.18 [1994]* | −2.8 |
| [2] | LogGDP2V | −1.63 | −3.03 [2001] | −4.17 [1993] | −4.10 [1998] | −3.1 |
| [3] | LogGDP3V | −1.41 | −3.47 [1984] | −4.08 [1991] | −4.37 [1991] | −2.3 |
| [4] | LogCPRV | −3.22 | −4.17 [1983] | −3.81 [1983] | −5.09 [1988] | −4.1 |
| [5] | logCPUV | −2.20 | −6.68 [1992]** | −5.54 [1992] | −5.74 [1996]** | −4.6 |
| [6] | LogIDV | −3.96 | −5.15 [1988]* | −5.28 [1988] | −5.65 [1987] | −4.8 |
| [7] | logMGSV | −4.18* | −4.16 [1995]* | −5.94 [1994]** | −4.97 [1991] | −2.0 |
| [8] | LogXGSV | −2.05 | −4.31 [1998] | −5.32 [1998] | −6.48 [1998]** | −2.6 |
| [9] | logYQDHR | −2.00 | −4.26 [1984] | −4.24 [2001] | −5.07 [1994] | −3.5 |
| [10] | logYQDHU | −0.57 | −3.17 [2000] | −3.12 [2000] | −4.61 [1994] | −3.8 |
| [11] | logET1 | −2.44 | −3.39 [1988] | −4.71 [1996] | −3.42 [1988] | −6.5 |
| [13] | logET3 | −3.68 | −5.74 [1987]** | −5.62 [1987] | −5.12 [1987] | −4.2 |
| [14] | log(POPU/POP) | −2.31 | −4.14 [1996] | −2.94 [1990] | −5.01 [1995]** | −2.6 |
| [15] | LogUWB | −0.83 | −3.82 [2000] | −3.82 [2000] | −5.23 [1999]** | −3.2 |
| [16] | LogPPI | −2.14 | −4.04 [1993] | −4.03 [1993] | −4.67 [1991] | −3.1 |
| [17] | LogPCPR | −2.14 | −4.01 [1994] | −4.25 [1996] | −4.96 [1994] | −3.4 |
| [18] | logPCPU | −1.88 | −3.99 [1994] | −3.47 [2002] | −4.08 [1997] | −3.2 |
| [19] | LogPCG | −2.18 | −4.50 [1985]* | −4.38 [1985] | −5.18 [1989]** | −3.4 |
| [20] | LogPI | −2.95 | −5.94 [1990]** | −6.59 [1990]** | −5.52 [1990]** | −3.5 |
| [21] | logPGDP1 | −3.12 | −5.68 [2003]** | −5.28 [2003]** | −5.68 [2003]** | −5.9 |
| [22] | LogPXGS | −3.09 | −5.33 [2002]** | −5.40 [1995]** | −5.56 [2000]** | −7.7 |
| [23] | logMONEYS | −2.97 | −4.56 [1993] | −5.17 [2001] | −5.70 [1992] | −1.7 |
| [24] | IRL | −2.97 | −3.50 [2000] | −4.53 [1998] | −3.64 [1996] | −4.8 |

Notes: The equations are listed in the same order as in the Appendix; CRADF is the statistic of the Engle and Granger (1987) test; $ADF^*_C$, $ADF^*_{CIT}$ and $ADF^*_{CIS}$ are the statistics of the tests by Gregory and Hansen (1996). The break dates are reported in brackets. BDM is the co-integration test statistic by Banerjee et al. (1998). One (two) asterisk indicates a 10% (5%) significant statistic.

with strongly significant Gregory–Hansen statistics.[10] Moreover, in another nine cases the Gregory–Hansen statistics are only marginally insignificant.[11] In these cases, we utilized as a further check the error correction model (ECM) cointegration statistic by Banerjee *et al.* (1998), which is simply the *t* statistic of the feedback coefficient in the ECM formulation; the non-cointegration hypothesis is generally rejected, i.e. the estimated dynamic equations do generally display a strong error-correcting behaviour.[12] This suggests that the lack of cointegration in the full sample estimates depends actually on the presence of structural breaks, possibly induced by the reform process, rather than on other forms of mis-specification of the model equations. Moreover, in the large majority of cases, allowing for a single break appears to restore the long-run relations. Strong evidence of multiple breaks was found only in the secondary sector labour demand equation (see below), and in some price equations, whose behaviour was probably affected by two major shocks, corresponding to the two bursts of inflation in 1988–89 and 1993–94. However, in most price equations, taking into account a single break results in strongly significant static and dynamic equations, with meaningful economic properties (see the Appendix). Therefore, we tentatively decided to include these equations in the model.

Besides improving the statistical properties of the long-run equations and of the associated ECM, the structural changes detected do generally coincide with known turning points in recent Chinese economic history. We examine in the following sections some of the more relevant breaks detected by the procedure.

### Aggregate supply

The sectoral production functions are specified using a Cobb–Douglas technology with constant returns to scale and Harrod neutral technical progress:[13]

$$Y_i = A_i \, K_i^{a_i} \, (e^{\lambda_i t} \, L_i)^{1 - a_i} \tag{1}$$

where the subscript *i* indicates the sector ($i = 1, 2, 3$). Real aggregate GDP follows from the sum of sectoral outputs, and the output gap is defined as the deviation of aggregate demand from potential output, the latter constructed as the sum of the sectoral GDP estimates coming from the three production functions.

Several features emerge from the estimation. First, the production functions of the three sectors undergo upward shifts in total factor productivity (TFP) at the beginning of the 1990s. These breaks coincide with the so-called 'Deng Xiaoping effect', i.e. the speed up of the reform process following the Fourteenth Party Congress, with the endorsement of the 'socialist market economy' (Smyth and Inder 2004). Second, in the tertiary sector labour-augmenting technical progress was found to be insignificant. This is consistent with the results of standard growth accounting: using the estimated parameters, the sample average of the Solow residual is found to be 1.0 per cent in the primary, 2.7 per cent in the secondary and −0.3 per cent in the tertiary sectors. Therefore, growth in the tertiary sector is explained mostly by the growth of the factors of production. In the primary and secondary sectors, instead, labour-augmenting technical progress is found to grow at a rate of $\lambda_1$ = 0.01/(1 − 0.21) = 1.3 per cent and $\lambda_2$ = 0.02/(1 − 0.79) = 9.5 per cent, respectively. By defining $n_i$ the growth rate of employment in sector $i$, and $\psi_i$ the share of sector $i$ over total output, the balanced growth rate implied by the model for the whole economy is $n = \psi_1(n_1 + \lambda_1) + \psi_2(n_2 + \lambda_2) + \psi_3 n_3$. By substituting in this formula the sample averages of $n_i$ and $\psi_i$ calculated in the second half of the samples (i.e. after the structural changes in the production functions), we get a long-run output growth rate of 6.5 per cent, which is below the observed sample value of 9.1 per cent. This is a plausible result, as the observed sample average is likely to reflect the catch-up process, during which, as the standard Solow model predicts, the rate of (transitional) growth exceeds that of steady state growth.[14] The simulation results reported below confirm that the model tracks accurately this transitional dynamic.

By way of comparison, note that if the production functions are estimated without taking into account an intercept shift, the once-and-for-all increase in TFP is captured by the trend term, resulting in much higher estimates of the rates of labour-augmenting technical progress (2.2 per cent in the primary, 13.9 per cent in the secondary and 2.5 per cent in the tertiary sectors, respectively).[15] These, in turn, imply a steady-state growth rate of 9.5 per cent, which is less plausible as an estimate of the growth rate to which China should converge in the next decades. In other words, ignoring the exceptional character of events like the 'Deng Xiaoping effect', with the associated one-shot productivity increases, leads to upward biased estimates of the rate of exogenous technological progress, possibly affecting the reliability of medium- to long-term forecasts.

### Aggregate demand

Rural and urban private consumption depends on the respective real house-holds' income and on a wealth effect. As stated above, wealth is defined as the sum of the money stock, government debt and net foreign assets, as in Dées (2001). The wealth effect therefore represents a channel of transmission from the external imbalances to aggregate demand, the prices level and competitiveness.

Aggregate fixed capital formation is specified as the sum of domestic and foreign investments. Domestic investment, in turn, depends on real demand, on real interest rates and on real exports. The equation undergoes a structural break in 1989 corresponding to the severe 1989 recession, which is shown to have induced a permanent downward shift in the long-run investment path. The investment flow is allocated in the three main sectors using a set of exogenous coefficients. We assume implicitly that the FDI flow is allocated between sectors using the same ratios as domestic investment (for a similar assumption, see Inada 2000). Therefore, foreign direct investment affects directly the production functions, and hence real growth, through the sectoral capital stocks.[16]

In the import function the scale variable was disaggregated into domestic absorption and exports. This specification takes into account the role of the Chinese economy in the Asian production chain: as China imports semi-finished products and capital goods from the other Asian economies, and exports finished goods to the rest of the world, a sizeable amount of its imports can be explained by processing trade, and is therefore likely to depend on world demand for Chinese goods.[17] The standard *J* test of encompassing (Davidson and MacKinnon 1981), performed on the error-correction models, favours this specification against the standard one (where imports depend on real GDP): the hypothesis that the standard equation encompasses our preferred specification is strongly rejected with a *t* statistic of 8.7, while the reverse hypothesis leads to a 10 per cent insignificant *t* statistic of −1.5.[18] Real exports depend on world aggregate demand and the real exchange rate. The stock of FDI was introduced in the long-run equation as a proxy for non-price competitiveness.

### Revenues

Rural income is placed in relation to the nominal primary sector output and per capita urban residents' disposable income, the latter considered as a proxy for the size of urban workers' remittances. Remittances are an increasingly important determinant of rural households' disposable income, with an estimated order of magnitude of around 2 per cent of GDP, i.e. about 10 per cent of reported rural households' income. This is reflected in the long-run estimates, which show a significant effect of the remittances on per capita rural income starting in 1995.

### Population and employment

The specification of labour demand equations differs across sectors. In the secondary sector, we adopted a conditional labour demand function consistent with Cobb–Douglas technology. This can be expressed in log-linear terms as:

$$\ln L = \ln Y + a \ln\left(\frac{1-a}{a}\right) - \ln A - a \ln\left(\frac{w}{r}\right) - (1-a)\lambda_2 t$$

where $w$ is the price of the labour input and $r$ the price of capital, and $a$ the capital elasticity of output. Using the estimate $\hat{a} = 0.79$ coming from the secondary sector production function,[19] measuring the relative factor prices term (*w/r*) as the ratio of average wage of staff and workers, *UWB*, to gross fixed capital formation deflator, *PI*, and taking all the known terms to the left-hand side, we get:

$$\ln Y - \ln L + \hat{\alpha} \ln\left(\frac{1 - \hat{\alpha}}{\hat{\alpha}}\right) - \hat{\alpha} \ln\left(\frac{w}{r}\right) = \ln A + (1 - \hat{\alpha})\lambda_2 t \tag{2}$$

The left-hand side of Equation (2) is represented in Figure 1.1. Its time series displays two structural breaks. This behaviour is consistent with either a stochastic or a (doubly-) segmented trend. By applying the test proposed by Clemente *et al.* (1998), we rejected with a statistic equal to −6.25 (significant at 2.5 per cent) the null hypothesis of stochastic trend against the alternative of a doubly-segmented linear trend. The breaks are consistent with the observed increase in secondary sector productivity, associated at the beginning of the 1990s with the liberalization of FDI inflows (Graham 2004), among other things, and with the subsequent slowdown determined by the Asian crisis at the end of the same decade. The Cobb–Douglas specification implies that the real wage elasticity of labour demand equals −79 per cent, a relatively large value when compared with previous estimates.[20] This can be construed as an effect of the increasing weight of market

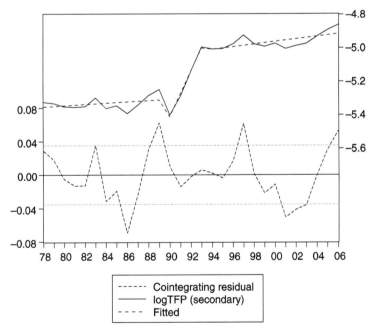

*Figure 1.1* The log of the total factor productivity estimate in the secondary sector long-run labour production function and the co-integrating residual.

mechanisms in labour allocation, reflected in the more recent sample adopted in our study.

In the primary and tertiary sector the same approach proved unsatisfactory from an empirical point of view. Therefore, labour demand was explained using real aggregate demand, as in Inada (2000), and the real wage. The latter was found significant only in the tertiary sector, with a long-run elasticity of –23 per cent.

As mentioned above, the rural–urban income differential explains the urban-to-total population ratio. The long-run elasticity of urban population to the wage differential increases significantly in 1996, a year that witnessed a persistent increase in the speed of rural–urban migration.[21]

### Wages and prices

The wage equation (Equation (15) in the Appendix) is specified in real terms, with real wages depending on aggregate labour productivity. The long-run elasticity of real wage to average labour productivity undergoes a structural break after 1999, rising from 68 per cent to 145 per cent. This behaviour reflects the operation of the wage reforms occurring in China at the end of the 1990s, and in particular those related to the Ninth Five-year Plan (Yueh 2004), which strengthened the relation between wages and productivity (see Figure 1.2).

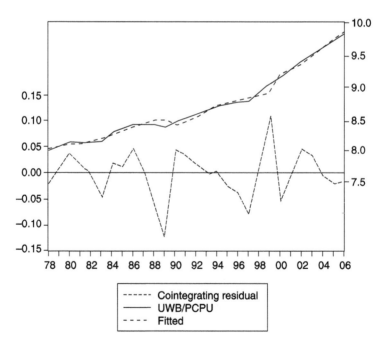

*Figure 1.2* The log of the real wage and its fitted value.

The deflators of urban and rural consumption undergo an upward shift in 1994. These breaks reflect the inflation outburst that occurred at the end of the dual-track price system. As explained by Chang and Hou (1997), price liberalization was accompanied by relative price adjustments that, given the downward rigidity of prices, were accomplished through increases in the prices of the previously undervalued products, thereby generating 'structural' inflation, correctly detected by the Gregory–Hansen procedure.

## The model's performance and properties

### *The model's tracking performance*

Table 1.3 reports the summary statistics of the full sample dynamic simulation for a subset of model variables. With the only exception of trade flows, the summary statistics of the model tracking performance are well below 10 per cent. This degree of accuracy is remarkable, if we consider that the simulation is performed over the period 1980–2006, during which the Chinese economy underwent a number of reforms and exogenous shocks, including the 1989 recession, the two inflationary outbursts in 1988 and 1994, the Asian crisis and the accession to the WTO, to quote a few.

*Table 1.3* Summary statistics of the full sample dynamic simulation

|       |                                      | *MAPE (%)* | *RMSE (%)* |
|-------|--------------------------------------|------------|------------|
| GDEV  | Real aggregate demand                | 3.6        | 4.2        |
| GDPV  | Real aggregate supply                | 2.4        | 2.9        |
| CPRV  | Real rural consumption               | 6.5        | 7.9        |
| CPUV  | Real urban consumption               | 6.3        | 7.1        |
| CPV   | Real private consumption             | 5.2        | 5.9        |
| IV    | Real investment                      | 5.1        | 7.0        |
| XGSV  | Real exports                         | 12.8       | 16.3       |
| MGSV  | Real imports                         | 9.4        | 12.5       |
| UWB   | Unit wages                           | 7.0        | 8.0        |
| YDHR  | Rural households disposable income   | 6.6        | 8.4        |
| YDHU  | Urban households disposable income   | 7.1        | 8.3        |
| PCPU  | Deflator of urban consumption        | 4.1        | 5.0        |
| PGDP  | GDP deflator                         | 3.2        | 3.8        |
| REER  | Real exchange rate                   | 3.2        | 3.9        |
| POPU  | Urban population                     | 1.0        | 1.2        |
| ET    | Total employment                     | 0.8        | 1.0        |
| MONEYS| Nominal money stock                  | 5.7        | 7.0        |
| NSGDPR| National saving-to-GDP ratio         | 5.1        | 6.3        |
| IGDPR | Investment-to-GDP ratio              | 2.3        | 2.9        |

*Note:* MAPE is the mean absolute percentage error, RMSE the root mean square error. Both statistics are expressed in percentages of the actual values of the variable.

*Some standard simulation experiments*

The model properties were further investigated through a set of standard simulation experiments, namely:

1   A permanent increase in real government consumption equal to 1 per cent of baseline real GDP.
2   A permanent increase in real FDI inflows equal to 1 per cent of baseline real GDP.
3   A permanent appreciation of the CNY/US$ nominal exchange rate equal to 10 per cent.

All the shocks were applied in 2002 and their effects were tracked in the following four years through to the end of the sample.

*Increase in government consumption*

The main results of this experiment are summarized in Table 1.4. The increase in real government consumption has persistent effects on real aggregate demand, *GDEV*, that converges quickly to about 0.6 per cent points above the baseline. The fiscal expansion has a positive effect on real supply, *GDPV*, basically through the effects of real investment, *IV*, on capital accumulation, but this effect is smaller than the effect on demand (a similar

*Table 1.4* An increase in real public expenditure by 1 per cent of baseline real GDP

|        |                                     | 1 | 2 | 3 | 4 | 5 |
|--------|-------------------------------------|------|------|------|------|------|
| GDEV   | Real aggregate demand               | 0.44 | 0.55 | 0.59 | 0.60 | 0.56 |
| GDPV   | Real aggregate supply               | 0.04 | 0.06 | 0.10 | 0.14 | 0.17 |
| CPRV   | Real rural consumption              | 0.03 | 0.07 | 0.08 | 0.08 | 0.05 |
| CPUV   | Real urban consumption              | 0.10 | 0.28 | 0.42 | 0.50 | 0.54 |
| CPV    | Real private consumption            | 0.07 | 0.19 | 0.28 | 0.32 | 0.34 |
| IV     | Real investment                     | 0.23 | 0.41 | 0.51 | 0.59 | 0.63 |
| XGSV   | Real exports                        | 0.00 | 0.00 | −0.01 | −0.04 | −0.08 |
| MGSV   | Real imports                        | 2.48 | 2.42 | 2.38 | 2.40 | 2.43 |
| UWB    | Unit wages                          | 0.37 | 0.72 | 1.02 | 1.29 | 1.46 |
| YDHR   | Rural households disposable income  | 0.07 | 0.16 | 0.26 | 0.36 | 0.43 |
| YDHU   | Urban households disposable income  | 0.32 | 0.62 | 0.86 | 1.06 | 1.18 |
| PCPU   | Deflator of urban consumption       | 0.00 | 0.05 | 0.14 | 0.25 | 0.34 |
| PGDP   | GDP deflator                        | 0.03 | 0.03 | 0.09 | 0.20 | 0.36 |
| REER   | Real exchange rate                  | 0.00 | 0.00 | 0.01 | 0.05 | 0.10 |
| POPU   | Urban population                    | 0.00 | 0.02 | 0.05 | 0.08 | 0.11 |
| ET     | Total employment                    | 0.01 | −0.01 | −0.03 | −0.04 | −0.06 |
| NSGDPR | National saving-to-GDP ratio        | −0.73 | −0.75 | −0.81 | −0.86 | −0.91 |
| IGDPR  | Investment-to-GDP ratio             | −0.10 | −0.06 | −0.04 | −0.03 | −0.01 |
| CAGDPR | Current account-to-GDP ratio        | −0.64 | −0.69 | −0.77 | −0.84 | −0.89 |

*Note:* Percentage deviations from baseline (deviations for the variable expressed as ratio to GDP).

pattern can be found in Inada 2000). Therefore, the output gap increase is quite persistent. This explains the sustained growth in unit wages, *UWB*, that by the end of the simulation period are about 1.5 per cent points above their baseline.

The increase in *UWB* has several effects: first, it determines an increase in disposable income that sustains the expansion of real private consumption, *CPV*; second, it widens the rural–urban income gap and therefore fosters rural–urban migration; third, it reduces total employment, *ET*; and fourth, it pushes up internal prices. As for the first two effects, note that rural and urban disposable income follow two different paths. Rural income, *YDHR*, depends on the value of primary output per capita, *GDP1V* × *PGDP1/ET1*, where *GDP1V* is the primary sector value added, *PGDP1* its deflator and *ET1* primary employment. Since primary employment depends on real demand, the increase in real demand dampens the positive effect of the increase in primary output. Urban income, *YDHU*, on the contrary, depends on *UWB*: therefore, an increase in *UWB* widens the rural–urban income gap and sustains urban consumption, *CPUV*. These two effects are both reinforced by rural–urban migration: at the end of the simulation, urban population has increased by 0.11 per cent over the baseline. However, by the end of the simulation horizon, the rise of urban income begins to foster rural income through the effect of an increase in remittances from urban to rural workers. The net result of these effects is an increase in total private consumption, equal to 0.34 per cent at the end of the simulation.

On average, the increase in private consumption is smaller than the increase in real disposable income, i.e. private saving rises, thus partially offsetting the decrease in public saving. This explains why the fiscal shock does not translate entirely on the current account balance, even though its effects on the investment-to-GDP ratio are only transitory. However, at the end of the sample almost 90 per cent of the fiscal shock is reflected in a worsening of the current account balance. From the point of view of trade flows, this behaviour of the current account balance is explained almost completely by a rise in imports, followed at the end of the sample by a moderate decrease in exports, as the rise in internal prices erodes the competitiveness of Chinese goods.

Consumption behaviour is affected also by stock/flow dynamics. The wealth effect operates from the beginning through the increase in public debt. Over time, the external imbalance causes a reduction in net foreign assets that dampens the wealth effect in private consumption by cancelling out almost completely the increase in domestic government securities.

### *Increase in foreign direct investment*

Table 1.5 presents the results of a simulation experiment that studies the effects of a permanent increase in real FDI equal to 1 baseline GDP point. This corresponds to an increase in the real FDI flow in a range between

*Table 1.5* An increase in real FDI by 1 per cent of baseline real GDP

|  |  | 1 | 2 | 3 | 4 | 5 |
|---|---|---|---|---|---|---|
| GDEV | Real aggregate demand | 0.42 | 0.50 | 0.52 | 0.56 | 0.59 |
| GDPV | Real aggregate supply | 0.45 | 0.79 | 1.07 | 1.31 | 1.53 |
| CPRV | Real rural consumption | 0.04 | 0.08 | 0.10 | 0.12 | 0.16 |
| CPUV | Real urban consumption | −0.03 | −0.09 | −0.16 | −0.20 | −0.25 |
| CPV | Real private consumption | 0.00 | −0.02 | −0.05 | −0.06 | −0.08 |
| IV | Real investment | 2.69 | 2.72 | 2.62 | 2.61 | 2.62 |
| XGSV | Real exports | 0.00 | 0.00 | 0.01 | 0.04 | 0.09 |
| MGSV | Real imports | 2.36 | 2.08 | 1.82 | 1.69 | 1.60 |
| UWB | Unit wages | −0.09 | −0.35 | −0.60 | −0.91 | −1.32 |
| YDHR | Rural households disposable income | 0.09 | 0.11 | 0.03 | −0.12 | −0.30 |
| YDHU | Urban households disposable income | −0.08 | −0.31 | −0.54 | −0.79 | −1.14 |
| PCPU | Deflator of urban consumption | 0.00 | −0.03 | −0.13 | −0.28 | −0.44 |
| PGDP | GDP deflator | 0.03 | −0.03 | −0.15 | −0.31 | −0.47 |
| REER | Real exchange rate | 0.00 | 0.00 | −0.01 | −0.04 | −0.11 |
| POPU | Urban population | 0.00 | −0.01 | −0.04 | −0.07 | −0.10 |
| ET | Total employment | 0.46 | 0.58 | 0.68 | 0.85 | 1.08 |
| NSGDPR | National saving-to-GDP ratio | 0.27 | 0.30 | 0.31 | 0.34 | 0.36 |
| IGDPR | Investment-to-GDP ratio | 0.87 | 0.89 | 0.90 | 0.92 | 0.93 |
| CAGDPR | Current account-to-GDP ratio | −0.60 | −0.59 | −0.59 | −0.58 | −0.57 |

*Note:* Percentage deviations from baseline (deviations for the variable expressed as ratio to GDP).

25 per cent (at the beginning) to 35 per cent (at the end of the simulation horizon). At the beginning of the simulation period, real FDI accounted for about 10 per cent of the baseline real investment, *IV*. The simulated increase by 25 per cent is therefore equal to about 2.5 per cent of total investment. However, the impact effect on total investment is larger, equal to 2.69 per cent. This is because the positive shock affects aggregate demand, *GDEV*, through the Keynesian multiplier, as well as aggregate supply, *GDPV*, through capital accumulation. The increase in aggregate demand determines an increase in domestic investment, hence a further increase in total investment.

The impact on demand is persistently smaller than that on supply: therefore, the output gap decreases, and wages and prices follow. The decrease in average wages, *UWB*, causes a decrease in the nominal disposable income of urban households, *YDHU*, which is only partially counterbalanced by the decrease in the urban consumption deflator: therefore, urban private consumption, *CPUV*, falls, in contrast to a moderate rise in rural consumption, *CPRV*. As a result, total consumption, *CPV*, decreases slightly: this contrasts with the positive effects of the shock and explains its relatively reduced impact on aggregate demand. As a consequence, private saving rises throughout the simulation horizon, thus partially counteracting the effect of the rise in national investment: in the medium run, only about half of the investment shock translates on the current account balance, which worsens by slightly more than 0.5 GDP points. Observed from the side of trade flows, this current account worsening is determined mostly by an increase in imports, counteracted, at the end of the simulation horizon, by an increase in exports, when the fall in domestic prices improves competitiveness.

## CNY revaluation

The last simulation experiment, described in Table 1.6, studies the effects of a 10 per cent nominal appreciation of the Chinese currency against the US dollar. Such a policy measure is insistently requested by policy makers and the public at large throughout the industrial world, with the support of leading economists (see Pisani-Ferry 2007), on the basis of the assumption that it will solve the problem of transpacific external imbalances.[22]

The impact of the revaluation on trade flows is quite large: real export volume falls by 1.18 per cent with respect to the baseline, while imports rise by about 1 per cent. The current account thus worsens by 0.57 GDP points. In the short run, the impact of this negative shock on aggregate demand is larger than its impact on aggregate supply: the fall in the output gap, together with the fall in import prices, induces an adjustment in domestic prices, which counteracts the negative effects of the nominal appreciation. Over time, the

*Table 1.6* A 10 per cent nominal appreciation of the CNY/US$ exchange rate

|        |                                  | 1     | 2     | 3     | 4     | 5      |
|--------|----------------------------------|-------|-------|-------|-------|--------|
| GDEV   | Real aggregate demand            | −1.14 | −1.66 | −1.96 | −1.95 | −1.70  |
| GDPV   | Real aggregate supply            | −0.19 | −0.47 | −0.78 | −1.11 | −1.37  |
| CPRV   | Real rural consumption           | −0.21 | 0.02  | 0.68  | 1.59  | 2.57   |
| CPUV   | Real urban consumption           | 0.20  | 0.71  | 1.28  | 1.72  | 2.02   |
| CPV    | Real private consumption         | 0.02  | 0.41  | 1.03  | 1.67  | 2.25   |
| IV     | Real investment                  | −1.41 | −2.27 | −3.25 | −3.87 | −3.86  |
| XGSV   | Real exports                     | −1.18 | −2.59 | −3.13 | −3.10 | −2.72  |
| MGSV   | Real imports                     | 0.99  | 0.59  | 0.08  | −0.23 | −0.13  |
| UWB    | Unit wages                       | −1.70 | −4.04 | −6.48 | −8.54 | −9.98  |
| YDHR   | Rural households disposable income | −1.20 | −2.94 | −4.52 | −5.61 | −6.12  |
| YDHU   | Urban households disposable income | −1.51 | −3.45 | −5.33 | −6.82 | −7.76  |
| PCPU   | Deflator of urban consumption    | −2.14 | −4.76 | −7.12 | −8.94 | −10.15 |
| PGDP   | GDP deflator                     | −1.65 | −3.10 | −5.05 | −7.14 | −8.86  |
| REER   | Real exchange rate               | 1.59  | 3.13  | 3.18  | 2.55  | 1.71   |
| POPU   | Urban population                 | 0.00  | −0.02 | −0.06 | −0.10 | −0.17  |
| ET     | Total employment                 | −0.08 | −0.17 | −0.24 | −0.26 | −0.27  |
| NSGDPR | National saving-to-GDP ratio     | −0.70 | −0.45 | −0.41 | −0.40 | −0.35  |
| IGDPR  | Investment-to-GDP ratio          | −0.14 | −0.23 | −0.35 | −0.44 | −0.45  |
| CAGDPR | Current account-to-GDP ratio     | −0.57 | −0.22 | −0.06 | 0.04  | 0.10   |

*Note:* Percentage deviations from baseline (deviations for the variable expressed as ratio to GDP).

shock affects also the aggregate supply, through the channels of investment and employment (that falls following the decrease in aggregate demand). At the end of the simulation period, the output gap narrows sensibly, although aggregate demand is slowly reverting to the baseline. In the medium run, the effects on import and export price competitiveness are different. As the GDP deflator decreases by 8.8 per cent in the fifth year with respect to the baseline, import competitiveness increases (i.e. *PMREL* increases) by about 1.2 per cent,[23] while export competitiveness decreases (i.e. *REER* increases) by 1.7 per cent, as the adjustment in export prices is slower. This relative price effect, together with the 'processing trade' effect (i.e. the dependency of imports on export demand) and the fall in domestic demand, counter-balances the rise in imports, which revert to the baseline by the end of the simulation horizon. As a consequence, the currency appreciation has only transitory effects on the current account balance, which at the end of the simulation period improves slightly by 0.1 GDP points. In fact, as time passes private consumption adapts to the fall in disposable income: this dampens the reduction in national saving induced by the revaluation (the reduction in national savings falls from −0.7 to −0.35 GDP points);[24] at the same time, the reduction in private investment is more persistent and offsets, starting from the fourth year, the reduction in national savings, thus improving, rather than worsening, the current account balance.

## Conclusions

In this chapter we have performed a systematic investigation of the structural breaks that have intervened in the Chinese economy since 1978 as a result of the transition process. The analysis was performed within the framework of a standard AS/AD specification, by testing each of its long-run equations for structural breaks of unknown date and shape, using the Gregory and Hansen (1996) procedure on a sample of annual data from 1978 to 2006. The estimation results show that the transition process has affected the specifica-tion of most of the behavioural and technical equations. In the vast majority of cases, a significant cointegrating relation emerges only after taking into account the possible existence of a structural break. At the same time, once allowance is made for some reform-induced structural changes, the AS/AD model tracks the historical performance of the post-1978 Chinese economy remarkably well (the root mean square error of GDP over the full sample dynamic simulation is equal to 2.9 per cent), and generates a meaningful steady-state growth rate. This confirms that a systematic analysis of the struc-tural changes is particularly useful when studying countries undergoing a transition process of whatever kind, as it allows the researcher to include data coming from different regimes, thus facilitating the detection of long-run relationships between the economic variables.[25]

The properties of the model have been investigated through a set of simula-tion experiments that confirm the importance of foreign direct investment as an engine of growth and competitiveness for the Chinese economy, and shed some light on the issue of the reduction of the so-called transpacific external imbalances. In particular, it is shown that the effects of an appreciation of the renminbi on the current account balance of China would be not only transitory (as already shown in the literature; see Dées 2001; Lee *et al.* 2006), but even (slightly) positive in the medium run. This result contrasts the hypothesis formulated, among others, by Pisani-Ferry (2007), according to which a 'big bang' revaluation would act as a trigger, favouring the shift to a pattern of growth supported by domestic, rather than external, demand. In fact, this hypothesis misses the point that, because of the structure of Chinese trade flows, the reduction in real exports determined by the revaluation would also over time induce a reduction in real imports, through the 'processing trade' effect mentioned above.[26] The most likely outcome of a 'big bang' renminbi revaluation is therefore a net reduction of the contribution of China to world economic growth, without any persistent effect on the Chinese current account balance.

At the same time, the fiscal expansion simulation shows that the Chinese economy displays a 'twin deficit' behaviour, because in the medium run a fiscal shock translates almost completely on the current account balance. This confirms the view that policies addressing the saving–investment gap are more effective in reducing the size of the external imbalances in China than policies aimed at correcting the price competitiveness of Chinese products (a similar view is expressed by Lee *et al.* 2006).

Before concluding, a few critical remarks on the methodology adopted and on some possible further developments are in order.

As is known, gradualism of the economic reform process in China has been pointed out by a number of scholars (e.g. Chow 2004; Prasad 2004) as a distinguished and successful feature of the Chinese transition, as compared for instance with the 'big bang' transitions of Central and Eastern European countries. Given this background, one may wonder whether a 'single break' methodology such as that adopted in the chapter, could lead to over-emphasizing some episodes, while overlooking some others. Once again, this is an open question. The first-best strategy for modelling a gradual transition would probably be that of adopting a variable parameter approach, as proposed recently by Park and Hahn (1999). A second-best strategy would be to allow for a set of multiple breaks.[27] However, the estimators for time varying parameters or multiple breaks are relatively cumbersome, and one should also weigh the expected benefits of following a similar research strategy against its costs. This is all the more true, considering that the 'gradualist' view of the reform process is questioned by the proponents of the so-called 'convergence school' (Sachs and Woo 2000). According to this school, Chinese institutions are converging to those of market economies, rather than to an original economic system 'with Chinese characteristics', and this process is characterized by a number of radical measures (the dismantling of the communes, the liberalization of the township and village enterprises, the creation of the Special Economic Zones, the liberalization of FDI inflows, . . .), all of which are occurring in a short period and affecting a large proportion of the Chinese population simultaneously (see also Kazakevitch and Smyth 2005). In a sense, the 'convergence school' validates our choice of adopting a relatively standard AS/AD economic structure to represent the (endpoint of the) Chinese transition. Moreover, by emphasizing the radical character of some reforms, it also warrants our 'single break' modelling strategy. In any case, irrespective of the relative merits of the two schools of thought, whose discussion would exceed the scope of this chapter, the accuracy of the model tracking performance suggests that the Chinese transition, be it gradual and experimental, or radical and converging to a standard market economy, can be represented reasonably well through a limited number of pointwise structural changes.

## Acknowledgements

This chapter is a substantially revised version of the *LLEE working document* No. 47 (www.luiss.it/ricerca/centri/llee/publications.html). An earlier draft was presented at the 18th CEA (UK) Annual Conference 'Integrating China into the World Economy', Nottingham, 16–17 April 2007, and at the joint CEA (UK) and CCES International Conference on 'Transition and development: governance, markets and growth', Fudan University, 15–16 September 2007. The authors thank Stefano Manzocchi, Aaron Mehrotra, Roberta Capasso, the editor and two anonymous referees for their useful suggestions. The usual disclaimers apply. Financial support from the Luiss Lab on European Economics on an earlier stage of this research, and from MIUR (PRIN 2005), is gratefully acknowledged.

## Notes

1  The reliability of the NBS statistics is an open matter. See, among others, Rawski (2001), Wang and Meng (2001), Xu (2004) and Scharping (2001).
2  A full description of the data sources is available upon request.
3  Since the WDI series end in 2004, in this as well as in some other cases we utilized the growth rates of the series in EIU for updating the WDI data up to 2006.
4  In this, as well as in some of the following cases, the NBS series were supplemented with the data reported by Inada (2000) for the years 1978 to 1988.
5  The hypothesis concerning the presence of two unit roots in the data-generating process is consistently rejected for all the $I(1)$ series utilized in the estimation. Detailed data are available upon request.
6  It should be stressed that Gregory and Hansen (1996) investigate the properties of their test in samples of at least 50 observations, while our sample consists of only 29 observations. However, although this point needs to be investigated formally, it is likely that the 'power versus frequency' problem (Otero and Smith 2000) remains also in the presence of structural breaks. This implies that using 29 annual observations is likely to provide more reliable estimates of the long-run parameters than using, say, 50 monthly observations.

7 We maintain that, in econometric research work, economic theory and history are legitimate sources of information, which should cooperate with mathematical statistics on an equal footing.

8 A full model listing, including the estimates of the error correction equations, is available upon request. Note that the labour demand function of the secondary sector (Equation (12) in the Appendix) was estimated using a different approach in order to take into account the existence of two structural breaks (see below).

9 This conclusion is reached by comparing the CRADF statistics with the critical values supplied by Engle and Yoo (1987), which consider a sample of 50 observations. However, our sample consists of 29 observations (from 1978 to 2006). The small sample critical values of Blangiewicz and Charemza (1990) would reject the null of non-cointegration at the 5 per cent level in another six cases (*CPRV*, *IDV*, *ET3*, *PGDP1*, *PXGS* and *IRL*), resulting in a more optimistic assessment of the model specification.

10 The equations that display cointegration-with-break are those of *GDP1V*, *CPUV*, *IDV*, *XGSV*, *ET3*, *POPU*, *UWB*, *PCG*, *PI*, *PGDP1* and *PXGS*. Moreover, by considering a structural break, the statistical significance of the cointegration statistic improves also in the import equation.

11 This happens in the equations of *GDP2V*, *CPRV*, *YQDHR*, *YQDHU*, *ET1*, *PPI*, *PCPR*, *PCPU* and *IRL*.

12 The test was applied to the ECM estimated conditional on the most significant structural break detected by the Gregory–Hansen procedure. This procedure is obviously subject to a pretesting problem. However, the resulting dynamic equations display generally very good statistical properties (the detailed estimation outputs are available upon request).

13 The hypothesis of constant return to scale is adopted in a number of macroeconometric models of the Chinese economy (Dées 2001; Inada 2000; Qin *et al.* 2006).

14 As a matter of fact, the steady-state growth rate should be expected to be lower, because most demographic projections envisage a diminution of the Chinese population, hence a reduction in $n_i$, starting in the second decade of this century (World Bank 2007). This adverse evolution should be partly offset, at the aggregate level, by the continuing migration of people from low to high productivity sectors. Nevertheless, Guest and McDonald (2007) forecast an average real growth rate of the Chinese economy over 2000–2025 equal to 4.9 per cent.

15 The resulting long-run equations are not cointegrating. Detailed results are available upon request.

16 Inada (2000) inserts separately the domestic and foreign capital stocks in the production function of non-state-owned industries, finding that the elasticity of output to foreign capital is greater than that to domestic capital (44 per cent and 37 per cent, respectively); Dées (2001) utilizes the FDI stock to explain TFP in the aggregate production function, and non-price competitiveness in the trade equations.

17 The share of processing trade imports over total imports has grown from 7 per cent in 1985 to 41 per cent in 2005 (NBS 2006).

18 The estimated elasticity of real imports to real exports is 25 per cent. A similar specification is adopted by Tsang and Ma (1997), who find a 97 per cent elasticity, and Qin *et al.* (2006), with an estimated elasticity of 83 per cent. Dées (2001) includes the FDI stock as a measure of non-price competitiveness; however, the significance of FDI, instead of real exports, in the import function is questioned by the Tsang and Ma (1997) results.

19 Inada (2000) reports a capital elasticity of output equal to 0.70 for the state-owned manufacturing sector, and to 0.81 for the non-state-owned manufacturing sector;

Qin *et al.* (2006) assume an 85 per cent elasticity for the whole economy (long-run trend of aggregate supply).

20 For instance, Dées (2001) finds a −30 per cent elasticity using a CES specification at the whole economy level, while Inada (2000) finds a −55 per cent long-run elasticity for the non-state-owned manufacturing industries.

21 Seeborg *et al.* (2000) survey the factors that prompted this structural change in rural–urban labour mobility by the end of the 1990s, among which are the rising rural–urban income differential and the decreasing weight of the state-owned enterprises.

22 An anonymous referee pointed out that since pressure for a CNY revaluation are spreading around the world, it would also be interesting to assess a revaluation of the CNY in nominal effective terms. We agree with this remark and we leave this development for future research.

23 Remember that *PMREL* is the ratio of *PGDP* to *PM*, and *PM* decreases permanently by 10 per cent following the CNY revaluation.

24 Note that the GDP ratios are evaluated as usual, taking into account nominal variables. In other words, the evolution of these ratios reflects also the movement in prices.

25 See, for instance, Bagnai and Carlucci (2003), for an application of this approach to a model of the European Union across the transition to the EMU.

26 An alternative, but complementary, explanation is that while the revaluation would foster domestic consumption, through its effects on real disposable income, it would at the same time induce a persistent reduction in domestic investment.

27 At the time when this research started there were no estimators for models with multiple breaks and non-stationary variables. Meanwhile, the estimator of Kejriwal (2008) has appeared: we leave its application for future research.

## References

Bagnai, A. (2004) 'Dynamic paths of the European economy: simulations with an aggregate model of the EMU as a part of the world economy', Chapter 9 in A. Deardorff (ed.), *The Past, Present, and Future of the European Union*, New York: Palgrave Macmillan.

Bagnai, A. and Carlucci, F. (2003) 'An aggregate model for the European Union', *Economic Modelling*, 20, 623–649.

Banerjee, A., Dolado, J.J. and Mestre, R. (1998) 'Error-correction mechanism tests for cointegration in a single-equation framework', *Journal of Time Series Analysis*, 19, 267–283.

Blangiewicz, M. and Charemza, W.W. (1990) 'Cointegration in small samples: empirical percentiles, drifting moments and customized testing', *Oxford Bulletin of Economics and Statistics*, 52, 303–315.

Chang, G.H. and Hou, J. (1997) 'Structural inflation and the 1994 "monetary" crisis in China', *Contemporary Economic Policy*, 15, 73–81.

Chen, B. (1997) 'Long-run money demand and inflation in China', *Journal of Macroeconomics*, 19, 609–617.

Chow, G.C. (2004) 'Economic reform and growth in China', *Annals of Economics and Finance*, 5, 127–152.

Clemente, J., Montañés, A. and Reyes, M. (1998) 'Testing for unit root in variables with a double change in the mean', *Economics Letters*, 59, 175–182.

Davidson, R. and MacKinnon, J.G. (1981) 'Several tests for model specification in the presence of alternative hypotheses', *Econometrica*, 49, 781–793.

Dées, S. (2001) 'The opening policy in China: simulations of a macroeconometric model', *Journal of Policy Modeling*, 23, 397–410.

Dickey, D. and Fuller, W. (1979) 'Distribution of the estimators for autoregressive time-series with a unit root', *Journal of the American Statistical Association*, 74, 427–431.

Dickey, D. and Fuller, W. (1981) 'Likelihood ratio statistics for autoregressive time series with a unit root', *Econometrica*, 49, 1057–1072.

Dolado, J.J., Jenkinson, T. and Sosvilla-Rivero, S. (1990) 'Cointegration and unit roots', *Journal of Economic Surveys*, 4, 249–273.

EIU (2006) *Economist Intelligence Unit Country Data*, online edition, https://eiu.bvdep.com/.

Enders, W. (2004) *Applied Econometric Time-series*, 2nd edition, New York: Wiley.

Engle, R.F. and Granger, C.W.J. (1987) 'Cointegration and error correction: representation, estimation and testing', *Econometrica*, 55, 251–276.

Engle, R.F. and Yoo, B.S. (1987) 'Forecasting and testing in co-integrated systems', *Journal of Econometrics*, 35, 143–159.

Fuller, W. (1976) *Introduction to Statistical Time Series*, New York: Wiley.

Graham, E.M. (2004) 'Do export processing zones attract FDI and its benefits: the experience of China', *International Economics and Economic Policy*, 1, 87–103.

Gregory, A.W. and Hansen, B.E. (1996) 'Residual-based tests for cointegration in models with regime shifts', *Journal of Econometrics*, 70, 99–126.

Guest, R.S. and McDonald, I.M. (2007) 'Global GDP shares in the 21st century: an equilibrium approach', *Economic Modelling*, 24, 859–877.

Holz, C. (2006) 'New capital estimates for China', *China Economic Review*, 17, 142–185.

IMF (2006) *International Financial Statistics*, 2006#12 CD-Rom edition.

Inada, Y. (2000) 'ICSEAD's econometric model of the Chinese economy – 1997 version', Chapter 2 in L.R. Klein and S. Ichimura, *Econometric Modelling of China*, Singapore: World Scientific Publishing, pp. 67–150.

Johansen, S. (1988) 'Statistical analysis of cointegration vectors', *Journal of Economic Dynamics and Control*, 12, 231–254.

Kazakevitch, G. and Smyth, R. (2005) 'Gradualism versus shock therapy: (re)interpreting the Chinese and Russian experiments', *Asia Pacific Business Review*, 11, 69–81.

Kejriwal, M. (2008) 'Cointegration with structural breaks: an application to the Feldstein–Horioka puzzle', *Studies in Nonlinear Dynamics and Econometrics*, 12, 1–37, www.bepress.com/snde/vol12/iss1/art3.

Knight, J. and Song, L. (1999) *The Rural–Urban Divide: Economic Disparities and Interactions in China*, Oxford: Oxford University Press.

Knight, J. and Xue, J. (2006) 'How high is urban unemployment in China?', *Journal of Chinese Economic and Business Studies*, 4, 91–107.

Kojima, R., Nakamura, S. and Ohyama, S. (2005) 'Inflation dynamics in China', *Bank of Japan Working Paper Series*, No. 05-E-9, Tokyo: Bank of Japan.

Laxton, D., Isard, P., Faruquee, H., Prasad, E. and B. Turtelboom (1998) *MULTIMOD Mark III, The core dynamic and steady-state models*, IMF Occasional Paper No. 164, http://imf.org/external/pubs/ft/op/op164/.

Lee, J.-W., McKibbin, W.J. and Park, Y.C. (2006) 'Transpacific trade imbalances: causes and cures', *The World Economy*, 29, 281–303.

Li, X. (2001) 'Government revenue, government expenditure, and temporal causality: evidence from China', *Applied Economics*, 33, 485–497.

NBS (2006) *China Statistical Yearbook 2005*, online edition, www.stats.gov.cn/tjsj/ndsj/2005/indexeh.htm.

OECD (2005) *OECD Statistical Compendium*, 2005#2 CD-Rom edition.

Otero, J. and Smith, J. (2000) 'Testing for cointegration: power versus frequency of observation: further Monte Carlo results', *Economic Letters*, 67, 5–9.

Park, J.Y. and Hahn, S.B. (1999) 'Cointegrating regressions with time varying co-efficients', *Econometric Theory*, 15, 664–703.

Pisani-Ferry, J. (2007) 'The RMB affair', 24 October 2007, www.pisani-ferry.net/article.php3?id_article=240.

Prasad, E. (ed.) (2004) 'China's growth and integration into the world economy: prospects and challenges', *IMF Occasional Paper* No. 232.

Qin, D., Cagas, M.A., Ducanes, G., Magtibay-Ramos, N., Quising, P., He, X., Liu, R. and Liu, S. (2006) 'A small macroeconometric model of the People's Republic of China', *Economic Research Department Working Paper*, No. 81, Mandaluyong (Philippines): Asian Development Bank.

Rawski, T.G. (2001) 'What is happening to China's GDP statistics?', *China Economic Review*, 12, 347–354.

Sachs, J.D. and Woo, W.T. (2000) 'Understanding China's economic performance', *Policy Reform*, 4, 1–50.

Scharping, T. (2001) 'Hide-and-seek: China's elusive population data', *China Economic Review*, 12, 323–332.

Scheibe, J. and Vines, D. (2005) 'A Phillips curve for China', *CAMA Working Paper Series*, No. 2, Canberra: Centre for Applied Macroeconomics Analysis, Australian National University.

Seeborg, M.C., Jin, Z. and Zhu, Y. (2000) 'The new rural–urban labour mobility in China: causes and implications', *Journal of Socio-Economics*, 29, 39–56.

Smyth, R. and Inder, B. (2004) 'Is Chinese provincial real GDP per capita non-stationary? Evidence from multiple trend break unit root tests', *China Economic Review*, 15, 1–24.

Sun, H. and Ma, B. (2004) 'Money and price relationship in China', *Journal of Chinese Economic and Business Studies*, 2, 225–247.

Sun, L. (1998) 'Estimating investment functions based on cointegration: the case of China', *Journal of Comparative Economics*, 26, 175–191.

Tsang, S. and Ma, Y. (1997) 'Simulating the impact of foreign capital in an open-economy macroeconomic model of China', *Economic Modelling*, 14, 435–478.

UNDP (2006) *Human Development Report 2006*, http://hdr.undp.org/hdr2006/.

Wallis, K.F. (2000) 'Macroeconometric modelling', in M. Gudmundsson, T. T. Herbertsson and G. Zoega (eds), *Macroeconomic Policy: Iceland in an Era of Global Integration*, Reykjavik: University of Iceland Press, pp. 399–413.

Wang, X. and Meng, L. (2001). 'A reevaluation of China's economic growth', *China Economic Review*, 12, 338–346.

Wang, Y. and Yao, Y. (2003) 'Sources of China's economic growth 1952–1999: incorporating human capital accumulation', *China Economic Review*, 14, 32–52.

World Bank (2006) *World Development Indicators*, CD-Rom edition, Washington: World Bank.

World Bank (2007) *World Development Indicators*, CD-Rom edition, Washington: World Bank.

Xu, X. (2004) 'China's gross domestic product estimation', *China Economic Review*, 15, 302–322.

Yao, S. (1996) 'Sectoral cointegration, structural break and agriculture's role in the Chinese economy in 1952–92: a VAR approach', *Applied Economics*, 28, 1269–1279.

Yueh, L.Y. (2004) 'Wage reforms in China during the 1990s', *Asian Economic Journal*, 18, 149–164.

Zhang, K.H. and Song, S. (2003) 'Rural–urban migration and urbanization in China: evidence from time-series and cross-section analyses', *China Economic Review*, 14, 386–400.

Zhao, Z. (2005) 'Migration, labour market flexibility, and wage determination in China: a review', *The Developing Economies*, 43, 285–312.

## Appendix: The model long-run equations

The *t*-statistics are reported in parentheses under the coefficients. $\varphi_{YY}$ indicates a dummy that takes value one after year $YY$ and zero elsewhere.

### [1] Primary sector production function

$$\ln(GDP1V/ET1) = \underset{(31.5)}{0.71} + \underset{(6.0)}{0.32\,\varphi_{94}} + (\underset{(5.6)}{0.62} - \underset{(5.0)}{0.41\,\varphi_{94}})\ln(K1V/ET1)$$
$$+ \underset{(2.5)}{0.01\,t}$$

$\bar{R}^2 = 0.98$

### [2] Secondary sector production function

$$\ln(GDP2V/ET2) = \underset{(3.3)}{-0.52} + \underset{(6.6)}{0.19\,\varphi_{93}} + \underset{(13.1)}{0.79\ln(K2V/ET2)} + \underset{(5.4)}{0.02\,t}$$

$\bar{R}^2 = 0.99$

### [3] Tertiary sector production function

$$\ln(GDP3V/ET3) = \underset{(4.4)}{-0.86} + \underset{(7.6)}{1.67\,\varphi_{91}} + (\underset{(13.1)}{0.97} - \underset{(7.7)}{0.50\,\varphi_{91}})\ln(K3V/ET3)$$

$\bar{R}^2 = 0.98$

### [4] Real consumption, rural households

$$\ln(CPRV) = \underset{(5.7)}{1.89} - \underset{(0.9)}{0.59\,\varphi_{88}} + (\underset{(1.7)}{0.22} + \underset{(1.9)}{0.33\varphi_{88}})\ln(YDHR/PCPR)$$
$$+ (\underset{(5.4)}{0.43} - \underset{(2.6)}{0.22\varphi_{88}})\ln(W/PCPR)$$

$\bar{R}^2 = 0.99$

**[5]  Real consumption, urban households**

$$\ln(CPUV) = \underset{(0.9)}{0.42} + \underset{(2.8)}{1.29\ \varphi_{96}} + \underset{(3.0)}{0.61\ \ln(YDHU/PCPU)}$$

$$+ \underset{(2.0)}{(0.25)} - \underset{(2.6)}{0.14\varphi_{96})\ \ln(W/PCPU)}$$

$\bar{R}^2 = 0.99$

**[6]  Total domestic investment**

$$\ln(IDV) = \underset{(7.7)}{-2.19} - \underset{(3.5)}{0.14\ \varphi_{88}} + \underset{(12.2)}{0.93\ \ln(GDE/PI)} + \underset{(4.3)}{0.23\ \ln(XGSV)}$$

$$- \underset{(2.4)}{0.006\ IRLR}$$

$\bar{R}^2 = 0.99$

**[7]  Real imports of goods and services**

$$\ln(MGSV) = \underset{(6.3)}{-7.04} - \underset{(3.9)}{0.34\ \varphi_{95}} + \underset{(6.2)}{1.43\ \ln(A)} + \underset{(2.0)}{0.25\ \ln(XGSV)}$$

$$+ \underset{(3.4)}{0.63\ \ln(PMREL)}$$

$\bar{R}^2 = 0.99$

**[8]  Real exports of goods and services**

$$\ln(XGSV) = \underset{(3.1)}{-25.08} - \underset{(4.6)}{7.78\ \varphi_{98}} + \underset{(3.7)}{2.46\ \ln(YROW)} - \underset{(2.9)}{1.13\ \ln(REER)}$$

$$+ \underset{(6.2)}{(0.26} + \underset{(4.4)}{1.01\ \varphi_{98})\ln(KFV)}$$

$\bar{R}^2 = 0.99$

**[9]  *Per capita* income of rural households**

$$\ln(YQDHR) = \underset{(358.4)}{6.15} - \underset{(1.2)}{3.17\ \varphi_{94}} + \underset{(36.3)}{(1.14} - \underset{(3.6)}{1.06\varphi_{94})\ \ln(GDP1V\times PGDP1/ET1)}$$

$$+ \underset{(2.81)}{0.52\ \varphi_{94}\ \ln(YQDHU)}$$

$\bar{R}^2 = 0.99$

**[10]  *Per capita* income of urban households**

$$\ln(YQDHU) = \underset{(13.5)}{-1.34} + \underset{(17.1)}{3.95\ \varphi_{94}} + \underset{(83.0)}{(1.13} - \underset{(17.4)}{0.45\varphi_{94})\ \ln(UWB)}$$

$\bar{R}^2 = 0.99$

## [11]  Total employment, primary sector

$$\ln(ET1) = \begin{array}{cc} 4.93 & + \ 0.10 \ln(GDEV) \\ (37.4) & (6.8) \end{array}$$
$$\bar{R}^2 = 0.63$$

## [12]  Total employment, secondary sector

$$\ln(GDP2V) - \ln(ET2)$$
$$- 1.04 - 0.79 \ln\left(\frac{UWB}{PI}\right) = \begin{array}{ccc} -5.35 & - \ 1.82 \ \varphi_{89} & + \ 2.04 \ \varphi_{93} \\ (247.4) & (7.9) & (8.6) \end{array}$$
$$+ \quad \begin{array}{ccc} (0.003 & + \ 0.13 \ \varphi_{89} & - \ 0.12 \ \varphi_{93}) \ t \\ (1.2) & (8.2) & (8.0) \end{array}$$
$$\bar{R}^2 = 0.96$$

## [13]  Total employment, tertiary sector

$$\ln(ET3) = \begin{array}{cccc} 1.39 & + \ 0.05 \ \varphi_{87} & + \ 0.60 \ln(GDEV) & + \ 0.07 \ln(IFV) \\ (7.0) & (2.0) & (4.1) & (3.7) \end{array}$$
$$- \quad \begin{array}{c} 0.23 \ln(UWB/PCPU) \\ (1.9) \end{array}$$
$$\bar{R}^2 = 0.99$$

## [14]  Urban-to-total population ratio

$$\ln(POPU/POP) = \begin{array}{cc} -1.78 - \ 0.16 \ \varphi_{95} & + \ (0.53 + 0.36\varphi_{95}) \ln(YQDHU/YQDHR) \\ (42.8) \quad (2.0) & (10.5) \quad (4.6) \end{array}$$
$$\bar{R}^2 = 0.98$$

## [15]  Unit wage

$$\ln(UWB/PCPU) = \begin{array}{cc} -7.24 & - \ 1.73 \ \varphi_{99} & + \ (0.68 + 0.77\varphi_{99}) \ln(GDPV/ET) \\ (163.0) & (5.4) & (27.6) \quad (6.5) \end{array}$$
$$\bar{R}^2 = 0.99$$

## [16]  Production price index

$$\ln(PPI) = \begin{array}{cccc} -3.28 & + \ 0.26 \ \varphi_{91} & + \ 0.49 \ \varphi_{91}\ln(PM) & + \ 0.51 \ln(ULC) \\ (17.0) & (8.0) & (12.6) & (13.3) \end{array}$$
$$\bar{R}^2 = 0.98$$

## [17]  Deflator, rural consumption

$$\ln(PCPR) = \begin{array}{cccc} -0.13 & + \ 0.10 \ \varphi_{94} & + \ 0.87 \ln(PPI) & + \ 0.13 \ln(PM) \\ (12.3) & (6.8) & (47.3) & (6.7) \end{array}$$
$$\bar{R}^2 = 0.99$$

### [18] Deflator, urban consumption

$$\ln(PCPU) = -0.30 + 0.24\,\varphi_{94} + 0.62\ln(PPI) + 0.38\ln(PM)$$
$$\quad\quad\quad\quad (16.5)\quad (9.5)\quad\quad (19.7)\quad\quad\quad\quad (12.3)$$
$$\bar{R}^2 = 0.99$$

### [19] Deflator, public consumption

$$\ln(PCG) = 0.16 - 0.16\,\varphi_{85} + \ln(PCP)$$
$$\quad\quad\quad (12.7)\quad (10.9)$$
$$\bar{R}^2 = 0.99$$

### [20] Deflator, total investment

$$\ln(PI) = -0.15 + 0.12\,\varphi_{90} + 0.81\ln(PPI) + 0.19\ln(PM)$$
$$\quad\quad\quad (9.8)\quad (6.5)\quad\quad (34.0)\quad\quad\quad (7.7)$$
$$\bar{R}^2 = 0.99$$

### [21] Deflator, primary sector value added

$$\ln(PGDP1) = -0.06 + 0.21\,\varphi_{03} + \ln(PCP)$$
$$\quad\quad\quad\quad (4.0)\quad (4.1)$$
$$\bar{R}^2 = 0.98$$

### [22] Deflator, export of goods and services

$$\ln(PXGS) = 0.002 - 0.03\,\varphi_{00} + (1.29 - 0.81\varphi_{00})\ln(PXF)$$
$$\quad\quad\quad\quad (0.1)\quad (0.6)\quad\quad (27.6)\quad (6.5)$$
$$\quad\quad + (0.13 - 0.38\varphi_{00})\ln(PPI)$$
$$\quad\quad\quad (1.3)\quad\quad (0.7)$$
$$\bar{R}^2 = 0.99$$

### [23] Money demand

$$\ln(MONEYS) = -7.33 - 0.41\,\varphi_{92} + (1.88 - 0.07\varphi_{92})\ln(GDPV)$$
$$\quad\quad\quad\quad\quad (8.7)\quad (0.4)\quad\quad (27.6)\quad (6.5)$$
$$\quad\quad + (1.01 - 0.68\varphi_{92})\ln(PGDP)$$
$$\quad\quad\quad (7.1)\quad (3.4)$$
$$\quad\quad - (0.016 - 0.008\varphi_{92}) \times 100\Delta\ln(PGDP)$$
$$\quad\quad\quad (1.4)\quad (1.7)$$
$$\bar{R}^2 = 0.99$$

### [24] Long-term interest rate

$$IRL = 6.57 - 1.61\,\varphi_{00} + 0.26\,[100\,\Delta\ln(PGDP)]$$
$$\quad\quad (16.1)\quad (2.5)\quad\quad (5.2)$$
$$\bar{R}^2 = 0.60$$

Legend of variables

| | |
|---|---|
| A | Domestic absorption |
| CPRV | Rural households' consumption, volume |
| CPUV | Urban households' consumption, volume |
| ET | Total employment |
| ET1 | Employment, primary sector |
| ET2 | Employment, secondary sector |
| ET3 | Employment, tertiary sector |
| GDE | Gross domestic expenditure, value |
| GDEV | Gross domestic expenditure, volume |
| GDP1V | Gross domestic product of primary sector, volume |
| GDP2V | Gross domestic product of secondary sector, volume |
| GDP3V | Gross domestic product of tertiary sector, volume |
| GDPV | Gross domestic product, volume |
| IDV | Gross domestic fixed capital formation, volume |
| IFV | Foreign direct investment, volume |
| IRL | Interest rate, one year nominal rate on loans |
| IRLR | Real interest rate, long term |
| K1V | Capital stock of primary sector, volume |
| K2V | Capital stock of secondary sector, volume |
| K3V | Capital stock of tertiary sector, volume |
| KFV | Foreign direct investments stock |
| MGSV | Imports of good and services, n.a. basis, volume |
| MONEYS | Money stock, value |
| PCG | Deflator, public consumption |
| PCP | Deflator, total private consumption |
| PCPR | Deflator, rural households' consumption |
| PCPU | Deflator, urban households' consumption |
| PGDP | Deflator, gross domestic product |
| PGDP1 | Deflator, primary sector value added |
| PI | Deflator, total investment |
| PM | Import price index (deflator of imports) |
| PMREL | Relative price of imports |
| POP | Total population |
| POPU | Urban population |
| PPI | Production price index |
| PXF | Export price of competitor countries |
| PXGS | Deflator, exports of good and services |
| REER | Real effective exchange rate |
| ULC | Unit labour cost |
| UWB | Unit wage, average wage of staff and workers |
| W | Stock of financial wealth, value |
| XGSV | Exports of good and services, n.a. basis, volume |
| YDHR | Rural households' disposable income |
| YDHU | Urban households' disposable income |
| YQDHR | Per capita rural residents disposable income |
| YQDHU | Per capita urban residents disposable income |
| YROW | World demand |

# 2 Do sentiment indicators help to assess and predict actual developments in the Chinese economy?

*Aaron Mehrotra and Jouko Rautava*

## Introduction

In 2005, China surpassed France and the UK in nominal GDP to become the fourth largest economy in the world after Germany, Japan and the US. If we apply GDP in PPP terms, only the US outranks China. China's global role is underlined by the fact that foreign trade plays a more prominent role in the Chinese economy than in most other large economies: its exports-to-GDP ratio is about 37 per cent.[1] In recent years, China's contribution to global economic growth has been particularly noteworthy.

The increasing importance of China for the world economy assures a growing demand for information on its macroeconomic developments. However, from the standpoint of economic monitoring and research, major problems remain regarding basic economic statistics. This is evidenced by the 17 per cent upward revision of GDP at the end of 2005; it is based on improved information on the role of the service sector in China's booming economy.[2] Moreover, even with the improvements in GDP data, their usefulness is still impaired by a lack of quarterly series on GDP components in real terms. On the expenditure side of GDP, the problems are even more formidable. Thus, quarterly consumption and investment data are available only as cumulative nominal data, which do not enable direct computation of actual quarterly figures.[3]

While one could in principle use some other indicators to proxy a national account item, there is also a lack of satisfactory proxies. For example, it has been argued that the monthly indicator on retail sales poorly captures trends in household consumption. The same applies to capital formation, as investment data published on a monthly basis (fixed asset investment) differ conceptually from the internationally comparable national account measure (gross fixed capital formation).[4] Besides the problems with real sector data, lack of proper price indices hinders the evaluation of actual developments.

To deal with concerns about the availability and reliability of data, one can use various survey indicators to gain insights into current developments and future trends in the real economy. While business sentiment indicators are widely used in developed industrial countries, their role in assessing Chinese developments has so far been very modest. Nevertheless, the National Bureau of Statistics (NBS) and the People's Bank of China (PBoC) have for several years been publishing a number of survey indicators for the consumer and business sectors.

In this chapter, we consider various business condition indicators reported by the PBoC in order to evaluate their usefulness in assessing and forecasting developments in the Chinese economy. We are not aware of any earlier studies focusing on the forecasting properties of Chinese survey indicators. Our contribution is to add to the existing literature on use of survey data for forecasting, which has predominantly focused on developed economies. Moreover, our approach provides an alternative method of assessing the reliability of the Chinese real sector 'hard' data. We find that our estimated bivariate vector autoregressive models, each composed of one diffusion index and one real sector variable, usually lead to an improvement in forecasting performance compared with a univariate autoregressive process. Similarly, principal components analysis, combining information from various diffusion indices, leads to enhanced forecasting performance. These results indicate that Chinese business sentiment indicators provide useful information about current and future developments in the Chinese economy. They also suggest that the official data provide a relatively accurate picture of the Chinese economy.

The chapter is organised as follows. In the next section, we provide a brief overview of the literature on forecasting properties of survey data. In the third, we discuss the availability of business condition indicators in China and the main characteristics of the indicators chosen for this study. The fourth section deals with the analytical framework, providing details of the empirical methodology applied in our exercise. The fifth section reports the results of our estimations, and the concluding section summarizes our findings.

## Literature review

The first business surveys go back at least to the 1920s and are widely used today in developed economies.[5] The classification of leading and business confidence (sentiment, climate) indicators appears to be somewhat arbitrary. However, leading indicators are often based on regularly published 'hard' data (money supply, asset prices, exports, etc.), while confidence indicators are built on certain consumer and enterprise surveys. Sometimes composite leading indicators include both hard and soft data. In principle, survey indicators that measure the judgements of economic agents about future prospects can provide valuable indications of possible turning points in the business cycle and hence may serve as leading indicators for economic developments. In practice, however, the situation is more complicated, as the forecasting properties of indicators may differ significantly, and track records are not always readily available for particular indicators. As noted by Brisson *et al.* (2003), some of the most important and interesting economic time series, such as GDP and investment growth, are particularly difficult to forecast. Here, we mention some studies that have used, or evaluated the use of, survey data for forecasting in various countries.

Previous research has often focused on use of survey data for forecasting industrial or manufacturing production. In his study of eight OECD countries, Madsen (1993) shows that survey expectations of production have predictive value for manufacturing output. For the euro area, Bodo *et al.* (2000) find that a conditional error correction model that includes the European Commission's business confidence index performs well in forecasting industrial production. Abberger (2004) evaluates the usefulness of the Ifo Institute's business cycle indicator ('business cycle clock') for German manufacturing based on two survey indicators of the current business situation and expectations. Using a circular-linear correlation method, he finds a high correlation between the Ifo business cycle indicator and output. Nevertheless, the interpretation of turning points within a business cycle is actually more difficult than assumed in the simple graphical representation of the business cycle indicator. Lemmens *et al.* (2005) show that business survey data can also assist in forecasting industrial production across different EU member states, i.e. one country's production levels can be forecasted by means of other countries' expectations. Using data for different industrial sectors, Kauppi *et al.* (1996) examine the forecasting ability of surveys for the severe recession in the Finnish economy in the early 1990s. Forecast errors were generally larger during the downturn, but models for the food and forest industries performed better than in normal times. Taking a more micro-oriented approach, Mitchell *et al.* (2005) use firm-level survey data in order to forecast manufacturing output growth in Britain. They find that this method improves forecasts relative to an approach using aggregated data.

Several studies have used business survey data for forecasting GDP growth. Mourougane and Roma (2003) examine the usefulness of the European Commission confidence indicators to forecast real GDP growth rates in selected euro area countries. They find that these indicators are useful for forecasting in Belgium, Germany, France, Italy and the Netherlands. Gayer (2005) also evaluates the forecasting potential of European Commission survey indicators in terms of aggregate euro area GDP growth. His findings suggest that the indicators' usefulness is restricted to the short term, namely one- or two-quarter forecast horizons. Langmantel (2007) considers the use of the Ifo business climate indicator for short-term GDP forecasting for Germany. He finds that the forecasting performance of the climate indicator depends on the forecast period; this makes it difficult to know *a priori* which model is more reliable. Hansson *et al.* (2005) use a dynamic factor model to filter noisy survey data and reduce dimensions in forecasting GDP growth in Sweden. They find that this procedure leads to improved forecasts compared to alternative specifications.

Survey data has proved useful beyond the forecasting of industrial production or GDP growth. In a recent study, Ang *et al.* (2007) examine four different methods of forecasting US inflation. They find that survey-based forecasts outperform time-series ARIMA models, specifications with Phillips-curve-motivated real activity measures, and term structure models. Regarding the use of survey indicators for policy work, Britton *et al.* (1999) explain how the Bank of England uses survey data in its economic assessment and policy decisions. Souleles (2004) provides a comprehensive analysis of the issues related to the use of US consumer sentiment survey data for testing the rationality of consumer expectations and the usefulness of survey data in forecasting consumer expenditures.

While the previous literature concentrates on advanced economies, we are not aware of any previous research focusing on the use of survey data for forecasting in China. Qin *et al.* (2006), however, include a consumer confidence index as part of a larger dataset in order to forecast GDP growth and CPI inflation in Mainland China, Indonesia and the Philippines. Their study compares the forecasting performance of an automatic leading indicator method with a macroeconometric structural model. The OECD composite leading indicator for China does not include any survey variables but instead uses 'hard' data from the real, external and financial sectors of the economy (Nilsson and Brunet 2006). Similarly, in order to forecast real GDP growth for Mainland China, Curran and Funke (2006) use an indicator based on data on exports, the real estate market and share prices.

## Data

In China, data limitations and economic reforms make it challenging to assess relationships between actual developments and sentiment indicator results, especially as compared with developed economies. Regarding business conditions in China, the NBS's quarterly Business Climate Index and the Confidence Index for Entrepreneurs are available for certain industrial, construction, transportation, real estate and service sectors. However, these indices have been reported only since the first quarter of 1998, which limits their usefulness for an econometric exercise.

The PBoC has published diffusion indices for the 5,000 largest industrial enterprises since 1992.[6] These quarterly series reflect judgements on developments experienced in the recent past, the current situation, and prospects for the next few months. The values for the indices range from −100 to +100, and a positive index number indicates that conditions are improving.[7] The diffusion index for general business condition (GBC) has tracked well the impact of the Asian crisis in the late 1990s and the ever-improving economic climate thereafter. Figure 2.1 displays the GBC and year-on-year growth rates for industrial production. An informal analysis suggests that the GBC could be considered a leading indicator for industrial production, as the two series are moderately correlated for 1, 2 or 3 lags of the GBC (coefficients between 0.58 and 0.65).[8]

Given the above considerations, in this chapter we consider the GBC and

*Figure 2.1* General business condition and industrial production (year on year growth rate).

three other diffusion indices (the current overseas and domestic order level, and lending attitude of bank) compiled by the PBoC to evaluate their ability to forecast developments in the Chinese economy. Domestic and overseas order levels were chosen for their presumably direct demand-pull link with our real sector variables. They measure demand in domestic and export markets, respectively (see, for example, PBoC 2007). Lending attitude of bank should indicate the role of financial factors in real developments. It reflects entrepreneurs' satisfaction over bank loans, and could be affected by both their cost and availability (see, for example, PBoC 2006, 2007). Indeed, Chinese news reports suggest that interest rate increases by the PBoC have impacted this variable (*China Economic News* 2007). These three other diffusion indices are illustrated in Figure 2.2.

Due to the aforementioned problems with GDP data and the fact that quarterly real GDP series are available only since 1998, we evaluate forecasting performances of the diffusion indices for developments in industrial output, retail sales and Chinese exports.[9] These three series feature prominently in public discussions and news about Chinese economic developments.[10] Consequently, it would be interesting to know whether diffusion indices could be used to provide forecasts for these three real sector indicators.

In order to obtain stationary time series data for econometric inference, the

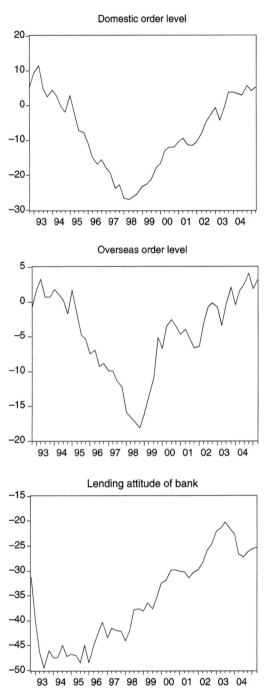

*Figure 2.2* Domestic and overseas order level and lending attitude of bank.

following transformations were applied. All the diffusion index variables were differenced once. Real exports and real retail sales in levels were first-differenced and transformed into logarithms.[11] The year-on-year growth rate of industrial production was differenced once, without logarithmic transformation.[12] Augmented Dickey–Fuller (ADF) tests for unit root generally suggest that the resulting series are stationary, as shown in the Appendix.[13]

## Methodology

Our approach for analysing the information content of the different diffusion indices is based largely on the vector autoregressive (VAR) framework. The formal presentation that follows draws on Lütkepohl (2004). A reduced form VAR representation can be written as

$$x_t = A_1 x_{t-1} + \ldots + A_p x_{t-p} + CD_t + u_t \tag{1}$$

where $p$ denotes the order of the model. In our VAR with $K$ endogenous variables, $x_t = (x_{1t}, \ldots, x_{Kt})'$ is a $(K \times 1)$ random vector, the $A_i$ are fixed $(K \times K)$ coefficient matrices and $D_t$ is a vector of deterministic terms. $C$ is the coefficient matrix associated with the deterministic terms. $u_t = (u_{1t}, \ldots, u_{Kt})'$ is assumed to follow a $K$-dimensional white noise process with $E(u_t) = 0$.

We commence with a discussion of bivariate vector autoregressions (BVARs). Every BVAR in the first part of the empirical study is composed of one indicator of the real economy (industrial production, retail sales or exports) and one diffusion index (overseas/domestic order levels, general business condition or lending attitude of bank). The particular pair of variables depends on the suitability of the series; for example, lending attitude of bank could *a priori* be considered appropriate to provide information about future growth of industrial production. All VARs are estimated for the time period 1993Q1–2004Q2.[14]

The estimated BVARs are then utilized in a forecasting exercise. After specifying a VAR model that passes the tests for mis-specification, we use it to obtain out-of-sample forecasts for the real sector variable one, two and four periods ahead, so that forecasts are generated for the period 2004Q3–2005Q2. An $h$-step forecast based on estimated coefficients yields

$$\hat{x}_{T+h|T} = \hat{A}_1 \hat{x}_{T+h-1|T} + \ldots + \hat{A}_p \hat{x}_{T+h-p|T}, \tag{2}$$

where for $\hat{x}_{T+j|T} = x_{T+j}$ for $j \leq 0$ and the $\hat{A}_i$ ($i = 1, \ldots, p$) are estimated parameters. The goodness of the forecasts is assessed by comparing them to forecasts from a univariate AR model in terms of the ratio of root mean square forecast errors (RMSE). In the univariate AR model, only the past developments in the real sector variable are used in order to obtain forecasts for this variable.

One obvious criticism of the BVAR approach is that more information could be obtained by using combinations of the diffusion indices. Therefore, we also estimate trivariate VAR models, each including one real sector variable and two diffusion indices, and compare the forecasting performance of these with the simple AR models. A problem here with the multivariate VAR models is the extremely high correlation between the three diffusion indices (general business condition and domestic and overseas order levels), as shown in Figures 2.1 and 2.2. This militates against using any combination of these in multivariate VAR models. Therefore, we also employ principal components analysis, where we generate new variables (the principal components) as linear combinations of the original variables (the diffusion indices). This is done by modelling their variance structure (see Johnson and Wichern 2002). The eigenvalue decomposition of the variance matrix is calculated, and the first principal component is obtained as the unit-length linear combination of the original variables with maximum variance. Going forward, the weights of the linear combinations – the factor loadings – are chosen by maximizing variance among unit-length linear combinations, so that the new principal components are always orthogonal to the previous components.[15] Given the orthogonality condition, we are able to use information derived from the different diffusion indices, even when those indices are highly correlated. In general, the use of principal components can also be seen as a way of summarizing information extracted from a large number of predictors.[16] This analysis allows us to determine the component with the highest variance proportion in the principal components analysis. In the BVAR framework, we estimate a model including this principal component and the real sector variable, and compare the forecasts from this model with univariate autoregressions.

A note on cointegration is in order. Our BVARs are estimated by using the stationary first-differenced variables. As the original (untransformed) variables are integrated of order one, possible cointegrating relations cannot be ruled out. However, we find little robust evidence of common stochastic trends in our short sample utilizing the Johansen trace test. We, therefore proceed on the assumption that no cointegration relationships exist among the untransformed (levels) data for the diffusion indices and real sector variables.[17]

## Empirical results

In this section, we present the results from the estimated models. We commence with evidence provided by the bivariate and trivariate VAR models using the individual business sentiment indicators. Finally, we look at results from the principal components analysis.

### *Forecasts with individual indicators*

The order of the VAR model is based mainly on the Akaike information criterion, with 8 as the maximum number of lags. In the case where misspecification tests provide evidence against the indicated order, another lag length is used. A constant is included as a deterministic term for all systems, whereas a linear trend is included only when it is statistically significant. The chosen systems using the business sentiment indicators perform quite satisfactorily in the conducted mis-specification tests.[18]

We next compare the *h*-step out-of-sample forecasts of the real sector variables yielded by our BVARs to simple AR models involving only the past values of the real sector variable. The forecasting ability of the model is determined by the ratio of the root mean square forecast error (RMSE) of the BVAR process to the AR model, one, two and four quarters ahead. The lag length of the AR model is based on the same considerations as the VAR model above. The results of this exercise are presented in Table 2.1.

The first four rows in Table 2.1 show that in seven cases out of nine, the BVAR models including a diffusion index outperform forecasts from a univariate AR-process with forecasts for one, two and four quarters ahead. This is suggested by values with magnitudes of less than 1 in the table. Specifically, in the case of exports and industrial production, the forecasting performance of the BVAR model is always superior to that of an AR-process. For retail sales, a simple AR-process produces the best one-quarter-ahead forecast, whereas the forecasting ability of the BVARs improves substantially when forecasting two and four quarters ahead. Lending attitude of bank seems to provide information that improves forecasts quite substantially, at least in the short run.

A comparison of the forecasting performance of the enterprise survey indicators with other plausible leading indicators is complicated in the Chinese

*Table 2.1* Relative RMSE of forecasts: BVAR, trivariate VAR and AR models 2004Q3–2005Q2

| Predictor | Exports | | | Retail sales | | | Industrial production | | |
|---|---|---|---|---|---|---|---|---|---|
| | $h=1$ | $h=2$ | $h=4$ | $h=1$ | $h=2$ | $h=4$ | $h=1$ | $h=2$ | $h=4$ |
| General business condition | 0.62 | 0.52 | 0.36 | 1.00 | 0.52 | 0.45 | 0.70 | 0.69 | 0.75 |
| Domestic order level | – | – | – | 1.86 | 0.55 | 0.57 | 0.86 | 0.84 | 0.86 |
| Overseas order level | 0.33 | 0.63 | 0.52 | – | – | – | 0.77 | 0.72 | 0.78 |
| Lending attitude of bank | 0.24 | 0.14 | 0.20 | – | – | – | 0.06 | 0.36 | 0.70 |
| OECD leading indicator | 0.07 | 0.36 | 0.43 | 2.73 | 1.09 | 0.73 | 0.41 | 1.08 | 1.04 |
| General business condition, Lending attitude of bank | 1.65 | 1.16 | 0.91 | – | – | – | 0.05 | 0.30 | 0.78 |
| Domestic order level, lending attitude of bank | – | – | – | – | – | – | 0.13 | 0.28 | 1.01 |
| Overseas order level, lending attitude of bank | 0.59 | 0.39 | 0.35 | – | – | – | 0.79 | 0.84 | 1.11 |

case by the paucity of data. However, the OECD publishes a composite leading indicator for China, which is available at monthly frequency.[19] The component series used in the compilation of this indicator are cargo handled at ports, enterprise deposits, chemical fertilizer production, non-ferrous metal production, monetary aggregate M2, and imports from Asia. Even though this composite variable is not designed to provide information on the series for retail sales and exports considered in our study, it does provide a benchmark against which the enterprise survey indicators can be examined. The fifth row of Table 2.1 shows the results from BVARs utilizing the OECD composite leading indicator.[20] The BVAR model outperforms the univariate AR model for all forecast horizons only in the case of exports. This is perhaps not surprising given that two of the components of the OECD indicator are directly linked to trade. As in the models with enterprise survey indicators, retail sales seem to be the most difficult variable to forecast.[21]

The vector autoregressive setup further allows us to examine the dynamics between diffusion indices and real sector variables by using impulse response analysis. In this framework, we introduce a shock to the diffusion index and trace the effects of this shock on the real sector variable in the BVAR setup. In most of our estimated BVARs, the model residuals are not contemporaneously correlated, which enables the use of forecast error impulse responses (for a discussion of impulse response analysis, see Breitung *et al.* 2004). However, in only three BVAR systems do we obtain a statistically significant impact of diffusion index shock on real sector variables. Acknowledging that 'shocks' to the diffusion indices are difficult to justify from a theoretical viewpoint, and that the statistical significance of these shocks may be limited in our short sample, we leave further causality analysis to future research.

The forecasting performance of the trivariate VAR models is evaluated in the last three rows of Table 2.1. We consider only combinations of those diffusion indices that are not closely correlated. In order to disregard a large number of statistically insignificant coefficients in these larger systems, we used subset models where the coefficients with *t* values below the threshold of one were eliminated from the system. The trivariate models outperform the univariate autoregressions at all forecast horizons in only two of five systems examined. Both systems include the lending attitude of bank, but this variable is also included in those cases where the multivariate systems are found to provide poorer forecasts than the AR models. Overall, the BVAR models seem to perform better in relative terms than the trivariate ones.

*Forecasts with principal components*

Finally, we use the principal components methodology to examine the forecasting ability of the variables created by this approach. Here, new variables are generated as linear combinations of the original variables by modelling their variance structure. The weights of the linear combinations – the factor loadings – are chosen so that the new principal components are always orthogonal to the previous components.[22] Table 2.2 depicts the results from the principal components analysis. The eigenvalues here result from orthogonalization of the sample correlation matrix, whereas the variance proportion indicates the share of a principal component in the total variance.

The first principal component (PC1), which has high negative factor loadings on domestic and overseas order levels and on general business condition, possibly reflects a broadly weak demand environment. As PC2 has a high negative coefficient on lending attitude of bank, this second component may capture the strength of demand relative to supply-side factors. The third principal component is admittedly more difficult to interpret, as it is comprised of a high negative loading on general business condition and high positive loadings on lending attitude of bank and domestic order level. Finally, PC4, with a large positive coefficient for domestic order level and a large-magnitude negative coefficient for overseas order level, could indicate the strength of domestic demand relative to external demand.

As most of the information from the diffusion indices can be summarized by the first principal component (55 per cent of the total variance), we use this first component in the BVAR setup with real sector variables, again comparing the resulting forecasts to the univariate AR models. The results are displayed in Table 2.3.

Table 2.3 shows that summarizing information from all four diffusion indices by the first principal component results in an improvement in the

*Table 2.2* Principal components of diffusion index variables, 1993Q1–2004Q2

|  | *PC1* | *PC2* | *PC3* | *PC4* |
|---|---|---|---|---|
| Eigenvalue | 2.19 | 1.20 | 0.40 | 0.22 |
| Variance proportion | 0.55 | 0.30 | 0.10 | 0.05 |
| Loadings: |  |  |  |  |
| Domestic order level | −0.57 | 0.36 | 0.38 | 0.64 |
| Overseas order level | −0.59 | 0.32 | 0.07 | −0.74 |
| General business condition | −0.52 | −0.38 | −0.74 | 0.18 |
| Lending attitude of bank | −0.24 | −0.79 | 0.55 | −0.10 |

*Table 2.3* Relative RMSE of forecasts, BVARs with first principal component and AR models, 2004Q3–2005Q2

| *Predictor* | *Exports* | | | *Retail sales* | | | *Industrial production* | | |
|---|---|---|---|---|---|---|---|---|---|
|  | *h = 1* | *h = 2* | *h = 4* | *h = 1* | *h = 2* | *h = 4* | *h = 1* | *h = 2* | *h = 4* |
| First principal component | 0.57 | 0.78 | 0.88 | 0.46 | 0.61 | 0.47 | 0.65 | 0.78 | 0.79 |
| First principal component (excl. GBC) | 0.48 | 0.74 | 0.81 | 0.38 | 0.63 | 0.47 | 0.75 | 0.84 | 0.86 |

forecasting exercise as compared with the univariate model. Notably, the relative RMSE values are less than one for all forecasting horizons and for all real sector variables, as shown in the first row of the table. As a robustness check, we re-estimated the first principal component by excluding general business condition (GBC).[23] One can argue that the inclusion of general business condition in the principal components analysis is unnecessary, as this variable may act as a summary variable of the different diffusion indices. Nevertheless, this robustness check does not change the conclusions from the principal components analysis, as shown in the second row of Table 2.3. It seems that the information content of the various diffusion indices can be meaningfully combined by principal components to form forecasts of the real sector variables. In particular, PC1 that accounts for over half of the total variance of the diffusion indices, forecasts the Chinese real sector variables quite satisfactorily.

## Conclusion

While business condition indices are regularly published in China, their role in economic monitoring is still very modest compared with the use of similar indicators in developed countries. In this chapter, we used various econometric techniques to study whether the diffusion indices published by the PBoC could be useful in assessing the short-term prospects of the Chinese economy. To our knowledge, while composite leading indicators have been constructed for China, no previous studies have evaluated the forecasting power of business sentiment indicators in the Chinese context.

We find that forecasts from our bivariate vector autoregressive models, each composed of one diffusion index and one real sector variable, generally outperform forecasts from univariate AR models one to four quarters ahead. In particular, the forecasts for industrial production and exports in the BVAR framework always beat the AR forecasts. These results suggest that the individual diffusion indices considered in our chapter could be meaningfully applied in a BVAR setup to predict future economic developments in China, which is of importance for macroeconomic decision making, including monetary policy. Similarly, principal components analysis, summarizing information from various diffusion indices, always outperforms the univariate AR models. However, the forecasting performance of trivariate VAR models, including two individual business sentiment indicators, does not differ markedly from the univariate models.

From the viewpoint of economic monitoring and research, there are still problems with basic Chinese macroeconomic statistics. This makes the comparison between 'soft' survey data and 'hard' macroeconomic time series particularly interesting. In fact, our results could be seen as support for the reliability of the hard macroeconomic time series considered in our chapter. We find that the trends in both soft and hard data are similar. Moreover, it seems that soft data can be satisfactorily used to predict the hard data.

Therefore, it is likely that both series reflect the same underlying economic dynamics.

The results are broadly in line with the existing literature concerning the use of survey data in various countries, as business surveys are found to be potentially useful in forecasting short-run real developments in China. For future research, it may be of interest to examine the forecasting ability of those Chinese survey indicators that are not investigated in this study, including the ones published by the National Bureau of Statistics. Nevertheless, one must be careful in choosing among numerous available survey indicators, and formal testing of their forecast properties is needed before they are brought into the actual forecasting work.

## Notes

1 The figure is based on data for 2006 from the National Bureau of Statistics (2007).
2 See PBoC (2005) for a detailed description of the revision and its implications for the structure of China's GDP.
3 In order to overcome problems with quarterly Chinese GDP data, Curran and Funke (2006) invoke some simple assumptions and time series techniques to construct a quarterly GDP series in real terms.
4 See World Bank's China Quarterly Update August 2005.
5 For more information on business surveys, see OECD (2003).
6 According to the NBS, in 2006 there were about 2,700 large and 30,200 medium-sized industrial enterprises in China.
7 The data are presented as the balance of positive replies over negative replies expressed as a percentage of positive plus negative replies.
8 It is of interest to compare the volatility of the GBC with the commonly-quoted Tankan index (business conditions, manufacturing) for Japan. We find that GBC volatility, measured by its standard deviation, amounted to 10.7 during 1993Q1–2005Q2, compared to 17.0 for the Tankan index. However, the higher volatility for Tankan is also partly reflected in the series for industrial production in the Japanese economy, where the standard deviation for the year-on-year growth rate of industrial production in the same period was 5.1 (4.8 for China).
9 As one of our aims is to assess the reliability of the Chinese real sector 'hard' data, we do not use unofficial constructed series for GDP in the forecasts.
10 Holz (2004) notes that the regular data reporting system is most highly developed for the industrial sector. Industrial statistics have moved to a two-class compilation system where industrial firms with accurate data report directly to the NBS (accounting for 60 per cent of industrial production) and all other firms are covered by sample surveys.
11 Real retail sales was constructed by deflating nominal retail sales by a proxy for the CPI index (which is not available directly and was thus built by the authors). Real exports was obtained by deflating US dollar export figures by the US CPI.
12 It would have been preferable to use as the raw series industrial production in levels, similar to real retail sales and real exports, as the year-on-year growth rates are by definition affected by historical developments, which may not be optimal in a forecasting exercise. However, the estimated systems did not perform satisfactorily in the mis-specification tests using the industrial production series in levels (again, constructed by the authors).
13 There are no clear structural breaks in the final series used in the estimation,

but we have taken their possible existence into account as follows. We use an automated procedure in the econometric software JMulTi to search for possible structural breaks (modelled as impulse dummy variables in the first-differenced series). Then, we use the Lanne *et al.* (2002) unit root test with a structural break, with the suggested break dates and corresponding impulse dummies by the automated procedure. Nevertheless, these do not change the conclusions from the unit root tests about the stationarity of the series.

14  Period 1993Q2–2004Q2 is used in the VARs with retail sales due to data availability.

15  The weights of the linear combinations are used to multiply the original time series variables in order to obtain the principal components.

16  Principal components analysis is utilized in Stock and Watson (2002), where diffusion indices are used to forecast US macroeconomic time series. Their forecasts outperform univariate autoregressions, small vector autoregressions and leading indicator models.

17  The Johansen trace test for the transformed variables in the BVAR systems (that include one diffusion index and one real sector variable), suggests a cointegration rank of two for all models. This finding is in line with our results from the unit root tests, suggesting that all final series are stationary.

18  These tests include the Portmanteau and LM tests for autocorrelation, the Doornik–Hansen (1994) test for non-normality and the ARCH-LM test. There is very weak evidence of autocorrelation (only at 10 per cent significance level) in the models consisting of overseas order level and industrial production, and domestic order level and industrial production. The performance of the models with the OECD composite leading indicator instead of the diffusion indices was somewhat poorer. There is now evidence of autocorrelation at certain lag orders even at 5 per cent level (and at 1 per cent level when exports are used as the real sector variable). However, the composite indicator is not the focus of our study. Detailed results from the mis-specification tests are available from the authors upon request.

19  For the purposes of our study, we aggregated this series from monthly to quarterly frequency by calculating the average value for each quarter. To ensure stationarity, the resulting quarterly series was included in the analysis in logarithms and differenced once.

20  It should be noted that our series for industrial production differs in construction from the one used as a reference series for China's composite leading indicators by Nilsson and Brunet (2006). We use the year-on-year real growth rate of industry value added provided by China Monthly Economic Indicators from 2002Q3 onwards and the IMF's series up to 2002Q2. Nilsson and Brunet consider a series constructed by combining the series for gross industrial output before 1994 and industrial value added for 1995–2004, converted to 1995 prices.

21  To again compare the Chinese diffusion indices with their Japanese counterparts, we constructed a BVAR model with Japanese industrial production (year-on-year growth rate) and the Tankan index (business conditions, manufacturing). However, in this brief analysis for Japan, the BVAR forecasts were not markedly different from those from a univariate AR model.

22  We acknowledge that if there is a non-linear relation between the diffusion indices, principal components may not be an optimal approach.

23  The variance proportion of the new first principal component amounts to 0.59 (excluding GBC).

# References

Abberger, K. (2004) Another look at the Ifo business cycle clock, *Journal of Business Cycle Measurement and Analysis*, 2(3), pp. 431–443.

Ang, A., Bekaert, G. and Wei, M. (2007) Do macro variables, asset markets, or surveys forecast inflation better?, *Journal of Monetary Economics*, 54, pp. 1163–1212.

Bodo, G., Golinelli, R. and Parigi, G. (2000) Forecasting industrial production in the Euro area, *Empirical Economics*, 25, pp. 541–561.

Breitung, J., Brüggemann, R. and Lütkepohl, H. (2004) Structural vector autoregressive modeling and impulse responses, in H. Lütkepohl and M. Krätzig (eds), *Applied Time Series Econometrics*, Cambridge: Cambridge University Press, pp. 159 pp. 159–196.

Brisson, M., Campbell, B. and Galbraith, J. W. (2003) Forecasting some low-predictability time series using diffusion indices, *Journal of Forecasting*, 22, pp. 515–531.

Britton, E., Cutler, J. and Wardlow, A. (1999) The Bank's use of survey data, *Bank of England Quarterly Bulletin*, May, pp. 177–182.

*China Economic News* (2007) Entrepreneurs' confidence index lower in Q3, 41, 22 October.

Curran, D. and Funke, M. (2006) Taking the temperature: forecasting GDP growth for mainland China, BOFIT Discussion Paper No. 6/2006.

Doornik, J.A. and Hansen, H. (1994) A practical test for univariate and multivariate normality, Nuffield College Discussion Paper.

Gayer, C. (2005) Forecast evaluation of European Commission survey indicators, *Journal of Business Cycle Measurement and Analysis*, 2(2), pp. 157–183.

Hansson, J., Jansson, P. and Löf, M. (2005) Business survey data: do they help in forecasting GDP growth?, *International Journal of Forecasting*, 21, pp. 377–389.

Holz, C.A. (2004) China's statistical system in transition: challenges, data problems, and institutional innovations, *Review of Income and Wealth*, 50(3), pp. 381–409.

Johnson, R.A. and Wichern, D. (2002) *Applied Multivariate Statistical Analysis*, 5th edition, Englewood Cliffs, NJ: Prentice Hall.

Kauppi, E., Lassila, J. and Teräsvirta, T. (1996) Short-term forecasting of industrial production with business survey data: experience from Finland's great depression 1990–1993, *International Journal of Forecasting*, 12, pp. 373–381.

Langmantel, E. (2007) Can the Ifo business climate indicator improve short-term GDP forecasts?, in G. Goldrian (ed.), *Handbook of Survey-based Business Cycle Analysis*, Cheltenham: Edward Elgar, pp. 159–173.

Lanne, M., Lütkepohl, H. and Saikkonen, P. (2002) Comparison of unit root tests for time series with level shifts, *Journal of Time Series Analysis*, 23, pp. 667–685.

Lemmens, A., Croux, C. and Dekimpe M.G. (2005) On the predictive content of production surveys: a pan-European study, *International Journal of Forecasting*, 21(2), pp. 363–375.

Lütkepohl, H. (2004) Vector autoregressive and vector error correction models, in H. Lütkepohl and M. Krätzig (eds), *Applied Time Series Econometrics*, Cambridge: Cambridge University Press, pp. 86–158.

Madsen, J.B. (1993) The predictive value of production expectations in the manufacturing industry, *Journal of Forecasting*, 12, pp. 273–289.

Mitchell, J., Smith, R.J. and Weale, M.R. (2005) Forecasting manufacturing output growth using firm-level survey data, *The Manchester School*, 73(4), pp. 479–499.

Mourougane, A. and Roma, M. (2003) Can confidence indicators be useful to predict short term real GDP growth?, *Applied Economics Letters*, 10, pp. 519–522.

National Bureau of Statistics (2007) *China Statistical Yearbook 2007*, Beijing: China Statistics Press.

Nilsson, R. and Brunet, O. (2006) Composite leading indicators for major OECD non-member economies, OECD Statistics Working Paper No. 2006/01.

OECD (2003) *Business Tendency Surveys: A Handbook*, Paris: OECD.

PBoC (2005) *China Monetary Policy Report, Quarter Four, 2005*, Beijing: China Financial Publishing House.

PBoC (2006) *People's Bank of China Quarterly Statistical Bulletin 2006–3*, Beijing: PBoC.

PBoC (2007) *People's Bank of China Quarterly Statistical Bulletin, 2007–2*, Beijing: PBoC.

Qin, D., Cagas, M.A., Ducanes, G., Magtibay-Ramos, N. and Quising, P. (2006) Forecasting inflation and GDP growth: Automatic Leading Indicator (ALI) method versus Macroeconometric Structural Models (MESMs), ERD Technical Note Series 18, Asian Development Bank.

Souleles, N.S. (2004) Expectations, heterogeneous forecast errors, and consumption: micro evidence from the Michigan Consumer Sentiment Surveys, *Journal of Money, Credit, and Banking*, 36(1), pp. 39–72.

Stock, J.H. and Watson, M.W. (2002) Macroeconomic forecasting using diffusion indexes, *Journal of Business and Economic Statistics*, 20(2), pp. 147–162.

## Appendix: Augmented Dickey–Fuller tests on final series used in estimation

| Series | Lags | Test statistic |
| --- | --- | --- |
| Domestic order level | 3 (AIC, HQ) | −1.40 |
| | 0 (SC) | −5.72*** |
| Exports | 8 (AIC, HQ) | −0.42 |
| | 3 (SC) | −5.31*** |
| Overseas order level | 0 (AIC, HQ, SC) | −6.16*** |
| General business condition | 7 (AIC) | −1.20 |
| | 3 (HQ) | −1.88 |
| | 0 (SC) | −7.85*** |
| Industrial production | 0 (AIC, HQ, SC) | −9.71*** |
| Lending attitude of bank | 0 (AIC, HQ, SC) | −6.35*** |
| Retail sales | 4 (AIC, HQ) | −3.04** |
| | 0 (SC) | −5.98*** |

*Notes:* Constant included as deterministic term in all models; information criteria in parentheses: AIC = Akaike, HQ = Hannan-Quinn, SC = Schwarz criteria; *10% significance level, **5% significance level and ***1% significance level.

# 3 Supporting China's GDP with ecologically efficient ultra high-speed freight transport systems

*John Kidd and Marielle Stumm*

## Introduction

This chapter proposes that regional and pan-continental arguments concerning China's infrastructure development should consider broad economic and ecological arguments so that it can sustain its growth pattern and do this with respect to both its near and more distant partners. As European and US manufacturers and consumers, and now Chinese consumers, become more closely interdependent, it is time to look to the balance of air, land and sea transport costs, especially those relating to freight, bearing in mind their propensity to pollute. We note that using a (traditional) railway train the end-to-end delivery time of containers from China to Europe is about 20 days, while our proposed Maglev ultra high-speed system could reduce this to three days. In comparison, air freight is limited to about 100 tonnes per plane (fast, but expensive per tonne/km), and Malaccamax boats carrying over 10,000 containers take 35+ days travelling from Asia to Europe, or 45+ days if the ships have to round the Cape of Africa if they are too large for the Suez canal. Overall, we expect the long distance Maglev freight system will offer low cost per kilometre; plus it can deliver huge volumes per day, and is very fast. The Maglev system will offer a new mode for freight forwarders to consider, which will maintain global GDP growth, as well as offer new opportunities along its route that current modes cannot.

As well as fast delivery, an additional advantage of the Maglev system is its very low ecological impact. The track has a low physical footprint, and Maglev's motive power comes from its superconducting electro-magnets' reaction against the fixed 'linear motors' in the guide track, requiring 50 per cent less power than conventional electrified railway systems. The Maglev system has very few moving parts or components that touch or slide upon each other so wear is minimal, there is no wear on the track, there is no motor noise, and as air friction is no higher than other comparable fast delivery systems the operating costs are low. The capital cost of Maglev systems is less than high-speed steel-wheels-on-railways, so it follows that the total costs of Maglev per tonne/km or passenger are very low.

But first, let us be clear: Maglev transportation systems are a new mode;

they are not '. . . a different form of railway'. Maglev is incompatible with other transport systems just as pedestrians are with respect to airplanes, or cars with shipping – all need multi-modal exchange points like stations, airports or freight yards. We accept that Maglev systems can integrate with existing multi-modal nodes, but more importantly we think that Maglev will offer a new 'hub and spoke system' delivering goods and people at 500km/hr over hundreds or thousands of kilometres with standard rail passing on the goods over a limited few hundred kilometres and road logistics being involved only for the 'last kilometre' when they can use their flexibility effectively.

Of great concern for this Maglev proposal is the political battle that will occur along the route as 'rights' are discussed and deliberated. The route between China and Europe crosses Kazakhstan, Russia and the border states of Europe and Russia which maintain some allegiance to Russia while they may look towards the EU; then there are the new accession states of East Europe now in the EU; and finally the nations in western Europe. All have their own agenda and political aims. Other, darker, aims may also be hidden by presidents wishing to line their own pockets with new money if corruption is a norm in their country. We discuss these enablers or detractors later in the chapter.

### Economic pressures

Asia continues to attract foreign direct investment but it was Europe (2005 data) that recently drew in the greatest FDI. According to UNCTAD (2007), there was continued growth in FDI globally, rising to US$ 916 billion (though the peak was US$ 1.4 trillion in 2000). Of this funding, Europe attracted US$ 421.8 billion, Asia US$ 199.6 billion and the US US$ 133.3 billion. China was a magnet for inwards FDI (US$ 72.4 billion) yet it exported US$ 11.3 billion, up from US$ 1.8 billion in 2004 – this money being spent not just in the US but also in Latin America, Africa and Europe.

We refer in Table 3.1 to the economies of Russia as well as India, as these are

*Table 3.1* Selected economic indicators

| Country | % annual change | | | Latest 12 months ($bn) | | |
|---|---|---|---|---|---|---|
| | GDP | Industrial production | Consumer prices | Trade balance | Current account | Foreign reserves |
| China | +10.4 | +15.7 | +1.5 | +143.6 | +160.8 | 897.9 |
| India | +8.9 | +9.7 | +6.3 | −41.8 | −13.2 | 158.3 |
| Russia | +7.4 | +5.6 | +9.6 | +142.3 | +91.4 | 258.7 |
| Czech Republic | +6.2 | +7.4 | +2.7 | +1.7 | −3.8 | 30.4 |
| Hungary | +3.8 | +9.0 | +5.9 | −3.1 | −7.6 | 20.9 |
| Poland | +5.5 | +11.7 | +1.6 | −3.6 | −6.6 | 46.7 |

*Source:* www.economist.com accessed January 2007 (*The Economist*, 2007c).

said to be 'growth tigers' that together with China (and Brazil) should outperform the (current) developed global nations (Wilson and Purushotha-man 2003) – which remains to be seen. Nevertheless, India and Russia have a major impact on the economy of China, not least with respect to its policies for energy acquisition in which the former Soviet Republics in Central Asia also play a major role.

### Infrastructure growth

#### Asian transport development

China is considered to be the world's premier low-cost assembler, and it is recognized that there are firms therein who are giants in their own right who feed the huge internal Chinese market, as well as outlets across the globe. However, with its seemingly limitless supply of cheap labour and rapid acqui-sition of technological prowess, China appears to be unstoppable: its share of the world's exported goods tripled between 1993 and 2005 (*The Economist* 2007a). To help move these vast volumes of goods, the ports of Asia have become the biggest and busiest in the world, but other forms of logistics competition might confront even these ports, especially as one has to consider hinterland transportation as an integral component of a nation's logistics network. For instance, the intensity of air freight to/from Asia is growing rapidly, as measured by tonnage or by the numbers of pure air-freighters on order (e.g. B747F or A380F), or by the numbers of older passenger planes being converted on retirement to air-freight use (e.g. MD77). However, the creation of ever-larger vehicles (A380F air-freighters or Malaccamax ships) will not solve the capacity constraints affecting China since global routes suffer from immovable pinch points. There is severe congestion along the air routes, and also in the Panama and Suez canals and through the Malacca and Sunda Straights. These pinch points will limit the trade volume arriving in or departing from China, notwithstanding its own (relatively poor) hinter-land infrastructures.

There seems to be potential for rail/road laying throughout China, and Asia in general, but the north and west regions of China are bounded by mountains and deserts, and the south-west by tropical forests (as well as mountains): so only three routes reach out from China to join to the Russian or Central Asian tracks. These logistics (re)development efforts are coordi-nated with the Chinese Ministry of Railways by several branches of the United Nations: for instance, UNDP (Development Programme); UNECE (Economic Commission for Europe); UNESCAP (Economic and Social Commission for Asia and the Pacific), as well as the ADB (Asian Development Bank). They concentrate their support on three main routes, broadly known as the Trans Asian Railway (TAR) feeders. These pass through eastern China and Mongolia (TAR1) to the Trans-Siberian Railway, which itself is being updated; TAR2 is the route from Lianyungang through central China to

Rotterdam, often referred to as the 'Eurasian Landbridge' or somewhat colloquially as the 'New Silk Road'; and TAR3, which ought to link Singapore to Scotland via routes passing south of the Himalayas. The TAR3 link crosses several politically difficult countries, with parts of the route having no planned track at present. It is assumed generally that this route will not come into existence, being perhaps superseded by the 'North–South route' from St. Petersburg through Russia via the Caspian Sea to the Iranian port of Bandar Abbas then onwards by sea to Asia, though this route too suffers from a clash of ideologies and leaders' aspirations.

One major issue facing coordinated Eurasian railway redevelopment is that of track gauge. In the beginning (in the UK) it was determined that the gauge had to be 4 foot 8½ inches (1435 mm – the so-called 'standard gauge') that China adopted, as well as the rest of Europe and the US. However, better load carrying and stability are realized with the wider gauge (1520 mm) deployed across Russia, and there is an even wider track in India (1676 mm). Moving goods between these gauges at borders is time consuming, and most often is done by exchanging axle units throughout the trains. The enforced six to eight hour delay is a frustrating issue for passengers, and also a security issue, as tampering is easier when freight and passenger cars are stationary – when they are officially 'inspected'.

It is necessary for the Chinese government to look to the future and consider how its trade flux will change as still more goods flow to/from Europe and the US, and in the light of commercial pressure to reduce the inventory cost cycle, which in the worst case may be well over 120 days. For instance, if goods travel by road from originators in mid-Europe to Rotterdam, go by Malaccamax ships round the Horn of Africa (being too large to pass through the Suez canal), reach China and have at least a 20-day production cycle, then repeat their trip back to middle Europe for sale, we have a tied-in inventory cycle of 50 + 20 + 50 = 120 days. Maglev can reduce this cycle time to 26 days (Table 3.2).

Within 'trains', we group all low speed designs which once were powered by coal to generate steam for their engines but which have become superseded by more powerful diesel-electric or the fully electric power units running up to 200 km/hr. A 'block train', however, is a special freight train carrying only containers with customs clearances organized in advance – common enough in Europe and the US, but not yet operational on the Eurasian route. Nowadays, there are the fast electric TGV (*train à grande vitesse*) in France (known by other acronyms in Germany, Spain and Japan). These are

*Table 3.2* Comparative Eurasian route times (days)

| | |
|---|---|
| Maglev | ~ 3 |
| Block trains | ~ 20 |
| Ship – Suez canal | ~ 35 |
| Ship – around Africa | ~ 45 |

almost 100 per cent limited to passenger carriage and generally run at 300 km/hr in commercial use (though one specially constructed French TGV reached a record 574 km/hr on 3 April 2007 – see http://en.wikipedia.org/wiki/TGV). Maglevs, however, are designed to travel at 500+ km/hr and will transport people as well as many different types of freight – all at the same high speed.

### *Structure of the remainder of the chapter*

The above brief review of the future of global logistics implied one way forward was to deploy Maglev transportation systems: we propose a three-pronged deployment strategy. Next we review the characteristics of Maglev systems, comparing these with the wheels-on-rail systems, and review the comparative costs of all rail systems. This leads naturally to a discussion section in which we review the pros and cons of Maglev. We return finally to the 'three strategies', noting that Maglev could satisfy China's transportation needs in the future and that foreign reserves and perhaps Sovereign Wealth Funds may support the deployment of Maglev infrastructures. We conclude that China, and the governments of other states, need to carefully consider an integrated approach to global transport infrastructure development.

## Three strategic deployments of Maglev

The demand for goods is increasing annually around the globe, especially between the core trading regions: the US, Europe and Asia. Much of this trade is centred on China as a low-cost assembler – but to be an assembler it has to receive many core components that originate in the US or Europe. To cope with its growth in trade volume, China has increased greatly its logistics capacity: (a) by building new railway lines or renovating existing track to higher standards more able to carry greater volume due to the greater maximum speeds; (b) roads have also benefited from investment, for example new highways have been built, and many rural roads given hard surfaces; (c) new ports have been built, and quay length increased in major ports; and (d) increased airport capacity has been constructed to cope with greater numbers of passenger and freight-only flights. Despite this growth, China is forecast to run out of logistics capacity quite soon (Callarman and Sprague 2007) and will need to rethink its strategy.

This chapter suggests three interconnected strategies to boost surface transportation systems capacity:

1    We propose that China installs Maglev because it will carry freight at the same high speed as Maglev passengers – at 500 km/hr. And China needs greater internal capacity.
2    We further propose that Central Asia, Russia and the EU also implement Maglev to link with the Chinese Maglev system, so boosting

pan-continental logistics capacity to maintain or increase global GDP growth into the future.

3    And furthermore, given the most recent Russian announcement that it intends to construct a tunnel under the Bering Strait (Humber and Cook 2007), we propose that they too implement Maglev in that project, linking to the Chinese Maglev routes and extending them into Middle America. At this point, Europe and China would then be integrated with the US by fast Maglev.

## Maglev vehicle systems

### Core components of Maglev systems

There are two types of levitation system: the EDS and the EMS (see below). Their magnets generate both lift and propulsion, while good engineering minimizes magnetic flux 'leaks', ensuring passengers are subject to weak magnetic forces no greater than those of the background of our ordinary lives. Moving magnetic arrays over a conductive loop will generate a current in the array, which will in turn create an opposing magnetic field, or force, which at a critical velocity will be strong enough to create levitation.

Basically the vehicles 'surf' along a track riding on an air gap, lifted by magnetism and guided by magnetic side panels: they cannot fall out of the track. They are also intrinsically safe – if by some odd circumstance two vehicles are on the same electrical segment of the track at the same time, the nature of the pulsation will determine they both travel in the same direction at the same speed: they cannot crash into each other.

### EDS: electro-dynamic systems

Electro-dynamic systems (EDS) have ferromagnetic or the much more power-ful superconducting magnets mounted along the lower sides and base of the vehicles. These vehicle magnets exert a force against coils, which are fixed in the upper floor or the sides of the support track. The track magnetic force repels the vehicle, lifting it and causing it to move forward, while the magnets along the sides of the vehicle maintain guidance. Generally, the EDS vehicles float with a gap of 150–200 mm (if superconducting magnets are used). These magnets do not have the ability to generate lift (to hover) when the train is stationary. Therefore an auxiliary wheel system (or air float system) is needed for low speed motion until the transition speed is reached; thereafter they levitate and quickly reach full speed. The EDS repulsive systems are inher-ently stable, as any decrease in air gap is met with a stronger repulsive mag-netic force – whether this is the levitating gap, or the side gaps maintaining directional stability. Modern superconducting magnets require cooling only by liquid nitrogen, not the much colder liquid helium. Liquid nitrogen is cheap to create, cheap to keep refrigerated, and is non-polluting when evaporating.

*EMS: electro-magnetic systems*

Electro-magnetic systems (EMS) use ferromagnets located on the upper sides of 'fingers on hands'. These 'hands' reach under the support track, forming the basic security system preventing cars falling off the tracks. Their magnets attract to fixed coils mounted on the underside of the track and, being attracted, lift the vehicle. They lift the vehicle by only 8–12 mm, but they have the ability to float the vehicle when stationary: so they do not require auxiliary wheels. They too have side guidance magnets. The EMS is dynamically unstable and requires complex and rapid computations to vary the attractive force to maintain their float gap, otherwise the gap decreases and the cars descend onto the track surface, which, at speed, is dangerous. Clearly, the civil engineering of this form of track must be to much closer tolerances than for the EDS system with its larger float gap. The EMS requires frequent, very rigorous, safety checks and adjustments to the track alignment to maintain safety and comfort.

*LSM: linear motors*

Linear synchronous motors (LSMs) consist of two electromagnetic members: the armature and the field windings. These can be likened to a standard electric motor if it is flattened into two component parts. And, just as with a normal motor, as electricity passes through the stator it reacts with the field coil magnetism and motion is generated.

Electro-magnetic ferromagnetic systems (EMS) make use of iron windings for both the field and the stator. The saturation of flux density in the iron limits the magnitude of the flux density that can be obtained in the air gap. This limits an EMS to small air gaps, typically of the order of 10 mm, as may be seen on the *Transrapid* (German system), which forms the basis of the Shanghai–Pudong Airport Maglev system. In contrast, the electro-dynamic systems (EDS) use superconducting field windings on the vehicle, which, being stronger, achieve very strong flux densities, so creating large air gaps – typically 150–200 mm.

**Additional Maglev capabilities**

As well as its 500+ km/hr (310+ mph) speed capability, Maglev systems offer significant performance advantages compared to steel-wheel-on-rail systems. The powerful Maglev LMS technology permits climbing or descending of grades steeper than 10 per cent, which is almost three times steeper than conventional rail systems that rely on the friction between wheel and rail to gain traction. As skidding occurs easily between the smooth hard rail and wheel surfaces, conventional rail systems are constrained to slopes of about 4 per cent in practice. Skidding also limits the ability of conventional rail to accelerate or come to a stop since friction is the only force linking their powered wheels to the passive rail – again, Maglev greatly outperforms, gaining top speed in only 5 km compared with the 35 km required by TGVs. Maglev vehicles can round 50 per cent tighter curves at the same speeds as conventional TGVs, since the Maglev guideway can be banked to ±30 degrees allowing travel at high speeds through tight-radius curves, whereas conventional rail systems must run on track that is almost flat. The heavy track banking for Maglev reduces uncomfortable sideward forces, ensuring ride comfort for passengers, and indeed, better stability for freight (Harding *et al.* 1999).

As Maglevs can climb harder and turn tighter than TGVs, its more flexible route alignment reduces the need for the many tunnels and bridges required by conventional railway systems, and it can easily follow the tight curves of the built environment in towns. And further, as the units do not need to gather power from overhead wires (like the TGVs) tunnels could be smaller in diameter, so will be much cheaper to construct than those for TGV tracks.

## Comparative costs of rail systems

Analysis shows that TGV systems offer high passenger capacity. For instance, signalling systems can usually handle a TGV train approximately every four to five minutes, with up to 1,000 seats per train. Maglev research suggests its capacity far exceeds that of TGV (Coffey 1991; Lever 1999; Maglev 2000). Its ultimate freight capacity can be considered a 'pipeline' of 15-metre units (two TEUs) end-to-end all moving at 500 km/hr (or 500,000 m/hr . . . 500,000/15 is ~33,000 units/hr or 800,000 units per day, i.e. 1,600,000 TEU per day). In practice, the Maglev units would not be pipelined, but 600,000 TEU/day is imaginable as the usual one-way delivery volume.

The cost of building high-speed rail tracks (TGV) over difficult terrain can be four to six times more expensive than if constructed over flat land. Their tracks are always expensive because they have to be dug deep and carefully back-filled with ballast to provide a more stable base than for slower-speed rail systems. Maglev systems, in contrast, use a cheap but solid construction system of vertical columns supporting concrete guide beams in which the electrical conducting circuits are mounted. The columns could be cast *in situ*, while the beams would be pre-cast and have their electrics embedded in the factory: they can be easily transported and placed on the columns.

The average high-speed TGV rail track costs a little over €34 million/km (Figure 3.1). However, for Maglev systems there are usually only estimated costs, except for the Shanghai–Pudong line, the true costs of which are a little shrouded (Table 3.3) or the proposed Shanghai–Hangzhou Maglev, which is an 'on/off/on' proposal. In addition to the track, we ought to recognize the cost of vehicles. The vehicles for Maglev cost about €1.5 million each (~US$ 2.2 million) comprising a lower magnet/motor section and the upper passenger or freight section. TGV passenger units cost between €1 to €2 million and their engine units about €3 million each – one usually at each end of a train (a consist, in 'US-speak').

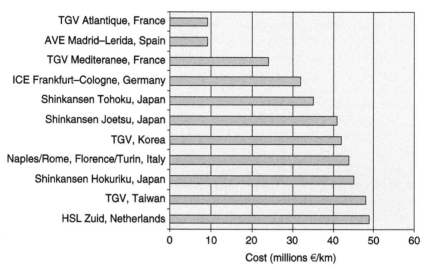

*Figure 3.1* Comparative costs of high-speed rail track construction.
*Source:* following CIT (2005).

*Table 3.3* Costs of rail systems (millions €/km)

| System | Cost estimates |
| --- | --- |
| Shanghai (track, signals, stations, cars and outbuildings) | 27.0 |
| Proposed Shanghai–Hangzhou route | 17.0 |
| Maglev-2000 (track, signals, stations: 2004 US prices) | 12.0 |
| Transrapid Maglev (6 European projects at 2004 prices) | 12.0 |
| High-speed TGV (present-day costs, track only) | 34.0 |
| 'Ordinary' rail track (present-day costs vary widely) | 10.0 |

*Source:* websites of Maglev 2000, Transrapid, and Railway-Technical.com/Finance and *China Daily*, 24 April 2007 (for the Hangzhou data).

## Discussion

### *Issues affecting Maglev take-up*

We suggest that it may now be opportune to build an ultra high-speed logistics link between the Chinese Pacific coast and Europe in order to promote trade, business passenger travel and tourism. Such an implementation will reduce current pollution levels. We discuss below several pros and cons – some factors relate to economic arguments, others to socio-political, aspects as illustrated in Figure 3.2.

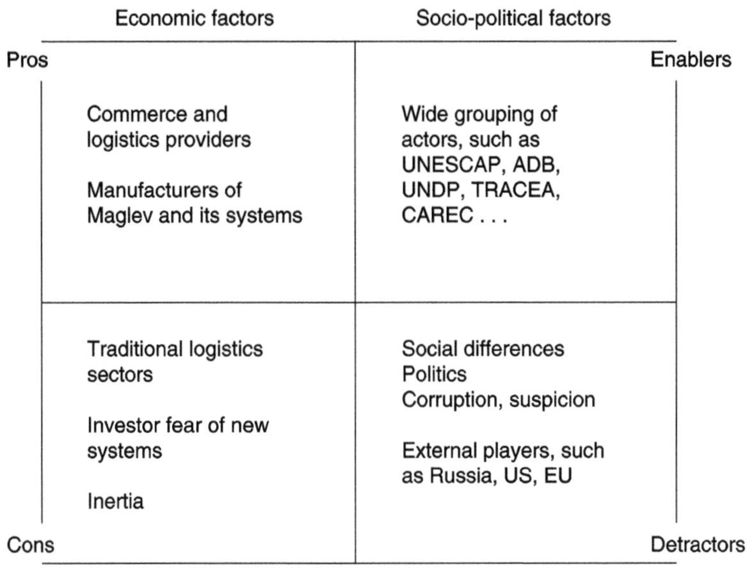

|  | Economic factors | Socio-political factors |  |
|---|---|---|---|
| **Pros** |  |  | **Enablers** |
|  | Commerce and logistics providers | Wide grouping of actors, such as UNESCAP, ADB, UNDP, TRACEA, CAREC . . . |  |
|  | Manufacturers of Maglev and its systems |  |  |
|  | Traditional logistics sectors | Social differences Politics Corruption, suspicion |  |
|  | Investor fear of new systems | External players, such as Russia, US, EU |  |
|  | Inertia |  |  |
| **Cons** |  |  | **Detractors** |

*Figure 3.2*  Factors affecting Maglev take-up.

*Economic pros*

We noted in Table 3.1, the economic indicators of some of the new states of Europe in the eastern part of the EU-25. These are not as strong as the Chinese data, but they are improving – partly due to investments by Taiwanese and Mainland Chinese firms. Rocks (2007) says over US$ 300 million has been invested in Central Europe by Asian firms to make electronics components (flat screen TV/monitors, computers, and so on), with the investor firms stating that: (a) they avoid tariff barriers by manufacturing in Europe, (b) there is a willing and educated workforce, and (c) logistics are both shorter to market and are well integrated throughout Europe. It makes sense, they say, to have a delivery to customer of only a few days compared to the extreme of 45 days by boat from Asia to Rotterdam and having then a further few days for final delivery.

We suggest that many multinational commercial interests will be served better by ultra high-speed Maglev logistics links. These businesses, while not directly lobbying for the links, will be strong consumers as soon as the Maglev links are open. For instance, freight forwarders are always balancing costs and speed of delivery, as well as looking to the security of the goods in transit. Manufacturers are always looking to the 'speed to market', which involves their final assembly being served with components 'just-in-time'. Even as China moves away from being an assembler to becoming more of an originator of globally marketed goods, it will not alter quickly its reliance on components sourced from other parts of the globe, notably Europe and the US. This is the nature of globalization.

The Industrial Revolution (based on steam power), the Information Revolution (based on the greater deployment of computers), and the Knowledge Revolution (dependant on the increasing integration of the Internet within business and leisure) spawned many new firms that in turn created requisite intermediaries. It will be the same for Maglev. There is much pent-up knowledge capital within Central Asia, India and China, and a high capacity for innovation in China. These regions will be able to compete in the development, building and operation of Maglev systems, thereby driving down costs. In addition, a wide set of related skills will develop in science and engineering, further benefiting their local economies.

*Economic cons*

The obvious opponents are the actors in the railway, roads, air and maritime sectors; plus the company owners, the shareholders and the mass of staff making, maintaining or operating the existing logistics systems. There is a huge sunk investment in these systems, and new steel-wheels rail tracks are being laid and ports expanded. China plans to spend at least two trillion Yuan (US$ 258 billion), at a rate of ~100 billion Yuan annually, to expand its rail network 35 per cent to 100,000 km by 2020 (as stated in its 11th Five-year Plan). However, vocal opponents have so far been strong enough to prevent even (capitalist) America developing wide-scale Maglev implementations not withstanding their forecast benefits (Lever 1999); though Japan plans to implement their Maglev links by 2025 (Takahashi *et al.* 2006). Perhaps the lobbyists in the US are to blame, 'since the national 79 mph rail speed limit was instituted in 1947, the migration to higher speeds in the US has been slow, consisting of small incremental increases in maximum safe operating speeds. To travel above 79 mph, a train must be equipped with cab signalling or automatic train protection' (DOT 2005). Somewhat weakly, the DOT authors conclude that more research is needed, notwithstanding cross-referencing in their report on transport systems in Europe and in Japan that regularly use much higher speeds.

High-speed trains like the TGV in France or the Shinkansen in Japan present factual economic arguments upon their deployment and observed operational costs, as well as arguments about the relocation of city workers to live in and commute to the countryside instead of crowding onto short in-city journeys. These high-speed rail systems are working at present, but for passenger traffic only, whereas the Maglev proposals have to rely upon estimates – which are often notoriously in error.

We have seen in Table 3.3, that Maglev systems are not as costly as passenger-only high-speed railways. Of course, there is the need to develop efficient transfer systems at the junctions of Maglev systems and traditional railways (notwithstanding the widespread acceptance of the operational costs of axle-swapping at the intersections of gauge changes in the existing traditional systems). We envisage these transfer hubs (multi-modal hubs) to be similar to those in use in major ports of the world, using a combination of cranes, hydraulic push/pull systems and robot stacking machines. It is not 'rocket science', and good exemplars may be found in the newly extended ports of Asia and Europe. There will be a large human cost associated with the change from one technology to another, the learning curve will be steep, and some people may be made redundant in the short term – a fact not desired by Chinese ministries.

And, as with all new technologies, a nearly silent opposition comes from the fear of the unknown. We say 'we are never as inventive as when we look for reasons not to change'. The idea of moving to Maglev causes anxiety for many, and scare-mongering is easy – 'high power magnets will kill, the passage of ultra high-speed trains will affect health', and so on. Such stories will be heard everywhere, and there will be many believers, even if these facts are unfounded, and they certainly are unproven. It is argued that one reason for the failure of Transrapid to extend to Hangzhou from Shanghai is due to its alleged high magnetic flux:

> citing unnamed officials, the official *Xinhua* news agency said on Saturday, May 26th 2007 that the 4.3-billion-dollar extension of the magnetic levitation train line, or Maglev, had been suspended amid worries the German technology could pose a radiation risk to communities along the new line.

This reasoning is weak as: (a) the Transrapid already running between Shanghai and Pudong can be tested easily, (b) the Transrapid experimental test site data in Germany declares that the radiation emitted is very low, comparable to the earth's own magnetic field strength, and (c) radiation is not a hazard in American Maglev systems (Lever 1999). However, other authorities in China consider the Shanghai–Hangzhou link to be viable and that it will be built using home-designed Chinese technology (*China Daily*, 24 April 2007) – que sera, sera!

### Socio-political enablers

'Big Businesses' will quietly push for faster logistics, but there are other enablers who have been in the Asian region for a while. Amongst these are: TRACECA (Transport Corridor Europe Caucuses Asia) with links to the European TEN-T (Trans-European Transport Networks) programme supported by the (UN)ECE, (UN)ESCAP, ADB and CAREC (Central Asia Region Economic Co-operation) (see ESCAP 2003; European Union 2002; Sims 2005; Parkash 2006, 2007).

We should note that CAREC reaches further geographically than the former Soviet 'stans' – incorporating Kazakhstan, parts of northern Iran and Afghanistan, the Xinjiang province of western China and the western part of

Mongolia. It is similar in extent to the old 'Turkestan', which roughly represented the Turkic-speaking area of Central Asia. This committee hopefully can speak for many of the involved actors and decision-makers who may become involved with our proposed 'Eurasian Maglev'. CAREC notes all aspects of infrastructure development in Central Asia and how these have fallen into disarray since 1991 (Sims 2005). It proposes reforms, partly fostered by TRACECA, partly by the OECD (with respect to its anti-corruption initiatives), and is in accord with the *Human Development Report* (UNDP 2006). All reforms are aimed at generating greater wealth for the local people through national and regional efforts in resource sharing and infrastructure development. The reforms embrace the oil, gas and mineral deposits in Central Asia, but also point to inequalities in supplies of (electrical) energy and water, which is needed for healthy living, and for irrigation.

### Socio-political detractors

As well as the 'fear of the unknown' and the fear of being a 'first mover', a major detractor is the difficulties of working with more or less corrupt governments and their agents (Table 3.4).

It is not too hard to imagine that firms from China, India or Russia will experience difficulties working with each other, and will find it even more awkward if working with firms from 'clean' nations who have a duty to their own shareholders to report verifiable financial statements. The history of informers and collaborators in Central Asia during the Soviet era (even now perhaps) has made it culturally challenging to accept accounting systems that expressly allow for informers, especially anonymous informers, to be 'whistleblowers'. The US Sarbanes–Oxley (SOX) Act of 2002 mandates informer hotlines from any point in the world, and US firms have a duty to report openly according to SOX rules. It has long been known by the Asian Development Bank that some 20–40 per cent of project finances in Asia are skimmed on receipt, making it impossible to achieve the target payback of projects. Further, in order to appear on target, build quality is sacrificed and quality assessors bribed to ignore all faults. Money earmarked for maintenance is often used instead to complete a project, so guaranteeing rapid performance degradation in operational use (Etienne 2003). Finding verifiable accounting data is difficult:

> it is said (with apparent sincerity) that some Chinese firms keep several sets of books – one for the government, one for company records, one for foreigners and one to report what is actually going on. By contrast, international accounting standards are built on foundations that China does not possess, such as truthful record-keeping and deep, clean, markets so that 'fair' valuations can be placed on financial instruments, property, or softer assets like brands and intellectual property.
>
> (*The Economist* 2007b)

There are large sociometric differences between the nations along the proposed Eurasia Landbridge route and between the actors who wish to cooperate in building infrastructure and also those who would use it later. Some of these aspects have been noted by Hofstede (1980, 1991), who says individual differences create organizational chaos if not managed transparently. We ask, therefore, given the secretive nature of corrupt people, how would transparency be promoted? Research indicates that both sides in a Russian and Chinese 'accord' look warily at each other, but for different reasons, and without open discussion their distrust may destroy any accord (Hutchings and Michailova 2004; Michailova and Worm 2003). There is therefore a real need to get staff in local, regional and international alliances to trust each other, but this is difficult to do, though not impossible (SOX 2006).

Trust and corruption and their interrelations are difficult to manage and are a serious hazard for businesses in Central Asia, more so than China, since the degree of trust between the people of Central Asia is much lower than in China, where institutionalized trust exists in the form of *guanxi*, which has been internalized since the time of Confucius (Li and Wu 2007). Li and Wu suggest that in countries where there is a low level of trust corruption becomes a severe economic burden, akin to robbery. But in countries where both the briber and the corrupt official can trust each other, it is not in either of their interests to be a whistleblower, so corruption volumes will be high as the process is almost risk free. This latter form of corruption is associated with the facilitation of business. See Table 3.4.

### Other positive aspects of Maglev

#### Ecological impacts

There are many heated arguments within 'carbon trading' discussions and all depend upon assumptions. Nevertheless the EU is determined to reduce its emissions overall and to address all transportation modes, which presently generate 24 per cent of its greenhouse gasses. This poses interesting questions, as the emissions in any one sector change as a passenger (or a tonne of

*Table 3.4* Indications of corruption and bribery

| Country | Corruption perception (ranked within 179 nations) | Bribery propensity (ranked within 30 nations) |
|---|---|---|
| China | 72nd | 29th |
| India | 72nd | 30th |
| Russia | 143rd | 28th |
| Czech Republic | 41st | – |
| Hungary | 39th | – |
| Poland | 61st | – |

*Source: Transparency International* (2007 reports): lower ranks are better.

freight) is moved singly or is 'consolidated'. There are also interesting questions to be posed as different forms of fuel are assessed for their total up- and down-stream pollution loadings. Taking an overall view is very important in the case of electricity since this fuel, very clean in use, has vast differences in upstream carbon costs depending on whether it uses nuclear fuel with an intrinsic very low carbon footprint, rising to a very high carbon cost if coal is used for electrical generation and, in the worst case, if that coal is delivered to the electricity generator by coal-burning trains, or by the lorry load. Following the Kyoto and now the Bali discussions on climate change, it is clear that nations will, for a long time yet, discuss the causes and remedies for climate change. In this chapter we simply note that Maglev systems are at least 50 per cent more efficient (in terms of electricity consumption) than TGV systems (in turn, these are more efficient than slower, older forms of rail transport), and so Maglev ought to be implemented as a nation's contribution to reducing their carbon footprint, no matter how they generate their electricity. On the latter point, it is evident that both the developed and the developing nations are now looking to the nuclear option for their near-term electricity generation since coal is too polluting.

All aspects of the Maglev systems are eco-friendly. The track has a low physical footprint, being simply a concrete beam mounted on columns so animals and people are not inconvenienced by its operation. And because of its raised height, the Maglev track is not as vulnerable to flooding or snow envelopment as a ground-level rail line. Their raised height makes them very safe as no at-grade crossings exist, with the attendant risk of collisions between the 'train' and other vehicles, pedestrians or animals. By the way, we discount terrorist attacks on Maglev specifically as it is no more vulnerable than ordinary rail systems, metro systems or buildings: determined terrorists will always attempt to create havoc. The Maglev technology is much quieter than other transportation systems as it does not produce any rolling, gearing or engine noise. The aerodynamic noise is low at speeds up to 250 km/hr (155 mph), and is significantly less than TGV trains at high speeds (Bariskow *et al.* 2002). Electromagnetic fields (EMF) produced by the Maglev system are negligible, being roughly equivalent to the earth's natural magnetic field, whereas the exposed sources of a conventional high voltage electrified train or subway system have about four to eight times the magnetic field strength of the Maglev system. Maglev systems emit no emissions to affect air quality, such as the sparking of the pantograph collectors of TGV, which produce ozone.

The Stern Review (2007) has indicated that if we collectively 'do nothing' the planet will be in grave danger, but for relatively little cost to our collective GDPs we can all contribute to a better future. This report shocked decision makers across the globe, and this chapter suggests on this point alone (climate change), decision makers ought to consider implementing Maglev as a way to address the problem. In addition, the Intergovernmental Panel on Climate Change (IPCC) adopted the 'Summary for Policymakers' from their Paris meeting in February 2007. Their report, *Climate Change 2007: The*

*Physical Science Basis*, assesses current scientific knowledge about the natural and human drivers of climate change (IPCC 2007). Its predictions are also grave. And the equally grave report by Hansen *et al.* (2007), speculating from the analysis of millions of years of Palaeoclimatic data, suggests that we may have indeed gone too far to save the globe since 'recent greenhouse gas (GHG) emissions place the Earth perilously close to dramatic climate change that could run out of our control, with great dangers for humans and other creatures.'

If this is true we ought not to berate ourselves and search fruitlessly for policies to 'save the world' but should adopt policies that mitigate the more deleterious effects of climate change. Herein we would say: install Maglev rather than standard rail or high-speed TGV transport systems, and move as much long-distance freight as possible to Maglev.

### Maglev for automatic delivery systems

Maglev units can be modified to carry dry bulk products, gas or liquids. And, as they can be programmed with destination and return addresses (just like data blocks on the Internet), they may be used to deliver minerals, fuels or water without the need for drivers or guards, having the empty units return automatically to be refilled, or in the case of container Maglev, to await new cargo.

CAREC studies have identified the need for China, Russia, India and the Central Asian states to move fuels and minerals across their borders for mutual regional benefit and for commercial sale to international markets. Of pressing concern, as noted in the *Human Development Report* (UNDP 2006), is the need to have a reliable supply of clean water. The Maglev bulk liquid units can transport all liquids quickly, reliably and cheaply in sufficient volumes to satisfy the varied needs of many customers.

### Maglev for rural development and tourism

As the high-speed steel-wheel Shinkansen trains expanded their reach in Japan, and other similar trains grew in scope in France, Germany and elsewhere in Europe, it became clear that city workers preferred to abandon their previous crowded and slow city commutes in favour of living in the countryside. They are willing to pay more for a seat on fast trains that deliver them to their city centre workplace as quickly as crowded commuter trains. There is no doubt that Maglev systems would create the same benefits for commuters in China or along its routes in general. At present, journeys in major towns take a long time. The local metros (if they exist) are slow and are very crowded at peak times, as are the roadways. For instance, a journey from the centre of Shanghai or Beijing to their residential outskirts takes at least two hours to complete. In contrast, an hour's Maglev trip would whisk one 2–300 km away, to tranquillity, clean air and a cheaper lifestyle.

The Maglev routes would also contribute to eco-friendly tourism in several ways. First, Maglev would offer non-polluting travel over long distances at high speed, allowing intermediate stops in interesting regions. Of course, aircraft can do this, but the tourist would have to connect a mix of long-haul and short-haul flights, probably involving incompatible schedules for individual tourists; and aircraft generate heavy carbon and other emissions. Second, as the Maglev becomes more commonplace and its network more extensive, it could offer pods of family size that might be removed from the Maglev track to become a road-based vehicle, like a camper van, for local exploration – even for urban/rural use (Reynolds 2000). In these cases, the overall carbon impact could be minimized further, as the rover vehicle could use a hybrid motor thus reducing its gasoline demands. These developments would support tourism growth, and bring new money to remote communities.

## The three strategies revisited

Given the various data above, it is reasonable to review the strategies we proposed earlier.

### *China installs Maglev for its internal logistics needs*

China is seriously addressing the need to move from a fossil-fuelled electricity industry to a nuclear one. Kidd (2007) notes that China has re-embraced a nuclear power plant construction programme aimed at the commercial, not military, market. Through the 2020s, they may be building reactors at the rate of ten per year – just in time, we suggest, to support a national network of Maglev transportation systems. Indeed, China has recently announced it will deliver Chinese-designed Maglev trains on two routes (Beijing–Tainjin and Shanghai–Hangzhou), the latter in time for the World Expo in 2010.

By installing Maglev along the Chinese section of the Eurasian Landbridge route from Lianyungang/Shanghai to Xi'an then to Urumqi (now with routes reaching beyond to Kazakhstan or to other states in Central Asia from Kashi), the authorities could absorb the goods from the road haulage, which runs up to 15,000 vehicles per day along the route (MOC 2004). This option would greatly reduce the diesel pollution, especially as many Chinese logistics firms use old, as well as over-laden, vehicles. We suggest other freight could be moved off the existing rail routes, benefiting overall pollution reduction. Trade volumes could be increased due to Maglev's high delivery speed and low headway between its vehicles. And further, bulks (minerals) as well as liquid fuels could be transported by Maglev from the resource fields in Xinjiang/Kazakhstan to the resource users on the coastal strip.

### The Eurasian Landbridge be converted to Maglev

This ~10,000 kilometre rail link is under active discussion with guidance by the UN and other agents. Of course, there are many issues to discuss and resolve, not least the 'rights of sovereign states' to control sections of the routes as well as to maintain them and to take rent from pan-continental traffic. But, as Table 3.2 indicated, the product cycle time using Maglev can be reduced from 120+ days to 26 days, which will foster the growth of global GDP through increasing trade. This substitution of delivery mode – moving from long-haul air-freight and deep-sea shipping to Maglev – will greatly reduce pollution.

The opening up of Central Asia, remote parts of China and also the Russian steppes through association with fast Maglev links will alleviate rural poverty (UNDP 2006). The development of new inland townships will also foster local exploitation of minerals without the need to tranship tonnes of overburden to existing refiners. This too is an example of the multiple ecological benefits that Maglev might bring to the global economy.

### Integrate Maglev in the Bering Straits project

By fully integrating Maglev from the planning stage, the overall costs may be reduced and hinterland development in northern China, the Russian Far East and in Alaska and northern Canada will be stimulated more thoroughly. And, though not shown in Table 3.2, the total product cycle time of freight passage to/from the US would reduce to ~26 days because the route from coastal China to mid-America is about 12,000 km. At present, the Pacific sea shipping takes about 20 days alone, then there is the onward time burden to/from originators and end-users within China and the US. A further boost to global pollution reduction initiated by this strategy would be the stimulation of the US to implement national coast-to-coast Maglev to move their freight away from the present very intensive use of lorry 'land trains' that currently congest and pollute all major US highways. In the US, Maglev has been proposed many times, but lobbyists have successfully delayed implementation, even in the face of strong research analyses that has indicated very positive benefits for the US (notably Lever 1999). Perhaps China's implementation will cause the US to implement Maglev.

## Funding for the Maglev projects

It is clear that these projects – the Maglev backbones inside China, from China to Europe and China to the US – are very major undertakings. They require the agreements of many heads of state, but above all they need a careful consideration of the funding.

The capital costs of building the 10,000 km of the Eurasia Landbridge from China to Europe can be considered to be €27 million/km; 10,000 km = €270,000 million ($415,000 million). We would expect, however, the final build cost to be something like $400,000 million, rising due to inflation, and falling due to moving down the 'learning curve'.

In passing we ought to recognize the magnitude of these costs – one trillion in the US has 12 zeros ($10^{12}$), although this is called billion in the rest of the world. We note:

| | |
|---|---|
| The Iraq war may have cost over | $3,000,000,000,000 |
| The Maglev Eurasian route might cost | $400,000,000,000 |

Stiglitz and Bilmes (2008) agree that the three trillion dollar cost of the war in Iraq to the US alone is an incredible amount, almost beyond comprehension, and certainly far beyond the figures provided by the Bush administration. They calculate what would have been saved if there was no war, that is, the 'opportunity cost'. Many of these costs are usually hidden, yet they are usually paid-out over time – to recompense the dispossessed and wounded, for instance.

Maglev implementation needs considerable cash injection over time. We note the huge foreign reserves held by some states. China is one such nation, with $898 billion – Japan's reserves are slightly higher (*The Economist* 2007c). Even Central Asian countries are not short of ready cash (Floerkemeier and Sumlinski 2008), and generally this is true globally (Aizenman 2007). These authors say the study of reserve adequacy and optimality provide valuable insights for policy makers and can help to guide monetary and reserve policies. Therefore, we surmise, if ministers are so minded to install Maglev, they have reserves in place, at least to commence the capital works:

> world foreign exchange reserves have surged from $2 trillion in 2001 to an unprecedented $5 trillion in early 2007. Of this total, the share of emerging Asia has risen from $600 billion to more than $2 trillion, as a result of reserves having increased at a rate of $200 to $300 billion per year since 2003. In addition, the reserve assets of oil-exporters boomed in 2005 and 2006 by more than $200 billion each year.
>
> (Noyer 2007)

There is another source of capital – the Sovereign Wealth Funds (SWFs). These have been around for a long time, at least since the 1950s but they seem to have grown in prominence recently – partly because some SWFs are involved in the 'bail-out' of a few US banks and other financial institutions following the late-2007 US sub-prime housing market collapse. We should note that the magnitude of SWFs worldwide has grown dramatically over the past 10–15 years, and is expected to rise from $2–3 trillion today to about $6–10, maybe $12 trillion, within five years. At present, the United Arab Emirates, Norway, Saudi Arabia, China, Kuwait, Russia and Singapore are among the countries that hold the world's largest SWFs (Europa 2008).

We further suggest that if the managers of the SWFs are so minded, they could invest with ease in both the capital and operational aspects of Maglev. As well as investing in the Eurasia Landbridge, they could include the China–US route under the Bering Straits. The total cost of building the tracks of the two backbone routes would be about $1.0 trillion, and adding adequate numbers of 'rolling stock' would cost maybe a further $0.5 trillion. Even if we postulate the cost to be $2.0 trillion, it is quite achievable under current conditions, and indeed far less costly than the Iraq war.

## Conclusions

In all countries, the implementation of Maglev will tax infrastructure planning and their fiscal ingenuity. But this new mode of transport will not work effectively until it reaches across each country and into the next one, too. There is a parallel to be drawn with the early telephone systems having but a handful of subscribers on the network – this only tested some aspects of the technology. Now there are millions connected by landline and wirelessly in every nation: we could not imagine work or leisure without the 'phone. It will be the same with Maglev, but its infrastructures needs to develop across many sectors – such as the research upon higher temperature superconductors and deploying this science quickly into practice; the development of high strength composite materials that will allow us to build a stronger Maglev and other transport vehicles having less dead weight and thus more commercial load capacity, so saving transportation energy; and the development of better primary energy systems so that the unit cost of motive power falls – presumably substituting fossil fuels for cleaner sources thereby benefiting society. All these tasks take time and have to be supported constantly by successive governments and by global leadership, too.

We must take the *big* decision soon – to implement a Maglev system over some considerable distance to offer a full service for freight, other containerized commodities and passengers. Ultimately, we will have to take what Möllering (2006) calls 'the leap of faith', noting data from all sources and exemplars, and to trust in our abilities to innovate. He notes we trust, often using constructs based on reason, routines and reflexivity, but ultimately, he says, we have to suspend our feelings of vulnerability and uncertainty, and take a 'leap of faith'. Simply going forward and 'doing it'.

We hope therefore this chapter will encourage China and its ministries, and the governments of other states and bodies such as the UN, to undertake a comprehensive, unbiased and fair review of the potential for Maglev, since we believe a decision on its deployment is needed 'like yesterday'.

## References

Aizenman, J. (2007) *Large Hoarding of International Reserves and the Emerging Global Economic Architecture*. National Bureau of Economic Research (NBER). July, Working Paper No. W13277

Bariskow B., Disk, D.R., Hanson, C.E., Hellmig, M., Joshi, A., Kupferman, A., Mauri, R., Roof, C.J. and Valihura, P. (2002) *Noise Characteristics of the Transrapid TR08 Maglev System*, US Department of Transport, DOT-VNTSC-FRA-02-13, July.

Callarman, T.E. and Sprague, L. (2007) All roads lead to Beijing, *Far Eastern Economic Review* 170(5): 57–59.

Coffey, H.T. (1991) *Maglev Design Considerations*, Argonne National Laboratory, Future Transport Technology Conference, Portland, OR., 5–7 August.

Commission for Integrated Transport (CIT) (2005) *High-Speed Rail: International Comparisons*, www.cfit.gov.uk/docs/2004/hsr/research/pdf/chapter4.pdf.

DOT (2005) *Human Factors in Railroad Operations*, Cambridge, MA: US Department of Transport, final report, DOT/FRA/ORD-04/12.

*Economist, The* (2007a) The problem with Made in China, 7 January.

*Economist, The* (2007b) China: country briefings, 10 January.

*Economist, The* (2007c) Cultural revolution, 11 January.

ESCAP (2003) Foreign direct investment in Central Asian and Caucasian economies: policies and issues, papers and proceedings presented at the Regional Round Table on Foreign Direct Investment for Central Asia, Dushanbe, 3–4 April.

Etienne, G. (2003) The economy of seepage and leakage in Asia: the most dangerous issue, in J. B. Kidd and F.-J. (eds), *Fighting Corruption in Asia: Causes, Effects and Remedies*, Singapore: World Scientific: 221–237.

European Union (2002) *Central Asia Strategy Paper*, http://ec.europa.eu/comm/external_relations/ceeca/rsp2/02_06_en.pdf.

Europa (2008) *Sovereign Wealth Funds: Frequently Asked Questions*, press release, MEMO/08/126, 27 February.

Floerkemeier, H. and Sumlinski, M. (2008) *International Reserve Trends in the South Caucasus and Central Asia Region*, IMF Working Paper, WP/08/41, February.

Hansen, J., Sato, M., Kharecha, P., Russell, G., Lea, D.W. and Siddal, M. (2007) Climate change and trace gases, *Philosophical Transactions of the Royal Society*, 365, 1925–1954.

Harding, J., Pollard, J.K., Katz-Rhoads, L., Mengert, P., Disario, R. and Sussman, E.D. (1999) *Passengers Acceptance of Alignments with Frequent Curves in Maglev or Other Very-High-Speed Ground Systems*, US Department of Transport, DOT-VNTSC-RR994-PM-99-1, March.

Hofstede, G. (1980) *Culture's Consequences: International Differences in Work-Related Values*, London: Sage.

Hofstede, G. (1991) *Cultures and Organisations: Software of the Mind*, London, McGraw-Hill.

Humber, Y. and Cook, B. (2007) Russia plans world's longest tunnel, www.blomberg.com.

Hutchings, K. and Michailova, S. (2004) Facilitating knowledge sharing in Russian and Chinese subsidiaries: The role of personal networks, *Journal of Knowledge Management*, 8(2): 84–94.

IPCC (2007) *Climate Change 2007: Fourth Assessment Report*, http://www.ipcc.ch.

Kidd, S. (2007) Fuelling Asia's growth: tapping the promise of nuclear, *Far Eastern Economic Review*, 170(7): 47–52.

Lever, J. (1999) *Technical Assessment of Maglev System Concepts: Final Report by Government Maglev System Assessment Team*, US Army Corps of Engineers, Special Report 98–12, October.

Li, S. and Wu, J.J. (2007) Why China thrives despite corruption, *Far Eastern Economic Review*, 170(3): 24–28.

Maglev (2000) www.maglev2000.com.

Michailova, S. and Worm, V. (2003) Personal networking in Russia and China, *Blat and Guanxi, European Management Journal*, 21(4): 509–519.

MOC (2004) *Developing Euro–Asian Transport Links*, Department of International Cooperation, Ministry of Commerce, China, www.unece.org/trans/main/eatl/docs/2nd_EGM_CHINA.ppt.

Möllering, G. (2006) *Trust: Reason, Routine, Reflexivity*, Amsterdam: Elsevier.

Noyer, C. (2007) *Foreign Reserve Accumulation: Some Systemic Implications*, Salzburg Global Seminar, 1 October.

Parkash, M. (2006) *Connecting Central Asia*, Manila: Asian Development Bank.

Parkash, M. (2007) *Challenges and Opportunities for Railways in the People's Republic of China*, Manila: Asian Development Bank.

Reynolds, F.R. (2000) Dualmode – transportation's future, *Intelligent Transportation Systems*, November/December: 78–79.

Rocks, D. (2007) Made in China – er, Velkiko Turnovo, *BusinessWeek*, 8 January, p. 43.

Sims, M. (2005) *Central Asia Regional Economic Cooperation (CAREC): Harmonization and Simplification of Transport Agreements, Cross Border Documents and Transport Regulations*, Manila: Asian Development Bank.

SOX (2006) http://complianceandprivacy.com/News-CNIL-SOX-whistleblowers.asp.

Stern, N. (2007) *The Economics of Climate Change: The Stern Review*, Cambridge: Cambridge University Press.

Stiglitz, J.E. and Bilmes, L.J. (2008) *The Three Trillion Dollar War: The True Cost of the Iraq Conflict*, New York: W. W. Norton.

Takahashi, M., Kwok, G. and Kubota, K. (2006) *Marketing Strategy of the HSST System*, a presentation to Maglev 2006 held in Dresden, 13–15 September.

UNCTAD (2007) *World Investment Report*, Geneva: United Nations.

UNDP (2006) *Human Development Report. Beyond Scarcity: Power, Poverty and the Global Water Crisis*, New York: United Nations and Palgrave Macmillan.

Wilson, D. and Purushothaman, R. (2003) *Dreaming with BRICs: The Path to 2050*, Global Economics Paper 99, Goldman Sachs Workbench, www.gs.com.

# 4 Dynamic evolution of regional growth disparity in China

## Evidence from 1978 to 2005

*Ru Zhang*

## Introduction

During the last 30 years since the reform and opening up, economic growth in China has been achieved at a glorious speed, which is regarded as the growth miracle; the contribution of China to world economic growth is considered the 'China factor'. Yet there is also suspicion about the persistence of the fast growth in China. As a result of the market-oriented reform and the continuous economic development policy, the output level of all the provinces in China has been significantly increased; yet at the same time, the regional growth disparity is also enlarged due to the different conditions of regions. Recent researches focus more on empirically testing the convergence hypothesis, as well as identifying the critical factors that determine regional growth disparity so as to make political suggestions. This chapter investigates regional growth disparity between mainland provinces during the period 1978–2005 from a dynamic point of view. Two critical questions are raised: (1) Do significant structural time differences exist and how important are geographical factors in the regional growth disparity? (2) What are the key factors that determine the regional steady-state position of output per worker? To stress question (1), stylized facts of regional growth and the evolution of provincial growth disparity are dynamically analysed. Multiple indexes, like the kernel density and Theil entropy, as well as the variance of $\sigma$-convergence, are introduced as the indicators of provincial growth disparity. Moreover, by introducing human capital and technology efficiency into the new classical framework, this chapter investigates regional characteristics of growth disparity and estimates provinces various speeds of convergence. To address question (2), a series of structural control variables are introduced into the Barro equation so that the provincial steady-state position of output per worker can be specified and the speed of conditional convergence estimated. The hypothesis of club convergence is also tested through introducing the dummy variables.

The rest of the chapter is arranged as follows. In the second section, some stylized facts about regional growth disparity in the past 27 years are statistically analysed to find the dynamic characteristics and the evolution of regional disparity patterns. The third section presents the theoretical model. The fourth section tests the absolute convergence hypothesis, as well as the time structural difference and the geographical factors that influence the provincial disparity patterns. In the fifth section, conditional convergence and factors that determine the steady-state position of output level are empirically identified and the club convergence testified; provincial convergence speed is also estimated. In the final section, some conclusions and political recommendations are given.

## Stylized facts of dynamic disparity patterns

The output level and its distribution have changed significantly since 1978 and especially during the market-orientated reform begun in the 1990s. Here, I use the statistical data to illustrate the evolution of disparity patterns in provinces and regions of China. All the data in this chapter are from the *China Statistical Year Books* and *Comprehensive Statistical Data and Materials on 50 Years of New China*, with some modification of price indexes. The database includes 29 mainland provinces, excluding Hong Kong, Macao, Taiwan and Tibet; the data of Chongqing since 1997 has been added to the province of Sichuan in maintain consistency with that before 1996. In this chapter, all the regional nominal value is converted to its real value, using the price in 1978 as the benchmark. The annual regional price index could also be referred to in the yearbook. Figure 4.1 shows the distribution dynamics of Kernel density of GDP per worker from 1978 to 2005. Based on the price level in 1978, the average income has increased from 902 RMB per worker in 1978 to 6720 RMB in 2005, while during the same period spatial inequality increased significantly too. The income gap between the richest and the poorest provinces is larger in 2005 than 1978. From Figure 4.1, it is explicit that the distribution of GDP per worker was significantly skewed to the right in 1978 and then the curve changed into a bell shape. In 2005, the curve is much the same as normal distribution, while compared to 1978, the range of the extreme values is larger and also the kurtosis of the curve is smaller, which means that there is more spatial inequality in the income distribution as time passed. Further focus on the relative income growth change is presented in Figure 4.2. This figure shows the dynamics of regional Kernel density of GDP per worker relative to Shanghai, the richest region throughout our research period. Another reason to choose Shanghai as the benchmark is that, it can always represent the technology frontier in China during the time period observed. From this figure, it is obvious that from 1978 to 1990, the speed of growth in provinces that have a relative lower initial output level is faster than provinces that are richer at the beginning. Also the shape of the income distribution curve is skewed to the right in 1978 and is approximately normally distributed in 1990. From 1990 to 2005, the range of extreme relative income values became larger and spatial inequality became more significant. The relative GDP distribution in 2005 is wider than in 1978. The

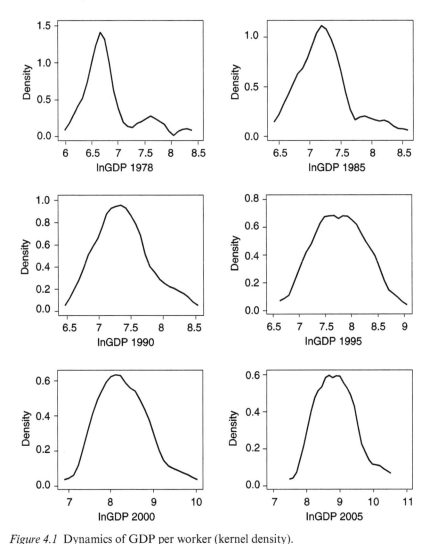

*Figure 4.1* Dynamics of GDP per worker (kernel density).

*Source:* All the data in this chapter are taken from the *China Statistical Yearbook* (various years) and *Comprehensive Statistical Data and Materials on 50 Years of New China.*

change reflects a shift of the median of relative provincial GDP per worker form the middle side toward the upper side and the ends. Also relative GDP distribution of the lower side seems to be worse in 2005 than 1978, which means some of the poorest regions in 1978 were growing slower than Shanghai during these 27 years and thus made the output gap wider. So, during the reform periods, not only is the absolute level of the income distribution gap between the richest and the poorest wide, that gap becomes larger

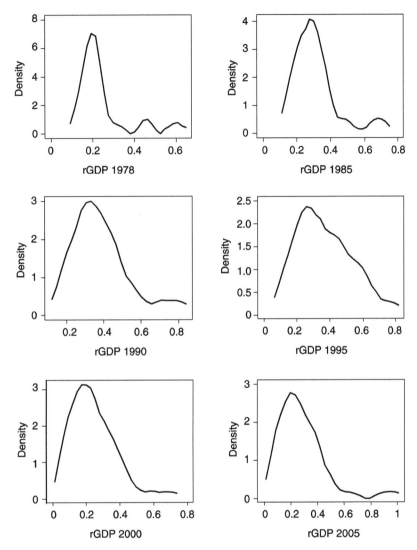

*Figure 4.2* Dynamics of relative GDP per worker (kernel density).

as time passes. And there seems to be significant structural change of provincial growth disparity before and after the 1990s.

Further, comparing the provincial relative growth rate from 1978 to 2005 shows that during this time period, 13 provinces experienced a faster growth rate compared to Shanghai, while the other 15 provinces underwent a declining relative growth level. Most of the regions with GDP per worker between 15 and 22 per cent that of Shanghai's in 1978, typically experienced an increase in relative income during the 27 years. These regions correspond to the upward shift of the median of relative GDP per worker in Figure 4.2. On the contrary, most regions with relative GDP of less than 14 per cent and larger than 23 per cent that of Shanghai's in 1978 experienced a decrease in relative income over the same period, which means that they grew more slowly than Shanghai. One way of interpreting these general movements is that there has been a trend of catching up or convergence among richer regions and a poverty gap or divergence at the bottom. During 1978–1990, 27 provinces grow faster than Shanghai, excluding Gansu, during 1990–2005, only Tianjin, Zhejiang and Jiangsu experienced a faster growth rate compared to Shanghai, and during 2000–2005, most provinces had a faster growth rate except Liaoning, Hunan, Hainan, Fujian and Hubei. Simply put, before the 1990s, there is a convergence trend between provinces; however, after 1990, the trend was reversed, and divergence is significant. Further, after 2000, the divergence trend was mitigated.

Let us take a further look at the total growth disparity of China and the three geographical districts of China (the east, middle and west) separately. The location of each province in China is presented in the Appendix. I use Theil entropy as an indicator of disparity of GDP per capita, which is calculated by $T_x = \sum Y_i \log(\frac{Y_i}{P_i})$ (Das and Barua 1996), in which $Y_i$ is the share of the GDP per capita in region $i$, $P_i$ is the share of population in region $i$. Further on, Theil entropy can be divided into two components, that is,

$$T_x = T_B + T_W = \sum_{i=1}^{n} Y_i \log \frac{Y_i}{P_i} + \sum_{i=1}^{n} Y_i \left( \sum_j Y_{ij} \log \frac{Y_{ij}}{P_{ij}} \right),$$ where $T_B$ is considered

the disparity between regions, and $T_W$ is the disparity within a specific region, $Y_i$ is the share of GDP per capita in region $i$, $P_i$ is the share of population in region $i$, $Y_{ij}$ is the share of GDP per capita of section $j$ in region $i$, $P_{ij}$ is the share of population of section $j$ in region $i$. As shown in Figure 4.3, the

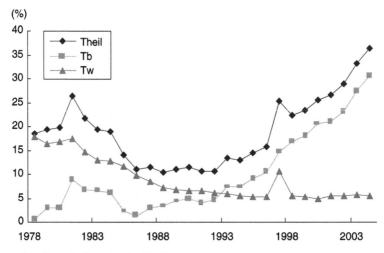

*Figure 4.3* Growth disparity by Theil entropy.

overall Theil entropy experienced a decrease from 1978 to the middle of the 1990s, and then increased ever since. Disparity between the eastern, middle and western regions of China has become more significant since the middle of 1980s, and, in contrast, the disparity within a region has been smaller since 1978. So, generally, there may not seem to be a trend of convergence among all the regions in China during the reform period 1978 to 2005; instead, some convergence clubs among regions may exist in different time intervals. In other words, all the regions may not experience absolute convergence but conditional convergence or club convergence, and time structural change may also be critical. We will test this hypothesis in the following sections.

Figure 4.4 shows the evolution of absolute difference of real GDP per worker and the dynamics of $\sigma$-convergence. The absolute difference of GDP per worker, which stands for the minimum level of regional real GDP per worker compared to the maximum level, is smaller when the disparity between provinces is more significant. From the evolution of the absolute difference of real GDP per worker, there is an inverse U-shape curve at the countrywide scale, which peaked in 1990. In other words, the regional disparity first declined and then increased. The trend in the eastern area is much the same as the countrywide trend, while the disparity in the western part has been constantly increasing since 1978, and the disparity in the middle area has kept steady during the period. If all the provinces are classified into two groups, coastal and interior (the location of each province is shown in the table in the Appendix), then during the reform period from 1978–2005, the evolution of disparity in the interior areas is just like the countrywide trend in general, while the coastal areas experienced convergence during 1978–1993 then divergence until 2000, and from 2000–2005, the disparity appears to be weakened. As Sala-i-Martin (1996) defined, a group of economies are converging in the sense of $\sigma$ if the dispersion of their real per capita GDP levels tends to decrease over time. It is also obvious in Figure 4.4 that there is significant time structural difference in the variance of real GDP per worker before and after 1990, which means $\sigma$-convergence existed between regions before 1990 and disappeared thereafter. The countrywide decline of disparity is mainly attributed to the convergence trend in the eastern or coastal areas, whereas the disparity in the middle and western areas, as well as the interior, remained steady during the time period.

To sum up, from the dynamics of provincial growth disparity, there is significant time structural change before and after 1990 and also critical are the geographical location factors. The growth disparity appears as an inverse U-shape, which means that the trend has transformed from convergence to divergence since the reform. Provinces that had a lower initial output level experienced a slower growth, while richer regions were convergent to clusters or clubs. Coastal and eastern areas appear convergent, while the disparity in the middle and western areas as well as the interior remained relatively constant. In the following sections of the chapter, I test the provincial disparity patterns empirically according to the convergence hypothesis.

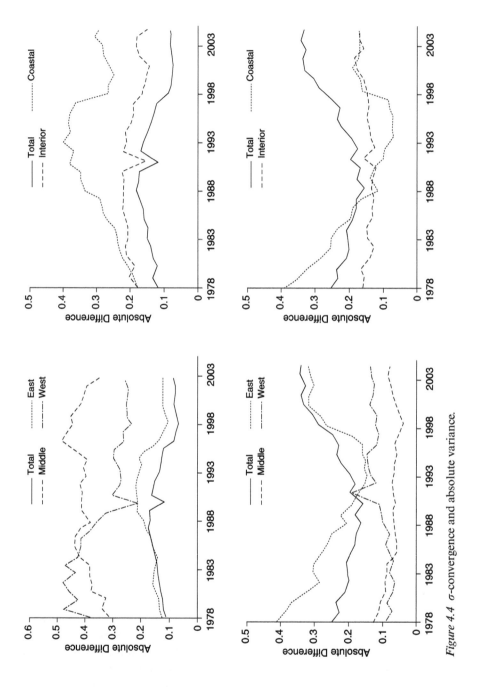

*Figure 4.4* σ-convergence and absolute variance.

## The model

The empirical study in this chapter is based on the augmented Solow model, also called the MRW model (Mankiw *et al.* 1992). The reason for choosing the new classical model is that the conditional convergence hypothesis is appropriate for explaining the evolution of the provincial disparity in China. In the MRW model, human capital was introduced to the production function, while the model in this chapter also includes a technology development factor. So the model in this chapter considers factors including physical capital accumulation, efficient labour and human capital accumulation, as well as technology efficiency. Therefore, using the new classical model, I assume that the fraction of output used in physical capital investment is constant and endogenous, and human capital and level of technology depreciate at the same rate as physical capital. Let the production function be:

$$Y(t) = K(t)^a H(t)^\beta TE(t)^\gamma (A(t)L(t))^{1-a-\beta-\gamma}$$

where $K$ is the stock of physical capital, $H$ is the stock of human capital, $TE$ is the level of technology and $AL$ is effective labour, which excludes human capital and technology progress. Also, I assume that $a > 0$, $\beta > 0$, $\gamma > 0$, $a + \beta + \gamma < 1$, with decreasing returns to scale in the production function. Labour force $L$ and technology level $A$ are assumed to grow exogenously at rates $n$ and $g$: $L(t) = L(0)e^{nt}$, $A(t) = A(0)e^{gt}$, the number of effective units of labour grows at rate $n + g$. The intensive form of production function is $y(t) = k(t)^a h(t)^\beta te(t)^\gamma$, $y$, $k$, $h$, $te$ are quantities per effective unit of labour. The evolution of the economy is determined by:

$$\dot{k} = s_k y(t) - (n + g + \delta)k, \quad \dot{h} = s_h y(t) - (n + g + \delta)h, \quad \dot{te} = s_{te} y(t) - (n + g + \delta)te$$

where $s_k$, $s_h$ and $s_{te}$ are the fraction of income invested in physical capital, human capital and technology development, respectively. Assume that the utility maximization problem of consumers is determined by:

$$Max \int_0^\infty e^{-pt} \frac{c(t)^{1-\sigma}}{1-\sigma} dt, \sigma > 0$$

On the balanced growth path, $\dot{k} = \dot{h} = \dot{te} = 0$, the economy converges to a steady state defined by:

$$k^* = \left(\frac{s_k^{1-\beta-\gamma} s_h^\beta s_{te}^\gamma}{n+g+\delta}\right)^{\frac{1}{1-a-\beta-\gamma}}, \quad h^* = \left(\frac{s_h^{1-a-\gamma} s_k^a s_{te}^\gamma}{n+g+\delta}\right)^{\frac{1}{1-a-\beta-\gamma}},$$

$$te^* = \left(\frac{s_{te}^{1-a-\beta} s_k^a s_h^\beta}{n+g+\delta}\right)^{\frac{1}{1-a-\beta-\gamma}}$$

Substituting the equation into the production function and taking logs gives an equation for income per capita:

$$\ln \frac{Y(t)}{L(t)} = \ln A(0) + gt - \frac{a + \beta + \gamma}{1 - a - \beta - \gamma} \ln(n + g + \delta) + \frac{a}{1 - a - \beta - \gamma} \ln(s_k)$$

$$+ \frac{\beta}{1 - a - \beta - \gamma} \ln(s_h) + \frac{\gamma}{1 - a - \beta - \gamma} \ln(s_{te})$$

which indicates that the income per capita depends on population growth, accumulation of physical and human capital and level of technology, as well as other exogenous factors. Factors that affect the productivity of labour may be human capital accumulation and technology progress, learning by doing, and institutional as well as structural factors. Through the specifications to the new classical augmented Solow model, the Solow residual are refined so that factors that determine regional long-run growth disparity could be specified and tested. We expect that both physical and human capital accumulation, as well as level of technology, would have positive effects on the growth rate, which we empirically test later in this chapter.

## Provincial empirics of growth disparity patterns

In the following part, we test the provincial disparity patterns empirically under the new classical framework applying the panel data of 29 mainland provinces in China during the reform period 1978–2005. As Sala-i-Martin (1996) defined, there is absolute $\beta$-convergence if poor economies tend to grow faster than rich countries, in which the key mechanism is the decreasing returns of physical capital. To test the provincial absolute $\beta$-convergence, we apply the method of Sala-i-Martin, and also include dummy variables to allow differences in the slope and intercept. The basic model is:

$$\gamma_{i,t,t+T} = a - \beta \log(y_{i,t}) + \varepsilon_{i,t,t+T} \tag{1}$$

where the growth rate, $\gamma_{t,t+T} \equiv \log(y_{i,t+T}/y_{i,t})/T$, $y_{i,t}$, $y_{i,t+T}$ is the GDP per worker in region $i$ at time $t$ and $t + T$, respectively and $T$ is the length of the time interval. The convergence speed $\lambda$ can be estimated by using the formula:

$$\beta = (1 - e^{-\lambda T})/T \tag{2}$$

There exists a convergence trend in growth if convergence speed is $\lambda > 0$.

Using the dummy variables that distinguish the geographical location of provinces as the eastern, middle and western areas and also the coastal and interior areas, the model would be:

$$\gamma_{i,t,t+T} = a - \beta_1 \log(y_{i,t}) + \beta_2 D_{east} \log(y_{i,t}) + \beta_3 D_{east} + \beta_4 D_{west} \log(y_{i,t})$$
$$+ \beta_5 D_{west} + \mu_{i,t,t+T} \tag{3}$$

$$\gamma_{i,t,t+T} = a - \beta_1 \log(y_{i,t}) + \beta_2 D_{coast} \log(y_{i,t}) + \beta_3 D_{coast} + \varepsilon_{i,t,t+T} \tag{4}$$

The data used in the empirical analysis is in the panel scale of the 29 mainland provinces excluding Hong Kong, Macao, Taiwan and Tibet in the reform period from 1978–2005. Data of Chongqing province have been added to Sichuan province. All the nominal variables are transferred into the real value using the price index in 1978 as the benchmark year. Moreover, the chapter divides the whole period into two time intervals, using 1990 as the turning point since the trend in income distribution seems to change in this year. The description of the location of the provinces is in the table in the Appendix.

The following empirical analysis tests the absolute convergence hypothesis using the initial output level to interpret the provincial growth rate during the reform period, and also tests whether in 1990 there was a time structural change. The results are reported in Table 4.1. In general, from 1978 to 2005, provincial growth appeared to diverge, although not so significantly. Yet during 1978 to 1990, there was a trend of significant absolute convergence between provinces; the speed of convergence is around 2.9 per cent per year. While during 1990 to 2005, there was a divergent trend in provincial growth, at the speed of 2.1 per cent per year. Moreover, to test the role of geographical location factors in provincial growth disparity, we use model 3 and 4 to verify the growth patterns in the eastern, middle and western areas, as well as the coastal and interior areas in different time intervals. The results are reported in Table 4.2. Testing the panel data from 1978 to 2005, allowing differences in both intercept and slope using dummy variables, I find that the coefficients are not significant. While only one kind of dummy variable is introduced, allowing either the slope or the intercept to vary, we would get significant results from all the coefficients. More specifically, to allow changes

*Table 4.1* Provincial absolute convergence: turning point

| Variable | Dependent variable: growth rate | | |
|---|---|---|---|
| | 78–05 | 78–90 | 90–05 |
| $\ln y_0$ | −0.002 | −0.025*** | 0.025*** |
| | (−0.46) | (−3.70) | (3.73) |
| Ad. $R^2$ | 0.01 | 0.31 | 0.32 |
| *F*-stat | 0.21 | 13.71 | 13.93 |
| implied $\lambda$ | 0.002 | 0.029 | −0.021 |

*Notes:* In this chapter, *T*-values are in parentheses under the estimated coefficients; *, **,*** indicate significant at the 10, 5 and 1% level, respectively.

*Table 4.2* Provincial convergence

| Variable | Dependent variable: growth rate 1978–2005 | | | | | |
|---|---|---|---|---|---|---|
| lny(78) | −0.013 | −0.009** | −0.010** | −0.004 | −0.009** | −0.010** |
| | (−1.16) | (−2.05) | (−2.24) | (−0.79) | (−2.25) | (−2.48) |
| Deast | −0.019 | 0.013*** | | | | |
| | (−0.23) | (2.54) | | | | |
| Dwest | −0.035 | −0.010** | | | | |
| | (−0.29) | (−1.98) | | | | |
| Deast*lny | 0.005 | | 0.002*** | | | |
| | (0.38) | | (2.55) | | | |
| Dwest*lny | 0.004 | | −0.002** | | | |
| | (0.20) | | (−2.00) | | | |
| Dcoast | | | | 0.087 | 0.022*** | |
| | | | | (1.57) | (5.13) | |
| Dcoast*lny | | | | −0.009 | | 0.003*** |
| | | | | (−1.18) | | (4.93) |
| Ad. $R^2$ | 0.45 | 0.38 | 0.38 | 0.48 | 0.51 | 0.49 |
| *F*-stat | 3.74 | 6.67 | 6.71 | 9.52 | 13.38 | 12.34 |
| implied $\lambda$ | E: 0.009 | 0.010 | 0.009 | C: 0.017 | 0.010 | 0.008 |
| | M: 0.016 | 0.010 | 0.012 | I: 0.005 | 0.010 | 0.012 |
| | W: 0.010 | 0.010 | 0.014 | | | |

| Variable | Dependent variable: growth rate 1978–1990 | | | | | |
|---|---|---|---|---|---|---|
| lny(78) | −0.031* | −0.031*** | −0.032*** | −0.024*** | −0.031*** | −0.032*** |
| | (−1.91) | (−4.66) | (−4.69) | (−2.76) | (−4.92) | (−4.92) |
| Deast | 0.001 | 0.013* | | | | |
| | (0.01) | (1.73) | | | | |
| Dwest | 0.011 | −0.007 | | | | |
| | (0.06) | (−0.88) | | | | |
| Deast*lny | 0.002 | | 0.002* | | | |
| | (0.09) | | (1.73) | | | |
| Dwest*lny | −0.003 | | −0.001 | | | |
| | (−0.1) | | (−0.91) | | | |
| Dcoast | | | | 0.112 | 0.019*** | |
| | | | | (1.31) | (2.95) | |
| Dcoast*lny | | | | −0.013 | | 0.003*** |
| | | | | (−1.08) | | (2.83) |
| Ad. $R^2$ | 0.48 | 0.48 | 0.48 | 0.53 | 0.50 | 0.49 |
| *F*-stat | 4.23 | 7.63 | 7.66 | 9.22 | 13.15 | 12.63 |
| implied $\lambda$ | E: 0.037 | 0.038 | 0.037 | C: 0.050 | 0.038 | 0.036 |
| | M: 0.040 | 0.038 | 0.040 | I: 0.028 | 0.038 | 0.040 |
| | W: 0.044 | 0.038 | 0.042 | | | |

| Variable | Dependent variable: growth rate 1990–2005 | | | | | |
|---|---|---|---|---|---|---|
| lny(78) | 0.007 (0.44) | 0.013** (2.01) | 0.012* (1.89) | 0.012 (1.65) | 0.012* (1.92) | 0.011* (1.76) |
| Deast | −0.081 (−0.60) | 0.010** (1.84) | | | | |
| Dwest | 0.032 (0.21) | −0.012*** (−2.07) | | | | |
| Deast*lny | 0.012 (0.67) | | 0.001* (1.87) | | | |
| Dwest*lny | −0.006 (−0.30) | | −0.002*** (−2.14) | | | |
| Dcoast | | | | 0.035 (0.33) | 0.021*** (3.98) | |
| Dcoast*lny | | | | −0.002 (−0.13) | | 0.003*** (3.96) |
| Ad. $R^2$ | 0.59 | 0.57 | 0.57 | 0.59 | 0.59 | 0.59 |
| F-stat | 6.7 | 10.85 | 11.21 | 12.02 | 18.73 | 18.61 |
| implied $\lambda$ | E: −0.017 | −0.012 | −0.013 | C: −0.010 | −0.011 | −0.013 |
| | M: −0.007 | −0.012 | −0.011 | I: −0.011 | −0.011 | −0.010 |
| | W: −0.001 | −0.012 | −0.010 | | | |

in slopes, we could find that during the reform period from 1978 to 2005, there is absolute convergence within the eastern, middle and western areas, as well as within the coastal and interior areas. The coefficient of $\beta$-convergence and the dummy variables is significant, which means that the speed of convergence in the eastern, middle and western areas as well as the coastal and interior areas is significantly different. Further estimating the speed of convergence, we could detect that during the reform period from 1978 to 2005, the western areas had the highest speed of convergence, while the speed in the eastern areas is the slowest; also, the speed in the coastal areas is higher than that in the interior areas. Using the model allowing a different intercept, we could find that the coefficient of $\beta$-convergence and the dummy variables are also significant. This means that under the assumption of identical convergence speed in different areas, there exist some fixed factors that make regions grow at a different rate even if the initial output level is similar. There may be absolute convergence within the eastern, middle and western areas, as well as the coastal and interior groups, while the trend is not significant between these regions. For the first time interval 1978–1990 the conclusion is much the same, while the coefficient of $\beta$-convergence is more significant and the speed of convergence is faster. The comparison of relative speed between regions is similar too. However, the disparity pattern in the second time interval, 1990–2005, is significantly different compared to the former interval. The coefficient of $\beta$-convergence is positive rather than negative, which means that there may be a divergent trend in regional growth. The model allowing variance in both the slope and the intercept is not so significant, while it is significant if either the slope or intercept is variable. The speed of divergence in the eastern areas is more remarkable than that in the middle and western areas, and the speed in the interior areas is faster than that in the coastal areas.

In addition, we can make cluster analysis of regions according to the real output level in the initial year, 1978, and in 2005, and also according to the growth rate during the period. We divide all the 29 provinces into five groups according to the real GDP level, the richest, upper, medium, lower and the poor, and also divide them into four groups according to the growth rate during the time period, the fast, upper, lower and slow. The results are reported in Table 4.3. From the movement of relative status of provinces between groups, it is obvious which provinces are catching up, relatively, and which ones have fallen behind during the past 27 years. It is interesting that provinces that are catching up locate mostly in the eastern and coastal areas while those falling behind are in the middle, western and interior areas.

## Conditional convergence: regional evidence

As the conditional convergence hypothesis shows, economies seem to approach some long-run level of income that is captured by the vector of some variables, and the growth rate falls as the economy approaches this long-run level. The prediction of the new classical model is that the growth rate of an economy will be positively related to the distance that separates it from its own steady state. Only if all economies converge to the same steady state does the prediction that poor economies should grow faster than rich ones hold true. Thus, the rest of this chapter tests some of the possible factors that could play a role in deciding the long-run steady state, based on the revised augmented Solow model in the third section of this chapter.

The Barrro equation used the initial output level and a vector of variables to interpret the disparity of regional growth rate, namely, the conditional convergence between regions. The Barro equation is as follows:

$$\gamma_{i,t,t+T} = a - \beta \log(y_{i,t}) + \psi X_{i,t} + \varepsilon_{i,t,t+T} \tag{6}$$

where $X_{i,t}$ is a vector of variables that hold constant in the steady state of region $i$. The speed of $\beta$-convergence can be estimated using formula (2). In the following section, we introduce a series of variables to clarify the factors that determine the conditional convergence between regions.

### Variables and data

In this section, we use a vector of factors from six elements, including physical capital accumulation, population and labour supply, human capital

*Table 4.3* Provincial cluster respecting output level and growth rate

| Cluster | Mean | Provinces |
|---|---|---|
| *Real GDP 1978* | | |
| Richest | 3906.77 | Shanghai |
| Upper | 2066.23 | Beijing, Tianjin, Liaoning, Heilongjiang |
| Medium | 1172.08 | Jilin, Qinghai |
| Lower | 812.32 | Hebei, Shanxi(Middle), Inner Mongolia, Jiangsu, Gansu, Ningxia, Zhejiang, Jiangxi, Fujian, Shandong, Shanxi(West), Hainan, Hubei, Sichuan, Xinjiang, Guangdong |
| Poor | 553.77 | Anhui, Henan, Hunan, Guangxi, Guizhou, Yunnan |
| *Real GDP 2005* | | |
| Richest | 27604.67 | Tianjin, Shanghai |
| Upper | 17001.06 | Beijing |
| Medium | 11125.19 | Inner Mongolia, Liaoning, Zhejiang, Shandong, Jiangsu, Guangdong |
| Lower | 8446.32 | Hebei, Heilongjiang, Jilin, Xinjiang, Shanxi(Middle), Fujian |
| Poor | 4514.64 | Anhui, Hunan, Sichuan, Gansu, Guangxi, Yunnan, Jiangxi, Hainan, Qinghai, Ningxia, Guizhou, Shanxi(West), Henan, Hubei |
| *Growth rate 1978–2005* | | |
| Fast | 9.47 | Tianjin, Fujian, Inner Mongolia, Xinjiang, Jiangsu, Zhejiang, Shandong, Guangdong |
| Upper | 8.17 | Hebei, Henan, Shanxi, Hubei |
| Lower | 7.15 | Beijing, Guangxi, Hainan, Anhui, Yunnan, Shanghai, Jiangxi, Liaoning, Jilin, Shanxi(West) |
| Slow | 5.97 | Heilongjiang, Sichuan, Guizhou, Ningxia, Hunan, Gansu, Qinghai |
| Catch up | | Tianjin, Inner Mongolia, Jiangsu, Zhejiang, Shandong, Guangdong |
| Fall behind | | Liaoning, Heilongjiang, Jilin, Qinghai, Gansu, Ningxia, Jiangxi, Shanxi, Hainan, Hubei, Sichuan |

*Note:* Real GDP is comparable in the price index relative to 1978.

accumulation, level of technology, institutional influence, and openness and structural factors, so that we can have a relatively comprehensive understanding of the factors that may determine regional growth disparity. We also use the panel data of 29 mainland provinces. The data set contains the available information for these regions, for 14 of the years between 1978 and 2005, that is, the years 1978, 1980, 1985, 1990, 1995, and from 1997 to 2005. According to the structural relationship of variables in the theoretical model, the vector of variables is devised as follows.

Dependent variable (GR): We use the growth rate of regional output per worker (Y/L), where Y indicates value of real regional GDP and L is the employed persons at the year end of each region.

The independent variables cover the following six aspects. Physical capital – capital accumulation is always regarded as the key point of economic growth in growth theory (Cai and Du 2000; Dong 2004). We further decompose this index into two components: investment rate (INVR) and investment efficiency (INVEFF). Investment rate is described as the proportion of gross fixed capital formation to GDP in a region. Investment efficiency is the ratio of gross fixed capital formation relative to gross capital formation, and the latter includes both gross fixed capital formation and change in inventories.

Population (POP) – as indicated in growth theory, the natural growth rate of population would be a better index as an explanatory variable of the growth rate.

Human capital (H) – we consider the role of human capital accumulation and level of technology separately from effective labour in the theoretical model. Considering the accessibility and availability of the data, we use the log scale of the initial total enrollment of higher education by region to describe the human capital stock in a region.

Technology (TE) – we use the log scale of the number of patent applications granted in a region as a proxy of the technology level in a region. So far, few researches have been concerned with this factor.

Market-oriented transition and the role of the government (GOV) – taking into account the transitional background of China, the role of institution and government intervention in the market economy should be considered. We use government expenditure relative to GDP as a proxy to measure the degree of government intervention in the economy.

Structure of property (PROP) – this index is denoted by the number of staff and workers in state-owned units relative to the total staff and workers.

Degree of opening (OPEN) – in the new growth theory, it is believed that human capital could lock in international trade, which makes the growth disparity between regions persist. We will use both dependence on foreign trade (TRADE) and actual rate of FDI (FDI) to describe this factor. The former is the total value of imports and exports relative to GDP, and the latter is actual FDI relative to GDP by region.

Industrialization (IND) – as a developing country, the diverse level of industrialization among regions might influence the provincial growth rate. We use gross regional industry product relative to gross regional product as the proxy of industrialization.

Other variables – we also add regional dummy variables to separate the geographical effects on growth rate to test the club convergence.

### Factors determining provincial steady-state growth

Considering the characteristics of the fixed factors that influence growth disparity, we use the fixed effects method to estimate the coefficients of variables. The results are presented in Table 4.4, in which factors that are not significant have been eliminated. In a model that does not include geographical location dummy variables, the effects of investment efficiency, human capital, level of technology, government expenditure, structure of property and FDI are significant at the 5 per cent level, the coefficient of conditional $\beta$ convergence is significant at the 1 per cent level, and the speed of convergence is about 2.2 per cent. After controlling the geographical dummy variables that indicate the location difference in the eastern, middle and western areas, the effects of investment rate, investment efficiency, government expenditure and structure property, foreign trade and regional dummy intercept variables are significant at the 5 per cent level. The effects of human capital and level of technology as well as regional dummy slope variables are significant at the 10 per cent level. The coefficient of convergence is significant at the 1 per cent level. The speed of convergence in the eastern area is significantly faster than that in the middle and western areas – 3 per cent compared to 1.9 per cent. It is obvious that, after controlling for a series of structural variables, there is club convergence in the eastern, middle and western areas; the speed of convergence is significantly higher in the east, while there is no remarkable difference of speed in the middle and western areas. Using the regional dummy variables that identify the coastal and interior areas, then the government expenditure, structure of property, foreign trade, industrialization and the slope and intercept dummy variables are all significant at the 5 per cent level. Investment

*Table 4.4* Conditional convergence and club convergence

| Variable | Dependent variable: growth rate 1978–2005 | | | | | | |
|---|---|---|---|---|---|---|---|
| lny(78) | −0.017*** (−8.86) | −0.015*** (−5.64) | −0.015*** (−6.65) | IND | | | −0.018** (−2.41) |
| INVR | | 0.018** (2.29) | | Deast | | 0.045** (2.05) | |
| INVEFF | −0.026** (−2.23) | −0.023** (−2.15) | −0.017* (−1.61) | Dwest | | −0.007*** (−3.67) | |
| H | −0.007*** (−3.08) | −0.003* (−1.62) | | Dcoast | | | 0.071*** (3.31) |
| TE | 0.007*** (3.64) | 0.003* (1.87) | | Deast*lny | | −0.005* (−1.72) | |
| GOV | −0.122*** (−5.48) | −0.114*** (−5.73) | −0.075*** (−3.76) | Dwest*lny | | Not significant | |
| PROP | −0.037*** (−3.04) | −0.023** (−2.39) | −0.028*** (−2.56) | Dcoast*lny | | | −0.007** (−2.47) |
| TRADE | 0.005 (1.17) | 0.009*** (2.91) | 0.007** (2.10) | $R^2$ | 0.45 | 0.51 | 0.59 |
| FDI | 0.079** (2.54) | | 0.029 (1.02) | F-stat | 38.2 | 42.4 | 48.1 |
| | | | | implied $\beta$ | 0.022 | E: 0.030<br>M: 0.019<br>W: 0.019 | C: 0.034<br>I: 0.019 |

efficiency is significant at the 10 per cent level. The speed of convergence is significant at the 1 per cent level. The speed in the coastal areas is approximately 3.4 per cent and in the interior areas is only 1.9 per cent. It is explicitly shown that, after controlling for a series of variables, there is club convergence in the coastal and interior areas and the speed of convergence in the coastal areas is faster than that in the interior areas. To sum up, there is significant conditional convergence between regions; factors that determine the steady-state output level include investment efficiency, human capital, level of technology, government intervention and structure of property. After controlling for a series of variables, there is club convergence within the eastern, middle and western areas, as well as the coastal and interior areas. The speed of convergence in the east is higher than in the middle and west, and the coastal area is higher than the interior areas, which is similar to conclusion reached in absolute convergence.

## Conclusion

This chapter investigates regional growth disparity between mainland provinces during the period 1978–2005 from a dynamic point of view. Two critical questions are raised: (1) Do significant time structural differences exist and how important are geographical factors in regional growth disparity? (2) What are the key factors that determine the regional steady-state output per worker? To examine question (1), stylized facts of regional growth and the evolution of provincial growth disparity are analysed, based on a dynamic perspective. Multiple indexes, like the kernel density and Theil entropy, as well as the variance of $\sigma$-convergence, are introduced to illustrate the changes of output distribution during various time periods in different groups. The conclusion is that there is significant time structural difference in regional disparity before and after the 1990s, in other words, the disparity patterns among regions acted differently in the two time intervals. Also, the geographical location factors are essential: regions that are in the eastern and coastal areas are expected to experience faster growth. Before 1990, there is absolute convergence between regions, and the speed of absolute convergence in the western areas and the interior areas is faster. After the 1990s, there is a trend of divergence between regions: the speed of divergence in the eastern and coastal areas is higher. From the dynamic evolution of growth disparity between regions, we can see that most regions that experienced catching up are located in the eastern and coastal areas, while regions that are falling behind are in the middle, west, northeastern and interior areas.

To address question (2), a series of structural control variables are introduced into the Barro equation so that the provincial steady-state position of output per worker can be specified and the speed of conditional convergence estimated. The hypothesis of club convergence is also tested using the dummy variables. The conclusion is that, after controlling for level of investment efficiency, human capital, technology efficiency, government intervention and property structure, economies with a higher level of initial output per worker will undergo a lower growth rate; the overall rate of conditional convergence is approximately 2.2 per cent per year. And there is also club convergence in the eastern, middle and western areas, as well as coastal and interior areas. The speed of club convergence in the eastern and coastal areas is higher. If the speed of convergence remains at approximately 2.2 per cent per year, then after 31 years, the distance between the real output level and the steady-state output level would decline to only half of the present level. Thus, the mechanisms that affect the convergence trend of regional growth in China not only include the decreasing returns of capital in the neoclassical scope but also technological progress in the scope of endogenous theory. One of the efficient ways for regions that follow behind to increase their growth rate in the long run is to change the structural characteristics that influence the steady-state growth level.

In conclusion, the key factor relating to conditional convergence is that the government can choose policies in order to harmonize the speed of development of different regions and districts, which in the long run would facilitate economic growth in China.

## References

Cai, F. and Du, Y. (2000) Convergence and divergence of regional economic growth in China, *Economic Research Journal*, 10: 30–37.

Das, S.K. and A. Barua (1996) Regional inequalities, economic growth and liberalisation: a study of the Indian economy, *Journal of Development Studies*, 32(3): 364–390.

Dong, X. (2004) Understanding the regional income disparity in China, 1952–2002, *Economic Research Journal*, 9: 48–59.

Mankiw, N.G., D. Romer and D.N. Weil (1992) A contribution to the empirics of economic growth, *Quarterly Journal of Economics*, 107: 407–437.

Sala-i-Martin, X.X. (1996) The classical approach to convergence analysis, *The Economic Journal*, 106: 1019–1036.

## Appendix: Location of mainland provinces

| Mainland province | Location | Location | Mainland province | Location | Location |
|---|---|---|---|---|---|
| Beijing | East | Interior | Henan | Middle | Interior |
| Tianjin | East | Coast | Hubei | Middle | Interior |
| Hebei | East | Coast | Hunan | Middle | Interior |
| Shanxi | Middle | Interior | Guangdong | East | Coast |
| Inner Mongolia | Middle | Interior | Guangxi | East | Interior |
| Liaoning | East | Coast | Hainan | East | Coast |
| Jilin | Middle | Interior | Sichuan | West | Interior |
| Heilongjiang | Middle | Interior | Guizhou | West | Interior |
| Shanghai | East | Coast | Yunnan | West | Interior |
| Jiangsu | East | Coast | Shannxi | West | Interior |
| Zhejiang | East | Coast | Gansu | West | Interior |
| Anhui | Middle | Interior | Qinghai | West | Interior |
| Fujian | East | Coast | Ningxia | West | Interior |
| Jiangxi | Middle | Interior | Xinjiang | West | Interior |
| Shandong | East | Coast | | | |

# 5 Growth, inequality and poverty in China

*Gopal Krishna Pal*

## Introduction

The low-income countries, at present, stress various social and economic indicators explaining their rapid economic development. But the objectives of development are changing over time to review economic factors like high national and per capita income, high saving, investment and capital formation to raise productivity: high total consumption is not sufficient to break the vicious cycles of poverty of these low-income economies. The 'low level of equilibrium trap' experienced by developing countries may be overcome, as the experiences of many countries suggest, by gaining high economic growth at the cost of inequality and mass poverty. Yet economic growth may not be the means for social sector development, e.g. health and education. It also may not generate capability of the people. First, the hypothesis that income inequality increases in the initial years of development but ultimately decreases (Fields 1995; Kuznets 1955) is also not found to be correct for many countries. Since 1820 global income inequality has increased steadily (United Nations 2006), while there has been economic growth in many countries. Income and consumption inequalities are found both in high-, upper middle-, lower middle- and low-income economies. Not only are income and consumption inequalities evident, but also inequalities in access to health and education, gender inequalities and uneven development of the regions are the problems in many countries. The analysis of these factors is quite problematic and leads to many critiques (see Nye *et al.* 2001). Inequality traps are the result of development at present.

Second, poverty is also an important issue in the development process of many countries (note Table 5.1). No definite relation is found between growth and poverty. From the experiences of the developing countries it may be found that a country with higher growth and per capita income has higher poverty than a low-income country. Sri Lanka had per capita income of $4,100, with per capita income growth of 6 per cent, in 2007, while the corresponding figures for China were $5,300 and 11.4 per cent in 2003–04; yet in China a higher percentage of its population live below $1 a day (the international poverty line). A similar, but less obvious, trend is found for India and

*Table 5.1* Selected national data on income and poverty

| Country | GDP per capita (PPP US$) 2007 | GDP growth (US$) 2007 | Poverty rate (various years) |
|---------|------------------------------|----------------------|------------------------------|
| Sri Lanka | 4,100 | 6.0 | 22.0 (2002) |
| China | 5,300 | 11.4 | 10.0 (2004) |
| Malaysia | 14,400 | 5.7 | 5.1 (2002) |
| Bangladesh | 1,400 | 6.0 | 45.0 (2004) |
| Pakistan | 2,600 | 6.3 | 7.5 (2007) |
| India | 2,700 | 8.5 | 25.0 (2002) |

*Source: CIA World Factbook* (2008).

Pakistan. An opposite relationship between growth and poverty is found if the performances of Bangladesh and Malaysia are compared. While per capita income in Malaysia was $14,400 and in Bangladesh was $1,400 in 2007, the poverty rate was less than 5.1 per cent in 2002 and 45 per cent in 2004 in the respective countries. A relatively high-income country had low poverty and a relatively low-income country had high poverty. The benefits of growth may not automatically percolate to the economically disadvantaged percentage of the population.

Third, no definite relation is found between inequality and poverty. Income and consumption inequalities are problems in high-income as well as low-income countries: in all the high-income OECD countries, high inequalities are found. Even in Norway, the country enjoying the highest per capita income ($52,030 in 2004), the Gini index in 2000 was 0.27. In the UK and US, the Gini indices, respectively, were 0.34 and 0.38. Contrariwise, many developing economies have less inequality than some developed economies at present. But in the high-income OECD countries, except Portugal and the Republic of Korea (for both the poverty rate is less than 2 per cent, as per the latest information), poverty is not found. The developed countries have been successful in eradicating poverty and so the people can enjoy minimum basic needs. Poverty is a problem for the developing economies; yet a developing country with high inequality may have low poverty and vice versa (Foster and Szekely 2001).

The developing countries' acute need at present is to create the conditions of equal opportunity for all. The neoclassical model of optimum utilization of resources through market forces is not always applicable in a developing economy on account of the presence of socio-economic rigidities and barriers. Development models were experimented with in a large number of countries for many decades, but since the 1950s they have been found to be insufficient to achieve high growth and high per capita income along with equity in distribution. The success stories of some countries in this regard are the outcome of government policies towards non-economic factors, together with the mechanism of market forces. For some low-income economies it can be found that in spite of low per capita income the value of the Human Development Index is higher than the countries with relatively higher per capita incomes. The countries that have placed greater stress on closing the opportunity gap have been successful in achieving economic and social sector development. Of course, the efficiency of a person engaged in the development process depends on his socio-economic position in the society (Bourguignon 2001). Therefore, we see that the opportunity to work, and the achieved level of education and skill, health, and extent of property rights are the factors contributing to individual and social gains.

Eradicating 'inequality traps' and opportunity gaps are the main objectives of economic development of any developing country at present. The World Bank in its *World Development Report 2006* stresses these factors. They ask:

> why does income distribution matter for poverty reduction? In a mechanical sense the rate of income poverty reduction in a country is a function of two things: the rate of its economic growth and the share of any increment of growth that is captured by the poor. Other things being equal, the larger the share of income captured by the poor, the more efficient the country is in converting growth into poverty reduction. Holding income distribution patterns constant and projecting current growth rates into the future, it would take three decades for the median household in poverty to cross the poverty line in Mexico. Doubling the share of the poor in future income growth would cut this time horizon by half. For Kenya the time horizon would be reduced by 17 years, from 2030 to 2013 – a transition that would bring the country within touching distance of an otherwise unattainable Millennium Development goal target of halving income poverty.
>
> (United Nations 2006: 228)

In the light of these objectives, an attempt is made in this chapter, first, to examine how far pre- and post-reform China was successful in achieving the goals of equality and removal of poverty while gaining economic growth. This may be a difficult target as distribution within China is wide and asymmetrically distributed between the urban and rural regions. Second, it is also proposed to examine the successfulness of its government's policies to close the inherited opportunity gap (Dreze and Sen 1989, 1997).

The hypotheses of the study are:

- A development strategy emphasizing economic growth increases economic inequality and poverty.
- A pro-poor strategy for development reduces economic inequality and poverty at the cost of economic growth.
- The variables and proxy indicators are: Gini-coefficients for measuring inequality; the population below the poverty line (as defined in the *World Development Report*: below $1 a day per person) for measuring poverty;

GDP per capita and GDP growth rates for comparing growth over time. Access to health and education are taken as the response variables for measuring the extent of opportunities available to a person to work with efficiency.

In this study these variables are analysed to identify the patterns of growth, inequality and poverty, and to locate the causes of such trends by evaluating the relevant government policies.

There are four further sections in this chapter. In the first, the socio-economic background of China during the pre- and post-revolution period is discussed, concentrating upon growth, inequality, poverty and backwardness. Also a comparison will be made in this section with some countries in East, South East and South Asia. Second, the development policies are considered. To identify the factors responsible for China's development concerning equity, equity and social opportunity since the revolution in 1949 are examined. Third, the findings of the study are highlighted, and finally, conclusions drawn.

## Socio-economic conditions in China

Records reveal that China was once one of the richest nations in the world (see Figure 5.1). A comparative picture of the percentage of world income during 1913–98 of China, India, some East Asian and South East Asian countries and the USA is presented in Figure 5.2. It shows that in 1950 the countries of East Asia and India had suffered worst, except for Japan, whose share rose continuously since 1913.

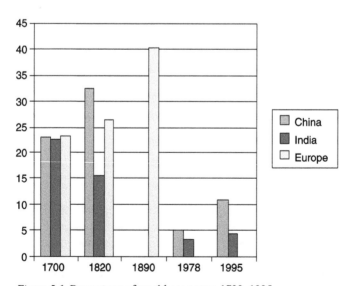

*Figure 5.1* Percentage of world economy, 1700–1995.

*Source:* Baru (2002: 2584).

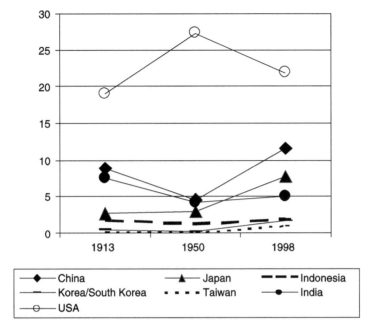

*Figure 5.2* Percentage of world economy, 1913–98.

*Source:* Maddison *et al.* (2002).

During 1914–71, as estimated by Dwight H. Perkins (1975), GDP over many years recorded an upward trend for China (Figure 5.3). Average annual rates of China's GDP growth in different sub-periods, from 1952 to 1974, are presented in Figure 5.4. It is seen that the first decade was marked by high rates of economic growth. During 1952–59, the GDP growth rate was 10.5 per cent and during 1957–59 it was 22 per cent. Growth was lowest during 1959–66, at 1.6 per cent.

China and India in the 1940s were approximately at the same stage of development, with very low levels of output per capita. They were technologically poor, with large rural sectors. While China held the advantage in agriculture, India was better in industry; annual per capita output for both of them was around $80 to $120 (Gill 1973: 114). In China, in 1936, about 90 per cent of the economy was comprised of scattered individual farming and handicrafts, while modern industry accounted for only 10 per cent. Only 0.6 per cent of the working population comprised industrial labourers in the same year. China in 1949 inherited a semi-feudal and semi-colonial economy. The rural landlords owned more than 70 per cent of cultivable land and charged 50 to 80 per cent of the crop as rent. In industry, the exploitation rate was high, varying between 200 to 1000 per cent. In the social sector, its performances were also very poor: the mortality rate was high and more than 90 per cent of the population was illiterate (Suinian and Quangan

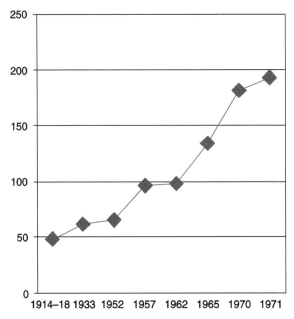

*Figure 5.3* China's GDP (1957 prices) in billion yuan.

*Source:* Perkins (1975).

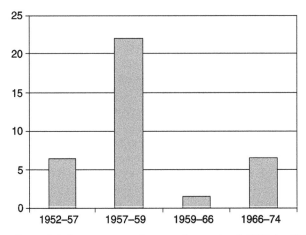

*Figure 5.4* Average annual rates of growth of GDP in China, 1952–74 (% per year, 1952 prices).

*Source:* Eckstein (1977: 225).

1986: 10–11). In 1933, about 64 per cent of GDP was produced in the agricultural sector, 17.8 per cent in industry and 18.2 per cent in the service sector (Richardson 1999) (see Figure 5.5).

It is observed from the development experiences of the East Asian countries

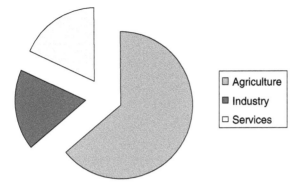

*Figure 5.5* Value added as percentage of GDP, 1933.

*Source:* Richardson (1999: 27).

that South Korea, Japan and Hong Kong developed at a faster rate than other countries during 1960–80. And the growth rates of most of the Latin American and African countries were comparatively low (on average) during the last few decades. But the developed countries were also growing at low rates. However, China made a major advance in this respect since its economic reform. During 1980–92, China's average annual per capita growth rate was 7.6 per cent and this increased to 8.8 per cent during 2003–04. Among the South Asian countries, India's per capita GDP growth rate began rising since the reform in 1991 and reached a respectable rate (5.4 per cent) during 2003–04. She was followed by Bangladesh and Pakistan.

In the social sector, China made tremendous progress. In literacy and life expectancy, the success of China, other countries of East Asia, and most of the countries of South East Asia are equally comparable to the high-income countries of the world. In this respect the progress made by the South Asian countries, except Sri Lanka, is disappointing.

In spite of faster economic growth in the East and South East Asian countries, the income distribution of these countries is notably below expectations. Except Taiwan, these countries, including China, display high inequality in income distribution. The Gini index for Taiwan was 0.24 in 2000, while it was 0.42 in 1995 and 0.45 in 2001 for China. South Asian countries, particularly Pakistan (0.27 in 2001), India (0.33 in 1999–2000) and Bangladesh (0.31 in 2000), have better records. Some former socialist countries, for example Russia (0.32 in 2002) and Poland (0.31 in 2002), were more equal than China (Table 5.2). As described in the *World Development Report 2006*, high income/consumption inequalities are found in Brazil, Haiti, Honduras and South Africa, and inequalities are also found in most of the high-income countries.

With respect to mass poverty or extreme poverty, as measured by the international poverty line, China, other countries of East Asia, and South East

*Table 5.2* Gini index for selected countries

| Country | Gini index | Year |
|---------|-----------|------|
| Taiwan | 0.24 | 2000 |
| China | 0.42 (0.45) | 1995 (2001) |
| Pakistan | 0.27 | 2001 |
| India | 0.33 | 1999–2000 |
| Bangladesh | 0.31 | 2000 |
| Russia | 0.32 | 2002 |
| Poland | 0.31 | 2002 |

*Source: World Development Report 2006.*

Asia, have done extremely well if their level of per capita income is considered. In the high-income market economies, extreme poverty is not found. Mass poverty is also at a minimum in some former socialist countries (<2 per cent in 2002 in Russia and Poland). China however is gradually progressing in reducing the extent of its mass poverty. In 1990, the poverty rate was 29 per cent in China; it fell to 16.6 per cent in 2001. South Asia's record in this respect is extremely poor, except Sri Lanka and Pakistan. The poverty rates for India, Bangladesh and Nepal were 35.3 (1999–2000), 36.0 (2000) and 39.1 (1995–96) per cent, respectively (see United Nations *Human Development Report* 2006 and other issues).

## Evaluation of development policies

Pre-reform (1949–78) China adopted a rapid development strategy that can be found in its socialist transformation programmes of land reform (1949–52), collectivization (1953–57), the policy of the 'Great Leap Forward' (1958–60) for industrialization, and the formation of people's communes (1958–84). Within a decade of the revolution of 1949, rapid and bold measures of institutional change were taken for socialist reconstruction of agriculture and industry. The primary task of the new government (formed on 1 October 1949), under the leadership of the Communist Party, was to deal with the factors hindering development by adopting a new democratic economic programme. The policy of the new programme was to allow initially a small private economy in rural and urban areas along with the formation of state controlled economic activities in modern sectors and in foreign trade. The new government adopted the path of socialism, the stage before communism, from the stage of a backward semi-feudal and semi-colonial economy.

    After the first phase of agrarian reform in 1952, by which the land relations were changed, the second phase, collectivization, started in 1953 along with the commencement of the First Five Year Plan. The objectives of collectivization were to abolish private property and private decision making in agriculture, and it was a step towards communism. Also through collectivization the government tried to increase agricultural production by large-scale farming. But this objective was only partly fulfilled since the peasants felt a lack of incentive in production by being deprived of their land and profit motive within the market economy. Disparity between agriculture and industry was large. As a corrective measure, in 1957, to enhance the performance of agriculture administrative decentralization was pursued by handing over major decision-making powers to the localities and provinces. But this measure failed to deal with the imbalances between agriculture and industry, and urban unemployment increased as many peasants began migrating to cities. To overcome this problem, the 'walking on two legs' policy was taken with the Great Leap Forward (GLF) programme. With this programme, China tried to maintain rapid growth in the modern industrial sector while mobilizing people in the rural areas to generate employment and increase output using labour-intensive techniques. It was the policy of technological dualism.

To speed up transition to communism and also to combine industry, agriculture, commerce, education and military affairs, the Rural People's Communes were initiated in the countryside in 1958. In return for communal labour, communal cafeterias provided meals and other necessities. Distribution was according to 'need' and not 'ability' of the workers. But in a developing economy with low production, the working of the communist principle of distribution was found to be self-contradictory. Both the commune system and GLF quickly faced difficulties in fulfilling their respective objectives because of the lack of incentives for the economic agents engaged in production.

To transform national consciousness in favour of socialism, another institutional change, the Great Proletarian Cultural Revolution, was introduced in 1965. Traditional forms of education were abandoned and physical work had to be done by everybody. The objective was that 'men in the society should work with the motive of social welfare instead of the self justice of capitalism'. The period of socialist transformation (1949–78) was a period of self-reliance. Since economic reform (1978), China has been trying to correct the mistakes of institutional change applied by socialist development by the socialist modernization of agriculture, industry, defence, science and technology. The government emphasized changes in the productive forces for economic development. It gradually introduced (essentially it 'allowed') the market forces for rapid economic growth. Two innovative systems, Household Responsibility System/Agricultural Responsibility System in agriculture, and Township and Village Enterprises in industry, were introduced, along with opening the economy to foreign capital by discarding the earlier 'closed-door' policy.

Different phases of reform are: rural and agricultural reform (1978–83), reform of the urban sector (1984–91) and more autonomy to state-owned enterprises (1991 to the present). Emphasis is now given to the light and consumer goods industries in lieu of the earlier policy stressing the growth of heavy industries. Economic equality is not the objective at present, as demonstrated by the slogans for development: 'To be rich is glorious' and 'as long as it makes money, it is good'. Foreign investment and technology has been playing a major role since 1978 in the industrial development of the country. At present, non-resident Chinese are also investing in the economy and they have a large share in the total capital investment within the present policy known as 'socialist market economy with Chinese characteristics'. With the opening up of the economy, China joined the WTO in December 2001, and has taken up the policy of 'export-oriented growth'.

China in 2004 was the fourth largest economy in the world, and in August 2005 its GDP (ppp) was $8,092 trillion. It is one of the fastest growing countries in recent decades. In the 1980s, China became self-sufficient in grain production and by 2006 about 12 per cent of GDP was produced in agricultural sector, 47 per cent in industry and 41 per cent in the service sector (World Bank 2008) (see Figure 5.6). Among the East Asian countries in recent years, foreign direct investment was highest in China. Its projected GDP per capita is $3000 by the year 2020 in the service sector.

## Explaining growth, distribution and poverty eradication

China's 'arguably moderate growth' but better social distribution before reform was on account of her policy of stringent government intervention in all economic activities. The withdrawal from market forces, 'closed-door' policy of self-reliance, abolition of property rights, emphasis on heavy industries at the cost of agriculture, inefficient management of macroeconomic variables and so on, resulted in moderate growth. The rapid experimentation of different socialist measures and the quick achievement of communism through distributional justice under the dictate 'to each according to his needs' under the commune system, did not work.

Second, production and distribution had no link to incentives. In a poor

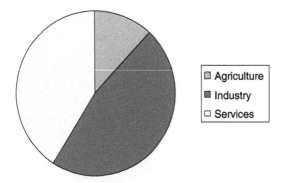

*Figure 5.6* Value added as percentage of GDP, 2006.

*Source: World Development Report 2008.*

economy like China after the revolution, the step towards an egalitarian society showed only an insufficient consumption basket; even the countryside was not successful in providing the basic needs of the people. To quote:

> For decades after the mid-1950s, life in rural China continued to be harsh. . . . And even in the 1970s hungry peasants swamped into cities to beg for food. In 1978 the government, concerned about rural poverty, carried out a special investigation that concluded that 260 million people lived below the poverty line – a third of the rural population.
>
> (United Nations 1997: 49)

> One of the most striking characteristics of Chinese society as seen by any visitor is its apparently egalitarian character in terms of income. . . . One certainly has the impression that the Chinese have succeeded in placing a floor on real income. . . . This impression is reinforced by the fact that one very rarely is exposed to extremes of luxury and high living. It is also particularly striking if one has been to India or some other parts of Asia.
>
> (Eckstein 1977: 299)

Third, failure in growth and removal of poverty were substituted by China's impressive records in the social sector and in human development, which narrowed the opportunity gap for the people during this period. The under–five mortality rate reduced from 202 (rate per thousand live births) in 1960, to 98 in 1970, and further reduced to 65 in 1980. In 1960, life expectancy at birth was about 36 years, but it had increased to 64 years by 1980. The number of physicians per thousand people was 0.6 in 1965 and this increased to 0.9 in 1980. For South Korea, the respective figures were 0.3 and 0.6; and for Malaysia 0.1 and 0.3. The adult literacy rate (percentage of population aged 15 and above) in China in 1977 was 66. This was quite high in comparison to India and other South Asian countries, except Sri Lanka. Adult illiteracy, which was 80 per cent in the 1950s, had fallen remarkably in the pre-reform period. Shortly after the revolution, China undertook campaigns to improve sanitation; extend health care services through a mass cadre of bare-foot doctors; and introduced extensive health insurance coverage for the people. Stress on the importance of universal basic education along with vocational and technical education has made China successful in improving human conditions. Higher education was less emphasized, though in engineering it had a strong following (Agarwala 2002: 67).

Post-reform China is marked by high growth, high inequality (its Gini coefficient rose from a low of 0.28 in 1981, to 0.38 in 1995, and to 0.45 in 2001), and with low poverty. Even so,

> while annually 1.5 million Chinese were lifted out of poverty between the years 2001 to 2004, the income divide among Chinese citizens has widened sharply. . . . The bottom 20 per cent of China's income-earners

earn a mere 4.7 per cent of the total income; while the top 20 per cent of China's income-earners take home 50 per cent of the total income. As of July this year (2005) Chinese rural areas still had over 26.1 million people living in absolute poverty, and China was still home to 18 per cent of the world's poor.

(Zheng 2005: 6–7)

The factors responsible for high rates of growth are modernization of agriculture and industry, improvement of the quality of productive forces through the modernization and adoption of science and technology, increasing the scope of utilizing the existing skills of the people (which were created before by human development), together with the introduction of a socialist market economy system. By going global, the economy earned the fruits of modern technology and foreign investment.

The adoption of the household responsibility system and withdrawal of communes introduced the concept of economic incentives. As a result, productivity in household agriculture increased by 40 per cent compared with collectives. Moreover, township and enterprises (TVEs) were encouraged by low taxes and by giving autonomy to them in production and marketing. As a result, the share of TVEs in industrial production increased from 12 per cent in 1978 to 39 per cent in 1992 (United Nations 1997: 49). The government also introduced price reform. The procurement prices for major crops and retail prices for other primary sector commodities were raised, resulting in a 20 per cent increase in rural per capita income during 1978–84. Rural sector development was also reflected in a reduction of the number of rural poor from 260 million to 97 million during this period.

Since the mid-1980s, however, the emphasis on industrial and export sectors increased poverty, lowered educational achievements, and enhanced income and regional disparities. As a corrective measure, the government in the early 1990s, via its Poverty Reduction Programme, aimed at eliminating absolute poverty by 2000. Even though the government was successful in its objective of the reduction of absolute poverty, income inequality is a matter of concern at present.

Let us now compare the factors for different rates of growth, varying income distributions and poverty in India and some Asian countries during the past few decades. In spite of less than moderate growth before reform, India had been successful in maintaining better equity in income distribution than China. There had been a disappointing record for poverty eradication for India, however. Since the second half of the 1980s, India had been experiencing rapid economic growth, but poverty reduction was not up to the mark. In most of the plans a greater emphasis was given to growth. Pro-urban industrial policies stressed the development of capital goods through capital-intensive technology. Though inequality in income was reduced by restrictive trade practices acts, and by national wage policies for urban and service sectors, no such strong measures were taken within the rural sector. The 'green revolution' favoured the rural rich and large landlords. Agriculture was not modernized for all. Lack of industrialization meant the rural sector suffered from an unemployed idle labour force. Lack of pro-poor development policy, a faulty anti-poverty programme and the neglect of rural development all added to the total number of people in poverty. India's 'trickle-down' policy in the early years after independence failed to eradicate poverty. In the education and health sectors, a comprehensive measure was lacking. Basic and technical education, and even primary health services, were neglected, resulting in extremely poor care in rural areas still present today.

India's social sector development is elitist in nature. In almost all the social sector indicators, India and other South Asian countries except Sri Lanka are lagging behind the East Asian and South East Asian countries. These countries have not been successful in creating opportunities for the masses and are suffering from an 'opportunity gap' in social and economic fields. Along with an emphasis on growth with market friendly development policy, the high performing countries of East and South East Asia adopted bold measures for eradicating poverty, and in creating opportunities for the masses.

Adult literacy rates (per cent) of some Asian countries are compared for the years 1977 and 1998–2004 in Figures 5.7 and 5.8. Life expectancies (in years) at birth for these countries are also shown for the respective years in Figures 5.9 and 5.10.

### Findings

Findings of the analysis of policies for development in different countries are highlighted. First, during the period of socialist transformation and institutional reform, China's objective of rapid economic development with high growth failed on account of excessive government intervention in the country's economic activities. Using traditional technology productivity in agriculture and industry could not be increased. As the government's main

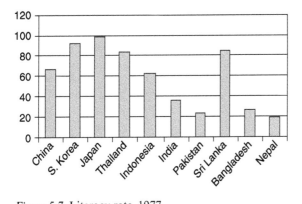

*Figure 5.7* Literacy rate, 1977.

*Source: World Development Report 1982.*

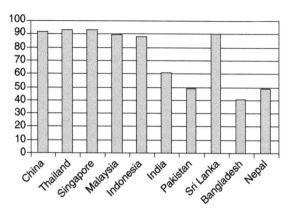

*Figure 5.8* Recent literacy rate.

*Source: World Development Report 2006.*

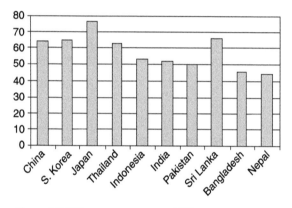

*Figure 5.9* Life expectancy rate, 1980.

*Source: World Development Report 1982.*

objective was to attain equity to build up an egalitarian society through various institutional reforms, this period was characterized by the pro-poor development strategy. Creating opportunities with social sector development was another objective of this strategy – and in this, China was partly successful.

Second, China did not depend on the 'trickle-down' effect of growth for eradication of mass poverty and income equality during this period. The government, without depending on market forces, tried to solve these problems by adopting specific policies. The government's pledge to the people could not generate any incentive to increase production. As a result economic growth was hampered before reform. The second hypothesis of the study, that pro-poor strategy for development reduces inequality and poverty at the cost of growth, is proven.

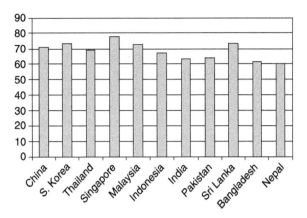

*Figure 5.10* Life expectancy rate, 1992.
*Source: World Development Report 2005.*

Economic reform is an attempt to rectify the earlier faults in development policies in China; it is a period of rectification rather than reconstruction. Depending on market forces, it has been able to attain higher growth through the utilization of the opportunities created earlier. This is characterized as the growth favouring the pro-rich development strategy and it proves the first hypothesis of the study. With this policy, China allowed inequality in income for economic growth. Income differences work as an incentive for production.

The countries that depended on the market for their economic development, for example East and South East Asian countries, were successful in achieving higher growth. But government intervention was necessary for reducing poverty and in generating equal opportunities for all through social sector development. Inequalities in income are also the result of market forces in these economies.

Most of the countries of South Asia are suffering from mass poverty and a lack of social sector development due to inappropriate policies. The governments of these countries, including India, relied on the 'trickle-down' effect. It is observed from the study that there is no direct link between growth and equity, and growth and poverty. Also inequality and poverty are not correlated in any way. The experiences of the developing countries suggest that growth, inequality and poverty are the three separate issues that should be taken care of with appropriate and specific policies. For market forces to operate properly, equal opportunities for the masses need to be created.

## Conclusion

China is one of the oldest civilizations in the world. Many articles in daily use were invented in its glorious past. But due to internal and external factors, the country has lost its glory. With the revolution in 1949 the majority of the people wanted to overcome socio-economic distresses by establishing a classless society, with no inequality traps or opportunity gaps. A poor country with technological backwardness and socio-economic rigidity requires it to adopt perfect policies; proper policy implementation is also necessary. The development experience of China suggests that, in a backward economy, where fully-fledged market forces are absent, the objective of attaining high growth with a self-reliance policy and with absolute government intervention may not be gainful. Abolition of property rights and distribution of basic needs on the principle of equity in an economy with moderate growth may invite socio-economic disorder. Moreover, low inequality in slow growth economies, e.g. in the countries of South Asia, may not solve the problem of poverty. Growth with equity, either in a market economy or in a command economy, cannot be achieved in the short run. Even in high-income countries, inequality is found. The high performing Asian economies also have the same problem. For higher growth, a self-correcting market economy is the alternative to absolute government intervention. The experiences of China and of other low-income countries during the period of economic reform are the current examples.

Growth may have some impact on reducing poverty; but for rapid and total poverty eradication, government intervention is urgently needed. Pro-poor growth with the production of basic goods and services is necessary for removal of poverty. So an absolutely free market economy in a less-developed country is not a proper means to eradicate poverty. A controlled market economy is needed for development with equity and without poverty. To quote:

> equating growth with poverty reduction is too simplistic. In the second half of the 1980s, for example, despite rapid growth [in India], income poverty fell little. Statistical analyses suggest that economic growth explains at best around 50 per cent of the reduction in income poverty.
>
> (HDR 1997: 52)

The task of the government is to generate conditions for utilizing the skills and efficiency of people for higher productivity, and also to create sufficient opportunities through social sector development. China's remarkable progress in recent decades is an opportunity for other developing countries. Through economic cooperation with China, these countries can yield the best results from their development efforts.

## References

Agarwala, R. (2002) *The Rise of China: Threat or Opportunity*, New Delhi: Bookwell.
Baru, S. (2002) Strategic consequences of India's economic performance, *Economic and Political Weekly*, 29 June: 2583–2592.

Bourguignon, F. (2001) *The Pace of Economic Growth and Poverty Reduction*, LACEA: www.nip-lac.org/programs_lacea/ Bourguignon.pdf.

Bozan, J., Shao, X. and Hu, H. (1981) *A Concise History of China*, Beijing: Foreign Languages Press.

Dreze, J. and Sen, A. (1989) *Hunger and Public Action*, Oxford: Oxford University Press.

Dreze, J. and Sen, A. (1997) *India: Economic Development and Social Opportunity*, Delhi: Oxford University Press.

Eckstein, A. (1977) *China's Economic Revolution*, Cambridge: Cambridge University Press.

Fields, G.S. (1995) The Kuznets curve, paper presented at the AEA Meeting, 6–8 June.

Foster, J.E. and Szekely, M. (2001) Is economic growth good for the poor? Tracking low incomes using general means, presented at the WIDER conference on Growth and Poverty, Helsinki, 25–26 May.

Gill, R.T. (1973) *Economic Development: Past and Present* (3rd edition), New Delhi: Prentice Hall.

Kuznets, S. (1955) Economic growth and income inequality, *American Economic Review* 45: 1–28.

Maddison, A., Rao, D.S.P. and Shepherd, W.F. (eds) (2002) *The Asian Economies in the Twentieth Century*, Cheltenham: Edward Elgar.

Nye, H.L.M., Reddy, S.G. and Watkins, K. (2001) A critique of 'dollar & kraay' trade, growth and poverty, www.maketradefair.com/en/assets/english/finalDK critique.pdf.

Perkins, D.H. (ed.) (1975) *China's Modern Economy in Historical Perspective*, Stanford, CA: Stanford University Press.

Richardson, P. (1999) *Economic Change in China, c. 1800–1950*, Cambridge: Cambridge University Press.

Suinian, L. and Quangan, W. (1986) *China's Socialist Economy: An Outline History (1949–1984)*, Beijing: Foreign Languages Press.

UNCTAD (2006 and other years) *World Investment Report*, Geneva: United Nations.

United Nations (1997) *Human Development Report*, New York: United Nations and Palgrave Macmillan.

United Nations (2006) *Human Development Report. Beyond Scarcity: Power, Poverty and the Global Water Crisis*, New York: United Nations and Palgrave Macmillan.

World Bank (2008) *World Development Report*, Washington, DC: World Bank.

Zheng, Y. (2005) The new policy initiatives in China's 11th Five-Year Plan, Beijing: China Policy Institute.

# Part II

# Labour market reform

# 6 The impact of technology adoption on employment

Exploration from the perspective of the manufacturing industry in transitional China

*Guangjie Ning*

## Introduction

Since executing economic reform and an open policy in the late 1970s, the Chinese economy maintains a high annual growth rate and technology innovation has also been improving. Technology adoption promoted economy growth, at the same time it exerted a great impact on employment quality and skill structure. Changes in employment quality and skill structure means a lot for China. We want to know if our future economic development demands more or less labour and more or less skilled labour. This will shed light on our educational development and the firms' training programmes. If the technological change has some adverse impact on employment, how can we coordinate the dilemma of relative backward technology and a high unemployment rate during the economic development period? Further technological change coincided with institution innovation in China. During the transitional process many previously state-owned enterprises were reformed into shareholding enterprises, combined with foreign companies or have been privatized. Do different ownership enterprises perform differently in the process of technology adoption and exert different impacts on employment? Answering these questions needs us to conduct some empirical analyses. This chapter tries to investigate the impact of technology input expenditure on the employment quantity and skill structure from the perspective of the manufacturing industry.

In an advanced market economy technical progress and labour productivity growth generally will exert an effect on wages, for example, leading to wage increases and then influencing employment further (resulting in employment reduction). Exploring technology's impact on wage and income inequality is an important channel and gains fruitful literature. However, if the wage's market mechanism is unhealthy and the wage itself cannot be sensitive to technology or becomes sluggish, the technology's impact on employment and skill structure should be considered seriously (Spitz-Oener 2006). Under the circumstance of imperfect labor market the direction and magnitude that technology influences employment will differ from that circumstance where wage adjusts to the technical change flexibly.

The wage-forming mechanism is not yet perfected in China, as the relationship between wages and productivity is not sufficiently strong, and the wage response to unemployment is lagged (Ning 2007). Under the circumstance that wages could not respond fully to technical change and labour productivity, directly investigating technology's impact on employment quantity and skill structure becomes essential.

This chapter uses the panel data in China to evaluate how industrial employment is affected by the technology innovation at the industry level. First, it examines the impact of technology adoption on employment quantity and skill structure from the perspective of manufacturing industry, considering the special institutional characteristics in transitional China: the impact of ownership structure, imperfect competition and interaction of institutional structure and technology adoption. Second, examines technology's effect on employment at the industry level, which will deepen our understanding of structural unemployment in China.

The plan of the chapter is as follows. The second section provides a literature review and establishes the analysis framework. The third section provides a theoretical foundation. The fourth section provides the econometric model and data description; the fifth section provides the results and discussion. Finally, we offer some conclusions and policy implications.

## The underlying mechanism of technology's impact on employment

Technologies are usually divided into two categories according to their adoption direction; one is process innovation and the other is product innovation. Process innovation is to reduce input cost and product price by means of productivity improvement in the manufacturing process. Product innovation aims to develop new kinds of final high-quality products to earn profit. There are no clear distinction between process innovation and product innovation in practice. At the enterprise level, product innovation is considered as output innovations to improve consumption by final consumers or the production processes of other firms. The firm who produces it often cannot use it. In parallel, process innovation will result from the use of new technology given by other firms. Therefore, one kind of technology innovation in one case acts as process innovation, while in other case it is product innovation. However, the different adoption direction is obvious even at the macro level and distinguishing these two technology categories in theory and empirical analysis is also necessary.

### Change of employment quantity

In essence, the employment change at the industry level resulting from technology innovation is employment structure change from the perspective of the macro level, that is, employment's industrial structure. Edquist *et al.* (2001)

states that process innovation exerts a greater shock on employment quantity, as process innovation relies mainly on increased labour productivity to reduce manufacturing cost and enlarge profit. The impact of process innovation in different industries varies, determined by the compensation mechanism. Technology progress can increase employment and compensate for the employment loss of replacing workers with machines by means of the enlarged investment or other mechanisms. Expanding industries' demand increases greatly and the employment quantity will also grow faster. Vivarelli (1995) divides the compensation mechanism into eight different channels: (1) increase demand by reducing price; (2) increase employment through new investment; (3) increase employment through reduced wage; (4) increase employment through new machine manufacturing and links among industries; (5) increase employment through new product innovation; (6) increased income turns into consumption and investment; (7) increase investment through the Schumpeter effect;[1] (8) increase investment by reducing price through the Pigou effect.[2]

Product innovation includes new material products and new service products. Generally its impact on employment reduction is comparatively modest or weak. If the new product spurs demand, it can also promote an increase in employment. For instance, in the era of the information economy, employment-expanding capability improves through Internet externality. Information technology can reduce the transaction cost and realize the high level of employment equilibrium (Weel 2006). However, if the new product to some extent replaces some old one, then employment may not increase. If the new product is used for another product's process innovation, it will also weaken the compensation mechanism.

In empirical fields, using the number of innovations a firm commercialized in a given year, Reenen (1997) investigated manufacturing firms in the UK and found that technology innovation has significantly positive effects on employment, even when one controls for fixed effects, dynamics and endogeneity. Yao and Xia (2005) analysed the impact of technology (the average of labour productivity and capital productivity) on employment using the provincial panel data from 2000 to 2002 in China and found that the coefficient is −0.434 and significant, suggesting that process innovation and capital deepening have adverse an effect on employment. Chen and Tang's study (2006) also demonstrates that China's industry tended toward heavy chemical industrialization during the periods 1991–95 and 1999–2003. In other words, process innovation dominates.

### Change of skill structure

Technology adoption demands the adjustment of labour's skill. Process innovation often requires the employee to improve skills or learn new skills, whereas product innovation often brings forth new occupations and leads to occupational structural change. We have to admit that the outcome of some new products does not rely heavily on technology and R&D; therefore the skill structure will not be doomed to great change.

Braveman (1974) argued that the power of technology adoption is controlled by the capitalist and used as a tool for appropriating the maximum profit. Even though the technology is widely used in the US, for the majority of workers their skills were downgraded or they became deskilled and worked as simple operators. Only the minority who research the advanced technology and grasp it become the leader in the firm's hierarchy and earn a high salary. Bauer and Bender (2004) analysed the effects of technology change on job and worker mobility from the perspective of micro firms in Germany. It promotes job creation and job destruction, increasing the hiring and firing activities. The results indicate that new information technology decreases both low-skilled and highly-skilled labour. Some management and technological employees are demoted to low-skilled occupations and the downgraded workers are more common than the upgraded ones. Most of the employment adjustment occurred outside of the firm and unemployment will arise.

Does technology adoption increase or decrease skill requirement? In fact, it depends on the direction of the technology process. Taking information technology as an example, what should be considered is whether it substitutes routine manual work or acts as a complements to analysis and interactive activity. If it is the latter, the skill requirement will grow. Spitz-Oener (2006) classified worker activities into five skill categories: *non-routine analytical tasks*, such as research, planning or evaluation activities; *non-routine interactive tasks*, such as selling or coordinating and delegating work; *routine cognitive tasks*, such as double-entry bookkeeping and calculating; *routine manual tasks*, such as machine feeding or running a machine; and *non-routine manual tasks*, such as housekeeping or restoring houses. His empirical results show that, as occupations have experienced a shift toward analytical and interactive activities and away from cognitive and manual routine tasks, occupations in western Germany require more complex skills today than in 1979 and that the changes in skill requirements have been most pronounced in rapidly computerizing occupations. Hence, we can learn that information technology acts as a complements to analysis and interactive activity. Garicono and Rossi-Hansberg (2006) suggest that if the technology reduces the cost of acquiring knowledge, the average worker's skill improves; if it reduces the communication cost, the worker's skill degrades.

Yao (2005) analysed the impact of technological progress on employment using the micro data from the manufacturing industry in the Zhejiang Province of China and found that technological progress makes the demand for skilled labour increase, and the proportion of skilled workers in both employment quantity and income share rises.

### Change of management structure and firm organization

In relation to employment change, we should also consider the effects of technological innovation on management structure and firm organization. For instance, information technology reduces transaction and communication costs and reduces the administration layers; which, in turn, impacts on the number of management employees. There exists a double link between new technology and management structure. The adoption of new technology needs some management structure innovation, and, on the other hand, the management structure innovation makes it easy for the new technology to be adopted. In China it is often the case that enterprises promote the adoption of new technology by means of firm ownership reform. Ownership reform involves radical change of management structure; for instance, many traditional state-owned enterprises are transformed into shareholding enterprises or acquired by foreign firms and become joint ventures. Chen and Tang's (2006) study shows that an industry with a high proportion of state-owned enterprises or a high degree of monopoly performs well in relation to technology change, but in relation to technology efficiency it is low and needs improving.

Furthermore, technological innovation and management structure are not two independent forces influencing employment; in fact, they often interact with each other and further affect employment quantity and structure. Wang *et al.* (2006) state that, information technology and organizational innovation complement each other and have great positive effects on production efficiency. He considers management structure from three perspectives: operational management, cooperation of manager and employee, and management of process innovation and product innovation.

### Industry aggregate analysis

Rothwell and Zegveld (1979) analysed the impact of technical change on various industries in the UK. Impacts on the textile industry included: integration and rationality reducing demand for labour; the deskilling of labour; and the need for skilled workers to operate electrical machinery. Computer-aided design and control also changed management structure, such as outsourcing and hiring technical workers from outside of the firm. As the main technological advances since the Second World War are in the micro-electronic (ME) and information technology (IT) industries, they examine the impact of ME on industry employment. In the case of the textile industry, the impacts include reduced employment quantity and increased proportions of skilled and unskilled workers. As for the technical researcher, the proportion has decreased.

Schettkat and Russo (2001) analysed the relationship between labour productivity and employment in different industries and found that for the majority of countries, the relationship in manufacturing industries is negative, while in transportation and communication industry the relationship is positive. Dobbs *et al.* (1987) considered the important role of market structure: as a result of the number of firms increasing and competition strengthening to expand labour demand elasticity, employment expands.

Most of the preceding study examined the impact of technology on employment in different industries. Our research centres on 38 manufacturing industries as a whole and investigates the average impact of technical change at the industry level on employment.

## Theory foundation

We obtain insights from the new economic growth theory. The source of applied technology comes from the work of the R&D sector, and developing new technology needs both capital and research workers. In turn, it has the production function of technology as $A = A(L_r, K_r)$, where $A$ is the output of technology, $L_r$ and $K_r$ are the labour and capital input incurred in the research department, respectively. The chapter argues that technological progress is an endogenous variable in the overall economic system. For a developing country, even if it does not own the original technology and has to resort to imports from a foreign country, during the process of technical adoption research workers are still needed to analyse and assimilate the imported new technology.

Technology can be put into force and embodied by capital and labour. We argue that technology's role depends fundamentally on skilled workers, which is consistent with human capital theory; in turn, we have $Y = K^\alpha H^\beta A^\theta L_o^{1-\alpha-\beta-\theta}$, where $Y$, $K$, $H$, $L_o$ is output, capital, human capital and ordinary labour, respectively. A skilled worker supplies both 1 unit of $L$ and some amount of $H$.

We can have a labour demand function such as below for our econometric analysis: $\ln L = \gamma_1 \ln Y + \gamma_2 \ln K + \gamma_3 \ln A$,[3] where $L$ is the sum of human capital and all kinds of labour.

Under imperfect competition, the explanatory variable of number of firms in this industry should be added. Moreover, the institution factors also exert an effect on labour demand. We incorporate an important institutional variable to consider whether enterprise reform has a great effect on industry employment.

Industry employment fluctuation is also influenced by macroeconomic performance; the real business cycle school regards technology shock as the main driving force of the macroeconomic cycle. If it is the case, we will have a better understanding of the macro economy's effect on employment when we explore the impact of technology on employment. However, we insist that macro price and inflation changes are separate forces from technological change. Studying employment change at the industry level should consider not only the technology at industry level but also the impact of macroeconomic shock.

## Data and econometric models

The data for econometric analysis comes from the *China Statistical Yearbook on Science and Technology* from 1999 to 2005. The National Bureau of Statistics and the Ministry of Science and Technology prepare the yearbook jointly. It reports on the development of China's science and technology activities. What we are concerned is the technological development condition and other economic indicators at the industry level. Only large and medium-sized industrial enterprises are included in the industrial data; that is to say, small firms' data is not available. Because of the change of ownership classification, we have to divide the data into two groups: one for 1998–2002, comprising state-owned enterprises and joint ventures (Chinese and foreign); and one for 2003–04, including state-owned enterprises, limited liability corporations, shareholding enterprises and joint ventures. For every year, we have data on 38 two-digit industries (according to standard industrial classification (SICC) code) for two or four ownership categories. For the former group, the sample size is about $38 \times 2 \times 5$, for the latter it is $38 \times 4 \times 2$.

First, we use the equation below to analyse the impact of the adoption of technology on employment quantity:

$$\ln L = \beta_0 + \beta_1 \ln TE + \beta_2 \ln LD + \beta_3 SZ + \beta_4 GY + \beta_5 GF$$
$$+ \beta_6 (\ln TE * SZ) + \beta_7 (\ln TE * GY) + \beta_8 (\ln TE * GF)$$
$$+ \beta_9 NF + \beta_{10} HY + \mu \tag{1}$$

$L$ stands for employment quantity at the end of a certain year in this two-digit industry. $TE$ is the technological input expenditure of this two-digit industry. The ratio of technology expenditure to output value is also useful, reflecting more accurately the direction of technology upgrading. We do not use R&D expenditure to represent technology, because it is the input occurring in the process of product experimentation, which cannot reflect accurately the condition of technology adoption.

Technical expenditure has the amount of capital stock (accumulating capital flow) and the amount of capital flow (expenditure occurred every year); as the change of ownership classification occurred since 2003 and the time longitude is relatively short, we only select the capital flow one and do not calculate the stock one. $LD$ represents the number of firms in this industry; if the coefficient is positive, it means that the strengthened market competition will result in employment expansion, otherwise it maybe that over-competition ruins employment growth or this industry should be a natural monopoly. $SZ$, $GY$ and $GF$ are the dummy variable to represent joint venture (if joint venture $SZ$ is defined as 1; for other firm categories, $SZ$ is 0), state-owned enterprise (if state-owned enterprise $GY$ is defined as 1; otherwise is 0) and shareholding enterprise (if shareholding enterprise $GF$ is defined as 1; otherwise is 0), respectively. The limited liability corporation is used for comparison. The next three variables are the interactive term of enterprise ownership and technical expenditure. $NF$ is the dummy variable for 1998–99 (during 1998–2002 group, if 1998 and 1999, $NF$ is defined as 1; for other years, $NF$ is 0) or 2003 (during 2003–04 group, if 2003, $NF$ is defined as 1; for 2004, $NF$ is 0) to reflect effects of macroeconomic conditions. $HY$ is the dummy variable of industries. We classify the 38 two-digit industries into eight categories according to their characteristics, The mining industry is used for comparison, so we have seven industry dummy variables. $HY_1$ is food and drink manufacturing (if food and drink manufacturing, $HY_1$ is 1; for other industries, $HY_1$ is 0; the same applies to $HY_2$, $HY_3$, $HY_4$, $HY_5$, $HY_6$ and $HY_7$). $HY_2$ is the textile and clothing industry. $HY_3$ is the wood, paper and printing industry. $HY_4$ is oil products, chemical products and medical products. $HY_5$ is the metal product industry. $HY_6$ is transportation machinery, information facilities and computers. $HY_7$ is the production and supply of electrical power, gas and water. Note that as the appropriate data on capital is not available, unlike theory foundation, the variable of capital is not included in our estimate equation.

The following equation demonstrates the impact of different kinds of technology adoption on employment:

$$\ln L = \gamma_0 + \gamma_1 \ln(WD / SB) + \gamma_2 \ln(XCP / Y) + \gamma_3 \ln LD + \gamma_4 SZ$$
$$+ \gamma_5 GY + \gamma_6 GF + \gamma_7 NF + \gamma_8 HY + \mu \tag{2}$$

where $WD / SB$ is the ratio of equipment controlled by micro-electronics to the original value of the equipment. It acts as an indictor of process innovation. $XCP / Y$ is the ratio of new product value to gross value of the output, which represents the developmental level of product innovation.

The equation for technology's effect on employment structure is as follow:

$$\ln (LS / L) = \lambda_0 + \lambda_1 \ln TE + \lambda_2 \ln LD + \lambda_3 SZ + \lambda_4 GY$$
$$+ \lambda_5 GF + \lambda_6 (\ln TE * SZ) + \lambda_7 (\ln TE * GY)$$
$$+ \lambda_8 (\ln TE * GF) + \lambda_9 NF + \lambda_{10} HY + \mu \tag{3}$$

$LS / L$ denotes the ratio of technical engineering personnel quantity to total employee quantity, an indicator of the skill structure of labour. The measure of skill requirement can be the proportion of skilled workers or educated workers. The shortcoming of the latter lies in the fact that, if the educated worker does not possess the corresponding skill owing to educational failure or scarcity of on-the-job training, the proportion of educated workers cannot reflect the skill requirement accurately. If we have other data such as job type or management worker structure, we will test which one is a good indicator for skill structure and use it to conduct econometric analysis.

To assess the impact of different technology on employment structure, the function is similar to function (2); in turn, we have:

$$\ln(LS \, / \, L) = \gamma_0 + \gamma_1 \ln(WD \, / \, SB) + \gamma_2 \ln(XCP \, / \, Y) + \gamma_3 \ln LD$$
$$+ \, \gamma_4 \, SZ + \gamma_5 \, GY + \gamma_6 \, GF + \gamma_7 \, NF + \gamma_8 \, HY + \mu \qquad (4)$$

## Interpretation of econometric results and discussion

### The impact of technical change on industry employment

Based on equation (1), the econometric results are listed in Table 6.1. First, we conduct pool model analysis.[4] Comparing column (1) with column (2), we see that the effect of technical expenditure on employment during 2003–04 is greater and the explanation power is stronger (as the adjusted $R^2$ is higher). This reflects the characteristics of developing countries' technology adoption: previous technology was backward. Upgrading technology can stimulate output expansion and have a positive impact on employment expansion.

It may also be that wages did not increase in relation to the technology adoption and labour productivity growth so that technical change could bring forth more employment. It is known that the bigger is the variable reflecting technological input–output efficiency, $Y/TE$, the stronger is the compensation impact, and the more obvious is the employment creation effect. However, the unreported econometric result indicates that the impact of $Y/TE$ on employment is negative, implying that technological development in China is still in the phase of relying on input increases to cope with the employment problem; the driving and spillover effect of technical change is not sufficient. Furthermore, with the number of firms in industry increasing and competition strengthening, the employment at industry level also rises. The ownership dummies show that employment in joint ventures is lower than in state-owned ventures during 1998–2002. During 2003–04, employment in shareholding enterprises is lower.

On the basis of column (1), we add the interactive term of technology expenditure and firm ownership to assess the effect of the interaction of technical change and management structure on employment. The results in column (3) show that the coefficient of interactive term is –0.167, significant at the 1 per cent level. The common notion is that the reformed enterprises place more weight on technology adoption and also lay off redundant workers. Technology and ownership change correlated with and influenced employment change. The impact of interactive terms of technical expenditure and number of firms is also negative and significant, showing that the interaction of competition and technical change reduced employment at the industry level. However, the interactive term of technology expenditure and firm ownership during 2003–04 is not significant.

In columns (4) and (5), we add the impact of time and industry differences. It is clear that employment growth during 1998–99 is 0.178 per cent lower than that during 2000–02 and the growth rate during 2003 is 0.908 per cent higher than that in 2004. Considering the industry difference, we find that compared to the mining industry, other industries' employment growth is slower,

Table 6.1 The impact of technical change on industrial employment

| Variable | Log(L)(1) 1998–2002 | Log(L)(2) 2003–04 | Log(L)(3) 1998–2002 | Log(L)(4) 1998–2002 | Log(L)(5) 2003–04 | Log(L)(6) 1998–2002 | Log(L)(7) 2003–04 |
|---|---|---|---|---|---|---|---|
| Constant | 5.930*** | 5.713*** | 2.860*** | 6.253*** | 4.829*** | 5.076*** | 7.135*** |
|  | (0.200) | (0.203) | (0.556) | (0.237) | (0.177) | (0.282) | (0.268) |
| Log(TE) | 0.219*** | 0.368*** | 0.523*** | 0.167*** | 0.351*** | 0.131*** | 0.189*** |
|  | (0.023) | (0.025) | (0.056) | (0.031) | (0.022) | (0.021) | (0.026) |
| Log(TE(−1)) |  |  |  | 0.108*** |  |  |  |
|  |  |  |  | (0.030) |  |  |  |
| Log(LD) | 0.752*** | 0.426*** | 1.290*** | 0.742*** | 0.673*** | 1.063*** | 0.509*** |
|  | (0.039) | (0.032) | (0.106) | (0.044) | (0.032) | (0.055) | (0.035) |
| Log(TE)*log(LD) |  |  | −0.053*** |  |  |  |  |
|  |  |  | (0.010) |  |  |  |  |
| SZ | −0.798*** | −0.071 | 1.024** | −0.558*** | −0.051 |  |  |
|  | (0.076) | (0.103) | (0.403) | (0.071) | (0.074) |  |  |
| SZ*log(TE) |  |  | −0.167*** |  |  |  |  |
|  |  |  | (0.036) |  |  |  |  |
| GY |  | 0.124 |  |  | 0.164** |  |  |
|  |  | (0.0991) |  |  | (0.070) |  |  |
| GF |  | −0.212** |  |  | 0.101 |  |  |
|  |  | (0.104) |  |  | (0.077) |  |  |
| NF(1998–99 or 2003) |  |  |  | −0.178** | 0.908*** |  |  |
|  |  |  |  | (0.080) | (0.071) |  |  |
| HY1 |  |  |  | −1.171*** | −0.900*** |  |  |
| HY2 |  |  |  | −0.494** | −0.287** |  |  |
| HY3 |  |  |  | −1.146*** | −0.723** |  |  |
| HY4 |  |  |  | −1.141*** | −0.993*** |  |  |
| HY5 |  |  |  | −0.932*** | −0.820*** |  |  |
| HY6 |  |  |  | −1.252*** | −1.090*** |  |  |
| HY7 |  |  |  | −0.977*** | −0.628*** |  |  |
| Hausman test (Fixed or random effect) |  |  |  |  |  | 16.292 Fixed effect | 129.204 Fixed effect |
| Observations | 343 | 287 | 343 | 269 | 287 | 343 | 287 |
| AdjR² | 0.841 | 0.841 | 0.855 | 0.874 | 0.921 | 0.984 | 0.984 |

Note: *, ** and *** indicate the variable is significant at the 10, 5 and 1% level, respectively.

especially in $HY_1$ (food and drink manufacturing), $HY_4$ (oil products, chemical products and medical products) and $HY_6$ (transportation machinery, information facilities and computers). To investigate the long-term impact of technology, in column (4) we add last year's technology expenditure as an explanatory variable and find its coefficient positive (0.108) and significant, showing that technical change exerts long and lasting impact on employment.

Considering the concrete differences between industries and year to year, we applied fixed or random effect models. We discovered that a fixed effect model is suitable through the Hausman test,[5] so we have columns (6) and (7). The basic conclusion does not change. The influencing coefficients of technology during 1998–2002 and 2003–04 are 0.131 and 0.189, respectively; the latter is higher. On average, the coefficient becomes smaller once we control every industry and every year's difference.

Finally we consider the problem of a possible co-relationship between technical expenditure and employment, i.e. the employment quantity gives rise to the change in technology. We use R&D input expenditure and number of inventive patents[6] owned as the instrument variables of technical expenditure in 2003–04. Applying two-stage least squares (an instrumental variables estimation technique), OLS methods and pool estimation, we find that the coefficient of technical expenditure hardly changed from that in OLS methods. Therefore the technical expenditure can be regarded as an exogenous variable in this case.

### The impact of different technology on employment

In Table 6.2, applying equation (2), column (1) explains that process innovation has a positive impact on employment and the coefficient is 0.097. Contrary to the traditional theory and other empirical results, the process innovation is beneficial for employment growth, while the product innovation's effect is significantly negative.[7] Column (2) uses the 2003–04 data and derives a similar conclusion but the coefficients are not significant. This is partly because in this phase of a developing economy, cost competition and price competition dominate; it is process innovation that makes a firm obtain advantage over other competitors. On the other hand, it is difficult for new products to enter the market and win the consumer's acknowledgement, so it has an adverse impact on employment. As before, the coefficients of number of firms and foreign ownership are significant.

Adding the dummy variables of industry and time, column (3) shows that the coefficient of process innovation is still positive. Compared to state-owned enterprises, the employment growth rate of joint ventures is lower by 0.703 per cent. Column (4) also illustrates that the growth rate of employment in 2003 is faster than that in 2004. Employment creation capability is lowest in joint ventures and highest in shareholding enterprises. This time, the effects of product innovation and process innovation are also not significant. This may be due to the relatively limited sample size during 2003–04.

Table 6.2 Different technology impact on employment quantity

| Variable | Log(L) (1) 1998–2002 | Log(L) (2) 2003–04 | Log(L) (3) 1998–2002 | Log(L) (4) 2003–04 | Log(L) (5) 1998–2002 | Log(L) (6) 2003–04 |
|---|---|---|---|---|---|---|
| Constant | 7.485*** | 8.338*** | 9.291*** | 7.196*** | 6.218*** | 8.716*** |
|  | (0.282) | (0.277) | (0.366) | (0.326) | (0.250) | (0.248) |
| Log(WD/SB) | 0.097* | 0.068 | 0.201*** | 0.073 | 0.046* | −0.039 |
|  | (0.052) | (0.060) | (0.047) | (0.046) | (0.024) | (0.033) |
| Log(XCP/Y) | −0.102*** | −0.052 | −0.038 | −0.040 | −0.059*** | 0.036 |
|  | (0.031) | (0.033) | (0.042) | (0.033) | (0.021) | (0.037) |
| Log(LD) | 0.941*** | 0.685*** | 0.943*** | 0.945*** | 1.120*** | 0.600*** |
|  | (0.041) | (0.034) | (0.038) | (0.034) | (0.045) | (0.041) |
| SZ | −0.811*** | −0.251* | −0.703*** | −0.251** |  |  |
|  | (0.091) | (0.134) | (0.078) | (0.098) |  |  |
| GY |  | 0.124 |  | 0.163* |  |  |
|  |  | (0.129) |  | (0.093) |  |  |
| GF |  | −0.052 |  | 0.279*** |  |  |
|  |  | (0.139) |  | (0.105) |  |  |
| NF (1998–99 or 2003) |  |  | 0.064 | 1.162*** |  |  |
|  |  |  | (0.071) | (0.093) |  |  |
| HY1 |  |  | Negative and significant at 1% level. | Negative and significant at 1% level. |  |  |
| HY2 |  |  |  |  |  |  |
| HY3 |  |  |  |  |  |  |
| HY4 |  |  |  |  |  |  |
| HY5 |  |  |  |  |  |  |
| HY6 |  |  |  |  |  |  |
| HY7 |  |  |  |  |  |  |
| Hausman test (Fixed or random effect) |  |  |  |  | 1.116 Random effect | 106.646 Fixed effect |
| Observations | 321 | 270 | 321 | 270 | 321 | 270 |
| AdjR$^2$ | 0.716 | 0.660 | 0.803 | 0.823 | 0.630 | 0.973 |

Note: *, ** and *** indicate the variable is significant at the 10, 5 and 1% level, respectively.

Columns (5) and (6) are the result of an optimal random effect model or a fixed effect model. As column (5) shows, process innovation contributes to employment growth, while product innovation leads to employment reduction. However, the impacts during 2003–04 still do not pass the significance test.

### Impact of technical change on employee skill structure

The results of analysis applying equations (3) and (4) are shown in Table 6.3. In the first two columns, technical input expenditure is positively related to the proportion of technical workers, and the impact during 2003–04 is greater, which illustrates that the labour skill requirement is upgraded with technical progress in recent years. We also investigate the effects of number of firms, ownership, industry and time on the proportion of technical workers. The number of firms in both periods has a negative impact on the skill structure. In principle, with the number of firms increasing and competition strengthening, firms should pay more attention to technical competition and increased their number of technical workers. However, the analysis indicates the opposite result. The reasons may be that, first, technical competition does not occupy an important role in current China. Second, it may also reflect the fact that, with the removal of industry entry barriers, the new firms entering the market are relatively weak in establishing technical employee teams. The proportion of technical workers in different industries also varies. Compared to the mining industry, the skill structure in the textile and clothing industry $(HY_2)$ is significantly lower, and in the production and supply of electric power, gas and water industry $(HY_7)$ is significantly higher. Similarly, using the instrument variable method, it is shown that technical expenditure can act as the employee skill structure's exogenous variable.

Columns (3) and (4) are the fixed effect models. Only during 1998–2002 does technical adoption have a positive effect on labour's skill structure. Columns (5) and (6) evaluate the effects of different technology changes on employment skill structure: process innovation increases the demand for skilled worker in both periods; while product innovation does so only during 1998–2002. It is partly because product innovation in the current phase concentrates mostly on the simple design and packaging of new products without demanding high technical skills. It may also be because product innovation is only the task of researchers in the R&D sector and does not influence the skill requirement of ordinary worker as does process innovation; consequently, the proportion of technical workers does not increase. These results correspond with those obtained by Borghans and Weel (2006) indicating that technical adoption aiming to reduce production time (which is similar to process innovation in the context of our analysis) demands upgraded skills. This also implies that, if technical change centres on process innovation, the employment skill structure needs greater adjustment, otherwise structural unemployment will result from skill mismatch. In the fixed effect models of columns (7) and (8), only product

Table 6.3 Impact of technical change on employment structure

| Variable | Log(LS/L) (1) 1998–2002 | Log(LS/L) (2) 2003–04 | Log(LS/L) (3) 1998–2002 | Log(LS/L) (4) 2003–04 | Log(LS/L) (5) 1998–2002 | Log(LS/L) (6) 2003–04 | Log(LS/L) (7) 1988–2002 | Log(LS/L) (8) 2003–04 |
|---|---|---|---|---|---|---|---|---|
| Constant | −3.011*** | −3.221*** | −2.139*** | −2.453*** | −1.710*** | −2.007*** | −1.832*** | −2.568*** |
| | (0.185) | (0.132) | (0.277) | (0.335) | (0.213) | (0.182) | (0.267) | (0.249) |
| Log(TE) | 0.120*** | 0.146*** | 0.036* | 0.032 | | | | |
| | (0.019) | (0.016) | (0.021) | (0.033) | | | | |
| Log(WD/SB) | | | | | 0.064** | 0.051* | −0.024 | −0.046 |
| | | | | | (0.027) | (0.029) | (0.024) | (0.034) |
| Log(XCP/Y) | | | | | 0.110*** | −0.010 | 0.049** | −0.028 |
| | | | | | (0.024) | (0.021) | (0.022) | (0.037) |
| Log(LD) | −0.134*** | −0.143*** | −0.137** | −0.061 | 0.016 | −0.053*** | −0.016** | −0.011 |
| | (0.027) | (0.018) | (0.054) | (0.044) | (0.022) | (0.016) | (0.053) | (0.041) |
| SZ | 0.565** | −0.244*** | | | −0.103** | −0.371*** | | |
| | (0.231) | (0.058) | | | (0.045) | (0.062) | | |
| SZ*log(TE) | −0.051** | | | | | | | |
| | (0.020) | | | | | | | |
| GY | | 0.092* | | | | 0.084 | | |
| | | (0.055) | | | | (0.059) | | |
| GF | | −0.016 | | | | 0.041 | | |
| | | (0.058) | | | | (0.064) | | |
| NF(98–99 or 03) | −0.239*** | | | | −0.104** | −0.005 | | |
| | (0.047) | | | | (0.041) | | | |
| HY1 | 0.080 | −0.008 | | | −0.155 | | | |
| HY2 | −0.682*** | −0.574*** | | | −0.975*** | −0.679*** | | |
| HY3 | −0.253*** | −0.116 | | | −0.496*** | −0.302*** | | |
| HY4 | 0.194** | 0.133* | | | −0.073 | 0.213* | | |
| HY5 | 0.070 | −0.003 | | | −0.108 | 0.089 | | |
| HY6 | 0.088 | 0.130 | | | −0.244* | 0.256** | | |
| HY7 | 0.509*** | 0.635*** | | | 0.788*** | 0.567*** | | |
| Hausman test | | | 37.903 Fixed effect | 18.959 Fixed effect | | | 12.176 Fixed effect | 12.188 Fixed effect |
| Observations | 342 | 287 | 342 | 287 | 321 | 270 | 321 | 270 |
| AdjR$^2$ | 0.442 | 0.585 | 0.848 | 0.791 | 0.472 | 0.516 | 0.828 | 0.815 |

Note: *, ** and *** indicate the variable is significant at the 10, 5 and 1% level, respectively.

innovation during 1998–2002 requires the skill structure to improve, which does not conform with the results in columns (5) and (6). This raises new concern about the technology category and skill structure.

As far as ownership is concerned, in most cases the proportion of technical workers in joint ventures is significantly lower than in other firm types, reflecting the fact that technological development in many joint ventures does not promote upgrading of skills. Moreover, in column (1), adding the interactive terms of ownership and technical expenditure, the coefficient during 1998–2002 is –0.051 and significant; it is clear that the interaction degrades the skill structure. During 2003–04, the impact can be ignored. The reform of enterprise ownership and technical changes did not promote simultaneous skill structure upgrading. Considering the low quality of labour, on average, and the mobility barrier existing in the labour market, these results are understandable.

### *Comparison of the relationship between technical change and employment in different types of firm*

Table 6.4 shows independent estimations for every firm ownership category and compares the coefficient differences in different types of firm ownership. All estimation functions are fixed or random effect models and the estimation functions with insignificant coefficients are omitted. For coefficient comparison, we list the related functions in one column. For example, in column (1) we have two separate functions for joint venture (SZ) and state-owned enterprise (GY) and compare the coefficients of log(TE) and log(LD), constant, observation and AdjR$^2$ from top to bottom responding to these two functions. In column (2), we have three separate functions, for state-owned enterprises, shareholding enterprises and limited liability corporations; constant, observation and AdjR$^2$ from top to bottom respond to these three functions. The same applies to other columns. From column (1), we can see that the coefficient of technical change in joint ventures is lower than that in state-owned enterprises, which may be attributed to the different direction of technical adoption in joint ventures. In column (2), apart from joint ventures, in the other three types of enterprise technical change has a positive impact on employment expansion. This further demonstrates the weak relationship between technical investment and employment growth in joint ventures. Columns (3) and (4) concern the impact of different types of technical change on employment quality. Column (3) illustrates that the process innovation of joint ventures has a positive impact on employment, while that of state-owned enterprises has a negative impact on employment, which is inconsistent with the anticipated outcome. In column (4), neither category of technology has a significant effect on employment in the four types of firm ownership, a finding that deserves attention.

Second, we examine the effect of technical change on employment skill structure. In column (5), only the technical change in joint ventures has

Table 6.4 Comparison of the relationship between technical change and employment in firms with different ownership

| Variable | Log(L) (1) 1998–2002 | Log(L) (2) 2003–04 | Log(L) (3) 1998–2002 | Log(L) (4) 2003–04 | Log(LSIL) (5) 1998–2002 | Log(LSIL) (6) 2003–04 | Log(LSIL) (7) 1998–2002 | Log(LSIL) (8) 2003–04 |
|---|---|---|---|---|---|---|---|---|
| Constant | 3.932***<br>6.005*** | 6.977***<br>7.634***<br>6.988*** | 5.084***<br>7.087*** |  | −2.836*** | −4.387***<br>−3.165*** | −3.556*** | −2.509***<br>−1.504** |
| Log(TE) | SZ<br>0.124***<br>GY<br>0.156*** | GY<br>0.258***<br>GF<br>0.167***<br>YX<br>0.191*** |  |  | SZ<br>0.045** | SZ<br>0.152***<br>GY<br>0.112*** |  |  |
| Log(WD/SB) |  |  | SZ<br>0.082*<br>GY<br>0.029 |  |  |  | GY<br>−0.011 | GY<br>−0.115***<br>YX<br>0.100 |
| Log(XCP/Y) |  |  | SZ<br>0.021<br>GY<br>−0.077*** |  |  |  | GY<br>0.079*** | GY<br>0.136**<br>YX<br>−0.128** |
| Log(LD) | SZ<br>1.262***<br>GY<br>0.880*** | GY<br>0.435***<br>GF<br>0.406***<br>YX<br>0.544*** | SZ<br>1.341***<br>GY<br>0.996*** |  | SZ<br>−0.008 | SZ<br>0.014<br>GY<br>0.024 | GY<br>0.275 | GY<br>0.059<br>YX<br>−0.176 |
| Observations | 158<br>185 | 73<br>72<br>74 | 139<br>182 |  | 157 | 68<br>73 | 182 | 72<br>71 |
| AdjR$^2$ | 0.982<br>0.976 | 0.978<br>0.982<br>0.983 | 0.967<br>0.975 |  | 0.905 | 0.949<br>0.855 | 0.776 | 0.881<br>0.769 |

Note: *, ** and *** indicate the variable is significant at the 10, 5 and 1% level, respectively; SZ stands for joint venture, GY is state-owned enterprise, GF is shareholding enterprise, YX is limited liability corporation.

an impact on skill structure. In column (6), technical change demands the improvement of skill structure in both joint ventures and state-owned enterprises. The coefficient in joint ventures is larger. Their technical changes match closely with the skill structure improvement inside the firm. These firms are relatively large scale and run formally, emphasizing labour quality improvement. It needs to be mentioned that, for a long period of time, some joint ventures relied on hiring temporary or part-time technical workers from outside; thus their employee skill structure did not respond to technical change and a low employee skill structure resulted. In 2004, the proportion of technical workers in shareholding and state-owned enterprises was 11.03 per cent and 11.12 per cent, respectively. The figure for limited liability corporations is 9.01 per cent, and for joint ventures is only 5.11 per cent.[8] According to Yao and Zhang's study (2001), the technology spillover effect in China works through labour mobility rather than imported technology, which also demonstrates the limitation of relying on imported technology for developing countries. Joint ventures played little role in improving labour quality. It is often the case that they seek out talented workers from other types of firm. In the era of new technology competition, however, they now have to place greater emphasis on their skill structures.

Finally, different types of technology have different impacts on labour skill structures. In column (7), the product innovation of state-owned enterprises demands labour skill improvement. In column (8), aside from the positive effect of product innovation, the process innovation of state-owned enterprises degrades the skill structure. For the limited liability corporation, product innovation lowers the skill structure. It seems that the impact of technology on the skill structure of different types of firm is heterogeneous and not confirmed.

## Summary

Using the manufacturing industry's panel data from 1998 to 2004 in transitional China, this chapter empirically analyses the impact of technology adoption on employment quantity and employment structure at the industry level. The econometric results indicate that, basically, technology adoption has a positive impact on employment quantities. This is mainly because, as a developing country, China's technology adoption can improve competition power, expand product demand and increase employment. Technical change also demands the improvement of the labour skill structure. However, the impact of different types of technology varies. Contrary to the prediction of traditional theory, the impacts of process innovation on employment quantity are positive, whereas the impacts of product innovation on employment quantity are virtually negative or insignificant, which implies that our industries still rely on labour productivity improvement to win competition; product innovation is not performing well and cannot bring forth employment expansion.

During the transitional period, the technical adoption acted together with enterprise ownership reform and market structure (competition) and will in future generate negative shocks on employment. The performances of different ownership enterprises also vary. The coefficient of the impact of technology on employment quantity in joint ventures is low or insignificant. Regarding the coefficient of the impact of technology on employment skill structure, for state-owned enterprises it is lower. When the joint venture works as a dummy variable, the impacts on both employment quantity and skill structure are often negative, showing the limited ability of joint ventures to create employment. It should be mentioned that we take a conservative attitude toward our results owing to the relatively small sample size.

The chapter places great emphasis on the role of employment in economic development. Its policy implication is that strengthening the manufacturing industry's technology processes and upgrading international competition power can effect employment expansion. Apart from persisting in developing process innovation, we should carry out meaningful product innovation in order to expand employment. Technology adoption raises the demand for skilled workers, though in some technology categories the impact is not obvious and definite. This challenges the education system and enterprise training programme. If graduate students and employees cannot make an adjustment to the skill requirement, skill mismatch and structural unemployment will occur. In the transitional period, technological progress and institutional structural adjustment are concomitants, which places greater pressure on employment. Therefore we should consider this problem seriously. The policy for joint ventures should also be adjusted accordingly so that the spillover and employment creation effects of technology can be undertaken smoothly.

## Acknowledgements

I am grateful to two anonymous referees and several seminar participants of the Seventh Forum for Chinese Youth Economic Scholars. Remaining errors and omissions are our own.

## Notes

1 The 'Schumpeter effect' refers to the positive impact on employment resulting from the entry of new firms and higher levels of entrepreneurship.
2 The 'Pigou effect' means that a large fall in prices would stimulate an economy and create the 'wealth effect' that will generate full employment.
3 Technology here refers to the technological input expense in the real manufacturing process; it is rarely influenced by employment quantity or structure, and hence can be regarded as an exogenous variable when considering its impact on employment. We will test its validity by using a method of instrument variable later.
4 Even though we know fixed or random effect models should be established after the $F$ and $LM$ tests, as our pool model design (ownership and industry dummy vari-

ables) will shed some new insights we retain them and compare them with fixed or random effect models.

5 Given a model and data in which fixed effects estimation would be appropriate, a Hausman test tests whether random effects estimation would be almost as good. In a fixed-effects case, the Hausman test is a test of $H_0$: that random effects would be consistent and efficient, versus $H_1$: that random effects would be inconsistent. (Note that fixed effects would certainly be consistent.) The result of the test is a vector of dimension k (dim(k)), which will be distributed chi-square (k). So, if the Hausman test statistic is large, one must use FE. If the statistic is small, one may get away with RE.

6 The employment quantity constraint can lead to technological adoption in manufacturing, in turn increasing technology expenditure. However, it will not inevitably lead to a rise in R&D input expenditure and patent quantity.

7 There is an absence of strong multicollinearity between product innovation ($xcp/y$) and process innovation ($wd/sb$).

8 *China Technology Statistics Yearbook* (2005).

## References

Bauer, T.K. and Bender, S. 2004. Technological change, organizational change, and job turnover. *Labour Economics*, 11, 265–291.

Borghans, L. and Weel, T.B. 2006. The division of labour worker organization and technological change. *Economic Journal*, 116, F45–F72.

Braveman, H. 1974. *Labour and Monopoly Capital: The Degradation of Work in the Twentieth Century*, New York: Monthly Review Press.

Chen, Y. and Tang, Z. 2006. Technology choice and technical progress of China's industries: 1985–2003. *Economic Research Journal*, 41(9), 50–61.

Dobbs, I.M., Hill, M.B. and Waterson, M. 1987. Industrial structure and the employment consequences of technological change. *Oxford Economic Papers*, 39(3), 552–567.

Edquist, C., Hommen, L. and McKelvey, M. 2001. *Innovation and Employment: Process Versus Product Innovation*, Cheltenham: Edward Elgar.

Garicano, L. and Rossi-Hansberg, E. 2006. Organization and inequality in a knowledge economy. *Quarterly Journal of Economics*, November, 1383–1435.

Ning, G. 2007. Wage forming mechanism in the market transition process of China (1993–2004). *Finance and Economic Study*, 33(2), 119–131.

Reenen, J.V., 1997. Employment and technological innovation: evidence from UK manufacturing firms. *Journal of Labour Economics*, 15(2), 255–284.

Rothwell, R. and Zegveld, W. 1979. *Technical Change and Employment*, London: Frances Pinter Limited.

Schettkat, R. and Russo, G. 2001. Structural dynamics and employment in highly industrialized economies, in P. Pascal and L. Soete (eds) *Technology and the Future of European Employment*, Cheltenham: Edward Elgar, pp. 111–141.

Spitz-Oener, A. 2006. Technological change, job tasks, and rising education demand: looking outside the wage structure. *Journal of Labour Economics*, 24(2), pp. 235–270.

Vivarelli, M. 1995. *The Economics of Technology and Employment*, Cheltenham: Edward Elgar.

Wang, M., Zhang, W. and Zhou, L.-A. 2006. Information technology, organization reform and product performance. *Economic Research Journal*, 41(1), 65–77.

Weel, B. 2006. Feature: IT diffusion and industry and labour market dynamics. *Economic Journal*, February, F1–F9.

Yao, X. 2005. Technical progress, skill demand and employment structure: skill biased basing on micro data of manufacturing industry. *China Population Science*, 19(5), 47–53.

Yao, Y. and Zhang, Q. 2001. Analysis of technical efficiency of the manufacturing industry in China. *Economic Research Journal*, 36(10), 13–19, 28.

Yao, Z. and Xia, J. 2005. Empirical analysis on capital argument, technical progress's impact on employment. *World Economy*, 28(1), 58–67.

# 7 Evaluating job training in two Chinese cities

*Benu Bidani, Niels-Hugo Blunch,*
*Chor-ching Goh and Christopher O'Leary*

## Introduction

Over the past decade, traditional job guarantees and economic security provided by urban state-owned enterprises (SOEs) in China have been reduced as
part of a nationwide economic reform effort. To help workers transition to
the free labour market, China instituted what was called the *xiagang* system.
Xiagang were redundant workers who remained attached to the SOE and to
whom the SOE provided subsistence income payments along with contributions to public health insurance and pension funds, and often times housing.
While the aim was to smooth labour adjustment, many redundant workers
have experienced significant income losses and difficulty finding new jobs.
The xiagang system has been dismantled, and much restructuring has already
occurred. Still, even the most optimistic observers recognize that China faces
more labour adjustment challenges, especially with reforms called for by
China's accession to the World Trade Organization (WTO). China – like
virtually all countries and especially transition countries – is increasingly
facing difficult policy questions about how to address the problem of laid-off
workers, in order to provide effective social protection and maintain social
stability.

How well can publicly provided training works influence policy decisions in
a range of programmes, including social security, unemployment insurance
and public employment services designed to help workers find new jobs and
restore their incomes? These latter interventions are collectively known as
'active labour market programmes' (ALMPs) and include retraining programmes, employment services (e.g. labour exchange, counselling, etc.), job
creation through loans or subsidies, public service employment, public works
and self-employment assistance. ALMPs such as these have been used extensively in developed and transition economies for many years. They represent
an attractive policy approach because they are intended to provide jobless
workers with a 'trampoline' for getting back into productive employment, as
opposed to simply providing them with a financial 'safety net'.

However, as international experience has clearly demonstrated, implementing an effective active labour market policy poses many challenges. The

immediate challenge is to design and implement retraining and other ALMPs that actually benefit participants in a cost-effective manner. Indeed, it is apparent from many studies in developed and transition countries that this is very often not the case. For this reason, there is growing emphasis on scientifically evaluating the effects and cost-efficiency of these programmes and basing future programme expenditures on such results.

In turn, this has lead to a surge in the academic literature on impact evaluation of training programmes. While a large literature has now been established for developed countries, the evidence for developing and transition economies is scarce.[1] For China, in particular, no evidence is presently available. Given the extent of recent decades' economic reforms in China and associated massive lay-offs and accompanying public retraining programmes, this is paradoxical, as these events virtually cry out for rigorous evaluation of the impact of job training.

This study evaluates retraining programmes for laid-off workers in the Chinese cities of Shenyang and Wuhan, using a carefully designed comparison group methodology. To our knowledge, this is the first evaluation of its kind in China. The results suggest that retraining helped workers find jobs in Wuhan, but had little effect in Shenyang. The study raises questions about the overall effectiveness of retraining expenditures and offers some directions for policy-makers about future interventions to help laid-off workers. The structure of the chapter is as follows. The next section presents the institutional context and labour market context of training for laid-off workers in China, focusing on the experiences of workers in Shenyang and Wuhan. The third section discusses the methodology underlying the analyses in this chapter, while the fourth section presents the data. Results follow in the fifth section, while the sixth concludes and provides suggestions for future research on the possible impact of active labour market programmes in China.

## The institutional and labour market context of training[2]

To understand the potential for job training, it is important to know the institutional framework and labour market context of training for laid-off workers in China. We first discuss national government policies promoting re-employment of laid-off workers, and then review the economic conditions at the national and provincial levels. This is followed by a brief examination of the economic conditions in the cities of Shenyang and Wuhan around the time retraining programmes there were evaluated.

In May 1998, the Central Party Committee and the State Council jointly organized a conference on safeguarding the Basic Living Standards of Laid-off Workers in SOEs and their Re-employment. After the conference, the Central Party Committee and the State Council jointly issued an outline of various policy measures adopted. These included setting up re-employment service centres (RSCs) and establishment of programmes to promote the re-employment of laid-off workers. Registration with an RSC established an institutional membership for the jobless distinct from being either xiagang or openly unemployed.

Beginning in 2001, programmes for laid-off workers started to change in Liaoning province, of which Shenyang is the capital city, and in some other provinces piloting social security reform. Wuhan, capital of Hubei province, was not among the cities where social security reforms were tried. In the pilot cities, including Shenyang, no additional RSCs were created starting in 2001, and newly laid-off workers unable to find new jobs joined the ranks of the unemployed as soon as they were separated from their prior employer. Current RSC registrants retained their institutional affiliation during the pilot test period. In Wuhan, newly laid-off workers were required to register with an RSC between 2001 and 2003, right up until the final closure of all RSCs in 2003. By 2003, all workers who were registered with RSCs terminated their membership and became unemployed unless they had found new jobs.

When RSCs were closed, a range of new active labour market policies (e.g. training, job information, job referrals, career information, etc.) was adopted to strengthen labour market development. These were available at public labour bureaus not requiring compulsory registration by the jobless. For example, in both Shenyang and Wuhan, the government required that the labour bureau offer at least three opportunities for employment for laid-off workers who demonstrated a great need. Special services in Wuhan were also targeted to households in which both husband and wife were laid-off and unemployed. Arrangements for publicly funded job training were handled differently.

Other policy measures included development of tertiary industries, particularly community services; encouraging the development of small and medium enterprises; facilitating self-employment including credit support; and expediting social security reform particularly in the areas of pensions, health care and unemployment insurance. The contribution rate for unemployment insurance was increased to 3 per cent from 1 per cent beginning in the latter half of 1999, with the 2 percentage point increase shared equally between employers and employees.

In Wuhan, 40,000 laid-off workers were employed in community services by the end of June 1998. By May 2001, in Shenyang there were over 600 grass-roots level organizations providing employment to about 90,800 laid-off workers. During the same period, the Shenyang municipal government set up various markets employing over 170,000 workers. Additional local efforts were also undertaken to encourage workers to set up businesses. These included tax reductions and exemptions, a temporary reduction in municipal administrative fees, and credit support.

China's GDP growth rates over the past few years have been enviable, but employment growth rates were more modest. Urban employment has been growing, albeit at a slower rate in recent years, while rural employment has declined significantly. However, provinces differ from the national averages in GDP and employment growth rates, unemployment rates and the number of xiagang. Unemployment rates in both Liaoning and Hubei provinces have been higher than the national average since 1996, even though their provincial GDP growth rates have exceeded the national average since 1997. Despite the relatively high output growth, employment has been falling in Liaoning and Hubei, with even larger reductions in their urban areas in 1998 and 1999.

Nationwide, SOEs continued to be the dominant employer in 1999, with a 55 per cent share of all urban employment in 1999, with another 11 per cent of the workforce employed in collectively-owned enterprises. By 1999, the private sector share of all urban employment nationwide had risen to 22 per cent. In the provinces of Liaoning and Hubei, a somewhat larger share of total employment was in the private sector.

Regions vary in the share of the workforce who is xiagang, with the magnitude dependent on the extent of the SOE reform and the industrial composition of employment. By the end of 1999, laid-off workers in Liaoning, Heilongjiang, Hubei and Hunan constituted 41 per cent of all lay-offs nationwide, with Liaoning and Hubei accounting for 13 and 7 per cent, respectively. As shares of the total employed nationwide, Liaoning and Hubei account for 3 and 4 per cent, respectively, so that these two provinces have disproportionately high shares of the nation's laid-off workers. In Liaoning and Hubei provinces, 57 and 59 per cent, respectively, of xiagang were from SOEs, while 38 and 29 per cent, respectively, were from the urban collectively-owned enterprises. Nationally, 70 per cent of xiagang workers were from the SOEs and 28 per cent from collectively-owned enterprises.

Job lay-offs are also concentrated in certain industries. Textiles, coal mining, armaments and machinery are the harder hit industries.[3] Data on the industrial distribution of laid-off workers in SOEs in 1998 and 1999 reveal that the industrial classification is broad – and shows that over half the laid-off workers are from the manufacturing industry in Wuhan. Supplemental information indicates that the manufacturing sectors impacted greatest by lay-offs were textiles and general machinery manufacturing. In certain categories of manufacturing, for example, cultural, educational and sports products, leather, fur and rubber manufacturing, the ratio of laid-off workers to total workers was between 40 and 50 per cent.[4] Evidence for Shenyang identifies four sectors with relatively high redundancies – light industry, textiles, petroleum and chemical and agricultural machinery.[5]

When we examine employment growth rates across sectors, we find that between 1996 and 1999, while employment in the manufacturing and mining/quarrying sectors declined significantly, in the financial services, estate agency activities and social services rose. Employment in the wholesale and retail trades grew between 1996 and 1998, but contracted between 1998 and 1999.

Among laid-off workers registered with RSCs in 1999, about 47 per cent were female in both Wuhan and Shenyang, while the proportion of female in the urban labour force was only 28 and 29 per cent, respectively, in Hubei and

Liaoning provinces. The vast majority of workers were less than 46 years old and among the less educated, with most having attained no higher than a junior middle school level.

Turning to benefits, laid-off workers in the Hubei RSCs are much more likely to be paid all basic living expenses (88 per cent) than those in Liaoning (59 per cent). Nearly 16 per cent of Liaoning workers in the RSCs do not receive any basic living expenses, while only 4 per cent in Hubei go without basic support. About half of the laid-off workers in Hubei belonged to an RSC for less than a year, with none staying more than two years. In Liaoning, about 37 per cent of the laid-off stayed with an RSC for less than a year, while 12 per cent stayed for over two years.

Were economic conditions in Shenyang and Wuhan different? Wuhan had a more dynamic economy than Shenyang. GDP per capita in 2000 in both cities was about the same – 16,111 yuan in Wuhan and 16,333 yuan in Shenyang. GDP growth rates have exceeded 10 per cent annually in both cities over the period 1996–2000, though growth rates in Wuhan have been higher. Wuhan's growth exceeded that in Shenyang by 5–6 per cent between 1996–97 and 1–2 per cent between 1998–2000. Higher growth rates provide greater opportunities for creating jobs. But, did the jobs actually materialize? Employment elasticities show the responsiveness of employment to economic growth, and are calculated by dividing the net new job growth rate by the economic growth rate. The employment elasticity was higher in Wuhan than in Shenyang. Between 1996 and 2000, Shenyang's employment elasticity was −0.001, while Wuhan's employment elasticity was 0.069. Thus, despite growth rates exceeding 10 per cent annually over this period, Shenyang did not experience net new job creation. Over this five-year period, while growth rates were high in both cities, Wuhan succeeded in creating significantly more jobs than Shenyang.

The employment structure across primary, secondary and tertiary industries in both cities was similar in 1999, with about 36 per cent employed in the secondary industry, around 41 per cent in the tertiary sector and the remainder in the primary sector. However, the pattern of employment growth differed by city over the period 1996–2000. From 1996 to 2000, the growth rate of employment in the primary industry was negative in Wuhan, while it was positive (5.7 per cent) in Shenyang. In both Shenyang and Wuhan, employment in the secondary industry declined; it declined by an average of 0.27 per cent annually in Wuhan between 1996 and 2000, while in Shenyang the decline was more substantial (4.1 per cent annually). The tertiary industry was the engine of employment growth in both cities, with employment growth in Wuhan over the 1996–2000 period averaging 3.03 per cent annually, while it was 2.07 per cent in Shenyang. The higher growth rate in the tertiary industry provided better employment opportunities in Wuhan.

Wuhan also enjoys better connections to the rest of China; with better-developed rail and communications systems, there are better opportunities for developing trade and commerce. The tourism sector is also better developed in Wuhan, providing an important impetus for the development of self-employment. Wuhan has also invested significantly more than Shenyang in fixed assets. In 2000, Wuhan spent 46.2 billion yuan (or 6,166 yuan per capita) on investments in fixed assets, compared to 26.2 billion yuan (or 3,824 yuan per capita) in Shenyang. Foreign investment in 2000 in Wuhan (1.3 billion US dollars) also exceeded that in Shenyang (1.04 billion US dollars).

The average annual disposable income of urban residents in 2000 in Wuhan was 6,763 yuan, while it was only 5,850 yuan in Shenyang. However, despite lower incomes, Shenyang residents saved more in the aggregate than Wuhan residents. The differences in saving rates indicate either a scarcity of investment opportunities or reduced consumer confidence leading to lower spending. These savings represent a resource that could help create jobs given the right incentives. Individually owned businesses saw strong growth in both Wuhan and Shenyang over this period, though overall development was stronger in Wuhan.

## Methodology

This section presents our methodology. First, we discuss the economic theory underlying the analyses, and then we discuss the empirical strategy.

The theoretical framework for this chapter is standard human capital theory, according to which an individual builds up knowledge and skills through education, experience and training (formal and/or on-the-job) and subsequently gets rewarded in the labour market in terms of wages (Becker 1964; Mincer 1974). This leads to the following simple model:

$$Y_i = Y(S_i, E_i, T_i, O_i), \tag{1}$$

where $Y$ is the employment outcome for individual $i$, $S$ is schooling, $E$ is experience, $T$ is training and $O$ is other individual characteristics, for example gender, for individual $i$. Schooling and experience are thought to affect employment prospects positively, since these factors positively affect the marginal product of an individual's labour services. Training may or may not affect employment prospects positively. This depends on, for example, whether the training in question is perceived by prospective employers to affect workers' productivity positively. If the training is thought to be of low quality or to be given to workers of low quality, thereby acting as a negative 'signal' to prospective employers (Spence 1973), training might have no effect on employment and may even stigmatize trainees.

Rigorous evaluations of social programmes, such as training, are needed to learn if a programme achieves its intended objectives. The central design issue in the evaluation is constructing a proper counterfactual. That is, what would have happened in the absence of the programme? In the case of a training programme, the evaluation must attempt to assess the employment outcomes of participants against what would have been the outcomes if they had not participated in the programme. The counterfactual is approximated by the experiences of a 'comparison group' of workers, who are similar in all respects except programme participation. Programmes that are evaluated on the basis of techniques that do not use a comparison group, relying only on statistics of programme participants alone (e.g. employment rates of graduates), are of little use in measuring whether programmes are generating positive net benefits.

Lacking a field experiment involving random assignment, our approach is based on a quasi-experimental design, whereby participant and comparison groups are selected after the programme has commenced (how this is done in practice is discussed in detail in the next section). Because of non-random selection into participation, one cannot simply compare means on outcomes between participants and non-participants. Adjustments must be made in the estimation process to account for the differences in the characteristics of the participant and comparison groups.

To examine more closely whether results are robust to the choice of estimator, our approach here is to use several techniques to adjust for differences in observable characteristics of workers from the participant and treatment groups when estimating the empirical counterpart of equation (1). First, we estimate the effect of training as simply the coefficient for $\beta_1$ in the regression:

$$y_i = \beta_0 + \beta_1 T_i + other\ controls + \varepsilon_i, \tag{2}$$

where $y_i$ is the employment outcome for individual $i$, one if employed, zero otherwise, $T_i$ is a binary indicator for whether individual $i$ received training or not, 'other controls' include additional controls – such as age (to proxy potential general experience), gender and education – to ensure that the impact estimate (i.e. the estimate of $\beta_1$) is valid, and $\varepsilon_i$ is an error term that takes into account measurement error on the dependent variable $y_i$ and other (unobserved) factors that may affect the dependent variable $y_i$. Equation (2), therefore, effectively is the empirical counterpart of equation (1). We estimate (2) as a probit model outcome. Additionally, to provide a robust alternative to the probit estimation, we also estimate the employment regression by OLS, thereby effectively estimating (2) as a linear probability model.

As yet another alternative, we apply propensity score matching methods. The intuition behind this method is to compare the mean values of outcomes across the participant and comparison groups. The comparison group is constructed in this case by a two-stage approach, where participants and non-participants first are pooled and a regression of the determinants of participation is performed. Based on this, the individuals are ranked across to their predicted probability of participation in the programme, i.e. their (predicted) 'propensity score'. When a participant and a non-participant are 'close' in terms of their propensity score, we have a match. This procedure is carried out for the entire sample and the impact estimate – which corresponds to the estimate of $\beta_1$ in (2) from the regression case – is then calculated as the difference in means on employment outcomes between matched participants and non-participants. There are several different ways to do the matching, for example 'nearest neighbour', where the match is based on only the closest non-participant; '$k$-nearest neighbours' matching, where the match is based on a weighted average of the $k$-nearest matches of non-participants in terms of their propensity scores; as well as kernel based and other methods (for details on propensity score matching, see Dehejia and Wahba 1999, 2002; Heckman *et al.* 1997, 1998; Rosenbaum and Rubin 1983, 1984, 1985).

Another widely used estimation method is to use instrumental variable (IV) techniques or two-stage least squares. However, since we do not have any instruments in our dataset which affect selection into programmes without at the same time affecting the outcome(s) of interest (here, employment), we cannot apply these methods. Consequently we must treat all observables, including assignment to training, as predetermined.

## Data

This section discusses the data and survey methodology, and also provides descriptive statistics on the samples for analysis. Tests for homogeneity in observable characteristics between the participant and comparison groups are presented. Additionally, the nature of training is discussed.

The survey was designed and implemented by the Chinese Institute of Labour Studies and the World Bank. Respondents for the survey were selected from lists of laid-off workers who had received training (the treatment group) and laid-off workers who had not received training (the control group) from lists provided by the Shenyang and Wuhan Labour Bureaus, as well as local training institutions (for details on the sampling procedure, see Bidani *et al.* 2004, 2005). The World Bank team prepared a draft questionnaire, which was revised by counterparts in the Chinese Institute of Labour Studies (the text of the final questionnaire is provided in Annex 4 of Bidani *et al.* 2004). The team from the Institute of Labour Studies then carried out the data collection. Fielding of the survey began towards the end of May 2000, and was completed the following month. Successful interview rates were highest for the Shenyang participant group (61 per cent) and lowest for the Shenyang comparison group (48 per cent). Wuhan's response rates were 51 per cent for the participant group and 55 per cent for the comparison group. The survey teams indicated that inaccurate contact information was the primary cause of non-response. The address on the identity card of workers differed from their actual residence in many cases.

Two anomalies related to this dataset were discovered by and discussed in Betcherman *et al.* (2002). First, a substantial fraction of workers report working in July 1998, when they were assumed to have been xiagang. This is addressed by deleting these workers to yield a 'true' xiagang-only sample. Second, the dataset contain 'late xiagangers', that is, individuals reporting having become xiagang after July 1998. These persons therefore were employed immediately prior to the intervention, and were still in their old firms. This second group was also deleted from the sample for analysis since they too were not 'true' xiagang. Another contamination issue was that some individuals in the comparison group reported having received training. Since these more appropriately belong in the participant group, they were reassigned (see Bidani *et al.* 2004 for details).

We find significant (statistically and substantively) differences between the comparison and participant groups in terms of the demographic variables occupation, industry and other separating firm characteristics (firm type, firm size) in samples from both cities (see the Appendix). The differences are more pronounced in Shenyang than in Wuhan. Training participants in both cities were more likely to be female and younger. Participants in Shenyang were less likely to be married but more likely to have a high educational attainment than the comparison group members. Such differences were not observed to the same extent in the Wuhan sample. The occupational structure of the participant and comparison groups was more similar in Wuhan. In Shenyang, occupational structure differed more significantly, with a higher share of the participant group in the professional, clerical and services categories, and a lower percentage in the craft and machine operator categories. Thus, it would be misleading to use unadjusted means to compute impacts of the training programme. We will therefore adopt methodologies that allow us to control for observable differences when computing the programme impacts.

In 1998, there were 113 schools to train skilled workers and 199 enterprise-based training units in Shenyang. The municipal government launched an ambitious training plan that year which provided free training to all laid-off workers, and a budget of 10 million yuan was allocated for this purpose. The city's re-employment training centre administered the programme, which was implemented by training organizations under the district labour bureaus. In Shenyang, the allocation of funding prior to training had recently been replaced by an after-training expense reimbursement contingent on training results. For training programmes with attendance rates of over 80 per cent, a passing rate of over 90 per cent and a re-employment rate of over 70 per cent, training expenses were reimbursed in full. When the re-employment rate fell below the required level, a 10 per cent deduction was made in the reimbursement for every 10 per cent difference. Training institutions could be disqualified if they did not meet the performance standards set.

In Wuhan, the government's role in retraining of laid-off workers was less active. In 1998, there were 32 job skills schools and employment training centres within the labour system. The city's labour bureau administered the city's re-employment training programme for laid-off workers and unemployed persons. The training was conducted by the labour bureau training organizations (such as the city employment training centre and district employment training centres). Other organizations that satisfied the qualification requirements also undertook this training, for which they were compensated to cover part of their expenses.

Training programmes in Shenyang were conducted on a significantly larger scale (Bidani *et al.* 2004, 2005). Between 1998 and 2000, 279,000 workers were trained in contrast to around 64,000 workers in Wuhan. Shenyang offered its workers a larger menu of training courses; 59 courses in 1999 compared to 34 different courses in Wuhan. The gross re-employment rates, according to administrative data, were in the 60–70 per cent range for both cities, increasing steadily in Wuhan over the three-year period.

Nearly all training in Shenyang was of one-month's duration, with 132 hours of study. In Wuhan, training lasted between one and six months, with the usual duration being two to three months of full-time study. Between July and December 1998, the average number of course hours was 255, of which 55 per cent were practical. In Shenyang, training courses with a minimum duration of one month were eligible for the government subsidy of 100 yuan per trainee. Laid-off workers did not contribute to the training courses. However, in Wuhan, only courses of two to three months were eligible for the government subsidy, and government policy was to provide 50–100 yuan from the re-employment fund for every laid-off worker trained and 300–400 yuan for every unemployed worker trained. Trainees in Wuhan were charged part of the training costs – they were exempt from paying the training fees but were expected to purchase textbooks and practice materials. Most trainees contributed about 200 yuan to the cost of their training.

Despite the more ambitious xiagang training programme by the Shenyang government, the quality of programmes varied widely across training institutions. Training institutions differed greatly in capacity, space, classroom set-up, workshop facilities, and laboratory and mechanical equipment. A number of training institutions only provided theoretical instruction without any practical training in their vocational courses. Some of the training courses did not provide skills demanded in the local labour market, and there were not even minimal standards governing the content of curricula and the qualifications of instructors.

The survey also asked about the nature of training. Information on the training provider, the duration of training, the type of training and whether individuals paid for training are shown in Table 7.1. Training was different across the two cities. As indicated, we restricted our list to three district training schools run by the labour bureau in Shenyang. So, the training there was almost exclusively provided by the labour bureau. In contrast, training in Wuhan was more varied. The Labour Bureau provided about three-quarters, with the rest provided by other organizations. The training in Shenyang was substantially shorter than that in Wuhan, averaging about one month, while the average duration of training in Wuhan was two to three months. Only about 3 per cent of the participants in Shenyang paid all or part of the costs of training, whereas about 21 per cent of participants paid at least part of the cost in Wuhan. The training organizations in Wuhan included colleges, universities and secondary technical schools, with presumably better ability to deliver quality training.

*Table 7.1* Characteristics of training

| Characteristic | Value | Shenyang | Wuhan |
|---|---|---|---|
| Training location | Labour Bureau | 0.956 | 0.716 |
| | Other | 0.044 | 0.284 |
| Duration | Months | 1.074 | 1.892 |
| Type of training | Computers | 0.363 | 0.325 |
| | Driving | 0.015 | 0.105 |
| | Repair | 0.057 | 0.086 |
| | Management, accounting, business | 0.069 | 0.284 |
| | Cooking | 0.293 | 0.088 |
| | Sewing and toy-making | 0.168 | 0.014 |
| | Beauty, massage and haircutting | 0.193 | 0.023 |
| | Other | 0.051 | 0.133 |
| Financing of training | Paid for training | 0.028 | 0.212 |
| | Did not pay for Training | 0.972 | 0.788 |

There were also variations in the type of courses that the participants attended. In Shenyang, about 37 per cent of the sample took computer courses, 29 per cent cooking, 19 per cent beauty, massage and hair cutting, and another 17 per cent sewing and toy making. In Wuhan, about 33 per cent took computer courses, 28 per cent took management courses, 9 per cent cooking, 9 per cent repairs and 11 per cent driving. There is some evidence that the types of training courses conducted in Wuhan, especially those run by the private sector, were selected by the organizers to accommodate the labour market demand for certain skills.

## Results

Our analyses focus on one key outcome, namely, current employment.[6] We use various estimators in this study to examine impacts of training on re-employment among xiagang workers. Additionally, we also examine more closely the determinants of training and briefly discuss determinants of reemployment beyond training.

Table 7.2 presents impact estimates for training computed by several different estimators: OLS/linear probability model, probit, and four different propensity score matching estimators. Training has a significantly positive impact on the likelihood of finding employment in Wuhan, but no significant effect on employment in Shenyang. Specifically, the numerical estimate for Shenyang is nil, but an employment rate gain of 9 to 12 percentage points was estimated for training in Wuhan by OLS and probit, respectively. The impact estimates are robust across the different estimators in both cities.

One potential problem with the propensity score matching methods is that they use markedly fewer observations than the regression approaches (see the

*Table 7.2* Training impact estimates (on employment) from a series of alternative estimators (standard errors in brackets)

| Estimator | Shenyang | Wuhan |
| --- | --- | --- |
| Ordinary least squares (OLS) | 0.03 | 0.090*** |
| | [0.022] | [0.027] |
| Probit, marginal effect | 0.019 | 0.119*** |
| | [0.032] | [0.034] |
| *Propensity score matching:* | | |
| (1)  Nearest neighbour matching | 0.032 | 0.087* |
| | [0.047] | [0.049] |
| (2)  Five nearest neighbours matching | −0.001 | 0.066* |
| | [0.040] | [0.037] |
| (3)  Kernel matching | −0.005 | 0.080** |
| | [0.032] | [0.032] |
| (4)  Local linear regression matching | −0.001 | 0.084** |
| | [0.034] | [0.033] |
| (Max) Observations[7] | 1821 | 1278 |

*Notes:* All estimations include a rich set of control variables (the results for these have been excluded due to space constraints but are available upon request); see the table in the Appendix for information on the full set of control variables included in the estimations. Standard errors for the OLS and probit impact estimates are robust, i.e. allowing for heteroskedasticity of unknown form (Huber 1967; White 1980), while the standard errors for the propensity score impact estimates are bootstrapped, using 200 replications. *Statistically significant at 10%, **statistically significant at 5%, ***statistically significant at 1%. Kernels used are as follows: (3): epanechnikov kernel, (4): tricube kernel. For the propensity score matching estimators, common support is imposed by excluding participant observations whose propensity score is higher than the maximum or less than the minimum propensity score of the comparison group. For the probit regression for Wuhan, one observation is dropped from the estimation due to 'Firmtype, other' being a perfect predictor for employment. For the propensity score matching estimations, to impose common support, observations outside the region of common support are dropped from the estimations in amounts as follows: 39 (Shenyang) and 9 (Wuhan).

bottom of Table 7.2). This reflects the fact that the overlapping area between the distributions of participants and comparison group observations, the so-called 'region of common support', is limited. This problem enhances the appeal of the more traditional regression-based methods (OLS and probit), where all observations are retained in the calculation of the training impact estimates. Since the impact estimates are similar across the different estimators, and OLS more completely use our sample information, OLS is therefore also our preferred estimator.

While the impact estimates and their magnitudes clearly are of interest to policy-makers, there are other aspects of the programmes that would potentially be relevant for policy regarding the design of future training programmes in China, as well. In particular, it would be interesting to examine a bit more closely who actually participates in the training, in other words, 'who actually picks up the training offered to prospective participants'?[8] This amounts to examining the results from the 'first stage' of the propensity score matching estimations.

Among the main findings are that training programme participants are predominantly younger females who have visited an employment service centre at some point. Also, workers in industries other than manufacturing (the reference category) are more likely to participate in training. For workers' occupation prior to becoming xiagang, there are no strong results. However, workers who previously worked in SOEs (the reference category) are less likely to have participated in training. Workers who currently receive unemployment benefits are more likely to participate in training than are workers who do not receive unemployment benefits. In Shenyang, workers from households with more employed workers are more likely to receive training than other workers. For all samples except the employment sample for Wuhan, workers who were working in July 1998 are less likely to have participated in training than those who did not work in July 1998.

Based on the previous discussion, there appears to be mixed evidence on the targeting of the training programmes in Shenyang and Wuhan. On one hand, workers who were working in July 1998, that is, immediately prior to the intervention, are less likely to participate in training, while workers collecting unemployment benefits (and, therefore, presumably are unemployed) are more likely to participate in training, indicating effective targeting of the training programmes in Shenyang and Wuhan in terms of labour market status (presumably it would also be difficult to both work and participate in the programme, anyway). On the other hand, at least in Shenyang, workers from households with more working household members are more likely to participate in the training programme, which seems to indicate poor targeting, at least as measured by the presence of other earners in the household. Indeed, in a sense the targeting is worsened the better off the individual is in terms of the presence of other earners in the household.

It will also be interesting to shed additional light on determinants of employment other than training. In the evaluation of the effectiveness of the programme – which is the primary objective of this chapter – explanatory variables other than the training (participant) indicator were included mainly to reduce the overall variance of the estimator and increase the reliability of the inferences from estimated coefficients. In particular, to the extent that impacts from other factors are confounded within the training indicator variable, those factors should be controlled for in the estimation. For example it is possible that the participation in the programme is related to gender, education or other factors. However, even if the primary role of explanatory variables other than the training (participant) variable are to serve as controls, the results for the estimated parameters of these variables are interesting in their own right. In particular, it will be instructive for policy to know how other factors, such as gender, education, previous occupation, and so on affect the labour market prospects of laid-off workers in China. After having completed a review of the core evaluation results, we therefore now examine results on the secondary variables.

First, females and disabled workers are consistently much less likely to be employed in both Wuhan and Shenyang. This should be an issue of concern for policy-makers, particularly if equity is considered important but also since these two groups could potentially contribute significantly to their households' livelihoods. Second, there are strong positive education effects from tertiary education in Wuhan. Since job training works for those more prepared to benefit from it, more effort should focus on identifying ways to help those with less formal education prepare for success in the job market. In Shenyang, workers from households with more employed household members are also more likely to be employed themselves, which might be due to spill-over effects or social networks. In Wuhan, the time since becoming xiagang has a negative impact on being employed, that is, the longer one is unemployed, the less likely that person is to find employment.

## Conclusion

This chapter presents results of an evaluation of retraining programmes for laid-off workers in Shenyang and Wuhan. To our knowledge, this is the first evaluation of its kind in China. Training programmes were estimated to have markedly different impacts in the two cities. In Shenyang, workers who had taken training in 1998 were no more likely to be employed in mid-2000 than workers who had not participated in training programmes. In Wuhan, however, participation in training was estimated to have raised the probability of employment relative to the comparison group. These results are robust across alternative estimation methods.

Analyses of training determinants indicate mixed evidence on the targeting of the training programmes in Shenyang and Wuhan. On one hand, workers who were working in July 1998, that is, immediately prior to the intervention, were less likely to participate in training, while workers collecting unemployment benefits (and, therefore, presumably are unemployed) were more likely to participate in training, indicating effective targeting of the training programmes in terms of labour market status (presumably it would be difficult to both work and participate in the programme). On the other hand, at least in Shenyang, workers from households with more working household members are more likely to participate in the training programme, which suggests poor targeting, at least as measured by the presence of other earners in the household.

While this evaluation must be supported by further research, it does raise a number of issues regarding training policies for laid-off workers. Most obviously, the study suggests that policy-makers must adopt a critical approach to retraining and recognize that expectations should be moderate. Unless training programmes are carefully designed and targeted, there are no guarantees that impacts will be positive. This finding is consistent with the international experience.

The different results for the two cities should be of interest for policy-makers. Why did this occur? It may be due to factors that have nothing to do with training – for example, the stronger economy in Wuhan may explain the more positive outcomes for employment in that city. However, the different results may well be due to differences in the retraining offered in the two cities. The quality and the relevance of the training programmes being offered probably contributed to the different outcomes. Training that is more responsive to market conditions and equips workers for jobs that are being created has a greater likelihood of creating a positive impact. Compared to Shenyang, Wuhan's training programmes had certain features that may explain the more positive training outcomes. These include longer programmes with more practical content, and stronger supporting employment services (as indicated by the much higher proportion of workers going through Re-employment Service Centres).

This evaluation, in combination with the international literature, therefore suggests the following lessons for retraining policy. First, moderate expectations about the capacity of retraining programmes to reintegrate laid-off workers back into the labour market are in order. Second, diversification of the sources of training appears fruitful; public, non-profit and commercial providers may have comparative advantages in providing different types of training. Third, the focus should be on providing training that is responsive to labour demand. The best way of doing this is to involve employers in planning training. Fourth, the most important supporting services are job search, counselling and good labour market information. These not only can increase the returns to training but they tend to be the most cost-efficient of all active labour market programmes. For some workers, particularly those who are job-ready, these employment services should be the priority. Fifth, programmes should be carefully targeted to groups that are most likely to have a net positive benefit. Lastly, it seems fruitful to experiment with different financing schemes, including those that require some financial contribution from trainees.

These results should be compared to findings from future evaluations. The experience of other countries with long experience in labour adjustment programmes can help inform Chinese training strategies. But national characteristics do matter a great deal. Programme evaluation should become an intrinsic part of the active labour market strategy in China. Such evaluations need to be carried out in a range of municipalities with varying characteristics and on diverse programme designs. They must also take into account the costs of programmes, something that has not been analysed in this study. Only through such rigorous evaluations can policy-makers determine what works and for whom in supporting laid-off workers. In addition, it is important to compare training to other active labour market alternatives (such as employment services) and to highlight the costs and benefits of alternate interventions to support laid-off workers. It would also be useful to complement the quantitative survey information with qualitative information on the quality and relevance of training programmes from trainees, training institutes and employers. This would enrich the understanding of which training programmes work and why.

## Acknowledgements

We thank participants at the Eighteenth Chinese Economic Association (UK) Annual Meetings in Nottingham and an anonymous referee for helpful comments and suggestions. Remaining errors and omissions are our own. The views expressed here are those of the authors and should not be attributed to the World Bank or any of its member countries or affiliated institutions.

## Notes

1 See Heckman *et al.* (1999) for a comprehensive review of impact evaluations in OECD countries; Dar and Gill (1998) for a review of 11 studies covering the US, Sweden, Australia, Canada and France; Galasso *et al.* (2001) for a study on the Argentinian Proemplio experiment; Jimenez and Kugler (1987) for a study on Columbia's national in-service training systems; Revenga *et al.* (1994) for an evaluation of the Mexican Probecat programme; Fretwell *et al.* (1999) for an evaluation of training programmes in Hungary, Poland and the Czech Republic; and NEI (2001) for an evaluation of training programmes in Bulgaria.
2 This section draws heavily on Bidani *et al.* (2004, 2005), where all the tables with the background statistics discussed here may also be found.
3 In 1999, laid-off workers in textile enterprises directly affiliated to the central government numbered 600,000; there were 400,000 in coal mining, 200,000 in armaments and 200,000 in machinery enterprises. These figures are taken from the presentation, 'Situation of laid-off workers in state enterprise and policies on securing their basic living standards and promoting their re-employment' given by the Labour Bureau at the Labour Market Policies Seminar in Beijing in May 1999.
4 Survey Report on Employment Situation in Wuhan, 1997, mimeo. The statistics refer to 1996.
5 Presentation by the Shenyang Municipal Labour Bureau on 'forcefully implementing re-employment project: organizing and facilitating redundant workers for re-employment' at the Labour Market Policies Seminar in May 1999.
6 In an earlier version of this chapter, we also examined the effect of training on wages (Bidani *et al.* 2005). Based on the comments and suggestions of a referee, however, we exclude the training–wage analysis here and, hence, focus exclusively on the employment analysis.
7 To conserve space, the results discussed here and in the remainder of this section are not reported here; they are available upon request.
8 To impose common support, the propensity score methods exclude extreme (in terms of their propensity score) observations. See the notes to Table 7.2 for details.

## References

Becker, Gary S. (1964) *Human Capital*, New York: National Bureau of Economic Research.
Betcherman, Gordon, Amit Dar and Niels-Hugo Blunch (2002) China Retraining Evaluation: Some Further Analysis, Mimeo, Human Development Network, Social Protection, Washington, DC: World Bank.
Bidani, Benu, Gordon Betcherman, Niels-Hugo Blunch, Amit Dar, Chorching Goh, Ken Kline and Christopher O'Leary (2004) Has Training Helped Employ the Xiagang in China? A Tale from Two Cities, Report No. 24161-CHA, Poverty

Reduction and Economic Management Unit, East Asia and Pacific Region, World Bank, Washington, DC.

Bidani, Benu, Niels-Hugo Blunch, Chorching Goh and Christopher O'Leary (2005) Evaluating Job Training in Two Chinese Cities, Working Paper 05–111, W. E. Upjohn Institute for Employment Research, Kalamazoo, MI.

Dar, Amit, and Indermit Gill (1998) Evaluating Retraining Programs in OECD Countries: Lessons Learned, *World Bank Research Observer*, 13(1): 79–101.

Dehejia, Rajeev, and Sadek Wahba (1999) Causal Effects in Nonexperimental Studies: Reevaluating the Evaluation of Training Programs, *Journal of the American Statistical Association*, 94: 1053–1062.

Dehejia, Rajeev, and Sadek Wahba (2002) Propensity Score Matching Methods for on Experimental Causal Studies, National Bureau of Economics Research Working Paper No. 6829, *Review of Economics and Statistics*, 84(1): 151–161.

Fretwell, David H., Jacob Benus and Christopher J. O'Leary (1999) Evaluating the Impact of Active Labour Programmes: Results of Cross Country Studies in Europe and Central Asia, *Social Protection Discussion Paper No. 9915*, Washington, DC: World Bank.

Galasso, Emanuela, Martin Ravallion and Augustin Salvia (2001) Assisting the Transition from Workfare to Work: Argentina's Proempleo Experiment, mimeo, Washington, DC: World Bank.

Heckman, James J., Hidehiko Ichimura and Petra Todd (1997) Matching as an Econometric Evaluation Estimator: Evidence from Evaluating a Job Training Program, *Review of Economic Studies*, 64: 605–654.

Heckman, James J., Hidehiko Ichimura and Petra Todd (1998) Matching as an Econometric Evaluation Estimator, *Review of Economic Studies*, 65: 261–294.

Heckman, James J., Hidehiko Ichimura, Jeffrey Smith and Petra Todd (2000) Characterizing Selection Bias using Experimental Data, *Econometrica*, 66(5): 1017–1098.

Heckman, James J., Robert J. LaLonde and Jeffrey A. Smith (1999) The Economics and Econometrics of Active Labour Market Programs, in O. Ashenfelter and D. Card (eds), *Handbook of Labour Economics, Volume 3A*, Amsterdam: Elsevier.

Huber, P.J. (1967) The Behavior of Maximum Likelihood Estimates under Nonstandard Conditions, in *Proceedings of the Fifth Berkeley Symposium on Mathematical Statistics and Probability* Vol. 1, Berkeley: University of California Press.

Jimenez, Emmanuel and Bernardo Kugler (1987) The Earnings Impact of Training Duration in a Developing Country: An Ordered Probit Selection Model of Colombia's Servicio acional de Aprendizaje (SENA), *Journal of Human Resources*, 22(2): 228–247.

Mincer, Jacob (1974) *Schooling, Experience and Earnings*, New York: National Bureau of Economic Research.

Netherlands Economic Institute (NEI) (2001) Evaluation of the Net Impact of Active Labour Market Programmes in Bulgaria, Rotterdam, Netherlands.

Revenga, A., Riboud, M. and Tan, H. (1994) The Impact of Mexico's Retraining Program on Employment and Wages, *World Bank Economic Review*, 8(2): 247–277.

Rosenbaum, P. and D. Rubin (1983) The Central Role of the Propensity Score in Observational Studies for Causal Effects, *Biometrika*, 70, 41–55.

Rosenbaum, P. and D. Rubin (1984) Reducing Bias in Observational Studies Using Subclassification on the Propensity Score, *Journal of the American Statistical Association*, (79): 516–524.

Rosenbaum, P. and D. Rubin (1985) Constructing a Control Group Using Multivariate Matched Sampling Methods that Incorporate the Propensity, *American Statistician*, 39: 33–38.

Satterthwaite, F.E. (1946) An Approximate Distribution of Estimates of Variance Components, *Biometrics Bulletin*, 2: 110–114.

Spence, Michael A. (1973) Job Market Signaling, *Quarterly Journal of Economics*, 87(3): 355–374.

White, H. (1980) A Heteroskedasticity-Consistent Covariance Matrix Estimator and a Direct Test for Heteroskedasticity, *Econometrica*, 48: 817–830.

## Appendix: Sample means for training: participant and comparison groups

| Variable | Shenyang | | | Wuhan | | |
| --- | --- | --- | --- | --- | --- | --- |
| | Treatment | control | difference | Treatment | control | difference |
| Outcome variable | | | | | | |
| Employed | 0.457 | 0.560 | −0.103*** | 0.447 | 0.410 | 0.037* |
| Control variables | | | | | | |
| Age | 36.76 | 40.05 | −3.29*** | 36.98 | 38.28 | −1.30*** |
| Female | 0.780 | 0.473 | 0.307*** | 0.620 | 0.422 | 0.198*** |
| Disabled | 0.048 | 0.051 | −0.003 | 0.043 | 0.045 | −0.002 |
| Married | 0.834 | 0.888 | −0.054*** | 0.855 | 0.867 | −0.012 |
| Time since becoming xiag. | 4.465 | 4.815 | −0.350*** | 5.741 | 5.057 | 0.684*** |
| Ever visited empl. centre | 0.387 | 0.138 | 0.249*** | 0.440 | 0.291 | 0.149*** |
| Primary education | 0.015 | 0.015 | 0.000 | 0.005 | 0.016 | −0.011** |
| Junior education | 0.443 | 0.662 | −0.219*** | 0.342 | 0.347 | −0.005 |
| Senior education | 0.272 | 0.160 | 0.112*** | 0.455 | 0.421 | 0.034 |
| Vocational education | 0.125 | 0.098 | 0.027** | 0.135 | 0.123 | 0.012 |
| Tertiary education | 0.145 | 0.065 | 0.080*** | 0.064 | 0.093 | −0.029** |
| Industry, low-skilled | 0.100 | 0.036 | 0.064*** | 0.150 | 0.134 | 0.016 |
| Industry, manufacturing | 0.766 | 0.942 | −0.176*** | 0.758 | 0.808 | −0.050** |
| Industry, services | 0.083 | 0.015 | 0.068*** | 0.069 | 0.038 | 0.031*** |
| Industry, pub. adm/education | 0.049 | 0.006 | 0.043*** | 0.023 | 0.019 | 0.004 |
| Occupation, manager | 0.044 | 0.043 | 0.001 | 0.046 | 0.056 | −0.010 |
| Occupation, professional | 0.062 | 0.035 | 0.027*** | 0.031 | 0.027 | 0.004 |
| Occupation, technician | 0.132 | 0.095 | 0.037*** | 0.096 | 0.136 | −0.040*** |
| Occupation, clerk | 0.124 | 0.076 | 0.048*** | 0.138 | 0.117 | 0.021 |
| Occupation, service worker | 0.088 | 0.042 | 0.046*** | 0.067 | 0.051 | 0.016 |

| | | | | | | |
|---|---|---|---|---|---|---|
| Occupation, agric./fishery | 0.000 | 0.000 | 0.000 | 0.003 | 0.008 | −0.005 |
| Occupation, craft worker | 0.185 | 0.263 | −0.078*** | 0.165 | 0.200 | −0.035* |
| Occupation, machine op. | 0.278 | 0.337 | −0.059*** | 0.395 | 0.333 | 0.062** |
| Occupation, unskilled labour | 0.087 | 0.111 | −0.024** | 0.058 | 0.072 | −0.014 |
| Tenure as xiagang (mths) | 134.47 | 165.62 | −31.15*** | 140.48 | 156.22 | −15.74*** |
| Usual earnings, xiagang | 297.99 | 306.64 | −8.65* | 263.04 | 283.94 | −20.90*** |
| Firm type, state enterprise | 0.680 | 0.881 | −0.201*** | 0.876 | 0.966 | −0.090*** |
| Firm type, collective ent. | 0.262 | 0.112 | 0.150*** | 0.116 | 0.032 | 0.084*** |
| Firm-type, private enterprise | 0.024 | 0.003 | 0.021*** | 0.003 | 0.000 | 0.003* |
| Firm-type, joint venture | 0.024 | 0.002 | 0.022*** | 0.003 | 0.002 | 0.001 |
| Firm-type, other | 0.010 | 0.002 | 0.008*** | 0.002 | 0.000 | 0.002 |
| Benefits, medical | 0.380 | 0.446 | −0.066*** | 0.646 | 0.707 | −0.061*** |
| Benefits, pension | 0.398 | 0.423 | −0.025*** | 0.619 | 0.624 | −0.005 |
| Receives unemp. benefits | 0.057 | 0.010 | 0.047*** | 0.089 | 0.034 | 0.055*** |
| Working in July 1998 | 0.365 | 0.557 | −0.192*** | 0.369 | 0.381 | −0.012 |
| House owned by individual | 0.287 | 0.296 | −0.009 | 0.175 | 0.186 | −0.011 |
| House owned by enterprise | 0.102 | 0.163 | −0.061*** | 0.168 | 0.277 | −0.109*** |
| House owned by parents | 0.523 | 0.444 | 0.079*** | 0.418 | 0.357 | 0.061** |
| House owned by other | 0.088 | 0.097 | −0.009 | 0.239 | 0.181 | 0.058*** |
| Household size | 3.201 | 3.184 | 0.017 | 3.351 | 3.286 | 0.065 |
| Number of employed in HH | 0.703 | 0.536 | 0.167*** | 0.495 | 0.486 | 0.009 |
| Children age 6 or older | 0.652 | 0.855 | −0.203*** | 0.732 | 0.736 | −0.004 |
| Children below age 6 | 0.102 | 0.043 | 0.059*** | 0.098 | 0.094 | 0.004 |
| N | 882 | 939 | | 653 | 625 | |

*Notes:* T-tests are one-sided and allow the error variance for treatment and control groups to differ, using the Satterthwaite (1946) correction; *statistically significant at 10%, **statistically significant at 5%, ***statistically significant at 1%.

# 8 Job search with non-participation

*Teng Ge*

## Introduction

In this chapter, we add flow into and out of the labour market to the standard search-and-matching model to endogenize the aggregate labour force flows across different market states. In our framework, workers are heterogeneous with respect to home productivity, which will drive some of them out of the labour market. Furthermore, labour market conditions are stochastic, in that during good times the expected payoff of searching is higher relative to the value of home production, while in bad times the reverse is true. Therefore, agents in this model have to optimize the usage of time among the trade-off between employment, job search and home production. The stochastic nature of the model, with heterogeneous agents, can drive the flow of the labour force in and out of the market, thus generating additional variability of labour force participation and unemployment in the standard model. Qualitatively, we show that these flows into and out of labour markets are increasing in market-dependent state premiums (the capital gains (losses) from the switch of the aggregate state from bad to good (from good to bad); that is, the extra amount of payoffs to the agents whose market status is not changed. Specifically, functions (14) and (15) define its value), like wage payments, net searching income, but decreasing in non-market-dependent state premiums, say home productivity. We also show that, even under the assumption of risk neutral workers prefer persistent participation decisions when the shocks are transient, and flows in and out of the market are smaller than the case of persistent shocks. A quantitatively calibrated model shows that we can increase the standard deviations in variables such as participation, employment and unemployment and generate well-behaved time series to replicate the stylized facts in the labour market. This occurs because in addition to the standard variability of employment and unemployment there is now variability in the size of the market. In the set-up of this chapter, in comparing with the benchmark model calibrated by Shimer (2005), these in and out of market labour force flows account for more than 90 per cent of all variability in unemployment.

The benchmark model of the labour market developed by Mortensen and

Pissarides (1994) studies worker flows between employment and unemployment.[1] Despite its success in many aspects of the labour market, recent research has shown that with a fixed size of labour market, the standard model seriously neglects many major labour force flows in the market. A genuine model that describes the dynamics of the labour market is required so as to explain and understand the following six different flows:[2]

- Flows from employment to unemployment (*E–U* flows), for example quitting jobs or layoffs.
- Flows from unemployment to employment (*U–E* flows), for example successful job matching.
- Flows from unemployment to inactivity (*U–N* flows), for example withdrawal from the labour market.
- Flows from inactivity to unemployment (*N–U* flows), for example first entry or back to the labour market.
- Flows from inactivity to employment (*N–E* flows), for example a very fast job search or return from a short leave.
- Flows from employment to inactivity (*E–N* flows), for example withdrawal from the labour market.

Flows in and out of the labour market are sizeable and systematical, as has been shown in many empirical studies. Blanchard and Diamond (1989, 1990), Fallick and Fleischman (2004) and Jones and Riddell (1999) show that the average flows from non-participation to employment are as large as the flows from unemployment to employment. Furthermore, there are fundamental differences in the cyclical behaviours of these flows through the different phases of business cycles, as can be seen in Figure 8.1.[3] The dashed lines in the upper and lower panels plot rate of unemployment, whilst those in the middle represent the rate of employment. Flows like *E–U*, *U–E* and *N–U* show strong counter-cyclical movements, and flows like *N–E* and *E–N* represent pro-cyclical behaviors and are relatively weak. Pries and Rogerson (2004) emphasized that cross-country differences in labour market participation are often larger than differences in unemployment rate. The same holds true for the cross-demographic groups within a given country. Thus, they argue that non-participation is a necessary element for a precise picture of the labour market.

The labour force participation in the standard model only concerns the static trade-off between market production and home production. The implication of this view is that any factor that will increase returns on home production – e.g. positive shocks to productivity of home production – or any factor that will decrease returns on market production – e.g. lower wage payments, higher searching costs – will lead to lower participation. Although these static trade-offs play an important role in workers' participation decisions, the dynamic considerations also have a significant influence on workers' behaviour. For example, the empirical findings from

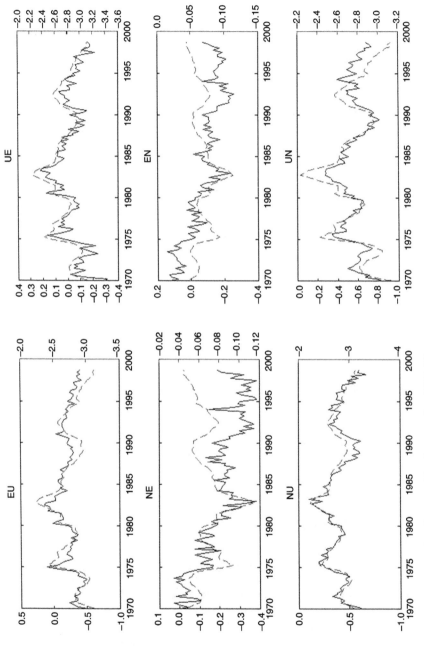

*Figure 8.1* US labour market flows and business cycles, 1970–98.

Abowd and Zellner (1985) and Poterba and Summers (1986) suggest that 'groups which have lower participation rates tend to have larger flows between participation and non-participation'.[4]

The model in this chapter is an extension of Mortensen and Pissirades' standard searching and matching model. We assume that the economy is subject to a series of shocks to firms' vacancy costs. In good times, the cost is low and in bad times it is high. Hence firms close existing vacancies or slow job creation in the down phase of the cycle, and re-open unfilled vacancies or accelerate job creation in up-turns of the cycle. Accordingly, a market boom will heighten job seekers' hazard rates and shorten their searching spells. Given that any active job seeker will bear certain strictly positive searching costs during a job search, only a tight market will be attractive to those who greatly value leisure, as an opportunity cost of participation. The model predicts a pro-cyclical behaviour of labour force flows in and out of the labour market and counter-cyclical flows in the labour market. These predictions meet with most of the empirical findings in Blanchard and Diamond (1989, 1990), Bleakley *et al.* (1999) and Fallick and Fleischman (2004).

## The model

The set-up in this section is an extension of Mortensen and Pissarides' (1999a, 1999b) standard searching and matching model. It follows the same participation principle as in Pissarides (2000) and Garibaldi and Wasmer (2005), and a comparison with these is given in a later section.

### The basic set-up

Time $t$ is infinite and continuous. There is a continuum of workers with a measure normalized to one. Each worker is characterized by his home productivity (value of leisure) $h$ uniformly distributed on $[0,1]$. The worker may be in one of two states: employed or unemployed, where $U_t$ denotes the measure of workers unemployed at time $t$. There is also a continuum of vacancies with measure $V_t$ which will be determined endogenously via a standard free-entry condition.

A matching function characterizes job-worker matching in a frictional labour market. The total number of matches at any point in time is a function of job vacancies $V_t$ and unemployment $U_t$, such as $M(V_t, U_t)$. The matching function is increasing in both arguments, decreasing marginal products to each input and constants return to scale,[5] such that $M(0, U_t) = M(V_t, 0) = 0$ and assumes $M_V(U_t, 0) = \infty$ for $U_t > 0$.

The vacancy–unemployment ratio $\theta_t = \dfrac{V_t}{U_t}$ measures the market tightness at time $t$. Each unemployed worker applying for a vacant job follows a Poisson process, with a rate of $\dfrac{M(V_t, U_t)}{U_t}$. Constant returns to scale in $M(.)$ imply workers apply for vacancies according to a Poisson process with a parameter $f(\theta_t)$, where $f(\theta_t) = M(\theta_t, 1)$ is worker's job-finding rate. Further $f(.)$ is strictly increasing and concave in $\theta$, and $f(0) = 0$, $f'(0) = \infty$. A vacancy contacts the unemployed, according to the same arguments, and also following a Poisson process with a parameter $\dfrac{f(\theta_t)}{\theta_t}$. We denote vacancy's matching probability by $q(\theta_t) = \dfrac{f(\theta_t)}{\theta_t}$.

The economy has two states: good ($G$) and bad ($B$). A firm's vacancy cost is lower in a good state than in a bad state, and it is publicly observed. Each active firm comes to the market with a vacant job and searches for an unemployed worker to fill it. Firms attempt to create vacancies by paying a strictly positive cost, $k_t dt$, where $k_t \in \{k^G, k^B\}$, for each time period $dt$. The market is subject to a series of aggregate shocks that switch vacancy costs. Suppose, further, that the vacancy cost shock is independent and identically distributed (i.i.d.) with an arrival rate of $\pi \in (0,1)$. Hence, the state of the market follows a two-state Markov process.

Labour is the only input. A good market is competitive, and market price is normalized to unity. A filled job generates flow revenue $p > 0$. A firm obtains net profit $(p - w)dt$ per period $dt$. Instead of the benchmark Nash bargaining solution, wage $w$ is a somewhat loosely determined fixed wage.[6] There are job separation shocks; each filled job is destroyed according to an independent Poisson process with parameter $\delta > 0$. Separation shocks terminate current matches, a firm makes no further profit and a worker becomes unemployed. Free entry determines the number of unfilled jobs in equilibrium such that expected payoff to a vacancy equals zero.

For simplicity, all agents are risk-neutral and have the same discount rate $r$. Workers derive linear utility from home production (leisure) and from market activity. At each point in time, the worker is either employed or unemployed. Unemployed workers are free to choose job search or home production (non-participant). Employed individuals are paid $w$ until separation. Unemployed workers gain a payoff; $b - c < w$; $b$ is unemployment insurance benefit and $c$ is searching cost. They meet job offers according to a Poisson process with parameter $f(\theta_t)$. A non-participating worker gains $h \in [0,1]$ only.

## Search equilibrium of the labour market

### Firms' searching problem

Let $J_F^i$ denote the present-discounted value of expected profit from a filled job, and $J_V^i$ the present-discounted value of expected profit from a vacant job, in state $i \in \{G, B\}$. In general, both $J_F^i$ and $J_V^i$ depend on state variable $\theta_t$. The Bellman equation for payoff in equilibrium is as follows:

$$rJ_V^i(\theta_t) = -k^i + q(\theta_t)[J_F^i(\theta_t) - J_V^i(\theta_t)] + \pi[J_V^j(\theta_t) - J_V^i(\theta_t)] \tag{1}$$

Equation (1) dictates that the present-discounted value of expected profit from a vacant job is a sum of three parts: first, the current vacancy cost; second, capital gains from job matching; and third, the capital gains (or loss) from state switching. For the purposes of distinction, we call the payoff gains from matching 'capital gains', and the payoff gains from state switching 'state premium'.

Following a similar principle, we can write down the rest of Bellman equations for a filled job in both a good and bad state, and a vacant job in a bad state:

$$rJ_F^i(\theta_t) = (p - w) - \delta[J_F^i(\theta_t) - J_V^i(\theta_t)] + \pi[J_F^j(\theta_t) - J_F^i(\theta_t)] \tag{2}$$

While the instantaneous cost of a vacant job will be influenced by aggregate shock, the wage and productivity are constant through the cycle. Under free entry $J_V^i = J_V^j = 0$, the payoff to a filled job can be solved from (2):

$$J_F^i = J_F^j = \frac{p - w}{r + s}$$

Then, from (1), the equilibrium job creation conditions, which will underpin market tightness, are given by:

$$q(\theta_t) = \frac{k^i(\delta + r)}{p - w}, \quad \text{where} \quad i \in \{G, B\} \tag{3}$$

As the free entry implies, $\theta_t$ will jump immediately to meet the job creation condition (3), and it is uniquely defined by constants such as $k^G$, $k^B$, $r$ and $s$. Hence, $\theta_t$ is a two-state Markov process that follows (3). Further, since $k^G < k^B$, it is not hard to show that $q(\theta^G) < q(\theta^B)$, which implies at a given level of unemployment firms post more vacancies in good times than in bad times. We have the following proposition.

**Proposition 1** *Market tightness is a Markov process, and in each state, it is uniquely defined by job creation condition. More vacancies will be created in good times when the vacancy cost is low than in bad times when the cost is high. For each particular state of the economy, vacancy rate increases in the firm's net payoffs $p - w$, and decreases in separation rate $s$ and discount rate $r$.*

### Workers' searching problem

Similarly, workers' searching payoffs are given by recursive Bellman equations. An employed worker's payoff is denoted by $W^i(h)$ if she is payed at $w$, her value of leisure is $h$, and state is $i$; and $Z^i(h)$ denotes the payoff to the same worker when she is unemployed. Hence, an employed worker's payoff in state $i$ is defined by:

$$rW^i(h) = w + \delta[Z^i(h) - W^i(h)] + \pi[W^j(h) - W^i(h)] \quad \text{where } i \neq j \in \{G, B\}$$

After a separation shock $\delta$, the worker becomes unemployed and is free to choose her job search decision $s \in \{0,1\}$ so as to maximize her payoff set down as the following:

$$rZ^i(h) = \begin{cases} (b-c) + f(\theta^i)[W^i(h) - Z^i(h)] + \pi[Z^j(h) - Z^i(h)] & \text{if } s = 1; \\ h + \pi[Z^j(h) - Z^i(h)] & \text{if } s = 0 \end{cases} \quad (4)$$

Unemployed workers choose to search ($s = 1$) or not ($s = 0$). A searching unemployed person enjoys unemployment benefits $b$, incurring searching cost $c$, and forgoing home production $h$. Accordingly, the worker's optimal searching strategy implies there exists a $\overline{h^i} = (b - c) + f(\theta^i)[W^i(h) - Z^i(h)]$ such that workers will choose $s = 1$ if, and only if, $h \leq \overline{h^i}$. More specifically we have the following hypothesis.

**Hypothesis 1** *With a given distribution of home productivity, there exists $\overline{h^B}$ and $\overline{h^G}$, such that $\overline{h^B} < \overline{h^G}$. An unemployed worker's optimal searching strategy satisfies the following:*

- Strategy 1 – search in both states if $h \leq \overline{h^B}$.
- Strategy 2 – search only in good state if $\overline{h^B} < h \leq \overline{h^G}$.
- Strategy 3 – never search if $h > \overline{h^G}$.

The following steps are necessary to prove a candidate strategy we presume is optimal: first, we need to solve the model for $\overline{h^B}$ and $\overline{h^G}$. Then, with these two critical thresholds and value functions for each candidate strategy, to show that it cannot be improved upon. With sufficient conditions for dynamic optimality, we can conclude that candidate strategies in hypothesis are optimal.

In order to solve the model, we need to define these payoffs to each strategy conditional on the state of the economy:

- Strategy 1 (*search, search*)

$$rW_1^G = w - \delta(W_1^G - Z_1^G) - \pi(W_1^G - W_1^B) \quad (5)$$

$$rZ_1^G = b - c + f(\theta^G)(W_1^G - Z_1^G) - \pi(Z_1^G - Z_1^B) \quad (6)$$

$$rW_1^B = w - \delta(W_1^B - Z_1^B) - \pi(W_1^B - W_1^G) \quad (7)$$

$$rZ_1^B = b - c + f(\theta^B)(W_1^B - Z_1^B) - \pi(Z_1^B - Z_1^G) \quad (8)$$

- Strategy 2 (*search, quit*)

$$rW_2^G = w - \delta(W_2^G - Z_2^G) - \pi(W_2^G - W_2^B) \tag{9}$$

$$rZ_2^G = b - c + f(\theta^G)(W_2^G - Z_2^G) - \pi(Z_2^G - H_2^B) \tag{10}$$

$$rW_2^B = w - \delta(W_2^B - H_2^B) - \pi(W_2^B - W_2^G) \tag{11}$$

$$rH_2^B = h_2 + \pi(Z_2^G - H_2^B) \tag{12}$$

- Strategy 3 (*quit, quit*)

$$H_3 = \frac{h_3}{r} \tag{13}$$

where $H_i$ denotes the payoff to home production, since we want to explicitly differentiate the states of searching unemployment and home production.

Notice that if we subtract (7) from (5) we get the expression of the state premium for an employed worker:

$$W_1^G - W_1^B = \frac{\delta[(W_1^B - Z_1^B) - (W_1^G - Z_1^G)]}{r + 2\pi} \tag{14}$$

Equation (14) states that the state premium of an employed worker is a proportion of the capital gains from job separation in two states. Similarly, the state premium of an unemployed worker can be found by subtracting (8) from (6):

$$Z_1^G - Z_1^B = \frac{f(\theta^G)}{r + 2\pi}(W_1^G - Z_1^G) - \frac{f(\theta^B)}{r + 2\pi}(W_1^B - Z_1^B) \tag{15}$$

Let $\Psi_1 = W_1^G - W_1^B$ and $\Phi_1 = Z_1^G - Z_1^B$, and lemma 1 shows that these two state premiums are both positive constants.

**Lemma 1** *Given the job creation condition by (3), the value of the state premium by choosing strategy one defined in (14) and (15) is positive constant, and uniquely defined in steady-state.*

*Proof.* See Appendix.

Further, to simplify equations (5) to (8) and solve the payoffs of each labour market state:

$$W_1^G = \frac{w[r + f(\theta^G)] + (b - c)\delta - [\pi\Psi_1(r + f(\theta^G)) + \pi s\Phi_1]}{r[r + \delta + f(\theta^G)]}$$

$$Z_1^G = \frac{wf(\theta^G) + (b-c)(\delta+r) - [\pi\Psi_1 f(\theta^G) + \pi\Phi_1(s+r)]}{r[r+\delta+f(\theta^G)]}$$

$$W_1^B = \frac{w[r+f(\theta^B)] + (b-c)\delta + [\pi\Psi_1(r+f(\theta^B)) + \pi s\Phi_1]}{r[r+\delta+f(\theta^B)]} \qquad (16)$$

$$Z_1^B = \frac{wf(\theta^B) + (b-c)(\delta+r) + [\pi\Psi_1 f(\theta^B) + \pi\Phi_1(s+r)]}{r[r+\delta+f(\theta^B)]}$$

A similar principle is also applicable to the workers who choose strategy 2. Through several steps of algebra, we have:

$$W_2^G - W_2^B = \frac{s[(W_2^B - H_2^B) - (W_2^G - Z_2^G)]}{r+2\pi} \qquad (17)$$

$$Z_2^G - H_2^B = \frac{(b-c) - h_2 + f(\theta^G)(W_2^G - Z_2^G)}{r+2\pi} \qquad (18)$$

Notice that the state premiums incurred by choosing strategy 2 are agent-dependent because the agent's outside option $H_2^B$ is increasing the agent's non-market productivity $h_2$. However, since for each agent his value of home production is a constant, his state premiums of $W_2^G - W_2^B$, and $Z_2^G - H_2^B$ are constant. Let us denote these vales $\Psi_2 = W_2^G - W_2^B$ and $Y_2 = Z_2^G - H_2^B$ and solve equations (9) to (12):

$$W_2^G = \frac{w[r+f(\theta^G)] + (b-c)\delta - [\pi\Psi_2(r+f(\theta^G)) + \pi s Y_2]}{r[r+s+f(\theta^G)]}$$

$$Z_2^G = \frac{wf(\theta^G) + (b-c)(s+r) - [\pi\Psi_2 f(\theta^G) + \pi Y_2(s+r)]}{r[r+s+f(\theta^G)]}$$

$$W_2^B = \frac{wr + h_2\delta + [\pi\Psi_2 r + \pi\delta Y_2]}{r(r+s)} \qquad (19)$$

$$H_2^B = \frac{h_2 + \pi Y_2}{r}$$

From the above group of equations, we have the following lemma characterizing the properties of these value functions.

**Lemma 2** *The value functions $W_2^G$, $Z_2^G$, $W_2^B$, and $H_2^B$ are monotonically increasing in $h_2$; $H_2^B$ is increasing faster. There exist unique cutoff points between $H_2^B$ and the other three.*

The proof of lemma 2 can be ascertained from Garibaldi and Wasmer (2005: Appendix). Lemma 2 implies that there is a trade-off between choosing strategies 1, 2 or 3. For some groups of workers, as their non-market productivity is low, payoffs from strategy 2 are lower than from strategy 1; for others, with a higher level of $h$, their optimal strategy is to adopt strategy 2. The rest of the workers, with extremely high levels of $h$, never participate in the market, hence they choose strategy 3. In equilibrium, there must be two cutoff agents who are indifferent between choosing between strategies 1 or 2, and choose strategy 2 or 3. Since the agents who choose strategy 2 will stop searching and quit the market in bad times, these two workers at the participation margin hence pin down the equilibrium rate of participation in bad state and good states. Additionally, combined with lemma 1, the marginal worker only participates in good times; his home production value must be no lower than the worker who is indifferent between searching and quitting in bad times, since the the state premium is non-negative.

To solve the model by setting $N_2^B = Z_1^B$ for the lower bound of the participation margin, $\overline{h^B}$, and $H_3 = Z_2^G$ for the upper bound, $\overline{h^G}$, respectively:

$$\overline{h^B} = \frac{wf(\theta^B) + (b - c)(\delta + r) + f(\theta^B)\pi\Psi_1 + \pi\Phi_1 (\delta + r)}{\delta + r + f(\theta^B)} - \pi Y_2 \tag{20}$$

$$\overline{h^G} = \frac{wf(\theta^G) + (b - c)(\delta + r) - [\pi\Psi_2 f(\theta^G) + \pi Y_2 (\delta + r)]}{\delta + r + f(\theta^G)} \tag{21}$$

By solving the participation margin $[\overline{h^B}, \overline{h^G}]$ one can characterize the size of different types of workers. $[0, \overline{h^B}]$ are active job-seekers, $[\overline{h^B}, \overline{h^G}]$ are marginal attached workers and $[\overline{h^G}, 1]$ are discouraged workers.

Equations (20) and (21) imply that the size of the labour force is increasing in wage $w$, net searching income ($z - c$); but other parameters have opposite effects on active job-seekers and marginal attached workers. First, $\overline{h^B}$ is increasing in $\Psi_1$, $\Phi_1$ but decreasing in $Y_2$ and $\overline{h^G}$ is decreasing in $Y_2$, $\Psi_2$. This result implies that the participation rate is decreasing with home productivity. From (14) and (15), $\Psi_1$ and $\Phi_1$ are independent of home productivity $h$; they stand for pure premium from market income. However, from (17) and (18) and lemma 2, both $\Psi_2$ and $Y_2$ are increasing the value of home production. The higher $\Psi_2$ and $Y_2$ represent a higher opportunity cost of participation, and hence a lower participation rate. Second, $h^B$ is increasing with $\pi$ but $\overline{h^G}$ is decreasing with $\pi$.[7] Our result implies that as $\pi$ increases, the state of the market will be switching back and forth frequently. In this case, more workers at the lower margin will adopt strategy 1 and less will choose strategy 2; and more workers at the higher margin will adopt strategy 3 over strategy 2. On the one hand, transitory shocks increase the number of active job-seekers, who are more willing to labour; on the other hand, they also increase the number of workers who quit the market permanently but who are willing to look for a job during economic booms – even the workers are risk neutral. A summary of workers' labour supply behaviour is shown in proposition 2.

**Proposition 2** *The equilibrium rate of participation in the labour force is increasing market wage* w, *net searching income* b − c, *and market dependent state premium* $\Psi_1$ *and* $\Phi_1$; *it is decreasing in the non-market production state premium* $\Psi_2$ *and* $Y_2$. *The number of marginal attached workers is increasing in the persistency of shock,* $\pi$, *but the active job-seekers are decreasing in* $\pi$.

Finally, we shall prove that, in relation to the above solution, given workers' home production *l*, the strategy we proposed in the above hypothesis cannot be improved upon by one-step deviation.

**Lemma 3** *The strategies proposed in hypothesis 1 cannot be improved upon.*

*Proof.* See Appendix.

Sufficient conditions for an optimal strategy in a dynamic programming problem (see Kreps 1990) require, first, that a candidate strategy cannot be improved upon; and second, that the flow of payoffs is bounded below. The following proposal concludes our proof.

**Proposition 3** *Strategies in hypothesis 1 are optimal.*

*Proof.* The first condition has been approved in lemma 3, and the second is oblviously met given $b - c > 0$, and $h \in [0,1]$. Hence we have proved that searching strategies in hypothesis are optimal.

Q.E.D

## Labour market flows

The search equilibrium of the labour market described in the last section pins down the equilibrium rate of participation in good times and in bad times: $\overline{h^G}$ and $\overline{h^B}$, respectively. We show that those flows into and out of the market, located in the range $(h^B, h^G)$, are marginally attached to the market. These flows are an equilibrium phenomena of the labour market since they reflect an optimum of switching between market production and home production for those who rationally choose strategy 2. We can thus transcribe the changes in unemployment with the following equation:

$$\dot{u}_t = (1 - u_t)\,\delta - u_t f(\theta_t) + n_t \tag{22}$$

where $n_t$ notes the effective factor of labour flows in and out of the labour market. It is a proportion of the marginally attached workers across the market, and may be either positive (flows in), negative (flows out), or zero (constant), depending on the nature of the state. Specifically, it is calculated as below:

$$n_t = \begin{cases} -(1 - u_t^M)_S + u_t^M & \text{if state switchs from good to bad} \\ -(\overline{h_t} - h^B)_S & \text{if state is bad and } h_t > \overline{h^B} \\ \overline{h^G} - h_t & \text{if state switchs from bad to good} \\ 0 & \text{otherwise} \end{cases} \tag{23}$$

where $u_t^M$ is the unemployment rate of marginal attached workers, which equals $u^G$ in steady state since active job-seekers and marginal attached workers are equally likely to be unemployed; $h_t \in [\overline{h^B}, \overline{h^G}]$ is thus a transition participation rate.

Given a current state, a steady state is achieved when inflows to equal outflows from unemployment, for example $\dot{u}_t = 0$. Hence a conditional steady-state unemployment rate is:

$$u^G = \frac{\delta}{\delta + f(\theta^G)} \qquad u^B = \frac{\delta}{\delta + f(\theta^B)} \tag{24}$$

Equations (20), (21) and (24) characterize two conditional steady-state equilibriums of the market when it is in a good and a bad state. Obviously, we have $u^G < u^B$.

The out of (conditional) steady-state adjustments of market tightness, unemployment rate and vacancy rate are shown in Figure 8.2. Suppose the initial condition of the economy is point *A*. $BC^B$ and $JC^B$ represent the Beveridge curve and job creation condition in a bad state. A favourable shock shifts the state from bad to good, and forward-thinking firms will adjust their vacancies. Since investment in opening of new vacancies is less

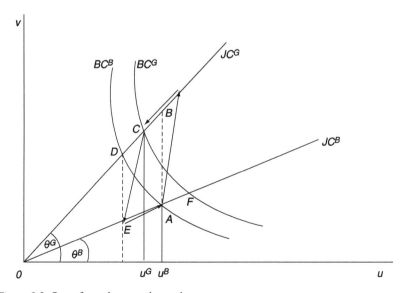

*Figure 8.2* Out of steady-state dynamics.

costly in good times, and current unemployment is high, it is relatively profitable for firms to open new vacancies and recruit employees. This implies that there will be a jump in the job vacancy rate and hence in market tightness $\theta$. In the meantime, it induces inflows of new entrants into the market. Such an increase in the aggregate size of the labour market shifts the Beveridge curve to $BC^G$, and the economy jumps to point B, which is a combination of a higher rate of vacancies and a higher rate of unemployment. After the participation rate jumps to its new equilibrium rate and the unemployment starts to converge with the conditional steady state, the adjustment will follow the $JC^G$ from point $B$ to point $C$. During this process, unemployment is decreasing, together with the matching probability for a new vacancy. Firms find it less easy to recruit, while holding market tightness constant, and they then start to close vacancies. As long as the vacancy rate is still above its steady-state level, unemployment will continue to decrease. At point $C$, the intersection of $BC^G$ and $JC^G$, both job vacancies and unemployment adjust to their new steady-state level. To summarize, when the labour market shifts from a bad to a good state, participation rates and job vacancies jump to their steady-state level; job vacancies will then overshoot the steady-state level and gradually converge. Unemployment initially increases, then decreases until it reaches the steady-state level; unemployment and job vacancy rates are characterized by a counter-clockwise loop to redistribute the labour force.

By a similar logic, a negative shock rotates the job creation curve from $JC^G$ to $JC^B$, and the economy jumps from point $C$ to point $E$ – an overshoot of the job vacancy rate. However, the unemployment rate will gradually increase to its new steady-state level by converging from the left. Further outflows from the labour force will continue until it shrinks to its steady-state level $\overline{h^B}$; during this process, the Beveridge curve keeps on moving towards the origin. Further adjustment will not rotate the curve of the job creation condition; the economy moves to its steady state on the saddle path from $E$ to $A$. In this process, the job vacancy rate first overshoots its steady-state level, while adjustments of the unemployment and job vacancy rates are not monotonic, and the relationship between job vacancy rate and unemployment shows a counter-clockwise loop.

Furthermore, this model could be employed to analyse the business cycle behaviour of an economy by introducing a series of shocks. The dynamics of business cycle analysis are similar to those discussed in the previous section. The adjustment path shown in Figure 8.3, considers a simple case whereby the economy is hit by a favourable shock followed by a negative shock. The unemployment rate, following the same economics, adjusts by first diverging during the period of shock, and then gradually converging. The same principle applies to the job vacancy rate, as depicted in Figure 8.3. Based on equations (22) and (23), our analytical discussions of dynamic adjustment in labour market provides an intuitive explanation of the market flows and cyclical behaviour of the labour market.

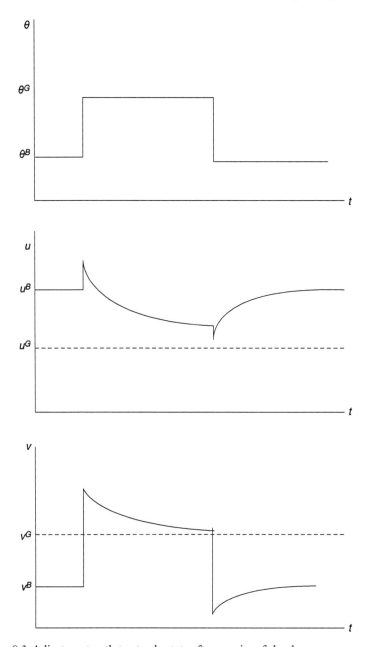

*Figure 8.3* Adjustment path to steady state after a series of shocks.

## A numerical exercise

The preceding sections provide analytical descriptions of the steady-state equilibrium and out of steady-state dynamics of labour market flows. These arguments are intuitive. To test the model's quantitative performance, we need to calibrate the model. In this section, we shall run a numerical experiment to compare the model's performance with the actual US data.

### *Simulation exercise*

The calibration exercise takes three steps. The first is to pin down the value of steady-state equilibrium characterized by $\overline{h}^G$, $\overline{h}^B$, $u^G$ and $u^B$. The second is to simulate a series of random market state variables: unemployment rate, employment rate and participation rate. The last step is to compare the time series properties of these artificial series with actual data.

We start by specifying parameter values and the functional form of matching functions. For simplicity, but without losing generality, we assume that the matching function is Cobb–Douglas,

$$f(\theta) = \theta q(\theta) = \mu \theta^{1/2} \tag{25}$$

where $\mu$ is the matching efficiency. The separation rate is equal to 0.04 for a quarterly level, which is the same as in Shimer (2005). Discount rate is set to be 0.012, the quarterly rate equivalent to an annual discount factor of 0.953. Unemployment insurance equals 0.4. According to Shimer, it lies below the upper-end of the income replacement rate range in the US, if interpreted entirely as an unemployment benefit. The vacancy cost is set to be 7.2 in good times and 10.8 for bad times.[8] All other parameters are left to be calibrated in the model, since they are unobservable in a real economy. Table 8.1 provides all the parameter values employed in the calibration and simulation exercises.

The first step was to determine the value of market tightness. We collected the data for the unemployment rate and vacancies from BLS (Bureau of Labor Statistics). The sample covers December 2000 to February 2006,[9] and

*Table 8.1* Calibrated values of parameter

| Parameter | Good state | Bad state |
|---|---|---|
| Discount rate $r$ | 0.012 | 0.012 |
| Separation rate $s$ | 0.04 | 0.04 |
| Unemployment insurance $z$ | 0.5 | 0.5 |
| Matching technology | $0.6\,\theta^{1/2}$ | $0.6\,\theta^{1/2}$ |
| Vacancy cost $k$ | 7.2 | 10.8 |
| Searching cost $c$ | 0.1 | 0.1 |
| Wage $w$ | 0.56 | 0.56 |

the mean value of the vacancy unemployment ratio is about 0.46. Next, we calculated the artificial value of market tightness with different values of shocks. By solving the free entry, one can pin down the value of market tightness. We picked the value of parameters, including the value of shocks, vacancy costs and wages, which gave the best estimation of the mean value of market tightness. We employed the simulated method of moments model, following the structural model – see the Appendix. The model generates a mean value of market tightness at 0.46, which minimized the distance from the empirical level. Following equation (24), the model gives equilibrium rates of unemployment for a good state and a bad state at 0.069 and 0.107, respectively. With these known parameter values, one can solve the extensive margin, which represents the locations of two marginal workers. Using a similar simulation method, we find that the payoffs for each state correspond to all searching strategies. The model generates the equilibrium participation rates for good and bad times as 0.552 and 0.515, respectively.

In the second step, we generated time series of unemployment, employment and participation. These series are given by a random series of aggregate states, according to the functions of equations (22) to (23), and we can locate those of unemployment and employment rates. We repeated this process 2,880 times to replicate 20 different samples, and then picked the sample which gave the best estimation of average unemployment.

The business cycle simulation result is depicted in Figure 8.4. The first panel of the first column is the index of state; '1' represents the good state and '2' the bad. The second panel is the adjustment path of the unemployment rate of active searching workers. As predicted in our theory, the unemployment rate of active searching workers is higher in bad times than in good times. The third panel represents the adjustment path of the participation rate; in good times it is high, and in bad times it is low. However, the adjustment to the steady-state level is not monotonic, as can be seen. There is initially a sharp decrease, followed by a gradual convergence to the new steady state, because the number of unmatched marginal attached workers shrinks if a negative shock is persistent.

The adjustment path of marginal attached workers is depicted in the first panel of the second column of Figure 8.4. The simulation result shows that in bad times, the unemployment rate of marginal attached workers is zero; while, as the state switches from bad to good, the unemployment rate first starts to increase sharply in response to a favourable shock, than gradually converges to its steady state. The second panel of the second column describes the adjustment of aggregate unemployment rate. Overshooting the aggregate unemployment rate is also captured in the figure as both periods show change. Correspondingly, the cyclical behaviour of the employment rate is described in the last panel of the second column. One can see the overshootings in this figure, too. Notice that the similarity in the adjustment path of the unemployment rate in Figures 8.5 and 8.4 offers evidence of the solid approximation of our model.

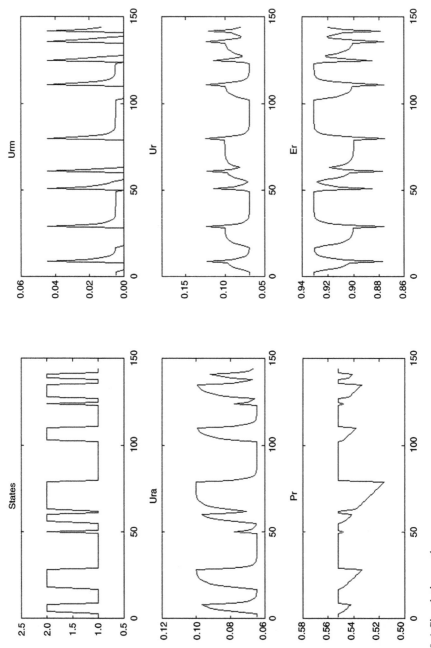

*Figure 8.4* Simulation path.

Furthermore, we can also generate the time series of six labour force flows from the model, and compare their cyclical behaviours with actual time series.[10] They are plotted in Figure 8.5. We can see that the model's prediction about labour force flows meets most of the facts from the actual data. In comparison with Figure 8.1, our simulation generates four out of six flows which are consistent with their corresponding empirical movements. The only counter-factual flows are $E$–$U$ flows and $N$–$U$ flows. In Figure 8.1, the actual data shows that these two are counter cyclical flows; however, in our model they are pro-cyclical. A pro-cyclical $E$–$U$ flow comes from a constant separation rate; throughout the cycles aggregate employment is pro-cyclical, hence the $E$–$U$ flow. However, the counter-factual feature of the $N$–$U$ flow in this model is unexplained.

We also wanted to know the descriptive statistic characteristics of this model. Hence we compared the corresponding first and second moments of the rates of employment, participation and unemployment. Results are given in Table 8.2. The first part represents the corresponding statistics from artificial data generated by the model, whilst the second part represents the actual data from CPS. Compared with the actual data, the quantitative performance of the model is good. We measured the volatility of the time series by their standard deviations. From Table 8.2, it is clear that the model generates very close standard deviations in terms of the rate of unemployment and employment, but it over-estimates the volatility of the participation rate. The model predicts that the most volatile variable is unemployment rate, followed by employment, whereas participation is the most stable of these three indicators; this prediction is consistent with the observations from actual data. However, the model under-estimated persistency, as measured by auto-correlation (AC), both in unemployment and employment; it matched persistency in participation rate very well. The model predicts a positive correlation between the rate of employment and participation, negative correlations between rates of unemployment with participation and employment, which is consistent with the actual data.

In comparison to Shimer's (2005) calibration, the model solves the problem inherited from the benchmark model. Shimer argued that the equilibrium rate of unemployment generated in Mortensen and Pissarides' model explains only about 10 per cent of the response in the vacancy–unemployment ratio, and only 5 per cent in unemployment rate.[11] However, in this chapter it has been found that extending the standard model with the third state, labour force, could reasonably improve performance of the searching and matching model. The volatility predicted in this chapter addresses almost every criticism from actual data, with certain sacrifices in persistency.

Veracierto (2004) tested the performance of the real business cycle (RBC) model with home production. The author replaced the single state of non-employment in the standard RBC model by search and non-participation, and found that the RBC model generates highly counterfactual labour market dynamics, such as unemployment being weakly pro-cyclical, and participation

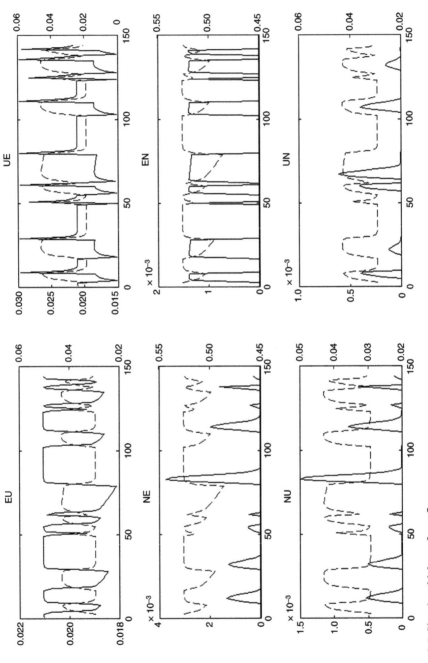

*Figure 8.5* Simulated labour force flows.

*Table 8.2* Statistics of simulated time series with 144 observers

|  | P | E | U |
|---|---|---|---|
| Statistics of simulated time series with 144 observers | | | |
| MEAN | 0.546 | 0.915 | 0.085 |
| ST DEV | 0.010 | 0.013 | 0.133 |
| AC(1) | 0.70 | 0.57 | 0.66 |
| AC(2) | 0.44 | 0.26 | 0.34 |
| Cross-correlation | | | |
| P | 1 | 0.227 | −0.279 |
| E | 0.227 | 1 | −0.98 |
| U | −0.279 | −0.98 | 1 |
| Summary of of US labour market, 1970 Q1 to 2005 Q4 | | | |
| MEAN | 0.647 | 0.938 | 0.062 |
| ST DEV | 0.003 | 0.008 | 0.11 |
| AC(1) | 0.70 | 0.90 | 0.90 |
| AC(2) | 0.46 | 0.70 | 0.70 |
| Cross-correlation | | | |
| P | 1 | 0.58 | −0.60 |
| E | 0.58 | 1 | −0.98 |
| U | −0.60 | −0.98 | 1 |

being more volatile than employment. However, we have seen that these problems can be solved by introducing the non-participation state into the matching model with the explicit searching cost.

In particular, there are two issues that need to be pointed out. The first is that the rates of unemployment and participation adjust in opposite directions. If the in and out of market flows dominate the inner market flow, we observe a pro-cyclical movement of unemployment. Therefore, this requires cross-market adjustment, or the number of marginal attached workers cannot be greater than unemployment in the bad state.

Second, the aggregate shock in this model could only generate flows in one direction. However, we observe from the real world that these flows may happen in both directions. We believe this is because the economy is experiencing multiple shocks. For example, if the economy in this chapter experienced two shocks – one in investment cost, increased from low to high, and the other a preferences shock related to individuals' domestic productivity – then we could observe labour force flows in both directions.

## Conclusion

In this chapter, we build a searching and matching model with heterogeneous workers. Workers are assumed to be free to adjust their participation decisions, facing a trade-off between market production and home production. We modeled workers' optimal searching strategies and characterized equilibrium in the labour market and steady-state unemployment and participation. Comparative statistical analysis with equilibrium solutions argue that greater worker participation in the market can be obtained with the higher wage, net searching income, and market dependent state premiums. However, workers' domestic productivity will genuinely discourage worker participation as it stands for the opportunity cost of searching. The comparative dynamic analysis describes cyclical behaviours of market flows. Qualitatively, the model's predictions are consistent with empirical findings.

Numerically, we calibrated the model, simulated its business cycle behaviours and generated six labour force flows across these cycles. We find the adjustment paths of the participation rate, unemployment rate and employment rate, and find that they are consistent with our analytical predictions. Descriptive statistics argue that, by comparing relative moments of time series properties generated by the model with the actual data from CPS, together with the additional market state and domestic production, the extended model genuinely avoids the problem of lack of unemployment volatility in the benchmark searching and matching model, and counter-factual cyclical facts of market indicators in the RBC model.

## Notes

1 See also Mortensen and Pissarides (1999a, 1999b) and Pissarides (2000).
2 According to the conventional definition of labour market states, for example CPS (2001), there are six flows across different market states (see Figure 8.1). For convenience of analysis, I omitted the job search, or $E$–$E$, flows in this chapter; the effect on cross-market flows is trivial.
3 This data was constructed by Bleakley *et al.* (1999) based on CPS. For additional details, please see this text.
4 Quoted from Pries and Rogerson (2004).
5 For empirical evidences on properties of the matching function, see Blanchard and Diamond (1989) and Pissarides (2000).
6 Because of the adverse selection in workers' type, a wage determined by a Nash bargaining solution becomes problematic, and can become even more complex in out-of-equilibrium cases. Wage is assumed to be determined by the Nash demand game, or auction. It adopted Hall's (2005a) 'metaphor'. Employer and worker simultaneously make an offer. If the worker's offer $w_W$ is no greater than the employer's offer $w_E$, the match is made and the contracted wage is agreed at $w = \gamma w_W + (1 - \gamma)w_E$, where $\gamma$ is represented by the worker's bargaining power. In equilibrium, the wage must be such that $w = w_W = w_E$. Given that there is no productivity shock to filled jobs, as far as both sides of the matching are 'happy' with the current wage, they do not renegotiate over the splitting rule. Hence, $w$ is a constant? For details on this Nash demand wage, see Hall (2005a) and Muthoo (1999).
7 In equation (20), the last term shows a decreasing relation in $\pi$, since we imposed

the condition $Z_1^B = H_2^B$ for this particular worker at the lower bound of the participation margin to pin down the value of $h^B$. By assuming that workers will take strategy 1 over strategy 2 in cases of indifference, then $Y_2 = 0$ and $h^B$ is strictly increasing in $\pi$.

8  This number is larger than other authors' estimations. However, these values are only used to pin down the participation rates and hence will not fundamentally influence the whole system's quantitative behaviour.

9  We only obtained the data for vacancy rates for 2000 onwards.

10  Notice that we missed the $N–E$ flow in our continuous model. However, we can conveniently 'create' this flow in a discrete version. A solution to our model in a discrete version can be supplied on request.

11  Hagedorn and Manovskii (2005) claim that Shimer's calibration failed to fully incorporate the opportunity cost of work. But their work has been proved to be true only in very extreme cases in which workers receive only 3 per cent profit from their work compared with large profits from home production. Mortensen and Nagypal (2005) claim that, even with investment cost and on the job search, however, Shimer's finding is still a robust consequence of the standard model.

# References

Abowd, John and Arnold Zellner (1985) Estimating gross labor force flows, *Journal of Business and Economic Statistics*, 3: 254–283.

Blanchard, Oliver and Peter Diamond (1989) The Beveridge curve, *Brookings Paper on Economic Activity*, 1: 1–76.

Blanchard, Olivier and Peter Diamond (1990) The cyclical behavior of the gross flows of US workers, *Brookings Paper on Economic Activity*, 1: 85–155.

Bleakley, Hoyt, Ann E. Ferris and Jeffrey C. Fuhrer (1999) New data on worker flows during business cycles, *New England Economic Review*, July/Agust: 49–76.

Fallick, Bruce and Charles A. Fleischman (2004) Employer-to-employer flows in the US labour market: the complete picture of gross worker flows, Working Paper, Board of Governors of the Federal Reserve System.

Garibaldi, Pietro and Etienne Wasmer (2005) Equilibrium employment in a model of an imperfect labour market, *Journal of the European Economic Association*, 3(4): 851–882.

Hagedorn, Marcus and Iourii Manovskii (2005) The cyclical behaviour of equilibrium unemployment and vacancies revisited, Working Paper.

Hall, Robert (2005a) Employment fluctuations with equilibrium wage stickiness, *American Economic Review*, 95: 50–65.

Jones, Stephen and Craig Riddel (1999) The measurement of unemployment: an empirical approach, *Econometrica*, 67(1): 147–162.

Kreps, David M. (1990) *A Course in Microeconmic Theory*, Englewood Cliffs, NJ: Prentice Hall.

Mortensen, Dale and Eva Nagypal (2007) More on unemployment and vacancy fluctuations, *Review of Economic Dynamics*, 10(3): 327–347.

Mortensen, Dale and Christopher Pissarides (1994) Job creation and job destruction in the theory of unemployment, *Review of Economic Studies*, 61(2): 397–415.

Mortensen, Dale and Christopher Pissarides (1999a) Job reallocation, employment fluctuations and unemployment, Chapter 18 in John B. Taylor and Michael Woodford (eds), *Handbook of Macroeconomics, Vol. 1B*, Amsterdam: North-Holland, pp. 1171–1228.

Mortensen, Dale and Christopher Pissarides (1999b) New developments in models of search in the labour market, Chapter 39 in Orley Ashenfelter and David Card (eds), *Handbook of Labour Economics, Vol.* 3B, Amsterdam: North-Holland.

Muthoo, Abhinay (1999) *Bargaining Theory with Applications*, Cambridge: Cambridge University Press.

Pissarides, Christopher. A. (2000) *Equilibrium Unemployment Theory*, second edition, Cambridge, MA: MIT Press.

Poterba, James and Lawrence H. Summers (1986) Reporting errors and labor market dynamics, *Econometrica*, 54: 1319–1338.

Pries, Michael and Richard Rogerson (2004) Search frictions and labour market participation, Working Paper.

Shimer, Robert (2005) The cyclical behaviour of equilibrium unemployment and vacancies, *American Economic Review*, 95(1): 25–49.

Veracierto, Marcelo (2004) On the cyclical behavior of employment, unemployment, and labour force participation, Federal Reserve Bank of Chicago Working Paper.

## Appendix

### *Proof of lemma 1*

Subtracting equation (5) from (6), and (8) from (7) results in:

$$W_1^G - Z_1^G = \frac{w - (b - c)}{r + f(\theta^G) + s + \pi} + \frac{\pi}{r + f(\theta^G) + \delta + \pi}(W_1^B - Z_1^B)$$

$$W_1^B - Z_1^B = \frac{w - (b - c)}{r + f(\theta^B) + s + \pi} + \frac{\pi}{r + f(\theta^B) + \delta + \pi}(W_1^G - Z_1^G) \qquad (26)$$

then we compare the difference between:

$$(W_1^G - Z_1^G) - (W_1^B - Z_1^B) = \frac{w - (b - c)}{r + f(\theta^G) + s + \pi} + \frac{\pi}{r + f(\theta^G) + \delta + \pi}(W_1^B - Z_1^B)$$

$$- \frac{w - (b - c)}{r + f(\theta^B) + \delta + \pi} - \frac{\pi}{r + f(\theta^B) + \delta + \pi}(W_1^G - Z_1^G)$$

$$(27)$$

From (3) we know that $f(\theta^G) > f(\theta^B)$, and if $(W_1^G - Z_1^G) > (W_1^B - Z_1^B)$ the left-hand side of (27) is positive. However, the right-hand side of the equation is negative, since the sign of the following expression follows:

$$\underbrace{\frac{w - (b - c)}{r + f(\theta^G) + s + \pi} - \frac{w - (b - c)}{r + f(\theta^B) + \delta + \pi}}_{-}$$

$$+ \frac{\pi}{r + f(\theta^G) + \delta + \pi}(W_1^B - Z_1^B) - \frac{\pi}{r + f(\theta^B) + \delta + \pi}(W_1^G - Z_1^G) \qquad (28)$$

$$\underbrace{\hphantom{+ \frac{\pi}{r + f(\theta^G) + \delta + \pi}(W_1^B - Z_1^B) - \frac{\pi}{r + f(\theta^B) + \delta + \pi}(W_1^G - Z_1^G)}}_{-}$$

given that $w > z - c$. It is contradictory. Similarly, one can prove that the equality does not hold here either. Hence it must be the case that $(W_1^G - Z_1^G) < (W_1^B - Z_1^B)$. Therefore, from (14) $\Psi_1 = W_1^G - W_1^B > 0$. Therefore it is not hard to prove that:

$$(W_1^G - Z_1^G) - (W_1^B - Z_1^B) < 0 \Rightarrow 0 < W_1^G - W_1^B < Z_1^G - Z_1^B$$

Hence we have proved that $\Psi_1 > 0$ and $\Phi_1 > 0$.

The second part of the lemma can be proved by a contraction mapping theorem. The preceding argument also proved the property of monotonicity of $[(W_1^G - Z_1^G) - (W_1^B - Z_1^B)]$. Since $\dfrac{\pi}{r + f(\theta^G) + s + \pi} < 1$ and $\dfrac{\pi}{r + f(\theta^B) + s + \pi}$ $< 1$, hence equation (27) also satisfies the property of discounting. Hence $[(W_1^G - Z_1^G) - (W_1^B - Z_1^B)]$ satisfies the Blackwell sufficient conditions for a contraction. The contraction mapping theorem ensures there exists a unique value (fixed point) of $[(W_1^G - Z_1^G) - (W_1^B - Z_1^B)]$ that satisfies (27). Further, given the job creation condition (3), the value of $[(W_1^G - Z_1^G) - (W_1^B - Z_1^B)]$ itself is a constant since it is recursively defined by constant parameters like $w, f(\theta^G), f(\theta^B), r, s\pi$. Insert the value of $[(W_1^G - Z_1^G) - (W_1^B - Z_1^B)]$ into (14) and (15) then one proved the lemma 1. QED.

### *Proof of lemma 3*

We prove that the strategy cannot be improved upon with a so-called single-step deviation. Candidate strategies are labeled with asterisks, as in the following equations:

$$Z^i(h^*) = \begin{cases} (b - c) + f(\theta^i)[W^i(h^*) - Z^i(h^*)] + \pi[Z^j(h^*) - Z^i(h^*)] & \text{if } h \le \overline{h}^i \\ h + \pi[Z^{j^*}(h^*) - Z^i(h^*)] & \text{if } h > \overline{h}^i \end{cases}$$

Now, suppose a worker with a domestic productivity such that $h \le \overline{h}^i$ chooses to deviate from the candidate strategy by arbitrary period $\Delta$. In other words, rather than searching for a job, he opts for home production in period $\Delta$. At the end of $\Delta$, he returns to the candidate strategy of job searching. A strategy that cannot be improved upon requires such a single-step deviation which cannot improve his payoff. By choosing deviation in period $\Delta$, his payoff will be

$$D(h) = h\Delta + \frac{1 - \pi\Delta}{1 + r\Delta} Z^i(h^*) + \frac{\pi\Delta}{1 + r\Delta} Z^j(h^*) \qquad (29)$$

On the other hand, the payoff to the same worker gained by following the candidate strategy is:

$$Z^i(h^*) = (b - c)\Delta + \frac{1 - \pi\Delta}{1 + r\Delta}\{f(\theta^i)\Delta W^i(h^*) + [1 - f(\theta^i)\Delta]Z^i(h^*)\}$$

$$+ \frac{\pi\Delta}{1 + r\Delta}\{f(\theta^i)\Delta W^j(h^*) + [1 - f(\theta^i)\Delta]Z^j(h^*)\}$$

$$= (b - c)\Delta + \frac{1 - \pi\Delta}{1 + r\Delta}f(\theta^i)\Delta[W^i(h*) - Z^i(h*)]$$

$$+ \frac{\pi\Delta}{1 + r\Delta}f(\theta^i)\Delta[W^j(h^*)$$

$$- Z^j(h^*)]$$

$$+ \frac{1 - \pi\Delta}{1 + r\Delta}Z^i(h^*) + \frac{\pi\Delta}{1 + r\Delta}Z^j(h^*) \tag{30}$$

by comparing (29) and (30), since $\Delta h \leq \Delta \overline{h}^i$. Further, knowing that $\overline{h}^i$ is solved by (21) and (22) satisfies:

$$\Delta \overline{h}^i = (b - c)\Delta + \frac{1 - \pi\Delta}{1 + r\Delta}f(\theta^i)\Delta[W^i(h^*) - Z^i(h^*)]$$

$$+ \frac{\pi\Delta}{1 + r\Delta}f(\theta^i)\Delta[W^j(h^*) - Z^j(h^*)]$$

Therefore, it is straightforward to show that $D^i(h) \leq Z^i(h^*)$. Hence any finite deviation from candidate strategy $Z^i(h^*)$ cannot improve his utility given that $h \leq \overline{h}^i$. On the other hand, following the same logic one can show that agents with domestic productivity such that $h > \overline{h}^i$ will be strictly worse off if they deviate from the candidate strategy. Hence we proved that the stratey could not be improved upon.

# 9  Youth unemployment in urban China

*Zhongmin Wu*

## Introduction

Although China has sustained high economic growth for a quarter of a century, unemployment has become a big problem in recent years. The unemployment rate in China is called the urban registered unemployment rate. The term 'registered unemployed persons' only refers to the persons who are registered as permanent residents in the urban areas engaged in non-agricultural activities. The rural labour force is outside the purview of unemployment statistics. The number of registered unemployed was only 5.95 million (3.1 per cent of the urban labour force) at the end of 2000 (NBS and MoL 2001: 67). To reduce a potentially explosive political situation, several new categories of joblessness were created, in addition to the registered unemployed. Thus, there are *xiagang* (laid-off workers) – employees who have been laid off but still have some link with their previous place of employment – the enterprise. Official sources put the number of laid-off workers at 9.11 million at the end of 2000 (NBS and MoL 2001: 402). The laid-off workers are not counted as unemployed as they still maintain a close link with and obtain a minimum payment from their enterprises. Such workers are not required to register for unemployment in order to obtain some benefits from the state or their firms (Gu 1999). Hence, the majority of officially recognized unemployed people are school-leavers in the cities. Over the last 20 years, 70 per cent of the total urban unemployed comprised youths, aged between 16 and 25. Youth unemployment data are more reliable than adult unemployment data in China, as youth unemployment data are not distorted by the exclusion of significant numbers of adult laid-off workers from the more familiar unemployment statistics.

Before the economic reform, it had not been admitted that unemployment existed in China. The logic is that socialism guarantees everybody food, housing and a job. Therefore, China had full employment. If some people did not have a job and wanted one, they were classified as 'waiting for employment'. Since the economic reform, the reality of unemployment has gradually been accepted. In 1994, China began to use the word 'unemployed'. In 1949, at the establishment of the People's Republic of China, there were 4.742 million unemployed and the unemployment rate was 23.6 per cent. The high unemployment rate was due to the war against Japan and the civil war. The economy of the Kuomintang had almost collapsed. In 1952, the number of unemployed fell to 3.766 million and the unemployment rate was 13.2 per cent. After China completed the transformation to socialism, 2.004 million were unemployed and in 1957 the unemployment rate was 5.9 per cent. The disaster began from the 'great leap forward' in 1958. China tried to realize the economic revolution in order to overtake Britain. From 1959 to 1963, the situation was very difficult for China, both economically and politically. After the economic recovery in 1965, 'the cultural revolution' began. The slump in the economy could not afford school-leavers to be employed. So from 1966 to 1977, about 17 million urban youth (the Red Guard) went to the rural areas to be re-educated by the peasants in response to Chairman Mao's call. Some of them did not even finish junior middle school and they spent most school time on 'revolution' rather than study. After the economic reform of 1978, youths gradually returned to the urban areas. They had been recruited through the government's intervention, although some of them were not qualified and poorly educated. They now form the majority of laid-off workers in contemporary China. From 1978 onwards, open unemployment changed to hidden unemployment and under-employment.

Chinese young people occupy an important position in the economic construction and social life of China. Since China adopted its policy of economic reform and opening up to the outside world, youths have been more conscious of social participation. At the start of the new century, youth employment problems continue to pervade China, with a disproportionately large number of young women and men exposed to long-term unemployment or else limited to precarious or short-term work. As a result, many drop out of the workforce or fail to enter it successfully in the first place and become inactive. Socially disadvantaged youth are particularly affected, thereby perpetuating a vicious cycle of poverty and social exclusion. In China, where very few can afford to be openly unemployed, the employment problem is more one of under-employment and low pay and low quality jobs in the typically large informal sector.

After the reform of the job-assignment system in Chinese universities, jobs are no longer guaranteed to the graduates. Some of these young elite find they do not have the right skills to match demands in the job market and become another part of the unemployed or under-employed army. The reason for this problem lies in the static university education system in China. As the country becomes more open to the global economy, the demand and supply in its employment market has undergone great changes in the past few years but educational reform has not kept up with it. Because there is usually a time lag between students choose their major subject and when they enter the job market, they might become victims of structural changes in the economy.

China is facing serious labour over-supply, with the number of people coming into the labour market reaching an unprecedented peak. College graduates who were formerly guaranteed jobs in the centrally controlled economy now must compete for work in an economy rife with laid-off workers caused by industrial reforms. The existence of large numbers of unemployed will exert severe pressures on the social security system, and will cause social instability. Many employers are reluctant to hire first-time job seekers with no work experience and unprepared for the challenges of work, particularly in a recession. Young people are disadvantaged because they lack experience, and when corporations are laying off staff they are not going to hire inexperienced youths.

Using simulation results, Zhai and Wang (2002) argue that if China adopts a policy of gradually relaxing its rural–urban migration control in conjunction with its labour market reform, it not only prevents a dramatic worsening of the urban unemployment problem, but also permits enough labour market flexibility to create more employment opportunities for rural unskilled labour shifted out of the farming sector. Econometric evidence from the US clearly does not support commonly expressed fears that undocumented immigration has caused a substantial increase in unemployment (Winegarden and Khor 1991). Evidence from the UK (Gregg 2001) suggests that those hit by youth unemployment, from any background, carry persistent effects from their past until at least age 33. Efforts to raise human capital once people become unemployed have rarely been successful in the past (Robinson 2000).

Youth unemployment is generally viewed as an important policy issue for many economies, regardless of their stage of development. The main purpose of this chapter is to analyse how rural–urban income inequality has affected urban youth unemployment. The underlying hypothesis is that the higher the rural–urban income gap, the more incentives rural people will have to migrate to the cities. Rural–urban migration will increase the pressure on job seeking, reducing the chances for urban school-leavers to find employment. The empirical work follows Okun's law and uses a panel data set of 29 provinces over a ten-year period from 1988–98. The results show strong evidence to support our hypothesis and validate Okun's law in the Chinese context. The rest of this chapter is organized as follows: the second section presents some stylized facts on youth unemployment in China, the third section discusses data and regression results, and the fourth section 4 draws conclusions.

## Stylized facts on youth unemployment in China

Youth unemployment forms the majority of total unemployment stock. Since the laid-off workers are not counted as unemployed, the majority of measured unemployed comprises school-leavers. Over the last 20 years, 70 per cent of total urban unemployed has been youths, aged between 16 and 25 (see Figure 9.1). Hence, the majority of officially recognized unemployed people are school-leavers in the cities. Youth unemployment data are more reliable compared to adult unemployment data in China, as youth unemployment data are not distorted by the exclusion of significant numbers of adult laid-off

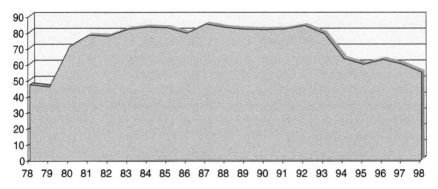

*Figure 9.1* Youth unemployment as a proportion of total unemployment.

*Table 9.1* The age level of urban unemployed in 1998 (millions)

|  | Unemployed | Total employees |
|---|---|---|
| Total number | 5.71 | 699.57 |
| Grouped by age |  |  |
| 16–25 years old | 54.7% | 20.1% |
| 26 years old and above | 45.3% | 79.9% |

*Sources: China Statistical Yearbook 1999; China Labour Statistical Yearbook 1999.*

workers from the more familiar unemployment statistics. As shown in Table 9.1, in 1998, of 5.71 million urban unemployed, 54.7 per cent are 16–25 years of age. Meanwhile, of total employees (both urban and rural), only 20.1 per cent are 16–25 years of age. The majority of adult jobless are the laid-off workers. The laid-off workers are not counted as unemployed, because they are still affiliated to their enterprise.

Lassibille *et al.* (2001) find that in Spain young workers are more likely to be under-utilized compared to their adult colleagues. Their results indicate that people with higher education have, all else being equal, a lower probability of being overeducated and a shorter length of unemployment. The labour market in China is very rigid and inflexible. The most important reason for rigidity is the political constraints both for official dismissals and the closure of loss-making state enterprises. The employee protection regulations in China mainly safeguard adults. Even though youths have been laid-off, they still do not count as unemployed. So only a few of the unemployed have had previous employment. Meanwhile, most unemployment outflow is to employment, not to leave the labour force.

The youth unemployment rate is much higher than the total unemployment rate. In urban China, as the majority of adult jobless people are laid-off workers who are not considered as being unemployed, the youth unemployment rate is more than three times that of the aggregate unemployment rate

(Figure 9.2). In addition, urban youth unemployment fluctuates more than aggregate unemployment over time. In times of recession, when aggregate demand falls, unemployment rates tend to grow. However, it has been demonstrated that under these circumstances the increase in the youth unemployment rate is often more substantial than the increase in the adult rate, implying that young workers are likely to suffer more than their adult counterparts. Gustman and Steinmeier (1981) use the local youth unemployment rate as a measure of job availability, which seems to influence youth labour supply and have the strongest effect on the labour supply for non-white males.

In 1979, there was a big increase in new urban employees; it lasted three years in an attempt to solve the problem of returning youths. Because of the returned youth, the new school-leavers got fewer opportunities than before. So youth unemployment (covering those aged between 16–25 years) increased rapidly in 1980 and 1981 (Figure 9.2). The decrease in new urban employment in 1989 led to the rise of both overall unemployment and youth unemployment. This was because, in 1989, *GDP* annual growth rates were only about 4 per cent (China has experienced an average 10 per cent annual growth rate in the last 25 years). The slump in the economy caused a decrease in labour demand, and new hiring decreased.

The provincial youth unemployment rate in the West has been much higher than that in the East. In 1996, the People's Republic of China comprises 30 provinces, municipalities and autonomous regions, 12 of which are in the eastern coastal region, nine in the middle region and a further nine in the western region. Tibet has been omitted from the empirical analysis, as unemployment data for Tibet is not available. The data set includes the remaining 29 provinces, municipalities and autonomous regions for the period 1988 to 1998. The top six provinces with the highest average provincial youth unemployment rates are Ningxia, Gansu, Qinghai, Guizhou, Inner Mongolia and Sichuan. They are all in the interior regions. Five of them are in the western region and only

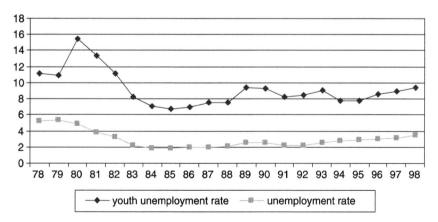

*Figure 9.2* Youth unemployment rate and total unemployment rate.

one is in the middle region. The bottom six provinces with the lowest average provincial youth unemployment rates are Beijing, Shanghai, Shanxi, Tianjin, Guangdong and Fujian. Five of them are in the eastern coastal region and only one of them is in the middle region. None of them is in the western region. Figure 9.3 shows that the provincial youth unemployment rates are much higher in the western than in the eastern region. All the higher unemployment rates occurred in the western region and they are much higher than those of the eastern coastal and middle regions. Lower unemployment rates only occurred in the eastern coastal and the middle regions (Wu 2004).

Youth unemployment is persistent. The provincial youth unemployment rates in 1988 and 1997 are presented in a scatter graph (Figure 9.4). The

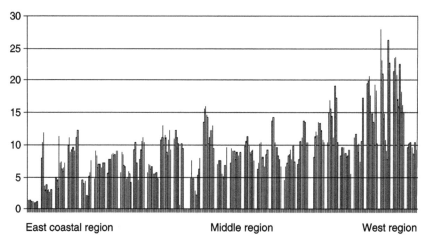

*Figure 9.3* Provincial youth unemployment rate panel data for 1988–98 in 29 provinces.

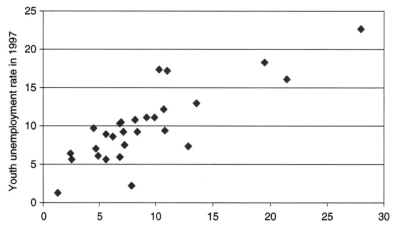

*Figure 9.4* Youth unemployment rate in 1988 and 1997.

ranking of provinces according to their youth unemployment rate has remained remarkably stable over the nine-year period. Table 9.2 shows a cross-correlation matrix for regional patterns of provincial unemployment rates. If the correlation below 0.7 is taken as indicating substantial change, it suggests that the regional pattern of youth unemployment altered in 1994 and 1998. Compared with OECD countries (OECD 1989), regional youth unemployment in China is more persistent than that in Australia and the US, less persistent than that in the UK and Italy, and is similar to that in Canada, West Germany and France (Wu 2003).

Youth unemployment is less persistent than total unemployment. Blanchard and Summers (1986) estimated an AR (1) process for the UK and USA, using the degree of first-order serial correlation to represent unemployment persistence. To measure unemployment persistence in China, their model is developed to:

Time series $U_t = \alpha + \beta U_{t-1} + \varepsilon_t$

Panel data $U_{it} = \alpha + \beta U_{it-1} + \varepsilon_{it}$

The empirical results are provided in Table 9.3. The persistence of youth unemployment is always smaller than the persistence of total unemployment. Youth unemployed mainly comprises school-leavers. They are actively searching for their first job. Adult unemployed mainly failed to keep their jobs. They find it difficult to maintain their skill and they have a disadvantage in learning new skills compared with youths. Just like physical capital, human capital is likely to depreciate in the absence of regular maintenance. Moreover, long-term unemployment may have a demoralizing effect on search behaviour, contributing to a less efficient matching process (Roed 1997).

It is necessary to run a unit root test for unemployment analysis. The augmented Dickey–Fuller (ADF) test is used to run regressions:

*Table 9.2* Correlation matrix of provincial youth unemployment rates

|    | 98 | 97 | 96 | 95 | 94 | 93 | 92 | 91 | 90 | 89 |
|----|----|----|----|----|----|----|----|----|----|----|
| 97 | **0.67** |    |    |    |    |    |    |    |    |    |
| 96 | 0.73 | 0.93 |    |    |    |    |    |    |    |    |
| 95 | 0.77 | 0.74 | 0.83 |    |    |    |    |    |    |    |
| 94 | 0.74 | 0.70 | 0.77 | 0.93 |    |    |    |    |    |    |
| 93 | **0.68** | 0.84 | 0.88 | 0.89 | 0.87 |    |    |    |    |    |
| 92 | **0.64** | 0.76 | 0.85 | 0.86 | 0.82 | 0.92 |    |    |    |    |
| 91 | **0.64** | 0.81 | 0.88 | 0.85 | 0.78 | 0.89 | 0.86 |    |    |    |
| 90 | **0.55** | 0.75 | 0.83 | 0.81 | 0.73 | 0.83 | 0.79 | 0.94 |    |    |
| 89 | **0.58** | 0.76 | 0.84 | 0.80 | 0.72 | 0.76 | 0.75 | 0.89 | 0.96 |    |
| 88 | **0.56** | 0.75 | 0.80 | 0.77 | **0.69** | 0.73 | 0.70 | 0.87 | 0.93 | 0.96 |

*Table 9.3* Persistence of unemployment

| Persistence of | Youth | Total |
|---|---|---|
| National unemployment rate | 0.732*** | 0.812*** |
| | (4.76) | (10.5) |
| log(national unemployment rate) | 0.758*** | 0.828*** |
| | (5.24) | (9.46) |
| Without year dummy provincial unemployment rate | 0.793*** | 0.820*** |
| | (19.9) | (15.3) |
| log(provincial unemployment rate) | 0.829*** | 0.870*** |
| | (14.7) | (28.6) |
| With year dummy provincial unemployment rate | 0.808*** | 0.842*** |
| | (21.8) | (17.4) |
| log(provincial unemployment rate) | 0.844*** | 0.891*** |
| | (15.7) | (32.7) |

*Notes:* Numbers in parentheses are *t*-ratios; * p < 0.10; ** p < 0.05; *** p < 0.01.

$$\Delta U_{it} = a_i + \gamma_i \, Time + \delta_i \, U_{it-1} + \Sigma \, \theta_{iL} \, \Delta U_{it-L} + \varepsilon_{it}$$

where $\Delta U_{i\,t} = U_{i\,t} - U_{i\,t-1}$. The ADF test evaluates the null hypothesis $H_0: \delta_i = 0$. Levin and Lin (1992, 1993) develop a unit root test for panel data, by performing the following regression:

$$\bar{e}_{it} = \delta \, \bar{v}_{it-1} + \mu_{it}$$

where

$$\bar{e}_{it} = \Delta U_{it} - \bar{a}_{1i} - \bar{\gamma}_{1mi} \, Time - \Sigma \, \bar{\theta}_{1iL} \, \Delta U_{it-L}$$
$$\bar{v}_{it-1} = U_{it-1} - \bar{a}_{2i} - \bar{\gamma}_{2mi} \, Time - \Sigma \, \bar{\theta}_{2iL} \, \Delta U_{it-L}$$

The null hypothesis for the panel unit root test is $H_0: \delta = 0$, which is to say that $\beta = 1$, or unit root. Here, the Levin–Lin test is used for panel data of both youth unemployment and total unemployment.

When $T = 10$ and $N = 25$, the 1 per cent critical statistics computed by Levin and Lin are −2.78. The computed *t* value is −6.20 for youth unemployment, which is smaller than the 1 per cent critical values. So the null hypothesis can be rejected at the 1 per cent critical level. That is, unit root does not exist in provincial youth unemployment in China.

Many experts have applied the Levin–Lin test. Maddala and Wu (1999) compare the Levin–Lin test, its extension by Im *et al.* (1997) and a simple alternative Fisher test. The Levin–Lin test gives us enough power to reject the unit root for regional youth unemployment in China. Unit root in unemployment normally has been termed as 'hysteresis'. The hysteresis is rejected but 'persistence' is accepted, which is in-between the hysteresis theory and the natural rate theory, NAIRU.

## Methodology and empirical findings

In recent years, rural people have been allowed to work in the cities. The primary motivation of rural–urban migration is huge rural–urban income inequality. Harris and Todaro's (1970) pioneering study on rural–urban migration in Africa suggests that rural-to-urban migration is driven by expected income. Migrants flow from the countryside of the poor regions to the more prosperous cities in the hope of earning higher incomes. The recent economic reforms in China have exaggerated the rural–urban income gap, providing strong incentives for the exodus of rural people into the cities. This has inevitably led to employment pressure, particularly on urban youth. Figure 9.5 shows a relationship between the provincial youth unemployment rate and the rural–urban per capita consumption ratio, which is an important measurement of rural–urban income inequality. It is obvious that there exists a positive relationship between the rural–urban income gap and the urban youth unemployment rate. The bigger the income gap between urban and rural areas, the higher the provincial youth unemployment rate.

Okun's law is an empirical law that relates short-run changes in output to changes in unemployment, and examines the sources of output changes that go along with changes in unemployment. When unemployment falls, more people tend to come onto the labour market to find work. For these reasons, reductions in unemployment and increases in output occur together. The empirical law that Okun discovered is that, in the short run, a 1 per cent change in the unemployment rate tends to accompany a 3 per cent reduction in the GNP gap. Figure 9.6 confirms that Okun's law fits in China. It also shows that the Okun curve is non-linear (Viren 2001).

Based on Okun's law and Edwards and Edwards (2000) methodology, the following regression equation is derived for China:

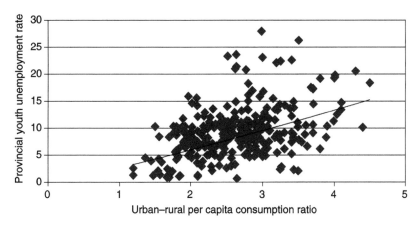

*Figure 9.5* The relation between unemployment and the income gap.

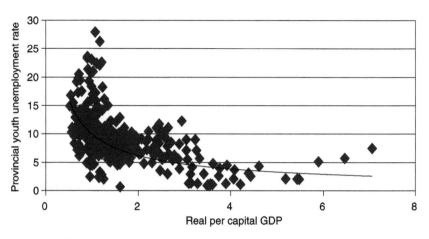

*Figure 9.6* Okun's law.

*Table 9.4* Summary statistics of variables

|  | Mean | SD | Min | Max |
|---|---|---|---|---|
| Urban youth unemployment rate (%) | 9.19 | 4.45 | 0.899 | 26.3 |
| Consumption ratio of nonpeasants to peasants | 2.64 | 0.616 | 1.191 | 4.50 |
| Growth rate of real per capita GDP (%) | 6.50 | 7.13 | −12.2 | 35.9 |

*Sources:* NBS (1989–99), *China Labour Statistical Yearbook*; NBS (1989–99), *China Statistical Yearbook*.

$$U_{it} = a + \beta\, U_{it-1} + \zeta \times Income\ Gap_{it} + \gamma \times GDP \text{ growth rate}_{it} + d_i + f_t + \varepsilon_{it}$$
$$i = 1, 2, \ldots, 29 \quad t = 1989, \ldots, 1998$$

The data are drawn from 29 provinces of China, over the period 1989–98. The consumption data are measured in constant prices, using provincial level and urban/rural deflators. The summary statistics and explanations of the dependent and independent variables are provided in Table 9.4. The explanatory variables are instrumented to avoid the problem of endogeneity. The instruments are the lagged values of the corresponding variables. The results for the simple linear form are given in Table 9.5, and those in double-log form in Table 9.6. The plain OLS, the random effect model, and the fixed effect model are estimated. Using Hausman's test, LM het. test, R-square and *t* ratios, we find that the random effect model without a year dummy is acceptable. It also performs better.

In both regressions, the results are quite consistent. There is strong empirical evidence of the rural–urban income inequality gap impacting on urban youth unemployment. A reduction in the rural–urban income gap will help reduce urban youth unemployment pressure. The results support our

Table 9.5 Regression results: dependent variable = youth unemployment rate

| Variable | OLS | FE | RE | OLS | FE | RE |
|---|---|---|---|---|---|---|
| (Youth unemployment rate)$_{t-1}$ | 0.764*** | 0.390*** | 0.664*** | 0.777*** | 0.337** | 0.634*** |
| | (17.4) | (2.77) | (16.7) | (17.7) | (2.41) | (14.9) |
| (Consumption ratio of nonpeasants/peasants)$_{t-1}$ | 0.487 | 0.258 | 0.689** | 0.527* | 1.525** | 1.047*** |
| | (1.47) | (0.52) | (2.24) | (1.88) | (2.34) | (2.90) |
| Growth rate of real per capital GDP | −6.554*** | −5.306*** | −6.670*** | −2.310 | −1.270 | −2.476 |
| | (−3.86) | (−3.43) | (−3.61) | (−0.79) | (−0.55) | (−1.02) |
| $R^2$ | 0.732 | 0.789 | 0.730 | 0.768 | 0.825 | 0.762 |
| LM het. Test | 6.87 | 12.5 | 7.51 | 4.19 | 8.92 | 4.46 |
| Haussman Test | | | 7.29 | | | 5.47 |
| Year dummies | | | | Yes | Yes | Yes |

*Notes*: Numbers in parentheses are *t*-ratios; * $p < 0.10$; ** $p < 0.05$; *** $p < 0.01$.

*Table 9.6* Regression results: dependent variable = log(youth unemployment rate)

| Variable | OLS | FE | RE | OLS | FE | RE |
|---|---|---|---|---|---|---|
| log(youth unemployment rate)$_{t-1}$ | 0.864*** | 0.466*** | 0.757*** | 0.879*** | 0.444*** | 0.759*** |
| | (22.7) | (4.61) | (21.1) | (24.2) | (4.25) | (20.3) |
| log(consumption ratio of nonpeasants/peasants)$_{t-1}$ | 0.087 | 0.041 | 0.168* | 0.080 | 0.305** | 0.223** |
| | (0.96) | (0.37) | (1.93) | (0.95) | (2.05) | (2.25) |
| Log(growth rate of real per capital GDP) | −0.760*** | −0.695*** | −0.825*** | −0.052 | −0.151 | −0.150 |
| | (−3.93) | (−3.35) | (−3.91) | (−0.17) | (−0.55) | (−0.53) |
| $R^2$ | 0.820 | 0.863 | 0.818 | 0.848 | 0.887 | 0.845 |
| LM het. Test | 3.68 | 2.21 | 12.9 | 2.90 | 2.25 | 12.1 |
| Hausman Test | | | 17.3 | | | 22.4 |
| Year dummies | | | | Yes | Yes | Yes |

*Notes*: Numbers in parentheses are *t*-ratios; * p < 0.10; ** p < 0.05; *** p < 0.01.

proposed hypothesis in this chapter. That is, the greater the rural–urban income gap, the more incentive rural people will have to move to the cities and look for jobs. This in turn will increase the pressure on job seeking in the cities, reducing the chances of employment for urban young people, particularly school-leavers.

A recent study by Roberts (2001) provides similar evidence. Roberts' study in Shanghai concludes that it is very hard for urban unemployed workers to compete with migrant workers who are willing to accept low wages and work long hours. The internal labour migration pressure has been constantly growing since China initiated its open door policy in the early 1980s. It is highly possible that this river will become an uncontrollable flood. The unequal distribution of foreign investment between the coastal and inland areas is one of the most important reasons leading to large-scale labour movement from the inland areas to the more prosperous coastal cities. These rural migrants are a more favoured choice for foreign-funded firms in the labour intensive manufacturing sector than the urban workers since they are cheaper, harder working and more willing to work overtime. Though a large number of laid-off workers live in the cities, the foreign-funded firms in the textile, electronic and other labour intensive industries in the suburban area are crowded with young migrant workers. This migration of rural labour has become a threat to the resolution of the urban employment problem.

It is also interesting to note that economic growth has a significant and negative effect on youth unemployment if there is no year dummy in the model. In other words, output growth will reduce youth unemployment. This means that Okun's law is validated in the Chinese context. If the year dummy is included in the empirical model, output growth is no longer significant in the model, although it still has a negative effect, as economic growth varies by year but not really by province.

## Conclusion

The problem of urban unemployment has become a major concern of policy makers and academic researchers in China. This chapter aims to understand the principal causes of urban youth unemployment. Following Okun's law, and using a panel data set, an empirical model is established to test an important hypothesis, that is, rising rural–urban income inequality can lead to higher urban youth unemployment. The results have important policy implications. They suggest that the reduction of urban youth unemployment could be brought about through rural economic development. Hence, government policies should emphasize how to raise rural income and reduce rural–urban inequality. Such policies may be expected to produce simultaneous win–win results for both the rural and the urban populations.

## References

Blanchard, O. and Summers, L. (1986) Hysteresis and the European unemployment problem, *NBER Macroeconomics Annual*, 1: 15–78.

Edwards, S. and Edwards, A.C. (2000) Economic reforms and labour markets: policy issues and lessons from Chile, *Economic Policy: A European Forum*, 30: 181–222.

Gregg, P. (2001) The impact of youth unemployment on adult unemployment in the NCDS, *Economic Journal*, 111(475): F626–F653.

Gu, E.X. (1999) From permanent employment to massive lay-offs, *Economy and Society*, 28(2): 281–299.

Gustman, A.L. and Steinmeier, T.L. (1981) The impact of wage and unemployment on youth enrolment and labour supply, *Review of Economics and Statistics*, 63(4): 553–560.

Harris, J. and Todaro, M. (1970) Migration, unemployment and development: a two-sector analysis, *American Economic Review*, 60: 126–142.

Im, K.S. Pesaran, M.H. and Shin, Y. (1997) Testing for unit roots in heterogeneous panels, mimeo, Department of Applied Economics, University of Cambridge.

Lassibille, G., Gomez, L.N., Ramos, I.A. and Sanchez, C.D. (2001) Youth transition from school to work in Spain, *Economics of Education Review*, 20(2): 139–149.

Levin, A. and Lin, C.F. (1992) Unit root tests in panel data, University of California, San Diego, Department of Economics discussion papers, pp. 92–23.

Levin, A. and Lin, C.F. (1993) Unit root tests in panel data, University of California, San Diego, Department of Economics discussion papers, pp. 93–56.

Maddala, G.S. and Wu, S. (1999) A comparative study of unit root tests with panel data and a new simple test, *Oxford Bulletin of Economics and Statistics*, 61: 631–652.

National Bureau of Statistics and Ministry of Labour, People's Republic of China (various years) *China Statistical Yearbook*, Beijing: China Statistical Publishing House.

OECD (1989) Regional unemployment in OECD countries, *Employment Outlook*.

Roberts, K.D. (2001) The determinants of job choice by rural labour migrants in Shanghai, *China Economic Review*, 12: 15–39.

Robinson, P. (2000) Active labour market policies: a case of evidence based policy-making, *Oxford Review of Economic Policy*, 16(1): 13–26.

Roed, K. (1997) Hysteresis in unemployment *Journal of Economic Surveys*, 11(4): 389–418.

Viren, M. (2001) The Okun curve is non-linear, *Economics Letters*, 70: 253–257.

Winegarden, C.R. and Khor, L.B. (1991) Undocumented immigration and unemployment of United States youth and minority workers: econometric evidence, *Review of Economics and Statistics*, 73 (1): 105–112.

Wu, Z. (2003) The persistence of regional unemployment: evidence from China, *Applied Economics*, 35(12): 1417–1421.

Wu, Z. (2004) Regional unemployment in transitional China: a theoretical and empirical analysis, *Economics of Planning*, 36(4): 297–314.

Zhai, F. and Wang, Z. (2002) WTO accession, rural labour migration and urban unemployment in China, *Urban Studies*, 39(12): 2199–2217.

# Part III

# Sustainable development and policy

# 10 Openness and productivity in China

*Maria Jesús Herrerías and Vicente Orts*

## Introduction

China's economy has been growing at an exceptional rate for almost four decades. Its strategy of growth throughout this period has undoubtedly been based on a number of different factors (investment policy, agricultural reforms, openness, etc.), although there seems to be fairly widespread agreement in the literature on the significant role played by two main factors, namely, capital accumulation and openness to trade from a long-run perspective. The economic reforms that were launched in the 1960s have played a major role in Chinese economic performance, the most important being the investment-orientated policy, which has had effects that have continued to grow since the open-door policy was introduced up to the present day. Investments in equipment (mainly imported from abroad) and transport infrastructures have been important factors that have encouraged economic growth. This phenomenon favoured an increase in the investment-to-GDP ratio from 20 per cent in the 1960s to 45 per cent in 2005. On the other hand, the Chinese economy has also progressively stimulated trade flows,[1] and Chinese exports and imports rose from an average 4 and 3 per cent of GDP, respectively, in the 1960s to values around 26 and 24 per cent of GDP, respectively, in recent years. In addition, the high annual GDP growth rates and the successful integration of China into international markets has favoured the growth of the contribution of Chinese exports and imports from values below 1 per cent of the world total in 1980 to 7 and 6.4 per cent, respectively, in 2005.

Openness to trade can stimulate growth and productivity through the positive externalities that it provides. Openness puts pressure on domestic producers, which results in more efficient resource allocation and stimulates productivity by increasing technological innovation and improving managerial practices. However, the mechanisms that operate through exports or imports are different. Exports mainly operate by economies of scale, learning-by-exporting, self-selection of firms and so forth, while imports mainly have to do with access to intermediate and final goods that will increase accessibility to foreign technology. Capital accumulation is another significant factor in accounting for economic growth. Regardless of whether we think in terms of the traditional or the endogenous growth models, capital accumulation has been considered a key factor in promoting economic activity and labour productivity. The new growth theory, however, highlights the role played by capital accumulation from the perspective of long-run growth. In particular, among the components of capital accumulation, investments in equipment (due to the embodied technological progress) and infrastructures have been considered as being the most important factors determining long-run growth. The reason for this is that both can have an effect on productivity, together with other relevant factors, such as R&D expenditure.

The endogenous relationship between openness, capital accumulation and productivity is a recurring issue in the empirical literature. On the one hand, the association between trade and productivity is mixed. Trade could be determining productivity, but productivity is also an important factor for establishing the pattern of trade, given the relationship between productivity and the probability of exporting (think of the Ricardian model of comparative advantage or of Melitz's model, where only more productive firms become exporters). A similar problem of endogeneity occurs in the relationship between capital accumulation and productivity, depending on whether supply or demand shocks predominate among the determinants of investment. But the problem of reverse causation also affects the relationship between trade and investment, thus making the relationship between openness, capital accumulation and productivity even more complex.

In this context, then, the purpose of this chapter is to analyse the importance of openness to trade and investment in explaining aggregate labour productivity performance in China.[2] We employ the methodology of the co-integrated VAR model to avoid the problem of endogeneity in the relationship between trade, investment and productivity. This methodology assumes that all potentially relevant variables that we are interested in analysing are endogenous prior to starting the analysis and we therefore allowed the data to reveal the nature of the relationship between them in our study. Furthermore, this methodology makes it easier to identify the short- and long-run structure in our estimated models. Finally, three indicators of openness (trade-to-GDP ratio, exports-to-GDP ratio and imports-to-GDP ratio) were employed in order to endow our results with a higher degree of robustness. Our results provide evidence that, in the Chinese economy, trade promotes labour productivity in the long run with our three different measures of openness, together with capital accumulation. In addition, we found that R&D expenditure stimulates investment in the long run.

The rest of the chapter is organized as follows. The second section contains a review of the literature on the relationship between openness, investment and growth; the third section describes the variables considered and the methodology that was followed; the fourth section shows the empirical results; and conclusions are given in the final section.

# Literature review

For a long time economists have attempted to account for the differences in growth rates and productivity among countries. Although there is some agreement that openness to trade and investment enhance economic growth and productivity, the evidence is nevertheless mixed and there is a certain amount of debate over the causal relationships among them.

Capital accumulation has long been considered an important mechanism for promoting growth and labour productivity. The theoretical literature, however, emphasizes that the most important factors for enhancing growth and productivity are to be found among the components of capital accumulation, equipment investment and infrastructure (Aschauer 1988, 1989; De Long and Summers 1991; De Long *et al.* 1992). In addition, the Schumpeterian version of the endogenous growth models proposed by Howitt and Aghion (1998) and Howitt (2000) stressed the possibility that capital accumulation is a significant source of growth due to the embodied technological progress. In other words, this relationship between capital accumulation and growth is possible because the supply factors predominate among the components of investment (Madsen 2002).

Openness to trade has also been considered to be a mechanism for enhancing productivity in both developed and developing countries (Lopez 2005). Among the channels identified in the literature as mechanisms for stimulating labour productivity through exports, the most immediate is that openness to trade induces the least productive firms to leave the industry and also leads more productive non-exporting firms to become exporters. Thus, market share reallocations contribute in a significant way to productivity growth (Bernard and Jensen 1999; Melitz 2003, among others). An additional channel is the strong competitiveness in the international market that forces firms to be more efficient and, as a consequence of this, their productivity improves. Furthermore, access to foreign markets favours firms by enabling them to obtain gains through economies of scale (Helpman and Krugman 1985). Finally, there are externalities and spillovers associated with exporting activities (such as efficient management and organizational styles, labour training and learning-by-doing) that ultimately improve the efficiency of firms and allow them to become more productive.

In the literature, imports are also considered to be a mechanism for encouraging labour productivity in the long run. As in the case of exporting activities, one of the most important channels in importing activities is the strong competitiveness that forces domestic firms to innovate and reallocate their resources in the most productive sectors (Grossman and Helpman 1991; Lopez 2006; MacDonald 1994; Traca 2002). Thus, there are also gains that derive from economies of scale, in a similar way to the case of exporting activities. In the endogenous growth models, on the other hand, imports are considered to be a mechanism for acquiring foreign technology (for example, R&D) and knowledge that can be incorporated into the domestic activity

(Ram and Keller 2007). New technologies and knowledge could be embodied in imports of intermediate goods or in capital imports, especially in investment in equipment, and thus lead to gains in the levels of productivity and output (Amiti and Konings 2005; Coe *et al.* 1997; Grossman and Helpman 1991; Lee 1995; Mazumdar 2001). Finally, there are externalities and spillover effects associated with importing that enhance productivity (learning-by-doing, managerial efforts, domestic knowledge, foreign contacts, learning of production methods, organizational structures, and so forth).

Nevertheless, and in spite of these arguments, there is also a certain amount of scepticism regarding openness to trade and its positive effects on economic growth (Rodriguez and Rodrik 2001; Rodrik 1999). On the one hand, the main prediction of the theoretical growth literature is that trade affects growth by influencing the rate at which productivity grows. However, the causality could also run in the opposite direction, that is, increases in growth induce more trade (Helpman 1988). In addition, according to the traditional theories on trade, an increase in trade flows can stimulate or reduce investment in an economy depending on whether the economy exports goods that are intensive in capital or in labour. On the other hand, the empirical evidence shows that openness to trade only seems to promote growth and productivity by promoting investment; that is, openness to trade raises investment rates and they account for the increase in productivity and economic growth (Balwin and Seghezza 1996; Barro 1991; Levine and Renelt 1992). Nonetheless, the opposite point of view is also feasible and an investment effort also influences economic growth and trade expansion (Rodrik 1995). Thus, the evidence for the relationship between openness, capital accumulation and productivity is mixed and the direction of the causality among the variables considered is ambiguous. The aim of this chapter is therefore to understand the nature of the relations and the direction of the causality between openness to trade and productivity, together with capital accumulation, which are important aspects of Chinese performance.

The effects of openness on growth in China have been subject to a great deal of analysis. Shan and Sun (1998) provide evidence of the positive effect of openness on growth in a wide range of empirical studies; similar results were found by Liu *et al.* (1997, 2002). In contrast, Hsiao and Hsiao (2006) found that exports do not cause the increases in China's GDP. Hence, it seems that evidence of the positive effects of openness on growth in China is inconclusive. The main indicator of openness employed in the literature, however, has been exports. Yet, when imports are included as an alternative measure of openness, we do not find any evidence regarding China, although in Thangavelu and Rajaguru (2004) we did find some empirical evidence supporting the idea that openness, as measured by imports, promotes economic growth for some Asian countries.

Finally, the effect of capital accumulation and economic growth on the Chinese economy has been studied by several authors, for example Chow (1993) and Yusuf (1994). These authors argued that capital accumulation is responsible for the fast growth and improved productivity in China. However, only Yusuf (ibid.) argued that technological progress has also played a significant role in that process. In contrast, Qin *et al.* (2005) found some evidence that output drives investment in the Chinese economy. Thus, the evidence for the relationship between capital accumulation and growth in China also seems to be ambiguous.

To sum up, the problem of endogeneity is a recurring issue in the empirical literature on openness, investment and economic growth, and for this reason the study of the relationships among them requires an empirical methodology that takes this issue into account.

## Data and methodology

In this chapter we examine the effects of openness with three different measures, together with capital accumulation, as the main determinants of labour productivity in China. The analysis starts by investigating the relationship between the trade-to-GDP ratio and labour productivity. In particular, in this model we studied whether trade and capital accumulation drive labour productivity in the long run. We then estimated the model again, this time analysing the effect of openness with the exports-to-GDP and imports-to-GDP ratios, which proved the robustness of our results.

The empirical analysis uses Chinese annual data for the period 1962–2004 from the Chinese National Bureau of Statistics (NBS). Our data set, which is common to all models, consists of labour productivity[3] – GDP per worker – (*lprod*), the real exchange rate[4] (*lrer*), R&D expenditure[5] (*lrd*), investment – Gross Fixed Capital Formation – (*linv*) and US GDP (*lgdpusa*). All variables are in logs and in real terms, and were deflated by the GDP deflator. The real exchange rate was calculated using the nominal exchange rate between the Chinese currency and the US dollar (Renminbi/$) and the consumer price indices (CPIs).[6] We estimated three models using the trade-to-GDP ratio (Exports + Imports/GDP) – (*tgdp*), the export-to-GDP ratio (*xgdp*) and finally the imports-to-GDP ratio (*mgdp*).

We focused on time series evidence in our empirical analysis and used the co-integrated vector autoregressive (VAR model) methodology, proposed by Johansen (1988, 1995) and Johansen and Juselius (1990, 1994). This methodology is based on the principle of 'general to specific', discussed in Juselius (2007) and Hendry and Mizon (1993). We started the analysis with a wide general specification (on which certain restrictions will later be imposed) of both a statistical and economic origin, until the most irreducible form possible was reached. We considered this methodology to be appropriate given the potential interdependence between the different variables that were considered. Furthermore, we also suggest joint modelling to distinguish between the short-run and long-run relationships, which in our case are the key elements of the analysis proposed here.

More specifically, we start with an unrestricted VAR model, a restricted linear trend in the co-integration space and an unrestricted constant ($\mu$) with a dimension of $r$ x 1:

$$\Delta Y_t = a\tilde{\beta}'_i \begin{pmatrix} Y \\ Z \\ t \\ D_s \end{pmatrix}_{t-1} + \sum_{i=1}^{k-1} \Gamma_i \Delta Y_{t-i} + \sum_{i=0}^{k-1} \omega_i \Delta Z_{t-i} + \sum_{i=0}^{k-1} \theta_i \Delta D_{st-i}$$

$$+ \varphi D_t + \mu + \varepsilon_t \tag{1}$$

$$\varepsilon_t \sim NIID\,(0,\,\Omega)\,t = 1\,\ldots.\,T$$

where $a\tilde{\beta}_i$ are the coefficients of the long-run matrix of dimension $p$ x $r$; $a$ gives the direction and speed of adjustment towards equilibrium and $\tilde{\beta}_i$ are the coefficients of the co-integrated vectors; $Y_{t-1}$ is the matrix of potentially endogenous variables in the model; $Z_{t-1}$ is the matrix of weakly exogenous variables; $t$ is the linear trend restricted to the co-integration space and $D_{st}$ is the matrix of the level shift dummy.[7] $\Gamma_i$ is the unrestricted matrix of dimension $p$ x $p$ of the coefficients of endogenous variables in the short run, while $\omega_i$ and $\theta_i$ are the coefficients of the variables that have been considered prior to analysing the weakly exogenous variables ($Z_t$) and the level shift dummy ($D_{st}$), respectively. Finally, the parameter ($\varphi D_t$) contains a vector of unrestricted permanent dummy variables and their corresponding coefficients. In addition, we assumed that the error term, $\varepsilon_t$, is an i.i.d. Gaussian sequence $N(0,\Omega)$ and the initial values, $Y_{-k+1}, \ldots Y_0$, are fixed. Since the co-integration property is invariant to the incorporation of additional variables in the model, we followed the procedure suggested by Juselius (2007). This method involves sequentially introducing several variables into the model, since according to Juselius, this process greatly facilitates the identification of the long-run structure in the simple model.

Finally, different standard root tests were used to look for the stationary process of variables required by our methodology.[8] From the information about the order of integration obtained in these tests we concluded that the best characterization of our variables is to accept that they are all integrated to order one. We rejected the order of integration equal to two in all cases.

## Empirical results

Given that our variables show a linear trend in levels, it seems reasonable to suppose that the model specification is based on our equation (1). Thus, 'this representation shows that all linear combinations of the process, such as the co-integrating relations and the common trends, could have a linear trend consistent with data' (Nielsen and Rahbek 2000: 13). The VAR model assumes that the residuals are not autocorrelated and are distributed as a normal distribution. To satisfy these assumptions, we have incorporated two level shift dummies in all the models.[9] The first level shift, $D_{s78}$, attempts to capture the beginning of the political and economic reforms in 1978. The second level shift, $D_{s94}$, is likely to be associated with the unification of the real exchange rate, fiscal reforms and liberalization of prices in 1994.

Additional unrestricted dummies were included in all the models estimated. We introduced two dummies that were common to all the models that were analysed here, i.e. a dummy for 1976, $dum_{76p}$, and another for 1989, $dum_{89p}$. The first dummy is associated with the Cultural Revolution and the second attempts to capture the political instabilities, the economic restrictions in 1989 and the events that took place in Tiananmen Square.

Model specification is one of the most important tasks in econometrics and, in particular, assuming the exogeneity of one or more variables in the methodology that is employed in this chapter could be risky. For this reason we have analysed the exogeneity of our variables, as can be seen in Table 10.1. The result of this analysis was that in the model that contains the trade-to-GDP ratio and exports-to-GDP ratio, the endogenous variables are labour productivity, investment and the real exchange rate. However, in the model that contains the imports-to-GDP ratio, only labour productivity and investment are endogenous. On the other hand, the LM test states that two lags are enough to capture the dynamic effects and to avoid autocorrelation problems in all our models.

Based on the information from the determination of the rank test and the roots of companion matrix (see Tables 10.2 and 10.3), we can determine the number of co-integrated vectors ($r$) and the number of common trends ($p - r$) by the LR test. In all models estimated, we found two co-integrated vectors. In addition, the root of the characteristic polynomial for each rank selected is less than unity, thus showing that our long-run relationships are stationary.

*Table 10.1* Determination of the rank test: productivity and trade-to-GDP ratio/ exports-to-GDP ratio

| | | Trade-to-GDP | | | | Exports-to-GDP | | | |
|---|---|---|---|---|---|---|---|---|---|
| $p-r$ | $r$ | Eig. value | Trace | 95% | p-value | Eig. value | Trace | 95% | p-value |
| 3 | 0 | 0.76 | 122.694 | 75.40 | 0.000 | 0.76 | 125.96 | 75.89 | 0.000 |
| 2 | 1 | 0.68 | 62.596 | 48.87 | 0.002 | 0.66 | 67.36 | 50.26 | 0.001 |
| 1 | 2 | 0.30 | 14.871 | 25.34 | **0.515** | 0.41 | 22.18 | 25.32 | **0.119** |

*Table 10.2* Determination of the rank test: productivity and imports-to-GDP ratio

| $p-r$ | $r$ | Eig. value | Trace | 95% | p-value |
|---|---|---|---|---|---|
| 2 | 0 | 0.74 | 97.49 | 54.18 | 0.000 |
| 1 | 1 | 0.63 | 41.46 | 28.20 | 0.001 |

*Table 10.3* Weak exogeneity test

| Vbles. | Trade | Exports | Imports |
|--------|-------|---------|---------|
| lrer | endogenous | endogenous | 0.35 |
| tgdp | 0.35 | | |
| xgdp | | 0.51 | |
| lrd | 0.26 | 0.18 | 0.12 |
| mgdp | | | 0.47 |

*Note:* Under the null hypothesis of weak exogeneity, this test is distributed as LR test, chi-square (r); p-values are in the table.

Our main result is that the relevance of openness in the process of labour productivity growth in China is independent of the measure or indicator employed, thus showing the robustness of our results. Moreover, we support the idea that openness boosts trade and encourages labour productivity in China.

We started the analysis by examining whether the trade-to-GDP ratio enhances labour productivity together with capital accumulation. Our results in equation (2) provide evidence that trade and investment stimulate labour productivity in the long run in China. Furthermore, we found that R&D expenditure and investment are complementary in the long run, as can be observed in equation (3). The causality[10] in the long run is only in one direction from trade and investment to labour productivity in the first co-integrated vector and from R&D expenditure to investment in the second co-integrated vector.

The long-run relationships that were found are as follows, where the restrictions imposed were accepted with a *p*-value of 0.145 (statistics in brackets):[11, 12]

$$lprod = 0.45linv + 1.38tgdp + 0.16D_{s94} \qquad (2)$$
$$[-22.15] \quad [-7.93] \qquad [-5.99]$$

$$linv = 0.26lrd - 0.18D_{s78} + 0.08t \qquad (3)$$
$$[-5.56] \quad [6.89] \qquad [-32.25]$$

However, one interesting aspect to study, instead of the broad measure of trade, is the role played by exports and imports independently of each other, since this can provide evidence of the robustness of our results with different specifications of openness. When exports were introduced into the model, we found that productivity, investment, real exchange rate and exports were co-integrated, as in equation (4). The two long-run relationships are as follows, where the restrictions were accepted with a *p*-value of 0.12 (statistics in brackets):

*Table 10.4* Dynamics of trade and labour productivity

| | Trade | | | Exports | | | Imports | |
|---|---|---|---|---|---|---|---|---|
| | $\Delta lprod$ | $\Delta linv$ | $\Delta lrer$ | $\Delta lprod$ | $\Delta linv$ | $\Delta lrer$ | $\Delta lprod$ | $\Delta linv$ |
| $\Delta lprod_{t-1}$ | – | – | 0.61 | 0.34 | 1.01 | – | 0.41 | 1.06 |
| | – | – | (4.07) | (4.75) | (6.45) | – | (5.19) | (5.83) |
| $\Delta linv_{t-1}$ | 0.13 | 0.37 | −0.21 | | | | | |
| | (3.7) | (4.31) | (−3.09) | | | | | |
| $\Delta lrer$ | | | | | | | −0.31 | −0.95 |
| | | | | | | | (−3.81) | (−3.86) |
| $\Delta lrd$ | 0.11 | 0.43 | – | 0.11 | 0.44 | – | 0.09 | 0.39 |
| | (6.2) | (8.26) | – | (5.73) | (8.64) | – | (3.91) | (6.81) |
| $\Delta lrd_{t-1}$ | 0.07 | – | – | 0.06 | – | – | 0.07 | – |
| | (3.46) | – | – | (3.60) | – | – | (3.68) | – |
| $\Delta lgdpusa$ | 0.44 | – | −0.40 | – | −1.08 | – | 0.53 | – |
| | (4.39) | – | (−1.92) | – | (−3.81) | – | (5.25) | – |
| $\Delta lgdpusa_{t-1}$ | 0.42 | 0.91 | – | 0.43 | 1.06 | – | – | – |
| | (3.19) | (2.45) | – | (3.26) | (2.89) | – | – | – |
| $\Delta tgdp_{t-1}$ | – | 0.66 | −0.42 | | | | | |
| | – | (2.94) | (−2.92) | | | | | |
| $\Delta xgdp$ | | | | – | −0.91 | 0.78 | | |
| | | | | – | (−2.37) | (3.33) | | |
| $\Delta xgdp_{t-1}$ | | | | −0.34 | – | −0.55 | | |
| | | | | (−2.32) | – | (−2.45) | | |
| $\Delta mgdp_{t-1}$ | | | | | | | −0.38 | – |
| | | | | | | | (−2.88) | – |
| $ecm_1$ | **−1.13** | – | – | **−0.89** | – | – | **−0.86** | – |
| | (−8.96) | – | – | (−7.83) | – | – | (−9.87) | – |
| $ecm_2$ | **−0.54** | **−0.87** | **−0.58** | **−0.31** | **−0.61** | **−0.18** | **−0.59** | **−1.12** |
| | (−6.68) | (−3.88) | (−4.7) | (−7.07) | (−5.13) | (−3.28) | (−9.73) | (−7.81) |

*Notes:* $ecm_i = \beta_i' X_t$ and the $t$-statistics in brackets. Deterministic components are available upon request. The restrictions imposed are accepted with a p-value of 0.20 for the trade model, 0.18 for the exports model and 0.059 for the imports model.

$$lprod = 0.40linv + 0.38lrer + 1.92xgdp + 0.19D_{s94} \qquad (4)$$
$$[-14.86] \quad [-2.94] \quad [-5.14] \quad [-5.53]$$

$$linv = 0.28lrd - 0.16D_{s78} + 0.08t \qquad (5)$$
$$[-5.55] \quad [5.91] \quad [-28.88]$$

Our results are consistent with an export- and investment-led labour productivity hypothesis. Openness leads to labour productivity and, unlike other studies, exports are seen to stimulate labour productivity exogenously. On the other hand, we found that the real exchange rate plays a significant role in long-run growth. In fact, an increase in the real exchange rate (depreciation) exerts a positive effect on labour productivity. This effect could be interpreted as gains in competitiveness, given that the Chinese government has employed the exchange rate to stimulate exports, which are at the same time used to finance imports, especially of equipment (Lardy 1993). Finally, our second co-integrated vector shows that R&D expenditure encourages investment, in a similar way to the previous models.

In the last model that we estimated, we found similar results when imports were examined as an alternative measure of openness. The two co-integrated vectors that were found are as follows, where the restrictions were accepted with a *p*-value of 0.071 (statistics in brackets):

$$lprod = 0.47linv + 2.04mgdp + 0.24D_{s94} \tag{6}$$

$$[-21.23] \quad [-6.14] \qquad [-8.41]$$

$$linv = 0.22lrd - 0.17D_{s78} + 0.09t \tag{7}$$

$$[-5.30] \quad [7.06] \qquad [-35.97]$$

These findings also suggest that openness led to growth. Once again, openness drives labour productivity exogenously in the long run. The direction of the causality runs from imports and investment to labour productivity in the long run in the first co-integrated vector and from R&D expenditure to investment in the second. An interesting result is the role played by the real exchange rate. As can be seen in our long-run relationships, the real exchange rate only improves labour productivity when the export-to-GDP ratio is included. However, it is not significant when imports or trade-to-GDP ratio are analysed. This finding is consistent with the economic policy carried out by the Chinese government in promoting exports, by maintaining a depreciated real exchange rate, to finance imports.

A result that is common to all the models analysed above, and which shows their robustness, is that both investment and openness to trade encourage labour productivity in the long run. In all the models estimated in this chapter, the direction of the causality runs from openness to labour productivity in the long run, regardless of the indicator employed in the estimation. Thus, unlike in other research, openness exogenously drives labour productivity. Moreover, capital accumulation causes labour productivity in the long run, and we did not find the causality running in the opposite direction. This finding supports the claim that capital accumulation has played a significant role in China from the 1960s to the present day. Furthermore, in all the models analysed, R&D expenditure encourages investment in the long run. The two findings are related to each other and are consistent with the Schumpeterian version of the endogenous growth theory.

Finally, given that an important aspect of the co-integrated VAR model is whether our variables grow together over time and converge into long-run relationships, we will briefly discuss the main dynamic aspects of the models under consideration.

In the first model, the labour productivity equation is error correcting with the two vectors found in equations (2) and (3). The alpha coefficient of productivity vector (2) indicates that the adjustment towards equilibrium is yearly and for the investment vector (3) the adjustment towards equilibrium is 18 monthly. We found that trade and investment have long-run effects on productivity, but only investment shows an additional, positive effect on the productivity equation in the short run. Thus, R&D expenditure is significant in both the short and the long run, while US GDP shows a positive effect in the short run. On the other hand, the investment equation is error correcting with its own vector in (3). The interpretation of the alpha coefficient is that almost every year investment adjusts towards equilibrium. In the dynamics, we observe a positive effect of one's own lag in investment, US GDP and trade in the short run. Moreover, R&D expenditure has a positive short- and long-run effect on the investment equation. Finally, the real exchange rate adjusts towards equilibrium when investment is below its steady state. In the dynamics we found that trade, US GDP and investment tend to appreciate the Renminbi and, on the contrary, productivity tends to depreciate it.

In the second model, the productivity equation is error correcting with the two co-integrated vectors found in equations (4) and (5). The alpha coefficient shows that almost every year the productivity vector in (4) adjusts towards equilibrium, while the investment vector shows a slower adjustment almost every two years in (5). In the dynamics, we found that exports show a negative effect in the short run, but in the long run this effect is positive. R&D expenditure plays a relevant role again in both the short and the long run. Finally, both US GDP and one's own lag in productivity display pro-cyclical behaviour in the short run. On the other hand, the investment equation is error correcting with its own vector (5). The adjustment towards equilibrium takes almost 18 months. In the dynamics, we observe that only R&D and productivity positively affect the investment equation. In contrast, US GDP and exports show a negative effect in the short run. Finally, the last equation in this model is the real exchange rate, which adjusts towards equilibrium when the investment vector is below its steady state. The adjustment is very slow. In the short run, we found that exports tend to depreciate the Chinese currency.

In the last model that was estimated, the productivity equation adjusts with the two vectors found in equations (6) and (7). The alpha coefficients show that the adjustment for the first vector is almost every year, while for the second it is almost every two years. We found that imports and investment stimulate productivity, while R&D expenditure encourages investment in the long run. In the dynamics, we found that one's own lag in productivity and US GDP both have a positive effect on the productivity equation, while imports and real exchange rate have a negative effect. Again, an important result is that R&D plays a significant role in both the short and the long run. Finally, the investment equation is error correcting with its own vector in (7) and adjustment towards equilibrium takes a year. In the dynamics, we found that only labour productivity and R&D have a positive effect on the investment equation, while the real exchange rate shows a negative effect in the short run.

## Conclusions

There is a debate in the economic literature over the relationships among openness, investment and productivity. Trade is considered to be an important channel as a potential generator of positive effects on growth and productivity. Economies of scale, self-selection firms, spillovers or externalities are some of the different arguments that can be found in the literature on trade and economic growth. Nevertheless, and despite these arguments, the empirical evidence for the positive effect of trade on growth seems inconclusive. On the other hand, economic theory also argues that capital accumulation stimulates growth and productivity, although some controversy exists about its effects in the long run.

In this chapter we have analysed whether the fast process of economic growth in China, especially in labour productivity, can be explained mainly through openness to trade. Unlike other studies, we have included investment in our models, given that capital accumulation has played an important role in China since the 1960s, together with other relevant factors such as R&D expenditure, the real exchange rate and US GDP level. These last two variables take into account the interactions of the Chinese economy with the rest of the world.

Our findings suggest that openness encourages labour productivity in the long run. This result is robust to different indicators of openness. In addition, we found that capital accumulation also plays a significant role in China's growth. However, this result is only possible when trade and capital accumulation are jointly considered in our estimations. Moreover, we found that R&D expenditure promotes capital accumulation in the long run. These results are interesting in the sense that the economic policies addressed to stimulate openness and capital accumulation enhance labour productivity. In addition, the innovation effort encourages investment and, as a consequence, capital accumulation. Both factors are crucial in the Chinese development strategy. Finally, we found that when trade and exports are included in the first and second models, the real exchange rate exerts a positive effect on labour productivity, which is probably related to an extra effect associated with gains in competitiveness.

In the dynamics, we found an interesting result that is common to all the models analysed and which consists in the role played by R&D expenditure in stimulating labour productivity in both the short and the long run. In addition, we found that in many models the US GDP, as a measure of foreign demand, and one's own lag in labour productivity both behave in a pro-cyclical manner in the short run.

The investment policy during the pre-reform period seems to have created favourable conditions for the gradual and successful implementation of the economic reforms carried out by the Chinese government since 1978. As a result, trade policy, the progressive deregulation of the market, R&D

investment and greater efficiency in resource allocation, among others, have encouraged economic growth in China for almost four decades.

## Acknowledgements

We are grateful to Dr Zhongmin Wu, Professor Alberto Bagnai, the participants at the 18th Annual Conference of the Chinese Economic Association at the University of Nottingham and two anonymous referees for helpful comments and suggestions. Financial support from the Spanish Ministry of Education and Science and FEDER (SEC 2005-08764 ECON) and the Generalitat Valenciana is gratefully acknowledged. The usual disclaimer applies.

## Notes

1 Source: National Bureau of Statistics of China.
2 This kind of average effect, of course, may disguise some of the processes actually taking place within an economy with the characteristics and the complexity of China's, although they could probably be revealed by an analysis with more disaggregate industry and geographical data.
3 In this chapter, productivity was corrected by applying the methodology suggested by Nielsen (2004).
4 The real effective exchange rate is not available from the NBS.
5 We took total expenditure on scientific research from the NBS as a proxy variable for R&D expenditure.
6 Real Exchange Rate = Nominal Exchange Rate ($CPI_{US}/CPI_{CHINA}$), where CPI is the respective consumer price index.
7 The shift dummies restricted to the co-integration space and the unrestricted permanent dummies were constructed following Juselius (2007, Chapter 6).
8 Available upon request.
9 The residual analyses of all models estimated in this chapter are available upon request.
10 Causality is assessed through significance tests on VECM parameters, as can be seen in the dynamics of the models estimated in Table 10.4.
11 In this chapter, all the models estimated are stable in the concentrated model version (R-form), but complete parameter constancy (X-form) is difficult to ensure in a period of important changes. In this regard, our estimates should be interpreted as an average effect. In all models estimated in this chapter, the recursive analyses are available upon request.
12 We have imposed the restriction of being equal to zero on the coefficients of the variables that are not significant until the most irreducible form is reached. In all cases, these restrictions are accepted, as can be seen in the *p*-value that we report, given that it is over 0.05.

## References

Amiti M. and Konings J. 2005. Trade liberalization, intermediate inputs and productivity: evidence from Indonesia, Centre for Economic Policy Research Discussion Paper No. 5104.
Aschauer, D.A. 1988. Government spending and the 'falling rate' of profit, *Journal of Economic Perspectives*, 12, 11–17.

Aschauer, D.A. 1989. Is public expenditure productive?, *Journal of Monetary Economics*, 23, 177–200.

Baldwin, R. and Seghezza, E. 1996. Trade-induced investment-led growth, National Bureau of Economic Research, Working Paper No. 5582.

Barro, R. 1991. Economic growth in a cross section of countries, *Quarterly Journal of Economics*, 106, 407–443.

Bernard, A.B. and Jensen, J. 1999. Exceptional exporter performance: cause, effect, or both?, *Journal of International Economics*, 47, 1–25.

Chow, G. 1993. Capital formation and economic growth in China, *Quarterly Journal of Economics*, 108, 809–842.

Coe, D.T, Helpman, E. and Hoffmaister, A.W. 1997. North–south R&D spillovers, *Economic Journal*, 107, 134–149.

De Long, J.B. and Summers, L.H. 1991. Equipment investment and economic growth, *Quarterly Journal of Economics*, 106, 445–502.

De Long, J.B., and Summers, L.H. 1992. Equipment investment and economic growth: How strong is the nexus?, *Brookings Papers on Economic Activity*, 23, 157–211.

Grossman, G.M. and Helpman, E. 1991. *Innovation and Growth in the Global Economy*, Cambridge, MA: MIT Press.

Helpman, E. 1988. Growth, technological progress and trade, *Empirica Austrian Economic Papers*, 5, 5–25.

Helpman, E. and Krugman, P.R. 1985. *Market Structure and Foreign Trade*, Cambridge, MA: MIT Press.

Hendry, D.F. and Mizon, G.E., 1993. Evaluating econometric models by encompassing the VAR, in P. C. B. Philips (ed.), *Models, Methods and Application of Econometrics: Essays in Honor of A. R. Bergstron*, Cambridge, MA: MIT Press.

Howitt, P. 2000. Endogenous growth and cross-country income differences, *American Economic Review*, 90, 829–846.

Howitt, P. and Aghion, P. 1998. Capital accumulation and innovation as complementary factors in long-run growth, *Journal of Economic Growth*, 3, 111–130.

Hsiao, S.T. and Hsiao, W. 2006. FDI, exports, and GDP in East and Southeast Asia: panel data versus time-series causality analyses, *Journal of Asian Economics*, 17, 1082–1106.

Johansen, S. 1988. Statistical analysis of cointegration vectors, *Journal of Economic Dynamics and Control*, 12, 231–254.

Johansen, S. 1995. *Likelihood-based Inference in Co-integrated Vector Auto-regressive Models*, Oxford: Oxford University Press.

Johansen, S. and Juselius, K. 1990. Maximum likelihood estimation and inference on co-integration, with applications to the demand for money, *Oxford Bulletin of Economics and Statistics*, 52, 169–210.

Johansen, S. and Juselius, K. 1994. Identification of the long-run and the short-run structure: an application to the ISLM model, *Journal of Econometrics*, 63, 7–36.

Juselius, K. 2007. *The Cointegrated VAR Model: Econometric Methodology and Macroeconomics Applications*, Oxford: Oxford University Press.

Lardy, N. 1993. *Foreign Trade and Economic Reform, 1978–1990*, Cambridge: Cambridge University Press.

Lee, J.W. 1995. Capital goods imports and long-run growth, *Journal of Development Economics*, 48, 91–110.

Levine, R. and Renelt, D. 1992. A sensitivity analysis of cross-country growth regressions, *American Economic Review*, 82, 942–963.

Liu, X., Burridge, P. and Sinclair, P.J.N. 2002. Relationships between economic growth, foreign direct investment and trade: evidence from China, *Applied Economics*, 34, 1433–1440.

Liu, X., Song, H. and Romilly, P. 1997. An empirical investigation of the causal relationship between openness and economic growth in China, *Applied Economics*, 29, 1679–1686.

Lopez, R.A. 2005. Trade and growth: reconciling the macroeconomic and microeconomic evidence, *Journal of Economic Surveys*, 19, 623–648.

Lopez, R.A. 2006. Imports of intermediate inputs and plant survival, *Economics Letters*, 92, 58–62.

MacDonald, J.M. 1994. Does import competition force efficient production?, *Review of Economics and Statistics*, 76, 721–727.

Madsen, J.B. 2002. The causality between investment and economic growth, *Economics Letters*, 74, 157–163.

Mazumdar, J. 2001. Imported machinery and growth in LDCs, *Journal of Development Economics*, 65, 209–224.

Melitz, M.J. 2003. The impact of trade on intra-industry reallocations and aggregate industry productivity, *Econometrica*, 71, 1695–1725.

Nielsen, B. and Rahbek, A. 2000. Similarity issues in cointegration analysis, *Oxford Bulletin of Economics and Statistics*, 62, 5–22.

Nielsen, H. 2004. Cointegration analysis in the presence of outliers, *Econometrics Journal*, 7, 249–271.

Qin, D., Cagas, A., Quising, P. and He, X. 2005. How much does investment drive economic growth in China? Queen Mary University of London, Department of Economics, Working Paper No. 545.

Ram, C.A. and Keller, W. 2007. Technology transfer through imports, Centre for Economic Policy Research, Discussion Paper No. 6296.

Rodrick, D. 1995. Getting interventions right: how South Korea and Taiwan grew rich, *Economic Policy*, 10, 53–107.

Rodríguez, F. and Rodrik, D. 2001. Trade policy and economic growth: a skeptic's guide to the cross-national evidence, in B. S. Bernake and K. Rogoff (eds), *NBER Macroeconomics Annual 2000*, Cambridge, MA: MIT Press.

Rodrik, D. 1999. *New Global Economics and Developing Countries: Making the Openness Work*, policy essay No. 24, Washington DC Overseas Development Council, Baltimore: Johns Hopkins University Press.

Shan, J. and Sun, F. 1998. On the export-led growth hypothesis: the econometric evidence from China, *Applied Economics*, 30, 1055–1065.

Thangavelu, S.M. and Rajaguru, G. 2004. Is there an export or import-led productivity growth in rapidly developing Asian countries? A multivariate VAR analysis, *Applied Economics*, 36, 1083–1093.

Traca, D.A. 2002. Imports as competitive discipline: the role of the productivity gap, *Journal of Development Economics*, 69, 1–21.

Yusuf S. 1994. China's macroeconomic performance and management during transition, *Journal of Economic Perspectives*, 8, 71–92.

# 11 Private sector development in Anhui Province

## The impact of regional spillovers from Jiangsu Province

*Genia Kostka*

### Introduction

Much of the recent literature on China's growth refers to the importance of foreign direct investment (FDI) (Huang 2003; Madariaga and Poncet 2007) and the privatization of state-owned enterprises (SOEs) (Garnaut *et al.* 2005). This chapter, however, focuses on regional spillovers from the coast to an adjacent province and the impact it has on private sector development (hereinafter 'PSD'). With rising costs of land and labour, as well as changes in environmental regulations in coastal areas, various resources have started to shift from the coastal provinces to adjacent interior provinces. By focusing on four counties in Anhui Province in central China, this chapter describes and analyses the different resource flows from Jiangsu and other coastal provinces to Anhui and the consequent economic impact on private sector development. Furthermore, this chapter analyses the steps taken by four different county governments to attract certain types of resource flow from the coast.

The topic of regional spillovers and PSD is particularly timely for several reasons. First, a deeper understanding of the various dynamics of PSD is important for gaining a fuller picture of China's economic transition process. The conventional view is that FDI liberalization played a key role in economic reforms. However, FDI was concentrated in the coastal areas throughout most of the reform period and only started to flow to the non-coastal regions at a later stage and in smaller quantities.[1] Therefore, while FDI was a driving force behind economic reform near the coast, one could argue that PSD *preceded* foreign investment inflow as well as SOE reform in non-coastal areas.

Second, analysing the economic impact of spillovers on PSD sheds light on the ingredients of regional economic growth. Private enterprises are widely regarded as being more profitable and efficient than SOEs (Dougherty and Herd 2005; Gao 2004; Jefferson *et al.* 1996; Phillips and Shen 2005). Consequently, regions with larger private sectors are hypothesized to have higher income levels. In addition, with the gradual removal of agricultural taxes and fees (*shuifei gaige*) since January 2006, local government finances have increasingly depended on taxation of private non-agricultural enterprises. This has placed considerable fiscal pressure on governments in central provinces like Anhui, where the agricultural sector still plays an important role.[2]

Third, given the large regional disparities in China, the question of how growth and development in one region influences the growth trajectory in neighbouring regions has become an important question for policy-makers and academics alike.

While resource flows affect enterprise development for all ownership types, including SOEs, collectives and foreign enterprises, this chapter focuses on private enteprises only. Private enterprises contribute the majority of GDP, especially after most industrial enterprises have been privatized under the policy of 'grasp the big, release the small' (*zhuada fangxiao*) during the late 1990s and early 2000s.

This research adopts a narrow definition of the private sector. The private sector is defined as domestic privately-owned enterprises with more than eight employees (*siying qiye*). This definition, based on registration status, excludes self-employed individuals and small private enterprises in the registration category of *getihu* (with up to eight employees). The adopted definition also excludes enterprises with mixed ownership, such as shareholding companies that include shares of private capital. As such, although this narrow definition of the private sector under-reports private sector activities, it allows one to focus on purely privately-owned enterprises. Finally, this research concentrates on non-agricultural PSD, whereby non-agricultural activities refers to the secondary industry (i.e. industry, construction) as well as the tertiary industry (i.e. services).

This chapter proceeds as follows. It begins with a literature review and an explanation of the research methodology used to measure the type and scope of resource flows towards the four selected counties in Anhui. The chapter then examines the different resource flows from Jiangsu and other coastal provinces to the four counties to explain the observed uneven growth patterns. This is followed by a discussion of different government policies at the county level to attract non-local resources to their localities.

**Literature review**

This section reviews the existing literature on theories of economic geography and regional spillovers, as well as the resource-based view of enterprise development.

One explanation for China's regional differences in economic development is that geographic location matters. Frankel and Romer (1999) argue that there is a positive relationship between access to major seaports and trade volume. Good infrastructure can compensate to some extent for poor geographical location by connecting customers and suppliers, thereby lowering transportation costs (Demurger 2001; Fleisher and Chen 1997).

New economic geographic research, moreover, shows industrial agglomeration effects and why clusters grow and prosper (Krugman and Venables 1995; Puga 1999). Mobility of inputs encourages firms to cluster together, thereby intensifying positive externalities such as the development of the division and specialization of labour among enterprises; the development of skilled labour markets; and information spillovers (Schmitz and Nadvi 1999). Porter (1990) points out that the expansion of a cluster makes market entry easier for new enterprises with little technical and managerial experience. Clusters have formed across China, and recent research on cluster formation has looked at the garment (Sonobe *et al.* 2002), motorcycle (Sonobe *et al.* 2006) and footwear (Huang *et al.* 2008) industries.Given that regional economic inequalities pose a potential threat to social stability, the question of if and how more developed regions provide spillovers to less developed regions is important. Brun *et al.* (2002) use provincial-level time series data for real per capita growth rates during 1981–98 and find significant spillovers from the coastal region to provinces in the central region, but no effect on the western region. Fu (2004) shows how coastal provinces which focus on processing-intensive exports received resource inflows from interior regions, but created only limited growth linkages to the interior regions. Fu argues that China's processing-export sector remains an enclave. Groenewold *et al.* (2008), using a six-region vector auto-regressive model, found the Yellow River and the *Changjiang* River regions to have significant spillover effects on other regions, while this was not the case for growth in other regions.[3]

However, by combining the Upper-*Changjiang* Region (Hubei, Hunan, Jiangxi and Anhui) and the Lower-*Changjiang* region (Shanghai, Jiangsu, Zhejiang) into one *Changjiang* River region, their results do not account for intra-regional spillovers, which could be large. In summary, further research is needed to analyse regional spillovers, as studies are few in number and partially conflicting. The literature has so far focused on output growth as an indicator of regional spillovers, but information on the types and channels of spillovers are still missing. This chapter addresses this research gap and describes the different types of spillover from Jiangsu to the four counties in Anhui in terms of resource flows. Resources, as the basic unit of analysis, can be defined as inputs into the production process through which the private enterprise can perform operations. The resource-based view of enterprises suggests that private enterprises can generate competitive advantages by applying core resources and capabilities, thus accelerating their development path (Nelson and Winter 1982; Wernerfelt 1984). Private enterprises can have different resources such as financial, physical, human and organizational resources (Barney 1991). Grant (1991) extended these by two other factors – technological resources and reputation. Additional 'invisible assets' are important, which Itami and Roehl (1987) introduced as 'information-based resources' such as management skills and experience, distribution control, corporate culture, consumer trust and brand image. The resource-based view distinguishes resources as *stocks* (inputs) and capabilities as resource *flows*, with the latter being the focus of this chapter.

Given that economic growth has been centred in the coastal region, local governments need to adopt policies that encourage selected resource flows from the coast to the interior. Government policies differ from policies targeting 'capital' flows to 'human resource' flows to 'information' flows. Fu (2004) suggests that government policies that encourage capital flow to labour surplus areas are more effective than policies encouraging migration. This chapter investigates the different types of resource flow from a coastal to an interior province, and links them with government policies adopted.

## Research methodology

This research analyses the different resource flows from Jiangsu to central Anhui and how local government policies have supported this resource flow to Anhui's interior counties in recent years. The focus is on three counties and one district (Tianchang, Nanqiao, Laian and Dingyuan) in Chuzhou Prefecture in central Anhui. These three counties and one district were selected in a three-fold process:

1　From the different central provinces, the pericoastal central provinces of Jiangxi and Anhui had the highest *siying qiye* share in total non-agricultural employment, with 12 and 10 per cent, respectively, whereas shares were much lower in the more interior provinces of Henan (5 per cent) and Hubei (8 per cent). This could indicate that, in terms of PSD, Anhui and Jiangxi benefited from their proximity to Jiangsu and Zhejiang. Anhui is particularly intriguing to study given its geographical proximity to its neighbouring coastal provinces, Jiangsu and Zhejiang, and the 'life blood' of the *Changjiang* River passing through the province. Despite its preferential geographical location, the private share in total non-agricultural employment in Anhui in 2005 was only 10 per cent, in contrast to 59 per cent in Shanghai, 28 per cent in Jiangsu and 22 per cent in Zhejiang (*China Statistical Yearbook 2006*).

2　The 17 prefectures in Anhui differ widely in terms of the role of the private sector. For example, in 2005 some prefectures, such as Fuyang and Bozhou, had only a small private share in total non-agricultural employment of 4–5 per cent. Other prefectures, such as Hefei and Huangshan, had a private share of 32 and 17 per cent, respectively. Among the 17 prefectures, *Chuzhou* Prefecture – with a 14 per cent private share in non-agricultural employment and located in north-central Anhui – was selected as an example of a prefecture bordering coastal provinces for three reasons. (a) Chuzhou shares similar geographical characteristics with other prefectures as it is hilly, does not have an access to a port (the closest is 130 km away), and no coal or copper resource endowments. (b) Tianchang County in Chuzhou Prefecture is surrounded on three sides by Jiangsu, which allows for the study of the impact of physical proximity to Jiangsu. Tianchang County is among the top ten counties in Anhui; since 1996 the county has grown at an average growth rate of 22 per cent and the GDP per capita doubled from 5,290 RMB in 1996 to 10,120 RMB in 2005 (Anhui Statistical Yearbook 1997, 2006). The success of Tianchang County is mainly due to a flourishing electronics industry that emerged in the 1980s in Qinlan Town, which is located at the border of Jiangsu. (c) The level of development of neighbouring coastal areas varies, with Zhejiang being slightly more developed than the Jiangsu border. Chuzhou Prefecture just borders Jiangsu, which minimizes this variation, although variation still exists whereby North Jiangsu is more developed than South Jiangsu. Chuzhou Prefecture has a total population of 4.4 million people and its administrative units consist of six counties and two districts. In Chuzhou, Nanqiao District and the three counties of Tianchang, Laian and Dingyuan were selected, which in the following will all be referred to as counties.[4] Figure 11.1 illustrates the location of the four counties.

3   Tianchang, Laian and Nanqiao are examples of bordering pericoastal counties. To test for differences with non-pericoastal counties, Dingyuan was selected. Tianchang is most exposed to Jiangsu, however the borders of Laian and Nanqiao are closest to Nanjing, the capital of Jiangsu.

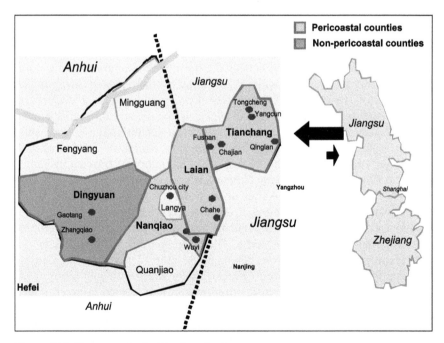

*Figure 11.1* Four counties in Chuzhou Prefecture.

*Source:* The author.

Since quantitative data on resource flows are not available, a qualitative approach was selected to describe the different types of resource flow from Jiangsu to Anhui. The results are based on 104 interviews in Anhui Province between 2006 and 2007, out of which 41 interviews were conducted in Chuzhou Prefecture during January to March and October to December 2007.[5]

Interviews were conducted with both sides – government officials (e.g. mayors and party secretaries, managers of industrial parks, managers of the local industrial and commercial bureaus) and private entrepreneurs (e.g. local owners and managers, as well as non-local investors). To increase reliability, data were collected in semi-structured interviews via open, indirect questions. To limit the selection bias, interviewees were acquired by two different channels: (a) introduced by the government (68 per cent) or (b) via private contacts (32 per cent). Interviews with business entrepreneurs are somewhat biased due to the fact that, if introduced by governments, the size of the enterprises was generally larger. As such, private contacts were then used to find smaller enterprises to complete the picture. Furthermore, if introduced by the government, the business–government relationship can be assumed to be better than average. Besides interviews, data were collected and analysed through multiple sources of evidence, such as government records, local gazetteers (*difang zhi*), statistical yearbooks, company brochures and websites, as well as through the author's own observations.

## Results

### Resource flows from coast to interior

Interior pericoastal provinces adjacent to coastal provinces can benefit from their developed neighbours. Looking at the four selected case studies, it is noticeable that pericoastal counties have faster GDP growth than the non-pericoastal counties. Tianchang and Nanqiao had higher GDP growth rates, reflecting a faster industrialization pattern. In contrast, Laian and Dingyuan grew at a slower rate, and their GDP per capita in 2005 was only half of the GDP per capita of Tianchang (see Table 11.1).

One explanation for different growth rates across counties is differences in the inflow and outflow of resources. Following Barney (1991), resources flows are distinguished as financial flows (F), human flows (H) and information flows (I). Possible factors explaining larger private enterprise growth in pericoastal areas are: (1) higher inflow of coastal enterprises and coastal investments; (2) higher share of returning migrants; and (3) larger formal and informal inflow of information resources. Table 11.2 summarizes the hypothesis regarding the types of flows from the coast to pericoastal counties. Note that the reverse resource flows from pericoastal counties to the coast are not addressed in this chapter but are referred to in the discussion section.

Table 11.1 Different economic growth among selected counties

| | | GDP per capita (RMB) | GDP per capita growth 96–05* (%) | Total GDP (100 mill RMB) | GDP growth rate 96–05 (%) | GDP structure | | | Sector area (km sq) | Pop. density (per km sq) |
|---|---|---|---|---|---|---|---|---|---|---|
| | | | | | | Primary (%) | Secondary (%) | Tertiary (%) | | |
| Tianchang County (618,000 people) | 1996 | 5,293 | | 31.0 | | 34 | 44 | 22 | | |
| | 2005 | 10,116 | 21 | 62.4 | 22 | 25 | 48 | 26 | 1,770 | 349 |
| Nanqiao District (270,000 people) | 1996 | 3,555 | | 8.1 | | 58 | 28 | 14 | | |
| | 2005 | 6,851 | 21 | 18.5 | 21 | 35 | 44 | 21 | 1,271 | 211 |
| Laian County (490,000 people) | 1996 | 4,685 | | 21.8 | | 35 | 41 | 24 | | |
| | 2005 | 6,824 | 16 | 33.4 | 17 | 28 | 38 | 34 | 1,481 | 331 |
| Dingyuan County (920,000 people) | 1996 | 3,369 | | 25.6 | | 40 | 38 | 22 | | |
| | 2005 | 4,246 | 14 | 38.8 | 17 | 45 | 21 | 34 | 2,891 | 318 |

Sources: Various County Level Statistical Bureaus; Anhui Statistical Yearbook (ASYB; 1997, 2006).

*Table 11.2* Hypothesis regarding resource flows

|  | *Kind of resource flow* | *From coast to interior* |
|---|---|---|
| Financial flow | Investment flow | +++ |
|  | Relocation of enterprise | +++ |
|  | Remittances from migrants | + |
| Human flow | Skilled labour from coast | –/+ |
|  | Returning migrants | ++ |
| Information flow | Formal, i.e. documents, patents | + |
|  | Informal, i.e. apprenticeship | ++ |

*Note:* +++ represents strong flow from the coast to the interior; –/+ represents no or small flow.

In the following, the financial, human and information flows are described in terms of type and size across the four counties.

*Financial flows*

Within the financial flows from the coast to the interior, there are three sub-categories characterized as: (1) investment flows, (2) relocation of enterprises, and (3) remittances from migrants. The levels of flows differ across the four counties.

*Investment flows*

Across all four counties, domestic investments have increased since 2001, as summarized in Table 11.3. The majority of these investments are from coastal provinces (more than 95 per cent), while the remaining are from other central or western provinces.

Table 11.3 shows that the highest level of domestic investment was in Tianchang, with 1.8 billion RMB (230 million USD). In contrast, FDI amounted to only 21 million USD in 2006. The second highest level of domestic investments was in Laian, followed by Nanqiao; while the lowest level was in Dingyuan. Most localities started to track domestic investment figures only after 2003, as prior to then there was too little to track individually. Overall, it can be concluded that investments from coastal provinces increased rapidly during recent years, and in Chuzhou this investment was more concentrated in pericoastal counties than non-pericoastal counties.

*Relocation of enterprises*

Relocation of private enterprises from coastal to interior pericoastal localities can be another positive resource flow. The largest share of coastal companies

*Table 11.3* Domestic investment in selected counties (actually used, in 10,000 RMB)

|  |  | 2001 | 2002 | 2003 | 2004 | 2005 | 2006 |
|---|---|---|---|---|---|---|---|
| Tianchang | Investment | N/A | 17,000 | 41,000 | 69,000 | 111,000 | 181,500 |
|  | Annual growth (%) | N/A | N/A | 141 | 68 | 61 | 64 |
| Nanqiao | Investment | 32,380 | 36,376 | 41,300 | 51,635 | 63,670 | 81,000 |
|  | Annual growth (%) | 11 | 12 | 14 | 25 | 23 | 27 |
| Laian | Investment | N/A | N/A | 20,000 | 51,000 | 107,000 | 147,000 |
|  | Annual growth (%) | N/A | N/A | N/A | 155 | 110 | 37 |
| Dingyuan* | Investment | N/A | N/A | 12,541 | 46,313 | 71,271 | 108,464* |
|  | Annual growth (%) | N/A | N/A | N/A | 269 | 54 | 52 |

* The large increase in Dingyuan in 2006 was due to a large salt project (non-coastal, initiated by the Anhui Provincial Government). Hence, the investment inflow of 2005 more correctly reflects the rather low level of coastal investment in Dingyuan.

*Source:* Various County Statistical Bureaus, 2007.

was found in Tianchang. In 2006 alone, 158 coastal enterprises were introduced in Tianchang. For example, in Yangcun Town, 14 out of 18 enterprises (78 per cent) originated from the coast. In Nanqiao, in Wuyi Town, 60 per cent of all enterprises are coastal (24 out of 40). From the 66 enterprises in Laian's Economic Industrial Park (*Laian xian jingji kaifaqu*), 61 enterprises are coastal enterprises (92 per cent) and 5 are foreign enterprises. In contrast, of the approximately 600 private enterprises in Dingyuan, less than 10 per cent are coastal enterprises. Most of them are located in an industrial park, where 80 per cent of the 50 enterprises are those from the *Changjiang* River Delta.[6]

The majority of coastal enterprises relocating to the four counties come from Jiangsu and Zhejiang, while fewer enterprises relocated from the more distant coastal provinces, such as Fujian and Guangdong. Relocation occurs via two mechanisms: (1) private enterprises are either 'pushed out' by changes in regulation and rising input prices in coastal areas; or (2) 'pulled in' by investment-attracting policies offered by local governments. In addition, coastal companies relocated to Anhui in order to gain access to local markets.

The push-out mechanism refers to the fact that, with increased economic development, coastal cities began to establish urban plans, and environmental and market standardizations. For example, Nanjing – the provincial capital of Jiangsu – has pushed out under-performing enterprises in an effort characterized as 'empty the cage to create more room for the beautiful birds' (*teng long huan niao*).[7] During the process of industrial replanning, a government official in Laian summarized the flow of relocating enterprises as follows: 'Some enterprises cannot meet the new standards in Nanjing, so the enterprises get dumped by their local governments. Some chose to leave, others were asked to leave. In Anhui we take them, but we also require that they meet our standards.' Moreover, rising costs of land and labour, as well as difficulties in obtaining land for industrial use, accelerated the relocation of enterprises from Jiangsu to central Anhui.[8]

The pull-in mechanism supports the relocation of coastal enterprises due to preferential taxation policies, and the availability and lower cost of land and labour. Details regarding preferential policies are discussed in the subsequent section on government policies supporting the resource flow. Finally, coastal enterprises have entered Anhui to gain better market access in the four counties.

*Remittances from migrants*

Migrants further support the financial flow from coastal provinces to interior counties by sending remittances in the form of money, commodities and equipment. In China, migrants often bring home these financial resources during the annual spring festival. According to World Bank (1997) estimates, migrants usually send 20–50 per cent of their income home. These remittance flows become an important source of income for rural counties such as Dingyuan, where half of the farming population has migrated to coastal areas.[9] Table 11.4 summarizes the numbers of out-migrants and remittances, based on estimates provided by local governments. Table 11.5 summarizes different government practices.

In Dingyuan County, for instance, 217 people out of 1,000 migrate to the coast, which is more than a third of the total workforce. The government estimates that each migrant brings home 5,000 RMB per year, which would amount to an additional inflow of 1 billion RMB for Dingyuan.

*Table 11.4* Outward migration and remittance

| Location | Population (000s) | No. of out-migrants (000s) | Ratio* (migrants per 1,000 population) | Estimated remittances (RMB million)** |
|---|---|---|---|---|
| Tianchang | 618 | 100 | 162 | 500 |
| *Qinlan Town* | 62 | 3 | 48 | 15 |
| Nanqiao District | 270 | 50 | 185 | 250 |
| Laian | 490 | NA | NA | NA |
| Dingyuan | 920 | 200 | 217 | 1,000 |
| *Gao Township* | 21 | 6 | 286 | 30 |
| *Zhangqiao* | 34 | 7 | 206 | 35 |

* The denominator should be based on agricultural population rather than total population, but data were lacking; **average of 5,000 RMB remittance per year was used for the estimation. Estimates by the Agricultural Bank of China in Tianchang range between 5,000–10,000 RMB as average remittance per year.

*Table 11.5* Government policies and measurable indicators

| Policy | Main policy purpose | Possible measurable indicators |
|---|---|---|
| (1) Industrial Park Policy | Improve infrastructure | Number of IPs near coastal province<br>Investment in IP infrastructure |
|  | Set up preferential conditions | Size and production output of IPs |
| (2) Relocation policy for Coastal Enterprises | Set up preferential conditions<br>Increase coastal investment | Preferential Policies (taxation, land)<br>Representative office in coastal cities<br>Promotion trips to the coastal areas |
|  | Increase availability of land | Village reorganisation to create land for industrial use |
| (3) Financial Policy | Increase bank loans to local enterprises | Organization of fairs between banks and enterprises<br>Encouragement to lend to local enterprises |
| (4) Migration Policy | Attract returning migrants | Preferential land policies for migrants<br>Organisation of fairs during spring festival<br>Development of personal relationships with migrants |

*Source:* Interviews, 2007.

Out-migration is lowest in Tianchang, with 162 people per 1,000 people migrating, followed by Nanqiao. No estimates were available for Laian County.

Finally, most of these remittances are deposited into local banks, which, in turn, transfer a large sum of this money back to the coastal areas as loans. As a result, the interior localities do not reap the benefits of the migrants' savings.

*Human flows*

In examining the labour flow from the coast to the interior, one must distinguish between (1) skilled coastal labour, and (2) returning migrants (skilled or unskilled). Unskilled labour flows mainly from the interior to the coastal regions, whereas reciprocal flows are small.

SKILLED LABOUR

All four counties experienced inward migration via skilled labour from the coast. In the early 1980s, *xiafang* intellectuals, as well as personal contacts in

Jiangsu, provided informal information for central Anhui.[10] In Qinlan Town in Tianchang, a *xiafang* technician established the first electronics factory, which later gave rise to many more electronics companies.

In the late 1980s and early 1990s, such information channels, although still informal, were expanded in scope by local governments inviting experts and engineers from Jiangsu to work in their free time for private enterprises (these are the so-called 'Sunday engineers'). By the mid-1990s, access to technicians became easier and, in addition to inviting engineers for short-term visits, localities began to hire laid-off engineers from transformed SOEs and retired SOE engineers from Jiangsu.[11]

Often these skilled coastal workers were hired in management positions or set up their own businesses. For example, a truck manufacturing enterprise in Wuyi Town in Nanqiao hired a Shanghai engineer and paid him a competitive salary, drawing upon the engineer's previous work experience in a large SOE in Shanghai.

Finally, attracting experts for long-term stays was – and continues to be – challenging in all four counties, as few talented people are willing to settle in small cities because of the inadequate provision of housing, entertainment, education and medical care. This is discussed further in the section on government policies.

RETURNING MIGRANTS

In addition to sending remittances, the localities in this study reported that 30–40 per cent of all migrants eventually returned to live in their home town.[12] These migrants return bearing a wealth of experience from working in the coastal cities (Murphy 2002). However, the impact of the migrants' know-how varies depending on the kind of job, industry and length of time of their stay. For example, in Tianchang some of the largest private enterprises such as *Tiansen* Wood Factory and *Shuangfeng* Stationery were founded by returning migrants.

Wang and Fan (2006) point out that many studies overemphasize the fact that returning migrants become hometown entrepreneurs and that returning migrants are negatively selected among migrants. Interviews from this study suggest that, in Chuzhou, only 4–5 per cent of all returnees engage in entrepreneurial activities.[13] This is supported by a study by Bai and Song (2002), which concludes that 2 per cent of returnees in Anhui and Sichuan become entrepreneurs. In summary, the flows of returning migrants are relatively large; however, the extent and nature of their impact remains open to debate.

*Information flows*

In addition to labour and capital, information flows are an important third part of resource flows from coastal regions to the interior. A differentiation needs to be made between: (1) formal information, such as that gained in meetings or documents, which can be measured; and (2) informal information, such as that acquired through personal friendships, which is harder to trace.

FORMAL INFORMATION

Organized meetings and study trips occur between entrepreneurs, between entrepreneurs and government, between government institutions, all of which facilitates information flows from Jiangsu to the four counties. Government study trips encompass a wide range of themes, including learning about industrial parks and clusters or credit-guarantee companies (*danbao gongsi*). County governments actively sought information from equivalent coastal bureaus, especially in Tianchang and Nanqiao. The county government in Nanqiao visited Jiangling industrial park in Nanjing and introduced some experts from Nanjing to their county, asking for their expertise in creating a local industrial park.[14] Tianchang also received advice from professors at Nanjing University on planning the local Qinlan industrial park in 1999. By early 2007, this industrial park, with its cluster focus on electronics, stood out in Chuzhou Prefecture.

Formal information flows are also increasingly occurring between research institutes in the coast and local enterprises in Anhui. For instance, private enterprises in Tianchang cooperated with different research institutions in Nanjing and Shanghai, such as Nanjing University and Shanghai Development and Research Centre. Cooperation with research institutions enabled Tianchang enterprises to draw upon know-how that is difficult to access otherwise.

INFORMAL INFORMATION

Informal information flows occur through informal channels, such as through personal friendships formed during study, work, shopping or visits to relatives. As Chuzhou Prefecture lacks its own university, students often go to Nanjing or Shanghai to study. These students serve as an information bridge between coastal provinces and the four counties, even if the students remain in the coastal provinces after their studies.

In Tianchang, the people's general willingness to learn from their better-off neighbours was especially high. Interestingly, the county government's business cards depict Tianchang using a full picture of the adjacent Jiangsu Province while cutting out the rest of Anhui. This reflects the county government's orientation towards its neighbouring pericoastal province. Many private enterprises reported that the benefits derived from being close to Jiangsu included easier access to the best practices in business operation and management. Closeness to Jiangsu also influenced local people's thinking, as locals wanted to do as well as, or even better than, their neighbours.[15]

## Government policies at the county level

This section describes the type of government policies adopted by the four county governments. It is hypothesized that county governments adopted different policies to influence the financial, human and information flows particular to their own region. Government policies vary in breadth and depth, but the most frequent policies can be grouped into the following categories: (1) industrial park policy, (2) relocation policy of coastal enterprises, (3) financial policy, and (4) migration policy.

Industrial park (IP) policy concerns the setting up and managing of industrial parks, which are areas of land set aside for focused industrial development. The relocation policy of coastal enterprises attempts to attract coastal enterprises to relocate to the four counties through preferential incentives. Financial policy aims to better direct the remittances stored in local banks towards local enterprises. Migration policy refers to policies targeted at increasing the share of returning migrants.

In linking government policies to resource flows, one can see that pericoastal government policies target different flows from the coast to Anhui. This is shown in Table 11.6.

The creation and management of industrial parks has the best overall effect on financial, human and information flows, relative to the other government policies. However, it is harder for certain counties such as Dingyuan to focus on IP policies and to attract coastal enterprises to relocate to such counties due to their remote locations.

### *Industrial park policy*

During the late 1990s and early 2000s, a primary focus of all four county governments has been the establishment of industrial parks in order to attract businesses.[16] Counties benefit from establishing an IP by gaining additional land for industrial use since land quotas are governed by different usage purposes by the Central Bureau of Land. Furthermore, through the establishment of IPs, local economies can benefit from other preferential central government policies, such as taxation.

*Table 11.6* Estimated impact of policies on resource flows

|  | *Financial flow* | *Human flow* | *Information flow* |
| --- | --- | --- | --- |
| (1) Industrial Park Policy | +++ | + | ++ |
| (2) Reallocation Policy | +++ | + | ++ |
| (3) Financial Policy | +++ | – | – |
| (4) Migration Policy | + | +++ | ++ |

*Note:* +++ represents strong impact of government policy on resource flow; –/+ represents no or small impact

However, the setting up of IPs entails costs which include: (1) the opportunity cost for the crop forgone on the former agricultural land; (2) the price for the land itself; (3) the reallocation of labour to the often remote location of the IP; (4) the construction of the logistics infrastructure such as roads or railroads; and (5) the establishment of electricity, water, energy and communication infrastructure.

The timing of constructing an IP is important. Counties like Tianchang or Nanqiao set up IPs in the late 1990s. As a result, they benefited from the larger financial inflows compared to counties such as Laian, which only recently established IPs. Furthermore, prior to 2003, there was a better chance to obtain official permission to create an IP. The mayor of a town in Nanqiao comments: 'The government is regulating IP creation more strictly and we cannot get approval. Instead, we have received another title, called "base to setting up business" (*chuang ye ji di*).'[17] Laian County has focused its strategy on IP in particular, creating two large industrial parks. The Laian *Chahe* IP was one of the biggest investments made by the county and Chuzhou Prefecture governments in the period 2005 to 2006. The *Chahe* IP is located just 300 metres from the Jiangsu border and has attracted coastal enterprises by offering land that is a quarter of the price of that in Nanjing.[18] *Chahe* IP has attracted heavy industry, with lower environmental restrictions than in Nanjing. An official in the Industrial Park Administrative Bureau explains:

> What is even more important than different land prices is that Nanjing is now getting rid of those old enterprises which are polluting or noisy and thereby contradicting current urban planning. We take in most of the Nanjing enterprises. From the 41 enterprises in this IP, already 85 per cent of them are from Nanjing.[19]

This shows that push factors are an important factor in explaining the rising reallocation of enterprises from Jiangsu to Anhui.

While Nanqiao and Laian have built 'general' IPs, Tianchang and Dingyuan counties have created 'themed' IPs with an industrial focus. Tianchang set up themed IPs in four selected key towns: Chajian Town for food-processing, Qinlan Town for electronics, Yangcun Town for pharmaceuticals, and Tongcheng Town for machinery and cable. Dingyuan County, on the other hand, has focused its themed IPs on resource-extracting industries such as salt and plaster.

### Relocation policy of coastal enterprises

Contrary to preferential policies such as IPs, which are generally standardized, relocation policies cover a range of areas including: (1) land and factory policies; (2) unofficial returns of local taxation ('rewards') in addition to standard preferential taxation; (3) creation of a suitable living environment for managers from the coast; and (4) marketing of the interior location through representative offices in coastal cities, or undertaking promotional trips to the coastal areas in order to attract investment. Interviews with investors from Jiangsu suggest that a supportive living environment is especially important for attracting managers and technicians away from coastal regions. The four county governments have supported such transitions by helping with the enrolment of children in schools, offering yearly toll tickets for traffic usage, and giving financial support for physical relocation.[20] Tianchang, in particular, built a modern residential park to retain enterprise managers.

### Financial policy

Local governments can increase access to capital for local enterprises by encouraging local banks and migrants to provide loans to domestic enterprises. To encourage the provision of loans to domestic enterprises, local governments organize a yearly fair for banks and local enterprises. Furthermore, in Dingyuan, migrants who deposit money in a bank are able to 'tick a box' when they open the deposit account stating that they wish for the deposit to be lent to local enterprises.

However, the impact of these incentives is rather low, since commercial banks still return large amounts of deposit funds to higher-level bank branches instead of giving it to local enterprises. For example, in 2005, the Agricultural Bank in Tianchang County received 1.2 billion deposits, but it only provided 700 million loans to local enterprises (58 per cent). The remaining deposits were used as a reserve and given to higher-level branches, who then lent the money to the most profitable investment (usually in coastal provinces).[21] The situation is similar in Dingyuan: incoming deposits were 4.3 billion RMB in 2006, while the outgoing balance of loans was only 2.7 billion RMB (62 per cent). Furthermore, the majority of loans was allocated to the salt-extracting SOE (300 million RMB in 2006) and various grain production stations, and did not boost the local private economy.

### Migration policy

Migration policy includes devices to attract returning migrants. Key important factors for migrants to return are social status and good education for their children. Social status plays a major role for migrants to return, as such returnees perceive their social status to be higher in their home town than in the big city where their enterprise is only one among many. Usually migration policies are less structured, and include, for example: (1) symbolic rewards for returning migrants; (2) favourable land policies; and (3) active support in setting up a business. Like other localities in Anhui, all four counties have adapted the phrase '*fenghuang huan chao*' (to welcome the phoenix to come back to the nest).

Among the four counties, Dingyuan had the most active migration policies. Dingyuan was the first county in Chuzhou Prefecture to organize a migrant business fair, in 2006, during the Chinese spring festival. During this annual fair, migrant workers who return to set up their own businesses are given an award by the county government. Some towns also organize migrant worker get-togethers to visit specific cities to see the latest developments and discuss opportunities for employment or business.[22]

Overall the decision of migrants to return depends mainly on family needs, over which local governments have limited influence. However, maintaining a link to migrants when they visit during spring festivals, as well as fostering a local culture and identity, might help to create a 'home complex', which potentially translates into more returnees. But from an economic perspective, while a 'home complex' might be beneficial to the locality, it is not always the most efficient allocation of resources. For example, in Juchao District in the neighbouring Chaohu Prefecture, a steel structure-producing company was set up in a rural environment because the founder wanted to give back to his home town. By choosing his hometown for the business, however, the founder created an unfortunate situation in which the company has had to struggle with long-distance transportation, rendering it harder to compete with similar enterprises located closer to highways and markets.

## Discussion

This research analysed the different resource flows into the four counties in Chuzhou Prefecture, Anhui. Tianchang has experienced the strongest economic development, followed by Nanqiao and Laian; while Dingyuan remains at the bottom. Reasons for this intra-prefectural gap between Tianchang and other bordering counties and interior counties are mainly due to differences in private sector development. Table 11.7 orders the four selected counties by *siying qiye* share in total non-agricultural employment.

The growth of Tianchang can be explained by a flourishing export-driven electronics private sector, and the output of *siying qiye* is three to four times as high in Tianchang as it is in other counties. The *siying qiye* share in non-agricultural employment was 20 per cent in Tianchang compared to only 6 per cent in Dingyuan. Nanqiao and Laian also did comparatively well with *siying qiye* shares in total non-agricultural employment of 10 and 12 per cent, respectively.

This chapter has argued that resource flows into the four counties partially explain different development trajectories. Counties benefited via three resource channels: financial flows, human flows and information flows. The type and scope of such inflows varied across localities, but direct pericoastal counties benefited more from resource flows than non-pericoastal counties such as Dingyuan.

In addition to standard economic geography theory, support for the developmental state theory is evident in China. At all levels, county governments played an important role in influencing capital, human and information flows. For example, due to regulatory changes in larger coastal cities such as

Table 11.7 Size of private sector in selected counties (2006)

| | Siying Qiye (no.) | Employees in Siying Qiye (000s) | Share of Siying Qiye in non-agricultural employment (%) | Output value of Siying Qiye (RMB billion) | Description |
|---|---|---|---|---|---|
| Tianchang (618,000 people) | 2,171 | 75 | 20 | 3.6* | The majority of enterprises are start-ups or previous 'red hat' enterprises in the electronics industry, originating from family-based workshops. In recent years, cluster formation in electronics helped to lower entry barriers for private enterprises. |
| Nanqiao (270,000 people) | 375 | 19 | 10 | 1.2 | The majority of private enterprises are start-ups, while approximately 20% are transformed from collectives. |
| Laian (490,000 people) | 696 | 30 | 12 | 1.7 | Only few enterprises are local start-ups; mostly enterprises are former SOEs, former collectives or coastal enterprises. |
| Dingyuan (920,000 people) | 605 | 26 | 6 | N/A (sales volume 2.3 billion RMB) | Only few enterprises are local start-ups; mostly enterprises are former SOEs and former collectives. Coastal enterprises are few in number, so county relies on extraction of salt and plaster. |

*Source:* Interviews, County Statistical Bureaus, 2007.

* Refers to 2005 instead of 2006.

Nanjing, coastal companies were pushed out of the coastal areas into the neighbouring county of Chuzhou in Anhui. At the same time, coastal enterprises were pulled into Chuzhou by preferential taxation and land offered by the four counties.

This research has ignored resource flows from Chuzhou to the coastal provinces. Here, the same categories of financial, human capital and information flow apply. First, with respect to financial flows, the inflow of money from migrants into local commercial banks in Chuzhou must be carefully analysed, as a large share of the financial resources from migrants will benefit larger enterprises in the coast rather than smaller local enterprises. In addition, there are some enterprises relocating from Chuzhou to the coast. For example, in Tianchang some research-intensive enterprises have started establishing research centres in Shanghai, seeking the benefits of first-hand information and international recognition from being located in a large city.

Second, as mentioned throughout the chapter, migrant flows from the four counties to the coast are large, including both skilled and unskilled labour, with sometimes half of the labour force migrating to coastal areas. Being located near coastal cities also makes it harder for the four counties to retain human capital, especially as many young and talented people prefer to commute to larger coastal cities.

Third, in terms of information flows, mainly apprenticeship flows were recorded from the interior to the coast. However, some enterprises also reported that after employees underwent training in the interior, these workers left for the coast in search of higher wages.

## Conclusion and further research

In summary, a new development trend has emerged since 2000, whereby peri-coastal counties (i.e. those adjacent to coastal provinces) developed faster than non-pericoastal counties. This growth is partially due to differences in terms of private enterprise development, which was influenced by resource flows from the interior to coastal areas.

Furthermore, this chapter has argued that local governments have been actively engaged in encouraging such resource flows, by adopting policies that target financial, human and information flows. This chapter concludes that county governments have 'turned eastwards' to further their economic development, albeit using channels that vary from one locality to another. Government attitudes and policies differ depending on local characteristics specific to each of the counties examined. Some county governments have focused on gaining benefits from the neighbouring coastal provinces by focusing on the creation of industrial parks directly on the border (Laian), while others have focused on policies targeting the return of migrants (Dingyuan). Table 11.8 shows that, based on a comparison of economic growth, the first policy seems to be the more effective. However, non-pericoastal interior counties such as Dingyuan are faced with more difficulties in attracting

*Table 11.8* Summary of indicators for government policies

| | Interior counties (without large areas adjacent to coastal province) | Pericoastal counties (adjacent to coastal province) |
|---|---|---|
| Higher economic growth (21–22% GDP growth rate 1996–2005)* | Nanqiao<br>(1) Focus on IP creation, early<br>(2) IPs next to border<br>(3) –<br>(4) –<br>Diversified domestic industrial base. Benefits from closeness to Chuzhou City | Tianchang<br>(1) Focus on 'theme' IP creation, early<br>(2) Theme IPs next to border<br>(3) –<br>(4) –<br>Strong focus on creation of industrial base in electronics. Successful cluster and supply chain creation |
| Lower economic growth (16–17% GDP growth rate 1996–2005)* | Dingyuan<br>(1) IPs focus on salt and plaster extraction<br>(2) No special policies to attract enterprises<br>(3) Tickbox at local banks<br>(4) Focus on migration policy (fairs, training to go out, etc.) The largest enterprise is a salt-producing SOE | Laian<br>(1) Focus on two large IPs, but late creation<br>(2) Create two IPs next to border<br>(3) –<br>(4) –<br>Strong reliance on collectives and SOEs, with only few start-ups |

*Source:* Interviews, 2007.

* GDP growth rates summarized in Table 11.1.

coastal enterprises. Therefore, one could argue that Dingyuan has less policy choice compared with a pericoastal county.

In summary, the primary aim of this chapter has been to describe the different resource flows from Jiangsu and other coastal provinces to four selected counties (Nanqiao, Tianchang, Dingyuan and Laian). Further research is needed as open questions remain. First, more research needs to be undertaken in terms of looking at the *timing, sequencing* and *duration* of resource flows. Although difficult, more attempts should be made to *quantify* the size of flows by using sample surveys. Moreover, while this chapter has focused on the positive *impact of the flows*, efforts to estimate the impact of environmental damage due to increased pollution by the coastal enterprises would shed more light on this topic. Finally, infrastructure investments largely influence resource flows and could be addressed in further depth.

## Notes

1 Up to 2003, 86 per cent of all accumulated FDI went to the coast, 9 per cent to central China, and 5 per cent to the west (China Foreign Capital Utilization Report 2004, quoted in Xiong and Guan 2005).

2  For agricultural localities, the removal of agricultural taxation provided contradictory incentives; on the one hand, local governments had greater incentives for PSD, but on the other hand, there was an immediate incentive to collect more funds from private enterprises to fill payment gaps (Kennedy 2007).

3  The *Changjiang* River is traditionally also known as the Yangtze River.

4  The main difference between a county (*xian*) and a district (*qu*) is that a district is directly linked with the prefecture government, and this matters in terms of local taxation; e.g. a local bank in Nanqiao directly submits certain taxes to the prefecture, whereas in a county a local bank pays it to the county.

5  Of the 41 interviews in Chuzhou Prefecture, nine interviews were government-organized conferences held in the four selected counties with six or more government officials, organized for the purpose of this research.

6  Interviews with the town mayor in Wuyi, 16 January 2007, Nanqiao District (No. 108); interview with local government officials from the Laian Industrial Park Administrative Bureau, 9 January 2007, Laian County (No. 92); and interview with government officials in the Dingyuan Industrial Park Administrative Bureau, 8 November 2007, Dingyuan County (No. 185).

7  Interview with town mayor and party secretary, 29 January 2007, Dingyuan County (No. 130).

8  Interview with government official, Dingyuan Industrial Park, 8 November 2007, Dingyuan County (No. 185).

9  Form and length of migrating time varies; some leave to fulfil seasonal demand in the coastal cities, whereas others are long-term migrants leaving for over six months.

10  The verb *xiafang* literally means 'sending down' and refers to the policy of transferring cadres and urban-educated youth to rural areas during the Cultural Revolution.

11  For the three stages of 'borrowing brains', 'hiring brains' and 'training brains', see Peng (2007).

12  Murphy (2002) quotes a study whereby 36 per cent of rural migrants returned to Jiangxi, Anhui, Hubei and Sichuan. Wang and Fan (2006) find that 28 per cent of migrants returned to Anhui and Sichuan after working in urban areas for an average of 2.9 years.

13  Source: Chuzhou Prefecture government and interviews in various counties (Interviews Nos. 113 and 130).

14  Interview with the DRC, 16 January 2007, Nanqiao District (No. 107).

15  Interview with the town mayor, 12 January 2007, Tianchang, Qinlan Town (No. 99).

16  IPs are set up at the national, provincial, prefecture, county and town level. In addition to the 88 provincial-level IPs in Anhui province, there are hundreds of IPs at the county and town levels. IPs usually provide an integrated infrastructure such as roadways, high-power electric supplies, communication cables, water and gas supplies.

17  Interview with the town mayor, 2 February 2007, Nanqiao (No. 139).

18  Interview with the vice manager of the Laian IP Administration Committee, 8 January 2007, Laian (No. 86).

19  Interview with the manager of the *Chahe* IP, 9 January 2007, Laian (No. 92).

20  Interview with the vice mayor of Tianchang County, 10 January 2007, Tianchang (No. 94).

21  Interview with a manager at the Agricultural Bank of Tianchang, 13 March 2007, Tianchang (No. 153).

22  County government conference on PSD, 18 January 2007, Dingyuan County (No. 113).

# References

*Anhui Statistical Yearbook* (various years) (Anhui tongji nianjian), Beijing: Zhongguo tongji chubanshe.

Bai, N. and Song, H. (eds) (2002) *Huixiang haishi jingcheng? Zhongguo nongcun waichu laodongli huiliu yanjiu (Out to the City or Back to The Village? The Study of Rural–urban Return Migration in China)*, Beijing: Zhongguo Caizheng Jingji Chubanshe.

Barney, J.B. (1991) Firm resources and sustained competitive advantage, *Journal of Management*, 17, 99–120.

Brun, J.F., Combes, J.L. and Renard, M.F. (2002) Are there spillover effects between coastal and noncoastal regions in China?, *China Economic Review*, 13, 161–169.

*China Statistical Yearbook* (various years) Beijing: China Statistical Publishing House.

Demurger, S. (2001) Infrastructure, development and economic growth: an explanation for regional disparities in China?, *Journal of Comparative Economics*, 19, 95–117.

Dougherty, S. and Herd, R. (2005) *Fast-falling Barriers and Growing Concentration: The Emergence of a Private Economy in China*, Paris: OECD.

Fleisher, B.M. and Chen, J. (1997) The coast-noncoast income gap, productivity, and regional economic policy in China, *Journal of Comparative Economics*, 25, 220.

Frankel, J. and Romer, D. (1999) Does trade causes growth?, *American Economic Review*, 89, 379–399.

Fu, X. (2004) Limited linkages from growth engines and regional disparities in China, *Journal of Comparative Economics*, 32, 148–165.

Gao, T. (2004) Regional industrial growth: evidence from Chinese industries, *Regional Science and Urban Economics*, 34, 101–124.

Garnaut, R., Song, L., Stoyan, T. and Yao, Y. (2005) *China's Ownership Transformation: Process, Outcomes, Prospects*, Washington, DC: International Finance Corporation and World Bank.

Grant, R.M. (1991) The resource-based theory of competitive advantage: implications for strategy formulation, *California Management Review*, 33, 114–135.

Groenewold, N., Lee, G. and Chen, A. (2008) Inter-regional spillovers in China: the importance of common shocks and the definition of the regions, *China Economic Review*, 19, 32–52.

Huang, Y. (2003) *Selling China: Foreign Direct Investment during the Reform Era*, Cambridge: Cambridge University Press.

Huang, Z., Zhang, X. and Zhu, Y. (2008) The role of clustering in rural industrialization: case study of the footwear industry in Wenzhou, *China Economic Review*, 19(3), 409–420.

Itami, H. and Roehl, T.W. (1987) *Mobilizing Invisible Assets*, Cambridge, MA: Harvard University Press.

Jefferson, G., Rawski, T. and Zheng, Y. (1996) Chinese industrial productivity: trends, measurement, and recent developments, *Journal of Comparative Economics*, 23, 146–180.

Kennedy, J.J. (2007) From the tax-for-fee reform to the abolition of agricultural taxes: the impact on township governments in north-west China, *China Quarterly*, 189, 43–59.

Krugman, P.R. and Venables, J. (1995) Globalization and the inequality of nations, *Quarterly Journal of Economics*, 110, 857–880.

Madariaga, N. and Poncet, S. (2007) FDI in Chinese cities: spillovers and impact on growth, *World Economy*, 30, 837–862.

Murphy, R. (2002) *How Migrant Labor is Changing Rural China*, Cambridge: Cambridge University Press.

Nelson, R.R. and Winter, S.G. (1982) *An Evolutionary Theory of Economic Change*, Cambridge, MA: Harvard University Press.

Peng, Y. (2007) What has spilled over from Chinese cities into rural industry?, *Modern China*, 33, 287–319.

Phillips, K.L. and Shen, K. (2005) What effect does the size of the state-owned sector have on regional growth in China?, *Journal of Asian Economics*, 15, 1079.

Porter, M.E. (1990) *The Competitive Advantage of Nations*, London: Macmillan.

Puga, D. (1999) The rise and fall of regional inequalities, *European Economic Review*, 43, 303–334.

Schmitz, H. and Nadvi, K. (1999) Clustering and industrialization: introduction, *World Development*, 27, 1503–1514.

Sonobe, T., Hu, D. and Otsuka, K. (2002) Process of cluster formation in China: a case study of a garment town, *Journal of Development Studies*, 39, pp. 118–139.

Sonobe, T., Hu, D. and Otsuka, K. (2006) Industrial development in the inland region of China: a case study of the motorcycle industry, *Journal of Comparative Economics*, 34, 818–838.

Wang, W.W. and Fan, C.C. (2006) Success or failure: selectivity and reasons of return migration in Sichuan and Anhui, China, *Environment and Planning*, 38, 939–958.

Wernerfelt, B. (1984) A resource-based view of the firm, *Strategic Management Journal*, 5, 171–180.

World Bank (1997) *Sharing Rising Incomes: Disparities in China*, Washington, DC: World Bank.

Xiong, J. and Guan, J. (2005) Comparison analysis of foreign capital used in China's northeast three provinces, *Nature and Science*, 3, pp. 81–87.

# 12 Does public ownership really help?

## China's TVE development and the change of ownership structure

*Jiannan Guo*

### Introduction and overview of the literature

Township and village enterprises (hereafter TVEs)[1] are a unique economic form in rural China, which are normally set up under local governments' initiative as a joint consequence of the self-reliance fiscal system, the gradual relaxation of restrictions on rural households in engaging in non-agricultural activities, and the imperative of government to absorb the abundant rural labour force freed by the adoption of the household responsibility system (HRS).

For more than 15 years since rural reform was initiated, public (and collective) ownership (of local government) was the dominant ownership structure of TVEs. By utilizing the ample labour force in rural areas and taking advantage of local governments' assistance in accessing scarce un-marketed resources, TVEs have experienced rapid expansion. From 1980 to 1999, the output of TVEs kept growing by nearly 20 per cent annually, double the growth rate of the state-owned enterprises (SOEs).[2] In the meantime, the labour force utilized by the TVE sector increased from 28.2 million in 1978 to 79.3 million in 1986, 123.4 million in 1993 and 138.7 million in 2004.[3] By the mid-1990s, output by TVEs constituted more than a quarter of total industrial output of the country.[4] Although the growth of TVEs was much slower after the mid-1990s than in the 1980s, the growth miracle of TVEs has nevertheless become 'the engine of growth' of China (Byrd 2003) and 'indeed an economic wonder of the world' (Wolf 1995).

There is a large volume of literature, both theoretical and empirical, on how TVEs created the miracle and most attributes their success to the positive role of local public ownership (e.g. Che 2002; Che and Qian 1998; Chen and Rozelle 1999; Li 1996; Lin and Yao 2001; Tian 2000). The literature normally concludes that the positive role of local public ownership is either 'a solution to a planning problem' considered by the central government (Che 2002; Lin and Yao 2001), a resource of 'managerial input' (Perotti *et al.* 1999), a vaguely defined form originating from the traditional cooperative culture in rural China (Weitzman and Xu 1994) or 'a second-best solution' when the first-best logic does not work or is even counter-productive in an incomplete market with imperfect information and distorted regulations (Che and Qian 1998; Rodrik 2004). So far most studies favour the last reason (see most recently, among others, Che 2002; Che and Qian 1999; Chen and Rozelle 1999; Li 1996; Peng 2001; Rodrik 2004; Sun and Che 2002; Tian 2000).

The main argument of this school of thought is based on the assumption that the market and institutions in rural China are far from complete and perfect. Under this assumption, public ownership becomes a second-best solution that not only provides TVEs with easier access to the input and output market, but also a commitment mechanism (Tian 2000) of local government that protects TVEs from being prey to central or provincial governments, as well as minimizes incentives for local governments to seek rent. Accordingly, these works have focused on exploring how the TVEs grab growth opportunities by utilizing the local governments' efforts. Therefore, although public and collectively-owned TVEs are often criticized for their vaguely defined property rights, which undermine managerial incentives, studies of this school of thought have proved in theory, with the support of empirical evidence, that public ownership's positive effects on TVEs outweighs the negative.

These studies offered satisfactory explanations for the success of TVEs while public ownership still dominated the structures, but little attention was paid to present this rationale formally, let alone to explaining the dynamics of the ownership structure in the TVE sector. They neglected a stunning feature of TVEs' restructuring process that took place in the 1990s – the fading out of public ownership – and hence failed to explain why TVEs performed heterogeneously across regions.

Table 12.1 depicts how the ownership structure of TVEs evolved from the early 1980s. From 1984 onwards, when the communist system was officially abandoned, a large number of TVEs were set up. The reform that took place in the urban areas in the mid-1980s further stimulated the expansion of

*Table 12.1* Development of private TVEs

| Year | Number of firms | | Number of employees | | Gross output | |
|------|-----------------|------|---------------------|------|--------------|------|
|      | Amount (m) | % | Amount (m) | % | Value (100m Yuan) | % |
| 1984 | 4.20 | 69.28 | 12.26 | 23.54 | 244.01 | 14.37 |
| 1985 | 10.37 | 84.87 | 26.52 | 38.00 | 667.06 | 27.13 |
| 1987 | 15.92 | 90.95 | 40.87 | 46.42 | 1251.63 | 31.33 |
| 1989 | 17.15 | 91.78 | 46.47 | 49.61 | 1543.35 | 32.17 |
| 1991 | 17.64 | 92.44 | 48.42 | 50.39 | 1887.47 | 33.14 |
| 1993 | 22.84 | 93.13 | 65.78 | 53.28 | 4748.83 | 35.80 |
| 1995 | 20.41 | 92.65 | 68.01 | 52.88 | 7744.31 | 38.13 |
| 1997 | 18.86 | 93.59 | 77.24 | 59.19 | 12139.30 | 50.25 |
| 2001 | 18.64 | 93.31 | 81.01 | 60.13 | 13535.44 | 53.15 |

private TVEs. By 1989, there were 17.15 million privately-owned TVEs, accounting for 92 per cent of the total number. Nonetheless, during the 1980s, private ownership was far from being a dominant structure in terms of economic size and employment scale. Private TVEs were generally small and inefficient. In 1989, the number of workers they employed was less than half the total number absorbed by all the TVEs, while their output value counted for a mere 32 per cent of the whole TVE output. With the improvement of the market and the institutional environment in the 1990s, TVEs were undergoing radical structural changes, of which one of the stark features was the fading out of public ownership: not only were many of the publicly (and collectively)-owned TVEs privatized, but the privately-owned TVEs also experienced accelerating growth in a less discriminatory market and institutional environment. By the first year of the twenty-first century, private TVEs not only outnumbered public ones (93 per cent of TVEs were privately owned), but also overtook their public counterparts in terms of output value (53 per cent) and employees (60 per cent). One may conclude that, although they are still smaller in size, private TVEs are nonetheless equally important as public ones. Why was public ownership fading out in TVE ownership structure? Is private ownership better nowadays? New questions are challenging the literature. Even though Sun (2002) first observed this change, his work is at most a comparative study contrasting public ownership to another form called 'joint-stock cooperative (*gufen hezuo zhi*)' – actually a variation of collective structure – and it offers limited insight.

This chapter aims to answer these questions and to depict this dynamic process by using a one-stage non-cooperative game model. Some earlier studies, such as Hsiao *et al.* (1998) and Tian (2000), also tried to adapt this approach to China's rural problem. However, Hsiao *et al.* focus on comparison with the quota profit system but do not tackle the gradual privatization of TVEs, whereas Tian confines his discussion to the setting of property rights, a hot topic at the time. Our analyses not only formalize the discussion of endogenous ownership arrangements in the context of rural China, but also develop econometric models and find empirical evidence supporting the prediction of the model.

The chapter is constructed in the following way. The second section presents the theoretical model generally. The third section builds econometric models based on previous discussions; two hypotheses about the public ownership structure are then tested using a panel dataset dating back to 1986 and covering 28 provinces. The fourth section concludes the main findings.

## Theoretical rationale and the hypotheses [5]

This section spells out our model of TVE production that will enable us to endogeniz the type of TVE ownership arrangement (private or public ownership) prevailing in a given setting and help us construct the testable hypotheses.

Our point of view is that, given China's rural institutional establishment, certain un-marketed resources are crucial to TVE production, and access to these resources is obtained by making their owners residual claimants. In our model, we focus on two specific un-marketed resources: the manager's ability to make management decisions and supervise labour (hereafter 'management ability'), and the ability to procure certain resources (hereafter 'procurement ability'), including government-owned or controlled factors of production and political favours (such as preferential policy treatment, and ways to resolve political and economic disputes with other firms or governmental units). In our model, the time that the TVE managers spend in management activities, denoted by $s$, is used as a proxy for managerial input.

In a transition economy with imperfect information and an incomplete market – especially an input market where access to certain essential factors are controlled by different levels of governments – procurement ability may be even more crucial for a firm to survive. This is the case in China's rural areas, and was especially so before the early 1990s. At that time, not only the production factors, but also some production activities were under government control. Such an irregular market resulted in *de facto* bottlenecks of factor supplies, which justified the involvement of government officials in TVE production processes. The process of obtaining these factors is a process of 'procurement' rather than a 'purchasing' process because the actual price, quantity and even quality of factors available to a firm are largely dependent on the firm's own ability – the ability to procure such materials. On the other hand, in the institutional environment TVEs face, the vagueness of policies and regulation leaves a wide margin to the government officials in interpreting and enforcing the rules. Therefore, stronger procurement ability resulting from better connections to government officials will create preferential policy treatment for a firm, which in turn may accelerate the firm's development. Normally the establishment of these connections is also a time-consuming process, and the wide margin of interpretation of the rules implies that the quality of certain resources procured depends largely on the effective time spent on such processes. Letting $H$ denote the resources a TVE needs to procure from such processes, and $t$ the time spent on the procurement ('special' procurement), we may define the 'effective procurement', $R$, by

$$R = g(t, H; \rho) \tag{1}$$

where $g(\cdot)$ is a homogeneous function which is increasing and concave in $t$ and $H$, and $\rho$ ($\rho \in [0,1]$) is introduced into the model to capture the effect of the market degree of perfection: $\rho = 1$ stands for a perfect and complete market where all the procuring resources are perfectly marketed and there is no margin for rule or policy interpretation, therefore the time spent specially on procurement is redundant; while a decreasing $\rho$ implies that 'special' procurement is increasing in importance; $\rho = 0$ is the opposite case where time devoted to procurement determines everything.

It is assumed that the entrepreneurs and bureaucrats each have one unit of time, which they may allocate between TVE production and their alternative activities, which gives an entrepreneur opportunity income $u_1$ and a bureaucrat $u_2$. (Note that here, and elsewhere in the chapter, $_1$ stands for entrepreneur and $_2$ for bureaucrat.)

The production function of a TVE may thus be written as:

$$q = F(s, R, K, L, Z) \tag{2}$$

By substituting effective procurement $R$ from (1) into (2), the production function may be written as:

$$q = f(s, t, H, K, L, Z; \rho) \tag{3}$$

where $f(\cdot)$ is linearly homogeneous, increasing and concave in its first six elements; $K$ is the capital investment needed for running the business, which can be made solely by the private entrepreneur, by the government, or jointly by the two parties; $L$ is labour input, which can be obtained from the competitive labour market at a wage of $w$ as a marketed resource. Thus the two kinds of agent considered are private entrepreneurs and government bureaucrats. Bureaucrats are local government officials, and private entrepreneurs are those who want to invest in a project to set up a TVE. An entrepreneur differentiates himself from normal managers by his unique ability to identify and grasp opportunities and his dedication to continuous innovation. Therefore, it is reasonable to assume that only entrepreneurs control the scarce project information, $Z$, which is crucial to establish a firm. Apart from the project information, $Z$, an entrepreneur also owns the expertise in management.

In contrast to entrepreneurs, bureaucrats have advantages in setting up connections with other bureaucrats and superior abilities in procurement, although an entrepreneur offering a higher price or devoting more time to the process may carry out such procurement. We quantify this idea of comparative advantage by means of a parameter, $\lambda$ ($\lambda \in [0,1]$), representing the procurement equivalence of an entrepreneur with respect to a bureaucrat, i.e. one entrepreneur hour in the procurement process is only equivalent to, in terms of resources obtained, a fraction ($\lambda$) of a bureaucrat hour. We shall assume that the provision of bureaucrats operates in a competitive market since, in rural China, entrepreneurship is normally in short supply because of the influence of the traditional Chinese culture which 'belittles the importance of commerce in society and does not seem to nurture entrepreneurship' (Fan *et al.* 1996) – an entrepreneur may choose to invest in other localities if he has the project or capital, and local governments often compete with each other in means to attract investment.

When an entrepreneur initiates a project, he may choose from one of the two organization forms to set up the business: a private firm solely on his own, or a public (collective) firm in collaboration with a government bureaucrat who has expertise in procuring 'special' resources (or has easier access to that market). The two types of organization stand for private ownership and public (collective) ownership, respectively.

Under private ownership, the entrepreneur faces the problem of deciding the amount of material, resources and time inputs needed to maximize net income:

$$\pi_1^{PR} = \max_{s_1, t_1, H, K, L} [Pf(s_1, \lambda t_1, H, K, L, Z; \rho) - bH - rK - wL] + (1 - t_1 - s_1)u_1$$

$$s.t \quad 0 \leq t_1 \leq 1, 0 \leq s_1 \leq 1, 0 \leq t_1 + s_1 \leq 1 \tag{4}$$

where $b$, $r$ and $w$ are prices for $H$, $K$ and $L$, respectively (here, and elsewhere in the chapter, $^{PR}$ stands for private ownership and $^{PU}$ for public ownership). The term in the square brackets represents the entrepreneur's expected income from running the TVE, and the other term, the 'income' from his alternative activities. The bureaucrat does not face decision problems under this arrangement so he may devote all of his time to his alternative (original) activities and will receive the opportunity income from his alternative activities. Under this ownership arrangement, private TVEs cannot 'buy' help from the officials in procuring special resources.

Under public ownership, both the entrepreneur and the bureaucrat are involved in TVE operations. This provides the opportunity for specialization – each agent may perform the task for which he has the absolute advantage. They cooperate by inputting the un-marketed resources (management or procurement ability) and sharing the profit. The sharing rule is endogenously determined and mutually agreed by the two parties, which takes the form of:

$$Share_2 = a + \beta \Pi$$

$$Share_1 = -a + (1 - \beta) \Pi \tag{5}$$

where $a$ and $\beta$ are coefficients determined endogenously in the system, which will be solved by backwards induction. Given the sharing rule (5), the bureaucrat will choose the amount of time he spent in procurement to maximize his expected income:

$$t_2 (s_1; a, \beta) = \arg \max_{t_2} a + \beta \Pi (s_1, t_2) + (1 - t_2)u_2 \tag{6}$$

Similarly, the entrepreneur must first choose his time devoted to management:

$$s_1 (t_2; a, \beta) = \arg \max_{s_1} -a + (1 - \beta) \Pi (s_1, t_2) + (1 - s_1)u_1 \tag{7}$$

where $\Pi(t,s)$ is the TVE's restricted profit function obtained by optimally choosing the amount of capital, labour and procurement input for given $t$ and $s$. In the non-cooperative game, the Nash equilibrium $(s_1^*, t_2^*)$ is obtained when each player chooses the best response to the choice actually made by the other, i.e. both equations (6) and (7) are satisfied simultaneously. Under our assumption of the concavity of the production function, it can be proven that the existence of a Nash equilibrium is assured.[6] We shall assume that the Nash equilibrium is unique for given $\alpha$ and $\beta$. It is easy to see that the entrepreneur will set $a$ at a level that holds the bureaucrat at his opportunity income for a given $\beta$, i.e. $a(\beta) = t_2^*(\beta) \cdot u_2 - \beta \cdot \Pi(s_1^*(\beta), t_2^*(\beta))$.

Therefore, the entrepreneur will choose $\beta$ so as to maximize his expected income:

$$\beta^* = \arg\max_{\beta} - a(\beta) + (1 - \beta) \cdot \Pi(s_1^*(\beta), t_2^*(\beta)) + (1 - s_1^*(\beta)) \cdot u_1 \qquad (8)$$

This completely endogenizes the parameters of the sharing rule in equation (5). Upon substituting for optimized value $\beta^*$, the entrepreneur's expected income under public ownership is:

$$\pi_1^{PU} = \Pi(s_1^*(\beta^*), t_2^*(\beta^*)) + (1 - s_1^*(\beta^*)) \cdot u_1 + (1 - t_2^*(\beta^*)) \cdot u_2 - u_2 \qquad (9)$$

which, as expected, is the joint profit of the two parties, less the opportunity income of the bureaucrat. The entrepreneur owns the scarce resource – project information – and hence will choose the ownership arrangement that maximizes his expected income ($\pi_1^{PR}$ vs. $\pi_1^{PU}$). This determines the dominant ownership structure type that can be observed in the real economy. In order to gain insight into this process, we solve the model for a Cobb–Douglas specification by assuming $q = As^{\delta_1} R^{\delta_2} K^{\delta_4} L^{\delta_5} Z^{\delta_6}$ and $R = H^p t^{1-p}$, where A and $\delta_i$ (I = 1,2,4,5,6) are positive constants, $\sum_{i \neq 3} \delta_i = 1$. Figure 12.1 shows the endogenized $\beta^*$ as a function of the degree of market perfection $p$.

The entire range of $\beta^*$ indicated in Figure 12.1, however, will not necessarily be observed when $p$ changes. If we allow the entrepreneur to choose the ownership structure rationally, public ownership will not always be the dominant contract. The bureaucrat has the tendency to participate in the TVE operation when there are more restrictions and government interventions in the market. Considering only the interior solution case, the proposition below shows the relationship of the dominant ownership arrangement in the extreme case.

**Proposition**[7] *When the institutional environment is sufficiently perfect (i.e. $p \rightarrow 1$), the private ownership arrangement will dominate its public counterpart.* Note that this proposition holds for any ownership share $\beta$, and the conclusion is drawn regardless of the setting of any other parameters, such as those of

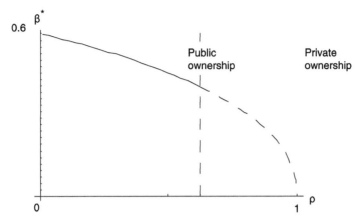

*Figure 12.1* Effect of the degree of market perfection on ownership share.
*Note:* The dashed part of the curve indicates that this range of $\beta^*$ is not observable.

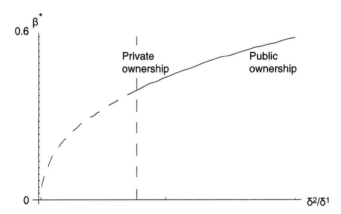

*Figure 12.2* Effect of the relative efficiency on ownership share.
*Note:* The dashed part of the curve indicates that this range of $\beta^*$ is not observable.

technology, procurement ability and opportunity income. The proposition suggests that the optimal ownership structure is endogenized in the institutional environment, which is the efficient response of the agents to the institution settings. If the institutional environment is not perfect, which ownership structure will dominate is bound to the entrepreneur's consideration of the technology used, both parties' opportunity cost, and the entrepreneur's ability to procure the 'special' resources compared to the bureaucrat's. The public ownership arrangement will be more likely to prevail when the market is far from perfect, the special resources more valuable and the procurement ability more important.

Figure 12.2 depicts the endogenized value of $\beta^*$ when the ratio $\delta_2/\delta_1$ varies. $\delta_2/\delta_1$ stands for the relative efficiency of the two resources – management time and procurement input – used in the production technology. Holding others constant, the more the technology that the TVE uses relies on procurement resources, the more the entrepreneur will prefer to run the firm jointly with a bureaucrat. As also shown in Figure 12.1, not the entire range of the curve will be observed in reality: public ownership may be the dominant structure only when the reliance of technology on the procurement reaches a certain level.

Following the discussion above, we can construct two hypotheses to test with empirical data:

- $H_{01}$ – the role that public ownership plays in the development of TVEs varies depending on the degree of market perfection. While TVEs may benefit from their public ownership structure when the market is far from perfect, progress will be impeded by this ownership structure as the market condition improves.
- $H_{02}$ – the optimal ownership arrangement of TVEs is endogenously determined by the market condition and the technology used.

## Empirical evidence

### *The data and the construction of the market perfection index*

In studies on China, because of the enormous differences existing among the provinces, 'province' has been widely used as the spatial unit. We follow this conventional approach to test our hypotheses with provincial aggregated data.

The examination, however, encounters serious problems in finding proper indicators reflecting the degree of market perfection. Such indicators are rarely seen in the existing literature. In recent work, Zhang *et al.* (2006) provide two variables to account for the business environment in which enterprises in rural areas operate: the ratio of fees charged to rural residents when applying for licenses to run enterprises to per capita net income of the village, and the approval wait time when applying for a license. These two variables, both collected from their micro-level field survey, are only for a given time point and certain areas. The only countrywide information appearing in the literature is from a project carried out at the National Economic Research Institute, China Reform Foundation (Fan *et al.* 2001). Their ranking and rating system, however, lowered the measurement scale of the statistics, which could very likely result in loss of information. Moreover, their indices published cover only the years from 1997 to 2000. Therefore they are not suitable candidates in our work: we will have to create our own.

We consider the market conditions of a province from three perspectives: (1) infrastructure development, reflected by the density of paved roads and the density of railway lines in a province; (2) degree of market openness, reflected by the export-to-GDP ratio and the ratio of FDI to the total amount of fixed investment; and (3) government interference, by the ratio of SOE output to the total industrial output of a province, and the ratio of government expenditure to total GDP. The basic statistics of these six variables are listed in Table 12.2.

*Table 12.2* Variables used to produce market perfection index

| Aspects reflected | Variables | N | Mean | SD | Min | Max |
|---|---|---|---|---|---|---|
| Infrastructure development | Paved road* density (km/km²) | 336 | 0.2052 | 0.1380 | 0.0106 | 0.7072 |
|  | Railway density (km/km²) | 336 | 0.0239 | 0.0567 | 0.0010 | 0.3615 |
| Market openness | Export/GDP | 336 | 0.1325 | 0.1448 | 0.0161 | 1.0827 |
|  | FDI/fixed investment | 336 | 0.0638 | 0.1009 | 0.0000 | 0.6561 |
| Government interference | SOE/industry output | 336 | 0.6435 | 0.1630 | 0.1792 | 0.9842 |
|  | Government expenditure/GDP | 336 | 0.1281 | 0.0525 | 0.0492 | 0.3480 |

It is straightforward to see why infrastructure is important when considering market conditions. In rural China, because the development of local business is often subject to insufficient roads linking to the outside, building a new road is normally given priority on the local government's task list. The higher the road density, the better infrastructure condition a market has. The same is valid for railway line density. The reasons for including the two market openness variables are twofold. On the one hand, the degree of openness itself indicates the degree of market perfection. On the other hand, it will affect the degree to which local government interferes with the economy. With the inflow of foreign capital, the government may reduce its control over the firms in the economy so that the foreign capital will not be scared away. Thus, the higher the FDI and export ratios, the more open the economy, implying a better market condition. The interference of government will make the market condition worse, though the selection of variables reflecting that interference is polemical. Some scholars, such as Byrd and Lin (1990) and Lin and Yao (2001), use the overall ratio of HRS to capture the effect. A careful scrutiny of the data reveals that the process of promoting HRS was completed in the mid-1980s, and that, in the following years, the ratio remained 100 per cent. Therefore the HRS ratio can only be helpful when dealing with data before 1985. The two variables we use are the ratio of SOE output to the total industrial output of a province, and the ratio of government expenditure to total GDP. SOEs are directly controlled by the government; thus the higher this ratio, the more the government may interfere in the economy. The ratio of government expenditure measures the power with which the government behaviour can affect the economy. Therefore, the perfection of the market condition should be negatively linked with these two variables.

In order to take all these variables into account, we resort to principal component analysis to combine them into six principal components and then choose the score of the first principal component, prin1, to index for the market perfection index, the variable to measure local market conditions. The results of the principal component analysis are reported in Table 12.3, and the loadings of the six principal components are shown in Table 12.4. There are a couple of reasons for choosing Prin1. First, it accounts for 51.37 per cent of the total variance, which means that more than half of the information is explained by it, more than the other five put together. Therefore, to choose the first principal component will produce a single index with the least loss of information. Second, a principal component is a linear combination of the variables participating in the analysis, with the loading assigning the coefficients of this combination. In Table 12.4, we find that the loading of Prin1 contains a very good property for explaining market perfection, contrary to the others. Prin1 is positively linked with the infrastructure variables and the market openness variables, but negatively with the variables standing for government interference, which is consistent with our discussion on variable selection. Moreover, there is no single variable dominating in the construction of Prin1, while this is the case for other principal components. The

*Table 12.3* Explanation capability of the principal components

| Prin. comp. | Eigenvalue | Difference | Proportion | Cumulative |
|---|---|---|---|---|
| 1 | 3.0822 | 1.9754 | 0.5137 | 0.5137 |
| 2 | 1.1069 | 0.2640 | 0.1845 | 0.6982 |
| 3 | 0.8428 | 0.3938 | 0.1405 | 0.8387 |
| 4 | 0.4490 | 0.1518 | 0.0748 | 0.9135 |
| 5 | 0.2972 | 0.0754 | 0.0495 | 0.9630 |
| 6 | 0.2218 | | 0.0370 | 1.0000 |

*Sources: China Statistical Yearbook* (various years); *China Rural Statistical Yearbook* (various years); *TVE Annual Performance Statistics*, http://zw.cte.gov.cn/tjxx/tjxx.asp.

\* Private firms include individually-owned firms and shareholding firms (including joint-stock cooperatives); gross output is the monetary value in real terms deflated with provincial deflators.

*Table 12.4* Loadings of the principal components

| Original variables | Prin1 | Prin2 | Prin3 | Prin4 | Prin5 | Prin6 |
|---|---|---|---|---|---|---|
| Paved road density | 0.4442 | 0.1691 | −0.2261 | 0.8228 | −0.1996 | 0.0788 |
| Railway density | 0.1835 | 0.7817 | −0.4034 | −0.4106 | −0.1506 | 0.0364 |
| Export/GDP | 0.4548 | 0.2449 | 0.4167 | 0.0049 | 0.5829 | −0.4687 |
| FDI/fixed investment | 0.4654 | −0.0288 | 0.4853 | −0.2118 | −0.1369 | 0.6953 |
| SOE/industry output | −0.4643 | 0.3651 | 0.0431 | 0.2791 | 0.5725 | 0.4936 |
| Government expenditure/GDP | −0.3606 | 0.4077 | 0.6125 | 0.1780 | −0.5012 | −0.2137 |

last two reasons make it easier to interpret the principal component chosen as the market perfection index. It is clear that a higher score of Prin1 indicates a higher degree of market perfection, and vice versa. For the convenience of analysis, we standardize the principal components into zero mean and unity standard deviation. Table 12.5 offers an overview of Prin1. The ascending trend over time is obvious, implying the improvement of market conditions.

With the market perfection index, Prin1, we can now examine the afore-mentioned hypotheses empirically by exploring the relationships between TVE performance, market condition and public ownership structure. For this, a panel dataset dating back to 1986 covering 28 (out of 31) provinces is constructed from the officially published statistics.

All the data on TVEs used in empirical analysis are taken from China's officially published statistics. Different provincial deflators are employed to deflate the financial measures to 1978 prices before further calculation.

The data did not date back to earlier years because some variables, such as FDI and paved road density, are not available for the years before 1986. We did not include data for the years after 1997 because there is a change of measurement of TVE output in 1998 for which documentation is not yet available, and because some TVE statistics are no longer published in the *Rural Statistical Yearbooks* from 1999. Among the whole 31 provinces, Hainan[8] and Tibet[9] are excluded because of the lack of proper data, and Chongqing is added into Sichuan as it did not become a municipality until 1994.

*Table 12.5* Summary of the market perfection index (Prin1)

|  | N | Mean | SD | Minimum | Maximum |
|---|---|---|---|---|---|
| By years |  |  |  |  |  |
| 1986 | 28 | −0.6078 | 0.6351 | −1.7784 | 0.5612 |
| 1987 | 28 | −0.4515 | 0.6972 | −1.6790 | 0.8276 |
| 1988 | 28 | −0.3415 | 0.6933 | −1.5707 | 0.9724 |
| 1989 | 28 | −0.3212 | 0.7024 | −1.5580 | 1.0237 |
| 1990 | 28 | −0.2538 | 0.7304 | −1.5977 | 1.2912 |
| 1991 | 28 | −0.2165 | 0.7882 | −1.4974 | 1.5104 |
| 1992 | 28 | 0.0523 | 0.9889 | −1.2854 | 2.6898 |
| 1993 | 28 | 0.2943 | 1.1883 | −1.2924 | 3.2501 |
| 1994 | 28 | 0.4409 | 1.2073 | −1.1788 | 3.8210 |
| 1995 | 28 | 0.4927 | 1.0788 | −1.1602 | 3.5313 |
| 1996 | 28 | 0.4217 | 1.1102 | −1.1805 | 3.3177 |
| 1997 | 28 | 0.4905 | 1.1080 | −1.1323 | 3.4906 |
| By year blocks |  |  |  |  |  |
| YB1 | 112 | −0.4305 | 0.6829 | −1.7784 | 1.0237 |
| YB2 | 112 | −0.0309 | 0.9549 | −1.5977 | 3.2501 |
| YB3 | 112 | 0.4615 | 1.1122 | −1.1805 | 3.8210 |
| Overall | 336 | 0 | 1 | −1.7784 | 3.8210 |

*Note:* YB1 is for 1986–89, YB2 for 1990–93, YB3 for 1994–97.

### The basic year model

Consider the model:

$$y = \beta_0 + \beta_1 \, Prin1 + \beta_2 \, PubShare + \beta_3 \, K + \beta_4 \, L + \sum_{k \geq 5} \beta_k \, x_k + \varepsilon \tag{10}$$

Here, the dependent variable $y$ is the per capita gross output value of all TVEs. There is only value-added data available for 1996, while for the other years we have gross output data.

Among the explanatory variables, Prin1 is the market perfection index, as discussed. *PubShare* is the number of employees in local publicly-owned TVEs as a share of the total number of provincial TVE employees, a proxy for public ownership structure. We have tried to use the output ratio of public TVEs with respect to the total TVEs as an alternative proxy. The empirical trial shows that there exists co-linearity between this alternative proxy and other variables that leads to undesirable results.

$K$ and $L$ stand for the input of capital and labour of TVEs, respectively. Empirically, $L$ is the size of the rural labour force (*rlabour*), while $K$ is measured by the lagged (for one period) per capita capital (*rural_k1*) for the rural area only, which actually is rural productive fixed assets. In the regression, lagged value is used in order to avoid the endogeneity of this variable.

$X_k$ are other variables controlled in the model. Table 12.6 summarizes these variables. Per capita TVE output value in 1978 (*TVE78*) is included to capture the effect of initial conditions. The importance of initial condition in a country's development has been emphasized in recent growth theory (Booth

*Table 12.6* Summary of the variables used in econometric models

| Variable | Label | N | Mean | SD | Min | Max |
|---|---|---|---|---|---|---|
| TVE | Per capita TVE output | 336 | 1482.16 | 2090.24 | 77.60 | 13887.01 |
| TVE78 | Per capita TVE output in 1978 | 336 | 77.38 | 88.89 | 13.86 | 441.45 |
| GDP1 | Lagged per capita GDP | 336 | 1275.39 | 1194.90 | 326.88 | 9479.90 |
| SOE | Per capita SOE output | 336 | 1211.45 | 1550.28 | 195.86 | 9628.65 |
| Lratio | Ratio of light industry | 336 | 41.28 | 11.63 | 16.44 | 65.83 |
| rural_k1 | Lagged pc rural fixed capital | 336 | 545.64 | 628.95 | 94.39 | 4381.84 |
| Rlabour | Rural labour | 336 | 1509.22 | 1194.36 | 121.60 | 5177.74 |
| PubShare | Public TVE labour ratio | 336 | 48.32 | 18.27 | 15.24 | 100.00 |
| Prin1 | Market perfection index | 336 | 0.00 | 1.00 | −1.78 | 3.82 |
| TVE_k | Per worker TVE capital | 336 | 2459.19 | 2315.08 | 341.09 | 15770.82 |
| indRatio | Ratio of industry TVE output | 336 | 59.37 | 56.32 | 3.27 | 100.00 |
| TVEtech_L | Ratio of technician in TVE labour | 336 | 3.65 | 1.70 | 0.24 | 9.93 |

1999), and attributes the effects to the externality caused by the uneven distribution of certain factors at the start-off stage. The reason for using 1978 as the starting point is that rural reform officially began in this year.

To control for geographical effects while preserving the impacts of the initial conditions, we follow Jin and Qian (1998) in dividing the 28 provinces into six regions (instead of using province dummies): large cities (the three municipalities including Beijing, Shanghai and Tianjin, referred to as D1), coastal (D2), north (D3), northwest (D4), southwest (D5) and south (D6).[10] Each region has its unique feature. The three municipalities stand out as a group because they are province-level units but their agricultural population ratios are much smaller than the others. The coastal areas have first-mover advantage in reform policies and are closer to overseas markets. Moreover, they have traditionally been areas for industry and commerce. The north and the south are mostly hinterlands, though the north has more heavy industries. The southwest and northwest are both underdeveloped, notwithstanding that the southwest has better conditions for agricultural development. In the regression, the south is used as the referral group.

Per capita GDP of a province is used in lagged (for one period) form (*GDP1*) to capture that province's market size, which accounts for its purchasing power. For a long period, TVEs were producing mainly for the provincial domestic market due to lack of transportation and information, and the provincial barriers to (unplanned) merchandise mobility. Therefore a province with larger purchasing power means a larger market and hence better potential for TVE development. Using the data in lagged value is a simple technique to reduce the side effect of endogeneity.

Finally, we capture the effect of the industrial structure of a province in the development of TVEs with the variable *lratio*, the ratio of light industry to total industry in terms of output value; while per capita SOE output value (*SOE*) is used to account for the interaction with the state sector.

While the reason for controlling the initial condition, the regional dummies and the variable standing for market size is obvious, why the other two variables are taken into account deserves further explanation.

TVEs' tie with the urban sector dates back to as early as the collective era (*prior* reform years), when the young students and technicians sent to the rural areas by the labour mobilization policy – called 'go up to the mountains, go down to the fields (*shang shan xia xiang*)' – were the main source of technology transfer for the rural brigade collectives, the prototype of TVEs. When the Cultural Revolution ended in the late 1970s, the mobilization policy was no longer adopted and rural firms had to seek new sources of technological progress and started hiring technicians retired from the urban sector – the SOEs. From the industrial structure point of view, light industry is more labour-intensive and requires less capital and relatively simpler technology. Hence, technology spillovers from the light industry SOEs can serve TVEs better, as they can utilize more effectively the rural areas' comparative advantage of an ample labour force while reducing the effects caused by lack of capital and technicians. With the development of TVEs, the SOEs in the urban sector started to subcontract simple and labour-intensive products to their neighbouring TVEs, providing them with better development potential. As TVEs enjoy technology spillovers from their neighbouring SOEs, and SOEs often subcontract simple products to their neighbouring TVEs, a larger SOE sector and a higher ratio of light industry make for better conditions for TVE development.

To examine the model, we regress using the OLS method for each year separately, and then for all the data as a whole. The results on the variables of interest are reported in Tables 12.7 and 12.8. Not surprisingly, with the improvement of market condition (depicted by the increase of the mean market condition index), the effects of public ownership (the regression coefficients of *PubShare*) decrease from 3.80 in 1986, to 2.75 in 1992, even becoming negative from 1993 onwards. While one may argue that the coefficients in most years are not robust, the *F* test does confirm that the change of the whole structure over time is significant. There are two possible reasons why this is the case. First, regressing for each year separately makes the sample size for each regression as small as 28, which seriously reduces the degree of freedom of the model and makes the model sensitive to disturbance, and vulnerable to the possible problem of model specification and co-linearity of regressors. Second, there might be correlations between the models of each year which makes the estimation inefficient.

To solve this problem, we adjust the model to:

$$
\begin{bmatrix} y_1 \\ y_2 \\ \vdots \\ y_T \end{bmatrix} = \begin{bmatrix} X_1 & 0 & \cdots & \\ 0 & X_2 & \cdots & \\ & & \ddots & \\ 0 & 0 & & X_T \end{bmatrix} \begin{bmatrix} \beta_1 \\ \beta_2 \\ \vdots \\ \beta_T \end{bmatrix} + \begin{bmatrix} \varepsilon_1 \\ \varepsilon_2 \\ \vdots \\ \varepsilon_T \end{bmatrix}
$$

$$= X\beta + \varepsilon$$

(11)

*Table 12.7* Cross-equation correlations of different years in the basic year model

|      | Y86   | Y87  | Y88  | Y89  | Y90  | Y91  | Y92  | Y93  | Y94   | Y95   | Y96   | Y97   |
|------|-------|------|------|------|------|------|------|------|-------|-------|-------|-------|
| Y86  | 1.00  | 0.86 | 0.87 | 0.68 | 0.63 | 0.49 | 0.49 | 0.42 | −0.05 | 0.23  | 0.20  | 0.14  |
| Y87  | 0.86  | 1.00 | 0.89 | 0.77 | 0.72 | 0.60 | 0.56 | 0.35 | 0.08  | 0.31  | 0.29  | 0.18  |
| Y88  | 0.87  | 0.89 | 1.00 | 0.92 | 0.84 | 0.64 | 0.57 | 0.41 | 0.16  | 0.31  | 0.26  | 0.21  |
| Y89  | 0.68  | 0.77 | 0.92 | 1.00 | 0.94 | 0.78 | 0.68 | 0.47 | 0.36  | 0.36  | 0.33  | 0.27  |
| Y90  | 0.63  | 0.72 | 0.84 | 0.94 | 1.00 | 0.90 | 0.74 | 0.56 | 0.45  | 0.22  | 0.20  | 0.12  |
| Y91  | 0.49  | 0.60 | 0.64 | 0.78 | 0.90 | 1.00 | 0.78 | 0.50 | 0.46  | 0.06  | 0.13  | 0.02  |
| Y92  | 0.49  | 0.56 | 0.57 | 0.68 | 0.74 | 0.78 | 1.00 | 0.66 | 0.38  | 0.10  | 0.23  | 0.18  |
| Y93  | 0.42  | 0.35 | 0.41 | 0.47 | 0.56 | 0.50 | 0.66 | 1.00 | 0.55  | 0.07  | 0.04  | −0.04 |
| Y94  | −0.05 | 0.08 | 0.16 | 0.36 | 0.45 | 0.46 | 0.38 | 0.55 | 1.00  | 0.19  | −0.00 | −0.06 |
| Y95  | 0.23  | 0.31 | 0.31 | 0.36 | 0.22 | 0.06 | 0.10 | 0.07 | 0.19  | 1.00  | 0.82  | 0.68  |
| Y96  | 0.20  | 0.29 | 0.26 | 0.33 | 0.20 | 0.13 | 0.23 | 0.04 | −0.00 | 0.82  | 1.00  | 0.90  |
| Y97  | 0.14  | 0.18 | 0.21 | 0.27 | 0.12 | 0.02 | 0.18 | −0.04 | −0.06 | 0.68  | 0.90  | 1.00  |

Table 12.8 Evolution of public ownership effects: the basic year model

| Year | Average of market perfection index | OLS model | | | | SUR model | | | |
|---|---|---|---|---|---|---|---|---|---|
| | | Prin1 | SD | Pub share | SD | Prin1 | SD | Pub share | SD |
| 1986 | -0.61 | 117.15 | 95.66 | 3.80 | 2.49 | 101.70 | 61.60 | 0.57 | 1.43 |
| 1987 | -0.45 | 145.88 | 91.62 | 3.00 | 2.63 | 89.64 | 57.05 | 0.68 | 1.59 |
| 1988 | -0.34 | 61.94 | 121.04 | 5.29 | 3.69 | 16.90 | 71.39 | 0.98 | 2.12 |
| 1989 | -0.32 | 71.12 | 121.25 | 6.95 | 3.88* | 14.38 | 63.95 | 2.76 | 2.34 |
| 1990 | -0.25 | 41.82 | 101.90 | 6.47 | 3.67* | 13.76 | 47.53 | 3.39 | 2.21 |
| 1991 | -0.22 | 26.92 | 99.47 | 1.76 | 3.04 | 48.99 | 43.44 | 0.53 | 1.84 |
| 1992 | 0.05 | -64.20 | 67.78 | 2.75 | 2.59 | -41.66 | 42.36 | -0.21 | 1.64 |
| 1993 | 0.29 | -310.60 | 122.96** | -2.16 | 7.44 | -279.13 | 91.84*** | -4.51 | 5.13 |
| 1994 | 0.44 | -770.64 | 185.50*** | -10.10 | 11.15 | -734.00 | 148.21*** | -7.00 | 7.25 |
| 1995 | 0.49 | 234.10 | 411.89 | -4.52 | 16.11 | 109.29 | 266.51 | -4.77 | 7.30 |
| 1996 | 0.42 | -11.84 | 746.26 | -15.32 | 24.68 | 322.04 | 481.94 | -12.39 | 8.32 |
| 1997 | 0.49 | -85.45 | 780.78 | -53.09 | 25.89* | 173.42 | 560.89 | -32.74 | 11.24** |
| Overall | | 170.68 | 91.55* | -17.05 | 4.51*** | 292.34 | 15.24*** | 1.52 | 0.76* |
| F test for no structural change | | 2.21 (p < 0.001) | | | | 50.70 (p < 0.0001) | | | |

Notes: Dependent variable: per capita TVE output; independent variables: tve78 GDP1 SOE lratio rural_k1 rlabour prin1 PubShare D1-D5; output for controlled variables and model statistics are not reported in the table; significance level (from this table onwards): *** 0.01; ** 0.05; * 0.10.

where $X_t = [1 \; Prin1_t \; PubShare_t \; K_t \; L_t \; TVE78_t \; GDP1_t \; SOE_t \; lratio_t \; D_{1,t} \ldots D_{5,t}]$ is the regressor matrix at year $t$, and $\beta_t = [\beta_{0,t} \; \beta_{1,t} \ldots \beta_{13,t}]^T$ is the coefficient vector at year $t$. $\varepsilon$ is the disturbance vector, which is generalized to allow the existence of contemporaneous correlation. Note that the second model is a generalized form of the first one, which can be obtained by applying stricter assumptions (CLRM) on the error terms.

We then apply seemingly unrelated regression (SUR)[11] on the model above by estimating the contemporaneous correlation matrix using OLS residuals. The SUR parameter estimates are reported in parallel in Table 12.8. Although the number of significant coefficients does not increase, it is easy to see that the SUR estimates have much smaller standard deviations, suggesting higher efficiency in regression. Taking into account the fact that the cross-model correlations presented in Table 12.7 are non-negligible, we have sufficient evidence to believe that the SUR estimation on this model is superior to the OLS one.

The SUR results provide a similar change pattern for the effects of public ownership. It helps the growth of TVEs in the years before 1992, especially in 1989 and 1990, when the positive effects reached their peak, and the market condition in terms of the market perfection index did not degrade. An explanation for this finding is that, after the political chaos of the summer of 1989, the government tightened its control over the market by other means than those reflected by the variables used in producing our market perfection index. Another interesting point of this model lies in the coefficients of Prin1 for 1992–94. During these three years, the market perfection index Prin1 shows negative effects on the development of TVEs. But this is contradictory to the construction of Prin1, for which a higher value means a better market condition that will result in better development opportunities for TVEs. We guess the problem arises because of the inconsistency of TVEs' ownership structures and market conditions. This will be tested later, together with the test for ownership structure endogeneity.

### Year block models

Another way to deal with the lack of degree of freedom is to increase the sample size for each regression. The data are grouped into three blocks, depending on the years: Block 1 (YB1) covers the years from 1986–89, YB2 1990–93 and YB3 1994–97. Each block covers a span of four years, containing 112 observations. The three blocks represent three different reform periods in rural China. The division of stages is a combination of Fan *et al.*'s (2002) and Lin and Yao's (2001).

Eight years prior to YB1, the rural reform began with the gradual adoption of the so-called Household Responsibility System (HRS). From then until early 1985, HRS gradually restored the family farming system in the agricultural production process – which had been abandoned for more than 20 years during the collective era – greatly boosting the agriculture sector and accumulating initial capital for the take-off of the TVE sector.

The period from 1985 to 1989 witnessed the take-off of the TVE sector against the background of the liberalization of both the pricing and the market systems. During that period, the rural commune system was officially abandoned, the government admitted the existence of private ownership as a type of economic unit, and the restrictions on rural households' non-farming activities were gradually relaxed. These changes of institution, together with the initial capital accumulated from the remarkable growth of the agriculture sector prior to this period, boosted the take-off of TVEs. A parallel reform policy adopted in this period started the 'dual-track' system, which partly opened the factor market to the economic units outside the central planned economy – such as TVEs. In this system, both the prices and quantities of the essential factors available to TVEs were not fixed and there was a wide margin for floating. Therefore, procurement ability became crucially important to TVEs. Nevertheless, this system gave the rural households access opportunities to materials that were never obtainable before (Lin and Yao 2001).

The period from 1990 to 1993 featured new developments in agricultural policy and conservativeness and cautiousness in development of TVEs. In this period, the government accelerated price and market reforms, the procurement system in agriculture products reduced its coverage on product types, and the prices for procured goods were largely increased. The government's policies in relation to TVEs, however, became quite conservative due to political chaos in 1989. As a result, the development of TVEs shrank. The trend did not reverse until 1993, a year after Deng Xiaoping's visit to the South.

In the years after 1993, TVEs expanded steadily, with the sector undergoing structural changes in both ownership arrangement and industrial structure. Institutions were improved and new laws (e.g. the Township and Village Enterprises Law) were published. In the last two years of this period, the number of TVEs declined. The decline may be because in an improved market the simple and labour-intensive technologies that TVEs adopted were no longer competitive, and the TVE sector had to be restructured (Wang and Yao 2002). Or, it could be a course correction of the over-heated investment after Deng's visit to the South.

The specification of the year block model is the same as that in the basic year model, except that the subscripts now stand for year blocks instead of years. The OLS results of the model are reported in Table 12.9, while Table 12.10 gives its SUR counterpart.

Unlike the case of year models, SUR does not greatly improve regression efficiency – there is a decrease in standard errors, but the magnitude of decline is minor for almost all the variables except in the restricted models, counting all blocks as a whole. Apart from the change of the standard errors, the estimates from OLS and SUR are consistent. Given the fact that the $F$ tests for no structural change are all highly significant, specific results from individual year blocks will attract greater attention from us. On the other hand, SUR does not necessarily give better estimates than OLS when the cross-model correlations are not large, although the consequences of specification

Table 12.9 Year block model: OLS results

| YB | 1 | | 2 | | 3 | | Overall | |
|---|---|---|---|---|---|---|---|---|
| TYPE | PARMS | Standard error | PARMS | Standard error | PARMS | Standard error | PARMS | Standard error |
| Intercept | -194.95 | 138.81 | 581.18 | 254.43** | 108.25 | 652.68 | 394.11 | 304.18 |
| TVE78 | 2.74 | 0.83*** | -0.23 | 2.13 | 22.85 | 5.49*** | 2.80 | 2.15 |
| GDP1 | -0.28 | 0.13** | -0.91 | 0.25*** | 0.02 | 0.26 | 0.92 | 0.13*** |
| SOE | 0.17 | 0.06** | 0.70 | 0.15*** | 0.06 | 0.29 | -0.07 | 0.11 |
| lratio | 0.86 | 1.95 | -12.64 | 3.93*** | 20.98 | 12.38* | -8.10 | 4.86* |
| rural_k1 | 1.67 | 0.18*** | 2.33 | 0.24*** | 1.18 | 0.43*** | 1.74 | 0.16*** |
| rlabour | 0.01 | 0.02 | 0.11 | 0.04** | 0.11 | 0.12 | 0.13 | 0.05** |
| Prin1 | 193.89 | 55.81*** | 380.34 | 80.82*** | -343.31 | 227.52* | 170.68 | 91.55* |
| PubShare | 3.58 | 1.73** | -0.82 | 5.03 | -29.78 | 8.98*** | -17.05 | 4.51*** |
| D1 | -59.83 | 154.30 | -578.93 | 447.06* | 400.49 | 1618.01* | -990.81 | 454.06** |
| D2 | 48.86 | 72.34 | 321.60 | 179.53* | 1750.98 | 536.14*** | 336.85 | 202.92* |
| D3 | 2.35 | 48.23 | -49.16 | 125.51 | -121.46 | 328.00 | -308.23 | 142.06** |
| D4 | 13.31 | 59.01 | -117.06 | 141.56 | -304.04 | 410.80 | -401.89 | 173.91** |
| D5 | 71.64 | 60.50 | 5.90 | 151.29 | -466.82 | 440.05 | -173.51 | 187.10 |
| $R^2$ | 0.97 | | 0.95 | | 0.90 | | 0.88 | |

Notes: dependent variable: per capita TVE output; $F$ test for no structural change over year blocks: $F_{(28,294)} = 7.11$, $p < 0.0001$.

Table 12.10 Year block model: SUR* results

| YB TYPE | 1 | | 2 | | 3 | | Overall | |
|---|---|---|---|---|---|---|---|---|
| | PARMS | Standard error | PARMS | Standard error | PARMS | Standard error | PARMS | Standard error |
| Intercept | -180.13 | 135.41 | 596.78 | 250.11** | 371.13 | 646.29 | -85.36 | 121.88 |
| TVE78 | 3.40 | 0.82*** | 1.16 | 2.10 | 20.94 | 5.44*** | 1.59 | 0.76** |
| GDP1 | -0.15 | 0.13 | -0.52 | 0.24** | -0.03 | 0.26 | 0.47 | 0.08*** |
| SOE | 0.08 | 0.06 | 0.46 | 0.14*** | 0.19 | 0.29 | -0.12 | 0.05** |
| lratio | 0.75 | 1.91 | -13.44 | 3.85*** | 13.31 | 12.28 | -2.70 | 1.76 |
| rural_k1 | 1.64 | 0.18*** | 2.10 | 0.23*** | 1.12 | 0.42*** | 1.82 | 0.09*** |
| rlabour | 0.00 | 0.02 | 0.11 | 0.04** | 0.10 | 0.12 | 0.01 | 0.02 |
| Prin1 | 200.09 | 52.75*** | 394.93 | 77.08*** | -148.85 | 222.98 | 337.00 | 40.55*** |
| PubShare | 2.53 | 1.67 | -2.91 | 4.84 | -27.46 | 8.77*** | 0.78 | 1.57 |
| D1 | -144.83 | 151.88 | -480.00 | 441.26 | 213.63 | 1591.61 | -630.68 | 134.73*** |
| D2 | 19.00 | 70.75 | 241.01 | 176.33 | 1601.55 | 530.01*** | -152.40 | 65.59** |
| D3 | -14.14 | 47.86 | -83.21 | 124.38 | -131.16 | 327.58 | -79.35 | 45.87* |
| D4 | 15.21 | 58.30 | -116.86 | 140.80 | -320.34 | 410.00 | -6.63 | 55.89 |
| D5 | 84.13 | 60.00 | 25.71 | 150.40 | -365.88 | 438.55 | 95.04 | 58.83 |
| $R^2$ | 0.9381 for block model | | | | | | 0.8815 | |

Cross-equation correlations of different year blocks

| | YB1 | YB2 | YB3 |
|---|---|---|---|
| YB1 | 1.00000 | 0.37618 | 0.19926 |
| YB2 | 0.37618 | 1.00000 | 0.17966 |
| YB3 | 0.19926 | 0.17966 | 1.00000 |

* Dependent variable: per capita TVE output; $F$ test for no structural change over year blocks: $F(28,294) = 9.60$, $p < 0.0001$.

error are more serious with SUR than with OLS. Table 12.10 reveals that the correlations range from 0.18 to 0.38; therefore, OLS is preferred to SUR in the year block models.

The variable of most interest is *PubShare*. In Table 12.9 it is found that the impact of *PubShare* is positive (3.58, robust at the 0.05 level) in the first year block. The impact declines to around nil (−0.82, not robust) in the second block. The trend remains in Block 3, where public ownership turns into a handicap in TVEs' development (−17.05, highly robust at the 0.01 level). Recall the change of market conditions over time in Table 12.5: the mean value of market perfection index in Year Block 1 is −0.43, which progresses to −0.03 in Block 2, and 0.46 in Block 3. This finding confirms the prediction of the $H_{01}$ hypothesis.

Among all the other variables controlled in the model, the effect of capital input *(rural_k1)* is the only one that is consistently significant and positive, showing that the capital factor is of crucial importance to TVEs' growth. The effect of labour input is not as robust as that of capital: it is positive for all years but not all are robust. As discussed before, labour is abundant in rural areas; it is their comparative advantage. Thus making good use of the labour resources did boost the progress of TVEs. While capital is relatively scarce, it turned out to be crucial in running a business. Just as in the basic year model, the effect of market condition does not always comply with what is expected – it gives a negative impact (significant at the 0.1 level) in Year Block 3, though the overall effect is positive (significant at the 0.1 level). We guess the problem arises because of the structural adjustment of the TVE sector and the inconsistency of TVEs' ownership arrangements and market conditions during the tide of privatization in the recovery period after Deng Xiaoping's trip to the South. Nevertheless, this assumption will be examined later, together with the test of ownership structure endogeneity.

### The structural equation system

Our theoretical model has suggested the possible existence of endogeneity between the variables, *Prin1* and *PubShare*. If the model matches reality, the optimal ownership structure should be endogenously determined in the system, by the market condition and technology used. This is also the $H_{20}$ hypothesis yet to be tested.

Following the theoretical model, we can set up the structural equation system:

Production equation:

$$y = \beta_0 + \beta_1 \, PubShare + \beta_2 \, K + \beta_3 \, L + \sum_{k \geq 4} \beta_k x_k + \varepsilon_y \tag{12}$$

Ownership equation:

$$PubShare = + a_0 + a_1 Prin1 + a_2 TVE\_k + a_3\, indRatio$$
$$+ a_4\, TVEtech\_L + \varepsilon_o \qquad (13)$$

where $X_k$ ($k > = 4$) is other variables controlled in the model, i.e. *TVE78, GDP1, SOE, lratio* and regional dummies D1–D5, as discussed in the previous section. The variable Prin1 is removed from the production equation because *PubShare* has endogenously captured the effect of Prin1. Three variables, *TVE_k, indRatio* and *TVEtech_L* are included in the ownership equation to capture the effect of technology used on the ownership structure arrangement. Here *TVE_k* is per worker-registered capital of TVEs, which differs from *rural_k1* in the production equation. The latter is more about the means put in the production process and is used in the production equation as a proxy of capital input, whereas registered capital *TVE_k* is better used as a proxy of a firm's reliance on procured capital because in the rural areas the amount of registered capital represents the entrepreneur's power and his connection with local government – larger registered capital normally means easier access to restricted resources such as credit. *IndRatio* is the ratio of industrial TVE output to total TVE output. A firm tightly linked with local government will normally follow its strategic plans, which in rural areas means that the firm should be in the industrial sector. Those firms will make use of their connections with the authorities and enjoy the benefit of strong capability in procurement. Therefore, higher *indRatio* implies higher reliance of the technology on procurement. The last variable included is *TVEtech_L*, the ratio of certified technicians to total labour in the TVE sector. TVEs are normally labour-intensive firms whose comparative advantage lies in making use of the low-cost less-skilled workers. It is assumed that a higher technician ratio implies higher technology, for which procurement resources may not be available through the traditional procurement process. This kind of firm will have to rely more on the market to find resources.

The endogenous determination of the ownership structure implies that the improvement of market conditions will reduce the optimal share of public ownership, while the technology requiring more procurement capability will be in favour of public ownership. Therefore, if the $H_{20}$ hypothesis is true, we will see the negative impact of *Prin1* and *TVEtech_L* on *PubShare* but a positive effect of *TVE_k* and *indRatio*.

In order to test the hypothesis, the structural equation system model is regressed for each year block individually and for all the years as a whole. The results of using 2SLS single-equation estimations and 3SLS systematic estimations are reported in Tables 12.11 and 12.12 separately. It can be observed from the tables that the estimates of 2SLS and 3SLS are very close in terms of magnitude, with 3SLS offering slightly less standard errors.

We first examine the results from the ownership equation. The parameter estimates in this equation do not give their full assent to the hypothesis. The equation is highly robust in each regression, as are most of the variables. The effects of *TVE_k* and *indRatio* are significantly positive over time, which is

Table 12.11 2SLS (two-stage least square regression) results for structural equations

| Variable | 1 | | 2 | | 3 | | All | |
|---|---|---|---|---|---|---|---|---|
| | Estimate | Standard error | Estimate | Standard error | Estimate | Standard error | Estimate | Standard error |
| **Production Equation** | | | | | | | | |
| Intercept | -473.20 | 144.79*** | 309.63 | 303.56 | 843.09 | 917.84 | 861.63 | 375.30** |
| TVE78 | 2.72 | 0.95*** | -1.59 | 2.34 | 19.70 | 5.89*** | 3.46 | 2.33 |
| GDPl | -0.39 | 0.16*** | -0.59 | 0.27** | -0.06 | 0.28 | 0.93 | 0.13*** |
| SOE | 0.22 | 0.08*** | 0.66 | 0.17*** | 0.50 | 0.32 | 0.05 | 0.12 |
| lratio | 1.79 | 2.07 | -8.42 | 4.40* | 19.16 | 13.05 | 0.81 | 5.46 |
| rural_k1 | 1.75 | 0.20*** | 2.39 | 0.28*** | 1.97 | 0.46*** | 1.98 | 0.18*** |
| rlabour | 0.04 | 0.02* | 0.18 | 0.04*** | 0.07 | 0.13 | 0.16 | 0.05*** |
| PubShare | 6.07 | 3.39* | -7.84 | 8.40 | -54.00 | 22.88** | -42.90 | 8.83*** |
| D1 | 129.30 | 160.48 | -36.89 | 479.98 | -2296.05 | 1366.22* | -812.93 | 453.55* |
| D2 | 173.42 | 67.17** | 733.44 | 172.21*** | 901.02 | 427.20** | 503.98 | 184.81*** |
| D3 | -26.84 | 51.17 | -134.65 | 134.27 | -231.86 | 358.89 | -288.67 | 151.22* |
| D4 | -81.83 | 57.59 | -326.03 | 147.14** | -489.58 | 431.61 | -536.55 | 178.71*** |
| D5 | -1.21 | 61.61 | -256.06 | 155.62 | -196.91 | 433.70 | -338.01 | 188.75* |
| Adj. R Sqr | 0.96352 | | 0.93337 | | 0.86344 | | 0.85516 | |
| F | 245.35*** | | 130.57*** | | 59.48 | | 165.83*** | |
| **Ownership Equation** | | | | | | | | |
| Intercept | 24.18 | 7.05*** | 37.07 | 3.30*** | 20.27 | 4.51*** | 47.31 | 1.94*** |
| Prin1 | 2.22 | 2.16 | 4.38 | 1.18*** | 2.43 | 1.12** | 4.48 | 0.81*** |
| TVE_k | 0.0106 | 0.0013*** | 0.0071 | 0.0006*** | 0.0037 | 0.0004*** | 0.0045 | 0.0004*** |
| indRatio | 0.33 | 0.10*** | 0.03 | 0.01*** | 0.26 | 0.04*** | 0.07 | 0.01*** |
| TVEtech_L | -3.68 | 0.86*** | -2.03 | 0.86** | 0.03 | 0.79 | -3.92 | 0.44*** |
| Adj R | 0.72212 | | 0.72765 | | 0.66213 | | 0.55655 | |
| F | 73.11*** | | 75.14*** | | 55.38*** | | 106.11*** | |

Table 12.12 3SLS (three-stage least square regression) results for structural equations

| Variable | 1 | | 2 | | 3 | | All | |
|---|---|---|---|---|---|---|---|---|
| | Estimate | Standard error | Estimate | Standard error | Estimate | Standard error | Estimate | Standard error |
| **Production Equation** | | | | | | | | |
| Intercept | −389.26 | 139.77*** | 302.78 | 303.28 | 1377.29 | 875.15 | 703.04 | 360.11* |
| TVE78 | 3.06 | 0.92*** | −1.32 | 2.34 | 21.75 | 5.62*** | 1.71 | 2.22 |
| GDP1 | −0.28 | 0.15* | −0.58 | 0.26** | −0.13 | 0.27 | 0.91 | 0.13*** |
| SOE | 0.17 | 0.08** | 0.65 | 0.17*** | 0.52 | 0.31* | 0.09 | 0.11 |
| lratio | 1.00 | 1.99 | −8.45 | 4.39* | 25.84 | 12.41** | 4.27 | 5.20 |
| rural_k1 | 1.60 | 0.19*** | 2.38 | 0.28*** | 2.38 | 0.44*** | 2.27 | 0.17*** |
| rlabour | 0.05 | 0.02** | 0.19 | 0.04*** | 0.03 | 0.12 | 0.11 | 0.05** |
| PubShare | 4.06 | 2.30** | −7.83 | 8.39 | −75.73 | 21.87*** | −39.71 | 8.51*** |
| D1 | 171.29 | 154.35 | −68.59 | 479.50 | −2942.61 | 1308.41** | −1407.90 | 432.97*** |
| D2 | 203.56 | 64.49*** | 725.99 | 172.05*** | 746.18 | 409.05* | 358.47 | 176.72** |
| D3 | −47.75 | 49.05 | −147.56 | 134.13 | −176.84 | 341.09 | −251.02 | 143.95* |
| D4 | −66.28 | 55.28 | −327.09 | 147.00** | −639.73 | 410.82 | −611.01 | 170.38*** |
| D5 | −14.29 | 59.25 | −252.00 | 155.47 | −263.66 | 412.93 | −362.18 | 180.07*** |
| **Ownership Equation** | | | | | | | | |
| Intercept | 22.99 | 6.87*** | 36.99 | 3.30*** | 17.87 | 4.41*** | 45.88 | 1.90*** |
| Prin1 | 2.28 | 2.12 | 4.52 | 1.18*** | 2.35 | 1.10** | 3.89 | 0.80*** |
| TVE_k | 0.0104 | 0.0013*** | 0.0071 | 0.0006*** | 0.0037 | 0.0004*** | 0.0046 | 0.0004*** |
| indRatio | 0.35 | 0.10*** | 0.03 | 0.01*** | 0.27 | 0.04*** | 0.08 | 0.01*** |
| TVEtech_L | −3.48 | 0.85*** | −1.97 | 0.86** | 0.43 | 0.77 | −3.65 | 0.43*** |
| System Weighted R-Square | 0.9500 | | 0.9037 | | 0.7894 | | 0.7609 | |
| Cross Model Correlation | −0.28580 | | −0.04520 | | 0.31405 | | 0.30747 | |

consistent with the prediction. The impact of *TVEtech_L* is negative in the first two blocks as well as for the overall data, but changes to positive but not significant in Year Block 3. This can be explained by the structural adjustment of TVEs in this period. As a result of the adjustment, the technological level of TVEs tends to be homogeneous. Therefore the technician ratio is no longer a determinant in ownership structure arrangement.

The variable Prin1, however, tells a different story. The 3SLS estimate of Prin1 in Block 1 is 2.28 (SD = 2.12), 4.52 (significant at the 0.01 level) in Block 2 and 2.35 (significant at the 0.05 level) in Block 3, whereas the overall effect for all years is 3.89 (significant at the 0.01 level). None of this complies with the $H_{02}$ hypothesis, which suggests the impact should be in the opposite direction. One possible explanation of the inconsistency is that the ownership arrangement is in reality not at the optimal state as determined endogenously in the system. Our interviews with officials from the Bureau of Small and Medium Enterprises (the former Bureau of TVEs) in different provinces reveal that there are often other factors affecting ownership selection, such as a plan of privatization made by the local government regardless of the institutional situation. The underdeveloped provinces see the prosperous private TVEs in the developed regions as good models to imitate, and regard privatization as a key to achieving parallel success. Hence, under the pressure of performance evaluation, local officials tend to set timetables to push privatization on the TVEs under their own jurisdiction, although the local institutional environment might not be well enough developed for such a purpose. Another possible reason is that our theoretical model does not consider the case in which the project is initiated by the government, i.e. the existence of bureaucrat entrepreneurs. In such a situation, the public share will be relatively higher because the bureaucrat himself is the residual claimer of the scarce resource project information. This situation, however, became increasingly unlikely in the years following the early 1990s due to the government administration reform that separates business entities from the government structure.

Taking a close look at the production model, we find that the coefficients of *PubShare* in different blocks are qualitatively the same as in the year block model. Therefore the results from all three models give evidence supporting the $H_{01}$ hypothesis empirically.

We will complete the empirical discussion by examining another interesting point – the effects of regional dummy variables. Comparing models with regional dummies to those without (not reported in the tables), we find that the effect of one of the initial conditions (*TVE78*) disappeared when regional effects were taken into account. This result suggests the regional pattern of this initial condition. Something similar happens to *lratio*, the ratio of light industry output. In models with regional dummies, coastal provinces lead all the others consistently; northwest provinces fall significantly behind, while the difference between the north and southwest and the bench group (south) is weak. If we break down the effects into year blocks, the coastal areas are leading because of their strong industrial background, entrepreneurial tradition and easier access to FDI and overseas markets. The insignificant difference between the north and southwest and the bench group implies that the underdevelopment of TVEs in these regions could be reasonably captured by the explanatory variables included in our model, but not by any unexplained intrinsic reasons uniquely inside the region. Large cities, surprisingly, lead only in the first year block, tie in the second, and then fall much behind in the third period (–2296 by 2SLS and –2942 by 3SLS, both robust). A likely reason is TVEs in these large cities are not at totally efficient – they could have done better if all the favourable factors were fully and effectively utilized.

## Concluding remarks

This chapter explains, using a formal model, why the role of public ownership in TVE development changed in rural China. The crucial idea is the existence of some un-marketed resources such as management and procurement that are crucial to TVE production. The result shows that, for some given imperfect institutional environments and certain technology used by TVEs, public ownership will dominate private ownership. With the improvement of market conditions, private ownership will become dominant regardless of the technology used, or put another way, the helping hand public ownership offers when the market is far from perfect will change to slow down the development of TVEs. This prediction is consistent with the empirical evidence obtained from all the regressions.

In the theoretical model, the ownership structure has been endogenized by solving the problem of optimal time allocation by each agent in terms of exogenous parameters such as degree of market imperfection, opportunity income and production technology. Although the empirical models have confirmed the endogenous determination of the ownership structure, the real process does not fully comply with the theoretical implications. We explain this by the possible existence of external intervention in the process of determining the optimal ownership structure.

An important implication of the model is that ownership arrangements cannot be changed effectively unless the institutional environment has been changed. For an economy with a high level of government intervention and bureaucratic corruption, public ownership may be the efficient ownership arrangement, while, vice versa, private ownership will only become efficient when the market has progressed to a certain completion level. Hence, reckless privatization regardless of the institutional situation will very likely lead to economic inefficiency, or put another way, retard the economy. This can explain why the gradual economic reform in China experienced better growth than the shock therapy experienced in Russia. This may also suggest that the growth of TVEs in China would have been even faster if the government interfered less in ownership structure arrangement.

This chapter has followed the literature in modelling this process as a one-period non-cooperative game, even though in reality it often tends to be of a long-running nature. For simplicity, we did not consider the case where the bureaucrat has the right to provide a licence for setting up a TVE, or can initiate a project and lease it to the entrepreneur, as happens in the fixed-rental form. Our assumptions rule out corruption, where the entrepreneur buys 'help' from the bureaucrat; in that case, it is more likely that the two parties will reach an arrangement. Nevertheless, the bargaining power of each party will depend on the non-cooperative equilibrium payoffs presented in our results. There might also be some implicit instrument outside of our model – such as credit control that results in difficulties finding start-up finance, or achievement bonuses that change the opportunity income – which the two parties may exercise to approximate the cooperative outcome. Though the provincial aggregate data give us satisfactory results in testing the model, firm-level data could improve the empirical analysis significantly. All of these problems could be tackled in future studies.

## Acknowledgements

I am grateful for helpful suggestions and detailed comments from Professor Keith Cowling and Dr Jeffery Round. Helpful comments were also received during the CEA 2007 and TED 2007 conferences, especially those of Dr Zhongmin Wu, Dr Chen Yang, Professor Eric Gerardin, Professor John Weiss and Professor John Knight. All errors and misinformation are my own.

## Notes

1 The term TVE in our work is generalized to refer to rural enterprises, including both community government-run enterprises and a growing number of private enterprises.
2 Calculated from the *China Rural Statistical Yearbook* and the *China Statistical Yearbook*, various years.
3 *China Labour Statistical Yearbook*, various years.
4 Calculated from the *China Rural Statistical Yearbook* and the *China Statistical Yearbook*, various years.
5 A full description of the theoretical model can be found in Chapter 3 of the author's doctoral dissertation – *Explaining Income Inequality in Rural China: A New Perspective.*
6 See Diewert (1973) and Eswaran and Kotwal (1985).
7 The proof of the proposition is available upon request.
8 The provincial data of Hainan Province is only available for years after 1988 when it was separated as an independent province from Guangdong. Since then, Hainan is treated as a special economic zone and therefore it is not appropriate to add Hainan data to the Guangdong data.
9 Because of the lack of a local support team, many indices in Tibet are left blank in various statistical yearbooks for years before the 1990s.
10 D1 – large cities: Beijing, Tianjin, Shanghai
D2 – coastal: Guangdong, Fujian, Liaoning, Shandong, Jiangsu, Zhejiang
D3 – north: Jilin, Heilongjiang, Inner Mongolia, Shanxi, Anhui, Hebei, Henan
D4 – northwest: Xinjiang, Qinghai, Ningxia, Gansu, Shannxi

D5 – southwest: Yunnan, Guizhou, Sichuan (including Chongqing)
D6 – south: Hubei, Hunan, Jiangxi, Guangxi

11 If there is no correlation across equations (the estimate of the contemporaneous correlation matrix is diagonal), SUR will produce the same results as OLS. However, SUR may improve the efficiency of parameter estimates when there is contemporaneous correlation of errors across equations. Therefore, theoretically, SUR parameter estimates will always be at least as efficient as OLS in large samples, provided that the equations are correctly specified. In our OLS model, correlations between the models of each year are likely to affect the estimation efficiency because, for instance, the variable we use to capture market size is lagged GDP, that is, calculated on the basis of the total added value across all the sectors, including the TVE sector, and hence is correlated with the model of the previous years. Actually, the evidence of the cross-model correlation matrix in Table 12.7 supports this argument.

# References

Booth, Anne (1999) Initial conditions and miraculous growth: why is South East Asia different from Taiwan and South Korea?, *World Development*, *27*(2), pp. 301–321.

Byrd, William A. (2003) Book review: *Power and Wealth in Rural China: The Political Economy of Institutional Change, China Journal*, *49*, pp. 166–169.

Byrd, William A. and Lin, Qingsong (1990) *China's Rural Industry: Structure, Development, and Reform*, Oxford: Oxford University Press and World Bank.

Che, Jiahua (2002) *From the Grabbing Hand to the Helping Hand: A Rent Seeking Model of China's Township–Village Enterprises*, Helsinki: United Nations University, World Institute for Development Economics Research.

Che, Jiahua and Qian, Yingyi (1998) Insecure property rights and government ownership of firms, *Quarterly Journal of Economics*, *113*(2), pp. 467–496.

Che, Jiahua and Qian, Yingyi (1999) Institutional environment, community government, and corporate governance: understanding China's township–village enterprises, *Journal of Law, Economics and Organization*, *14*(1), pp. 1–23.

Chen, Hongyi and Rozelle, Scott (1999) Leaders, managers, and the organization of township and village enterprises in China, *Journal of Development Economics*, *60*(2), pp. 529–557.

Diewert, W.E. (1973) Functional forms for profit and transformation functions, *Journal of Economic Theory*, *6*(3), pp. 284–316.

Eswaran, Mukesh and Kotwal, Ashok (1985) A theory of contractual structure in agriculture, *American Economic Review*, *75*(3), pp. 352–367.

Fan, Y., Chen, N. and Kirby, D.A. (1996) Chinese peasant entrepreneurs: an examination of township and village enterprises in rural China, *Journal of Small Business Management*, *34*(4), pp. 72–76.

Fan, Gang, Wang, Xiao-lu and Zhang, Li-wen (2001) Marketization index for China's provinces, *China and World Economy*, *9*(5), pp. 3–8.

Hsiao, Cheng, Nugent, Jeffrey, Perrigne, Isabelle and Qiu, Jicheng (1998) Shares versus residual claimant contracts: the case of Chinese TVEs, *Journal of Comparative Economics*, *26*(2), pp. 317–337.

Jin, Hehui and Qian, Yingyi (1998) Public versus private ownership of firms: evidence from rural China, *Quarterly Journal of Economics*, *113*(3), pp. 773–808.

Li, David (1996) A theory of ambiguous property rights in transition economies: the case of the Chinese non-state sector, *Journal of Comparative Economics*, *23*(1), pp. 1–19.

Lin, Justin Yifu and Yao, Yang (2001) Chinese rural industrialization in the context of the East Asian miracle, in S. Yusuf and J. E. Stiglitz (eds), *Rethinking the East Asian Miracle*, Oxford: Oxford University Press and World Bank.

Lin, Justin Yifu, Tao, Ran and Liu, Mingxing (2003) Decentralization, deregulation and economic transition in China, Working Paper, Beijing: Beijing University, CCER.

Peng, Yusheng (2001) Chinese villages and townships as industrial corporations: ownership, governance, and market discipline, *American Journal of Sociology*, *106*(5), pp. 13–38.

Perotti, Enrico C., Sun, Laixiang and Zhou, Liang (1999) State-owned versus township and village enterprises in China, *Comparative Economic* Studies, *41*(2/3), pp. 151–179.

Rodrik, Dani (2004) A practical approach to formulating growth strategies, *Barcelona Forum of September 2004: Thoughts on how to move forward from the Washington Consensus*, Barcelona.

Stel, Andre van (2004) Empirical analysis of entrepreneurship and economic growth, in H. L. F. d. Groot, P. Nijkamp and R. Stough (eds), *Entrepreneurship and Regional Economic Development: A Spatial Perspective*, Cheltenham: Edward Elgar.

Sun, Laixiang (2002) Fading out of local government ownership: recent ownership reform in China's township and village enterprises, *Economic Systems*, *26*(3), pp. 249–269.

Tian, Guoqiang (2000) Property rights and the nature of Chinese collective enterprises. *Journal of Comparative Economics*, *28*(2), pp. 247–68.

Wang, Yueping and Yao, Yang (2002) Market reforms, technological capabilities and the performance of small enterprises in China, *Small Business Economics*, *18*(1–3), p. 197.

Weitzman, Martin L. and Xu, Chenggang (1994) Chinese township–village enterprises as vaguely defined cooperatives, *Journal of Comparative Economics*, *18*(2), pp. 121–145.

Wolf, Martin (1995) China's socialist market economy: economic eye, *Financial Times*, 13 November, p. 26.

Zhang, Jian, Zhang, Linxiu, Rozelle, Scott and Boucher, Steve (2006) Self-employment with Chinese characteristics: the forgotten engine of rural China's growth, *Contemporary Economic Policy*, *24*(3), pp. 446–458.

# 13 Developing corporate social responsibility in China

## The impact of government regulations, market orientation and ownership structure

*Riliang Qu*

### Introduction

Recently, corporate social responsibility has received considerable attention from both academics and practitioners (see Durant 2006; Graafland *et al.* 2003; Griffin and Mahon 1997; Jones 1997; Maignan and Ferrell 2001; Maignan and Ralston 2002; Smith 1996; Waddock and Graves 1997). This may be explained by the fact that, although some studies postulated a negative relationship (e.g. Vance 1975) or no relationship (e.g. Aupperle *et al.* 1985) between corporate social responsibility (CSR) and business performance, more recent studies provided the empirical evidence that there is a positive relationship between those two constructs (Abratt and Sacks 1988; Russo and Fouts 1997; Waddock and Graves 1997). In addition, the empirical evidence suggests that CSR could have other benefits for a firm. For instance, a recent survey (Smith 1996) found that 88 per cent of consumers in the study were more likely to buy from a company that is socially responsible, suggesting that CSR could be an effective marketing tool in the future. It is also reported that corporate social responsibility could have positive effects in helping companies to attract more talented and committed employees (Maignan *et al.* 1999). In contrast to a growing body of research supporting the importance of CSR, the issues relating to the determinants and development of CSR are still relatively under-researched. In addition, most of the research to date has been conducted in the developed countries, mainly in the US and Europe. Consequently, there is limited knowledge about how CSR is perceived and implemented by companies in developing countries (Al-Khatib *et al.* 2004).

This chapter aims to contribute to the above under-researched areas by considering the relative impacts of government regulations, ownership structure and company's market orientation on the development of corporate social responsibility in China. Our focus on the impacts of government regulations is based on the fact that due to the well-known historical reasons, governments in China play a far bigger role in influencing corporate actions, compared with governments in the West. Another uniqueness of the Chinese economy is the dominance of state-owned companies in many industrial sectors. Traditionally, in accordance with socialist doctrines, Chinese state-owned companies actively engaged in many CSR activities, such as providing social housing and free medical services to employees and schooling services to the employees' children. Since the beginning of China's economic reform in 1978, many state-owned companies have significantly reduced their CSR activities due to increasing commercial pressures. To what extent do these state-owned companies still engage in CSR activities versus privately-owned companies and companies of other ownership structures, is therefore, an interesting question to be answered.

The chapter begins with a brief review of the literature and then discusses the development of hypotheses. The following section explains the research method and data collection procedures. Thereafter, the results of the data analysis are presented and the final section provides a discussion and conclusion.

## The determinants of CSR

As a broad concept, CSR has been given a variety of meanings. Along with the term corporate social responsibility, other terms such as corporate social responsiveness, corporate social performance, corporate citizenship and stakeholder management have also been extensively used (see Carroll 1979; Clarkson 1995; Griffin and Mahon 1997; Magnan and Ferrel 2001; Standwick and Standwick 1998; Turban and Greening 1996; Waddock and Graves 1997). Despite the existence of a variety of definitions, a review of the literature suggests that the classification framework created by Carroll (1979) has received wide acceptance. According to Carroll, corporate social responsibility is a multidimensional construct consisting of four types of responsibility: economic, legal, ethical and discretionary.

Economic responsibilities include the obligations for businesses to maintain economic wealth and to meet consumption needs. Legal responsibilities imply that businesses must fulfil their economic mission within the framework of legal requirements. Ethical responsibilities require that businesses abide by the moral rules defining appropriate behaviours in society. Discretionary responsibilities are tantamount to philanthropic responsibilities and reflect society's desire to see businesses contributing to its development. Compared with the previous attempts to define corporate social responsibility, Carroll's (ibid.) definition is quite a broad and inclusive concept, which may explain its universal appeal: not only is it used by researchers in the West, investigations in the developing countries also extensively use such a definition. As there is no previous research in China providing evidence to the contrary, given the breadth and increasing recognition of the definition by Carroll, we use this definition in our study.

Past research on CSR is mainly concerned with conceptualising it, as well as empirically assessing its impact on business performance. For example, a number of studies have been conducted in an attempt to link CSR with financial performance (i.e. Abratt and Sacks 1988; Aupperle *et al.* 1985; Russo and Fouts 1997; Waddock and Graves 1997). In addition to corporate performance, recent studies also examined the impact of CSR on other stakeholders of companies. For example, Mohr *et al.* (2001) looked at the impact of CSR on customer buying behaviour, while Turban and Greening (1996) examined its impact on organizations' attractiveness to employees.

Compared with the growing body of literature on the nature and consequences of corporate social responsibilities, however, the issue of how to improve companies' level of CSR has received relatively limited attention. Two noticeable exceptions are Thomas and Simerly (1995) and Maignan *et al.* (1999). Thomas and Simerly examined the relationship between the background of top managers evaluated in terms of internal versus external orientation and corporate citizenship, using a sample of 574 top executives in the US. A key finding of their research is that the internal orientation of top executives has a negative impact on a company's corporate social performance. Looking beyond the individual's effects on CSR, Maignan *et al.* investigate whether three specific dimensions of organizational culture affect corporate citizenship, including market orientation, humanistic orientation and competitive orientation.

This study continues along this line of enquiry. In addition to examining the influence of market orientation, we consider the effect of government regulations and ownership structure on a firm's level of CSR. Compared with market orientation, government regulations and ownership structure represent two external influences beyond management control. By considering their effects together with the impact of market orientation, it enables us to tell whether the company's level of CSR is more an outcome of alignment with market forces or a result of actions from governments and corporate owners. As such, the study also contributes to the debate on the effectiveness of government regulations and corporate governance.

### Government regulations

Government has long been viewed as among the most important change agent to influence corporate behaviour by defining the rules of the game for companies (Garwin 1983; Joseph 2002; Weidenbaum 1999). However, due to a lack of research attention focusing on the determinants of CSR, no empirical study has been found examining the effectiveness of various forms of government regulations in influencing companies' CSR.

On the other hand, although business self-regulation has been advocated (see e.g. Kolk and van Tulder 2002), it is argued that managers are largely unable to consider their firms' impact on society or to subordinate profit-maximization to social objectives due to bounded rationality (Maitland 1985). The recent corporate scandals surrounding the accounting firm Arthur

Andersen and its client firm Enron in the US provide an example of the failure of self-regulation by accounting professionals and highlight the potential pitfalls that might arise from the inadequacy of government regulations.

By setting up clear and strict guidelines and regulations on product quality, production processes and consumer protection, a government could send out clear signals to business of the necessity to remove the practices that are in contravention with the regulations, even though this may be an unsettling and even unpleasant process (Porter 1990). Therefore, we expect that:

**Hypothesis 1** *The higher the degree of government regulation pertaining to product quality and consumer protection is perceived by managers in a company, the higher degree of CSR a company will display.*

### Ownership structure

One of the major arguments against CSR is presented by Friedman (1970); he argued that profit maximization should be managers' sole responsibility in order to fulfil their obligations to the company owners. The argument is based on the assumption that profit is the only objective the company owners will pursue, which is becoming increasingly debatable. For example, research showed that institutional investors, being unable to move quickly in and out of funds without affecting share price, have strong interests not only in the financial performance of the firms in which they invest, but also in the strategies, activities and other stakeholders of those firms (Holderness and Sheehan 1988; Pound 1992). As the different owners may impose different expectations in terms of profits and corporate social performance, which in turn might influence management's perception as to the importance of engaging in corporate social responsibilities, we expect that:

**Hypothesis 2** *There will be significant differences in the degree of CSR exhibited among firms with different ownership structures.*

### Market orientation

Being market-oriented, a firm needs to constantly monitor and adapt to the changes in the environment in order to stay ahead of the competition (Kohli and Jaworski 1990; Narver and Slater 1990). Therefore, if we accept that CSR is becoming increasingly strategically important, as evidenced by the growing research interest and compelling findings in this area, arguably, the market-oriented companies will be among the first to appreciate it and act in accordance with the principles underlying the concept. Research in the US found that market-oriented cultures encourage firms to develop activities associated with CSR (Maignan *et al.* 1999). As there is no empirical research outside the US contesting the opposite, we, in accord with Maignan *et al.*, also hypothesize that:

**Hypothesis 3** *The more market-oriented a firm, the higher the degree of CSR it will display.*

## Research methodology

As previous studies suggest that there are significant industry differences in terms of CSR (Maignan *et al.* 1999), we concentrate on one industrial sector, the hotel sector, in China, to control for industry effects. The choice was made also because of the existence of a diversified ownership structure in this sector, allowing us to examine the effects of ownership structure.

### *Operation and measurement*

A five-stage iterative procedure, similar to the one used by Kohli *et al.* (1993), was followed to refine the existing scales and to develop new scales, including expert review, focus group critique and two rounds of pre-testing. The complete scales are provided in the Appendix. All the scales (except for ownership structure, which is nominal, i.e. the respondents were asked to identify their hotel's ownership structure) are measured using five-point Likert type scales, ranging from 'not at all' to 'very much'. The CSR instrument employed in the study (Cronbach's $a = 0.88$) was based on the one developed by Maignan *et al.* (1999), while the scale for market orientation (Cronbach's $a = 0.88$) was based on Kohli *et al.* (ibid.). Modifications were made, taking into account both the specific sector characteristics and Chinese business culture. The degree of government regulation is measured by a five-item scale (Cronbach's $a = 0.74$), measuring managers' perception of the adequacy and effectiveness of the current government regulations on product quality, production processes and protection of consumer interests.

### *Data collection*

The hotel sample consists of 600 hotels drawn randomly against the sampling frames of 2,935 hotels with more than one star listed in the *Directory of Chinese Star-Rated Hotels* (1999). A questionnaire, covering letter and a stamped return envelope was mailed to each of the hotels. The mail package was addressed to the hotel general manager. A total of 14 hotels could not be reached because of incorrect addresses, resulting in an effective base of 586 hotels. With a cut-off date four weeks after the mailing, 143 completed questionnaires were received, resulting in a response rate of 24.4 per cent. Following Armstrong and Overton (1977), non-response bias in the survey was assessed by comparing the early respondents' (two weeks prior to the cut-off time) and late respondents' values on a number of key variables including market orientation, CSR and government regulations. None of the differences was found to be significant by *t* tests, suggesting that non-response was less likely to be a cause for concern in subsequent analysis.

## Analysis and results

Hypotheses 1 and 3 were tested by the regression analysis and the results are provided in Table 13.1. H2 was tested by the ANOVA test. Table 13.2 provides the $F$ test result, together with a summary of means of CSR by ownership structure.

## Discussion

Support for hypothesis 1 in relation to the impact of government regulations is found ($b = 0.26$; $p = 0.000$), suggesting that managers' perception of the adequacy and effectiveness of government regulations has a direct impact on the level of CSR, hence demonstrating the positive role a government could play in fostering CSR. This finding has significant implications for governments in the developing countries, which normally either lack adequate regulations to control such aspects of business as product quality, production processes and protection of the interests of consumers, or simply do not have adequate resources to enforce those regulations. It appears important for those governments to recognize the need to strengthen those regulations in relation to such aspects of business as product quality, production process and consumer protection in order to raise the aspirations of business.

Support for hypothesis 3 in relation to the role of market orientation in developing CSR is also found ($b = 0.48$; $p = 0.000$). The finding is consistent with the empirical study in the US by Maignan *et al.* (1999), suggesting that market-oriented companies in China also realize the importance of

*Table 13.1* Antecedents of corporate social responsibility: standardized regression coefficients

| Independent variables | Standardized coefficients | T | Sig. |
|---|---|---|---|
| Government regulation | 0.26 | 3.67 | 0.000 |
| Market orientation | 0.48 | 6.75 | 0.000 |
| $R^2 = 0.37$ | | | |
| Adjusted $R^2 = 0.36$ | | | |

*Table 13.2* Ownership structure

| Variables | Ownership | N | Mean | SD |
|---|---|---|---|---|
| Corporate social responsibility | State-owned | 71 | 3.55 | 0.66 |
| | Shareholding | 21 | 3.72 | 0.63 |
| | Individually-owned | 6 | 3.42 | 0.39 |
| | Collective-owned | 20 | 3.65 | 0.65 |
| | Foreign-owned | 6 | 3.39 | 0.99 |
| | Joint venture hotels | 16 | 4.01 | 0.71 |
| $F = 1.61$; p = 0.16 | | | | |

responding to the demands and expectations of their stakeholders by developing a higher level of CSR.

Contrary to the hypothesis, corporate ownership did not seem to have a significant effect on a firm's level of CSR. Alternatively, it is possible that the effect does exist but was not detected because of the potentially insufficient power of the statistical test as a result of the relatively small sample size. This may be a direct effect of the fact that ownership may have little relationship to management decisions, although clearly more research on this topic is needed.

## Conclusions

This chapter has focused attention on the determinants of CSR in a major, but under-researched, economy – China. The research has evaluated both recognized antecedents based on the original work of Maignan *et al.* (1999) and proposed new factors that are expected to affect the development of CSR. A survey of 143 companies in China shows that, in the current research context, market orientation is the most significant predicator of CSR, followed by government regulations, suggesting that the development of CSR is an outcome of both market forces and government actions.

The findings have a number of theoretical as well as practical implications for policy-makers, especially those in the developing economies. A main theoretical contribution of our study is that it shed lights on the key determinants of CSR in the context of developing countries and highlights the government's role in the development of CSR. Given the tendency among developing countries to regard all forms of government regulation as excessive and restrictive to competition, therefore, a key practical implication of our study for policy-makers is that, while there is clearly a need to remove excessive regulations relating to competition, there may also be a case for tightening up the existing regulations or even developing new regulations that address enhanced levels of consumer protection, encourage increases in product quality and generally provide greater incentives for a move towards CSR.

## Limitations of this research and directions for future research

The results reported above provide some useful insights into issues surrounding the development of CSR in a developing economy. However, they are not without limitations. These relate to several areas. First, as an exploratory study, we only examined the impact of three factors. It is recognized that a variety of other factors, such as industry type, organizational life cycle, culture and quality of management, may also contribute to the level of CSR. Therefore, one future research task is to examine the effects of these additional factors on the development of CSR. Second, the cross-sectional design we adopted for this study enables the generation of important insights into the determinants of CSR but understanding of the change processes involved in improving it is very limited.

Future research could usefully adopt a more in-depth and longitudinal design to explore these change processes. Finally, as with many previous studies, data were obtained from top managers. It would be useful to obtain a broader sample of managers, and perhaps even non-managers, in future studies, so that any potential bias in the data resulting from the level of seniority of informants will be minimized.

## References

Abratt, R. and D. Sacks (1988) The marketing challenge: towards being profitable and socially responsible, *Journal of Business Ethics*, Vol. 36, No. 2, pp. 497–507.

Al-Khatib, Jamal A., Mohommed A. Rawwas and Scot J. Vitell (2004) Organizational ethics in developing countries: a comparative analysis, *Journal of Business Ethics*, Vol. 54, No. 4, pp. 309–322.

Armstrong, S. and Overton, S. (1977) Estimating non-response bias in mail surveys, *Journal of Marketing Research*, Vol. 14, No. 3, pp. 396–402

Aupperle, Kenneth E., Archie B. Carroll and John D. Hatfield (1985) An empirical examination of the relationship between corporate social responsibility and profitability, *Academy of Management Journal*, Vol. 28, No. 2, pp. 446–463.

Carroll, Archie B. (1979) A three-dimensional conceptual model of corporate performance, *Academy of Management Review*, Vol. 4, No. 4, pp. 497–505.

Clarkson, M. (1995) A stakeholder framework for analyzing and evaluating corporate social performance, *Academy of Management Review*, Vol. 20, No. 1, pp. 92–117.

Durant, Augusto (2006) CSR continues to define itself globally, *Caribbean Business*, Vol. 34, No. 18, p. 48.

Friedman, Milton (1970) The corporation's social responsibility is to increase its profits, *New York Times Magazine*, 13 September.

Garwin, D.A. (1983) Can industry self-regulation work?, *California Management Review*, Vol. 25, No. 4, pp. 37–52.

Graafland, Johan, Bert Van de Ven and Nelleke Stoffele (2003) Strategies and instruments for organising CSR by small and large businesses in the Netherlands, *Journal of Business Ethics*, Vol. 47, No. 1, pp. 45–60.

Griffin, Jennifer J. and John F. Mahon (1997) The corporate social performance and corporate financial performance debate, *Business and Society*, Vol. 36, No. 1, pp. 5–32.

Holderness, C.G. and D. P. Sheehan (1988) The role of majority shareholders in publicly held corporations: an exploratory analysis, *Journal of Financial Economics*, Vol. 20, No. 4, pp. 317–346.

Jones, Del (1997) Good works, good business, *USA today*, 25 April, p. 1B.

Joseph, E. (2002) Promoting corporate social responsibility: is market-based regulation sufficient?, *New Economy*, Vol. 9, No. 2, pp. 96–101.

Kohli, A.K. and B. J. Jaworski (1990) Market orientation: the construct, research propositions and managerial implications, *Journal of Marketing*, Vol. 54, No. 2, pp. 1–18.

Kohli, A.K., B. J. Jaworski and A. Kumar (1993) MARKOR: a measure of market orientation, *Journal of Marketing Research*, Vol. 30, pp. 467–477.

Kolk, A. and R. van Tulder (2002) The effectiveness of self-regulation: corporate codes of conduct and child labour, *European Management Journal*, Vol. 20, No. 3, pp. 260–272.

Maignan, I. and O. C. Ferrel (2001) Antecedents and benefits of corporate citizenship: an investigation of French businesses, *Journal of Business Research*, Vol. 51, No. 1, pp. 37–51.

Maignan, I. and D. A. Ralston (2002) Corporate social responsibility in Europe and the US: insights from businesses' self-presentations, *Journal of International Business Studies*, Vol. 33, No. 3, pp. 55–67.

Maignan, I., O. C. Ferrell and G. T. M. Hult (1999) Corporate citizenship: cultural antecedents and business benefits, *Journal of the Academy of Marketing Science*, Vol. 27, No. 4, pp. 455–470.

Maitland, I. (1985) The limits of business self-regulation, *California Management Review*, Vol. 27, No. 3, pp. 132–147.

Mohr, Lois A., Deborah J. Webb and Katherine E. Harris (2001) Do consumers expect companies to be socially responsible? the impact of corporate social responsibility on buying behavior, *Journal of Consumer Affairs*, Vol. 35, No. 1, pp. 45–73.

Narver, C.J. and S. F. Slater (1990) The effect of a market orientation on business profitability, *Journal of Marketing*, Vol. 54, No. 3, pp. 69–73.

Porter, M.E. (1990) *The Competitive Advantage of Nations*, New York: Free Press.

Pound, J. (1992) Beyond takeovers: politics comes to corporate control, *Harvard Business Review*, Vol. 70, No. 2, pp. 83–94.

Russo, M.V. and P. A. Fouts (1997) A resource-based perspective on corporate environmental performance and profitability, *Academy of Management Journal*, Vol. 40, No. 3, pp. 534–559.

Smith, Craig (1996) Corporate citizens and their critics, *New York Times*, 8 September, p. 11.

Standwick, P.A. and S. D. Standwich (1998) The relationship between corporate social performance and organisational size, financial performance, and environmental performance: an empirical examination, *Journal of Business Ethics*, Vol. 17, pp. 195–204.

Thomas, A.S. and R. L. Simerly (1995) Internal determinants of corporate social performance: the role of top managers, in Dorothy P. Moore (ed.), *Academy of Management Journal Best Paper Proceedings*, Madison WI: Omnipress, pp. 411–415.

Turban, D.B. and D. W. Greening (1996) Corporate social performance and organizational attractiveness to prospective employees, *Academy of Management Journal*, Vol. 40, No. 3, pp. 658–672.

Vance, Stanley C. (1975) Are socially responsible corporations good investment risks?, *Management Review*, Vol. 64, No. 8, pp. 18–25.

Waddock, S.E. and S. B. Graves (1997) The corporate social performance–financial performance link, *Strategic Management Journal*, Vol. 18, No. 4, pp. 303–319.

Weidenbaum, M.L. (1999) Business and Government in the Global Marketplace, 6th edition, Upper Saddle River, NJ: Prentice Hall.

# Appendix

| Scale | Scale items | Coefficient alpha (hotel sample) |
|---|---|---|
| Market orientation | 1. We are quick to detect changes in our customers' product preference | |
| | 2. We are quick to detect fundamental shifts in our industry (e.g. competition, technology, regulation) | 0.88 |
| | 3. We periodically review the likely effect of changes in our business environment (e.g. regulation) on customers | |
| | 4. We measure customer satisfaction systematically and frequently (Narver and Slater 1990) | |
| | 5. Our salespeople are instructed to monitor and report on competitive activity | |
| | 6. We regularly collect information about our employees' needs | |
| | 7. We have a sufficient number of interdepartmental meetings to discuss market trends and developments | |
| | 8. When something important happens to a major customer or market, the whole company knows about it in a short period | |
| | 9. Data on customer satisfaction are disseminated at all levels in this company on a regular basis | |
| | 10. When one department finds out something important about our competitors, it is slow to alert other departments | |
| | 11. Our salespeople regularly share information within our business concerning competitors' strategies | |
| | 12. We freely communicate information about our successful and unsuccessful customer experiences across all business functions | |
| | 13. We have measures in place to ensure the voices of the employees are heard by the top management | |
| | 14. It takes us forever to decide how to respond to our competitors' price changes | |
| | 15. For one reason or another, we tend to ignore changes in our customers' product or services needs | |
| | 16. We periodically review our product development efforts to ensure that they are in line with what customers want | |
| | 17. Several departments get together periodically to plan a response to changes taking place in our business environment | |
| | 18. If a major competitor were to launch an intensive campaign targeted at our customers, we would implement a response immediately | |

*(continued)*

| Scale | Scale items | Coefficient alpha (hotel sample) |
|-------|-------------|-------------------|
| | 19. The activities of the different departments in this business unit are well coordinated | |
| | 20. Customer complaints are not regarded as something crucially important in this company | |
| | 21. Even if we came up with a great marketing plan, we probably would not be able to implement it in a timely fashion | |
| | 22. We provide comprehensive training for our employees to teach them how to serve the customers | |
| Corporate social responsibility | We continually improve the quality of our products and services<br>Our company seeks to comply with all laws regulating hiring and employee benefits<br>We are recognized as a trustworthy company<br>Our salespersons and employees are required to provide full and accurate information to all customers<br>We give active support to programmes furthering social causes<br>We have programmes in place to reduce the amount of energy and material wasted in our business | 0.88 |
| Government regulation | 1. Compared with other regions in China, our city has stricter regulations to protect the consumers<br>2. Compared with other regions in China, our city has more effective regulations to encourage the hotels to improve their product and services quality<br>3. The current government regulations on the services standards of the hotel sector are very comprehensive<br>4. There are complete laws and regulations to ensure fair competition | 0.74 |

# 14 Technological entrepreneurship

## Regional variations and impacts of entrepreneurship policy

*Gang Zhang, Xuebing Peng and Jun Li*

## Introduction

As our society is moving towards a knowledge-based economy, competitive advantage of the firm as well as the nation is now virtually defined by its ability to innovate and exploit technological opportunities. Idea exploitation, new firm creation and growth are dependent upon a good supply of budding entrepreneurs, who either engage in entrepreneurial processes independently or within their place of work. Entrepreneurs are thus the catalyst for techno-logical innovation and economic vitality at all levels. To create an environment conducive to technological entrepreneurship, governments have a big role to play and many countries, including China, have formulated policies to sup-port technological entrepreneurship. Nevertheless, we still do not know the extent to which these policies work, as our understanding of why some regions become vital centres of technopreneurial activity while others lan-guish and of what role governments at regional level should play remains very limited. This is specifically hampered by a lack of empirical evidence on impacts of entrepreneurship policy in general and of technological entre-preneurship in particular.

Technological entrepreneurship refers to the creation of new firms by independent entrepreneurs and corporations to exploit technological dis-coveries. There are three main streams of literature in technological entre-preneurship: the study of entrepreneurial people and organizations in relation to opportunity exploitation (Bahrami and Evans 1995; Kenney and Burg 1999; Smilor *et al.* 1989); the study of public research commercialization and university spin-offs (Gregorio and Shane 2003; Hindle and Yencken 2004; Smilor *et al.* 1999); and the study of institutional structures and frame-work conditions conducive to technological entrepreneurship (OECD 2001; Spencer *et al.* 2005). The third stream has strong policy implications and is the focus of this chapter.

Entrepreneurship policy has its origins in SME policy. Early studies of SME policy investigated a range of economic policies such as macro-policy, deregulation, financial support, provision of consultant and advisory services, information services, sales opportunities, intellectual property protection, entry barriers, bankruptcy policy, registration procedures, and so on (Audretsch and Thurik 2001; Gnyawali and Fogel 1994; Verheul *et al.* 2001). However, it was gradually recognized that, although these policies do influence entrepreneurial activities in a region or nation, the broad definition of entrepreneurial policy makes it difficult to pinpoint the direct impact of a specific policy (Hart 2001). Despite a number of researches into the relationship between entrepreneurial policies and technological entrepreneurship, i.e. the Silicon Valley entrepreneurship ecosystem (Bahrami and Evans 1995), the contextual determinants of entrepreneurship (Reynolds *et al.* 2001), impact of entrepreneurial policy on the level of entrepreneurial activity (Lundström and Stevenson 2001a) and Taiwan's technological entrepreneurship practice and its supporting policy (Hung and Chu 2006), overall, little empirical research has been conducted.

Two gaps can be found in the literature on research into technological entrepreneurship and entrepreneurial policy. First, extant research focuses mainly on issues in the domain of high-technology entrepreneurship and tends to neglect innovation activities in conventional business sectors. Second, most of the studies on the relationship between entrepreneurial policy and technological entrepreneurship are case study based, with few using quantitative methods. This chapter sets out to redress these two issues in the context of Chinese technological entrepreneurship. In this chapter, we develop a conceptual framework to explore how entrepreneurship policies can affect activities of technological entrepreneurship. Cross-sectional data in 30 regions during 2003–04 in China were collected and the conceptual framework is tested through factor analysis and hierarchical cluster analysis.

The chapter is divided into four sections. First, we explore the relevant theoretical and empirical literature to develop an analytical framework that relates technological entrepreneurship to entrepreneurship policy. Second, we discuss the operationalization of key concepts and data collection. Third, we present the results of factor analysis, cluster analysis of regional technological entrepreneurship, and the testing of hypotheses. In the final section, we discuss the findings and limitations of this research.

## Technological entrepreneurship and entrepreneurial policy: an analytical framework

### Technological entrepreneurship

Entrepreneurship is a multidimensional concept, and there is no generally accepted definition (Lumpkin and Dess 1996). The main reasons, as Audretsch (2003) indicates, are twofold: the multiple organizational forms of activity involving entrepreneurship, and the benchmarking relative to the concept of change. It has also resulted from the multifaceted nature of entrepreneurship. Early scholars tended to define entrepreneurship from a single dimensional perspective, as illustrated in three economic traditions of entrepreneurship research: the German, Chicago and Austrian traditions (Hébert and Link 1989). The German tradition paid particular attention to the innovation aspect of entrepreneurship. Schumpeter (1934), for example, considered the entrepreneur an innovator who creates new products, new production processes and new forms of organization, and develops new markets and new inputs; the Chicago tradition emphasized risk-taking as a nature of entrepreneurship in an uncertain environment (Knight 1921); and the Austrian tradition emphasized the entrepreneur's alertness to profitable opportunities (Kirzner 1973). The common thread in these economic traditions, however, was an emphasis on the pursuit of opportunity as a distinct feature of entrepreneurship. This has led Sahlman and Stevenson (1991) to define entrepreneurship as, 'a way of managing that involves pursuing opportunity without regard to the resources currently controlled. Entrepreneurs identify opportunities, assemble required resources, implement a practical action plan, and harvest the reward in a timely, flexible way' (p. 1). Extending the concept to the corporate context, Sharma and Chrisman (1999: 18) define corporate entrepreneurship (CE) as, 'the process whereby an individual or a group of individuals, in association with an existing organisation, create a new organisation, or instigate renewal or innovation within that organisation.'

Recent research has shifted to appreciate the multidimensional characteristics of entrepreneurship. Taking established organizations as a unit of analysis, for example, Miller and Friesen (1982) and Covin and Slevin (1991) consider entrepreneurial organization a combination of three dimensions: innovativeness, proactiveness and risk bearing. Similarly, Guth and Ginberg (1990) and Zahra and Shaker (1991) explored corporate entrepreneurship in light of innovation, new business venturing and strategy renewal. While Lumpkin and Dess (1996) explored five dimensions of corporate entrepreneurship, namely autonomy, innovativeness, risk taking, proactiveness and competitive aggressiveness, Atoncic and Hisrich (2003) explored three dimensions of CE, namely new business venturing, product/service innovation and process innovation.

In effect, three approaches can be identified in defining entrepreneurship, i.e. entrepreneurial orientation, entrepreneurial output, and a combination of orientation and output. The entrepreneurial orientation approach examines the multidimensional factors that make an organization entrepreneurial. The output-oriented perspective defines entrepreneurship in line with the traditional emphasis on creation and its outcomes. Shane and Venkatarman (2000), therefore, argue that entrepreneurship research should focus on 'finding and exploiting profitable opportunity', namely, 'why, how and when some people, not others, discover, access and exploit opportunity to create future goods and services.' Based on the premise of 'opportunity discovery', Reynolds *et al.* (2001) distinguish the difference between need entrepreneurship and opportunity entrepreneurship. From the perspective of opportunity discovery and exploitation, technological entrepreneurship can be defined as the process of discovery and exploitation of the market opportunity of technology. Accordingly, the level of technological entrepreneurial activity can be measured in terms of output (e.g. number of new firms or new businesses, etc.) and characteristics/orientation (e.g. innovation, risk bearing and proactiveness, etc.). The commercialization of technology can be achieved either through the creation of a new business entity or by the establishment of a new venture within an existing company (Hindle and Yencken 2004). Taking into account individual and corporate entrepreneurship from the perspectives of entrepreneurial orientation and output, this chapter develops a measurement set of technological entrepreneurship, as shown in Table 14.1.

### Entrepreneurial policy

Entrepreneurial policy aims to foster a socially optimal level of entrepreneurship (Hart 2001). Entrepreneurship policy overlaps with SME policy, but they differ at least in one critical aspect. Entrepreneurship policy is primarily aimed at increasing business start-up rates; small business policy is aimed primarily at assisting those small businesses that have been established (Bridge *et al.* 2003). Thus, in contras to SME policy that is mainly concerned with existing SMEs, entrepreneurial policy is aimed at potential entrepreneurs as well as the existing stock of SMEs (Audretsch 2003; Hindle and Rushworth 2002). Generally speaking, government can employ two kinds of policy to promote technological entrepreneurship: policy to promote innovation of technological firms in a specific industry and policy to promote creation of new technological firms (Wennekers and Thurik 2001). Essentially, entrepreneurial policy is to implement measures that provide incentives, create opportunities and develop skills to encourage people to become entrepreneurs, and its ultimate goal is to make people more entrepreneurial (Lundström and Stevenson 2001b) (see Figure 14.1).

Verheul *et al.* (2001) argue that governments are able to influence the rate of entrepreneurship through five different methods of intervention: (1) demand-side intervention to influence the number and type of entrepreneurship opportunities, including income policy and income disparity, policies stimulating technological development, competition policy and establishment legislation; (2) supply-side intervention to influence supply of potential entrepreneurs, including immigration policy, regional development policy and social benefit policy; (3) intervention to impact the availability of

*Table 14.1* Measuring technological entrepreneurship

| aspects<br>modes | Output | Orientation |
|---|---|---|
| Independent TE | Birth of new firm | Innovativeness, etc. |
| Corporate TE | New business venturing | Innovativeness, etc. |

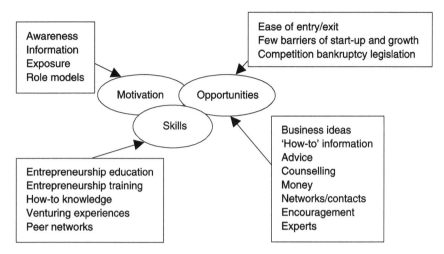

*Figure 14.1* Entrepreneurship policy foundation.

*Source:* Lundström and Stevenson (2001b).

resources, including policies aimed at the venture capital market, direct financial support, direct provision of relevant business information, i.e. advice and counselling, or the educational system; (4) intervention to influence individuals' preferences in relation to becoming an entrepreneur, including educational system and overlapping with culture; and (5) risk-reward profile, including taxation, labour market legislation regarding hiring and firing, and bankruptcy policy. Alternatively, the OECD (2001) categorizes entrepreneurial policy of its member countries into four groups: access to finance, regulation of simplifying the procedures of entry and exit, business support programmes, and encouraging people to be more entrepreneurial. In terms of promoting corporate entrepreneurship, there are four aspects of entrepreneurial policy: market pull, technology push, institution of technology entrepreneurship, and entrepreneurship spirit.

In view of technological entrepreneurship as the process of discovery and exploitation of the market opportunity of technology, we define entrepreneurial policy as measures that help entrepreneurs to discover and exploit opportunity. In the process of technological entrepreneurship, those factors linking with opportunity discovery are embodied in the market and technology, while those factors associating with opportunity exploitation are embodied in human resources and capital.

### Relationship model of technological entrepreneurship and entrepreneurship policy

It is generally held that policy measures can influence the level of entrepreneurship. But the extent of influence is a matter for debate. Some researchers argue that the characteristics of individuals are the primary driving force behind the dynamics of entrepreneurship, while background conditions, including policy, are just secondary determinants of it (Shane and Venkataraman 2000; Venkataraman 2004). Reynolds *et al.* (2001), on the other hand, found that governments play an important role in entrepreneurship by providing financial support, technology and intelligence, and offering information, consulting and educational assistance. Corman *et al.* (1988), on the basis of a survey of high technology firms in the Boston area, found that the motivational factors influencing high-technology entrepreneurship include: value structure of the entrepreneur, venture capital, perceptions of risk, and characteristics and traits of the high-tech entrepreneur. Bahrami and Evans (1995) also showed that new emergent technology, talent pool and venture capital have important impact on the Silicon Valley flexible recycling ecosystem. Other scholars found that the development and maturity of the marketplace plays an important role in technological entrepreneurship (Chao and Teo 2004; Kenney and Burg 1999).

It is acknowledged that creation of an entrepreneurial culture at the regional level is an integral part of an entrepreneurship policy that is aimed at qualitative, more intangible changes, such as changing mindset and nurturing social capital. Nevertheless, the development of an entrepreneurial culture would not be possible without tangible interventions. Our research is primarily focused on the tangible aspects of policy interventions. Evidence so far seems to suggest that technology, finance, human resources and marketplace are the four critical determinants of technological entrepreneurship. Thus, we develop the following relationship model to test relationships between technological entrepreneurship and entrepreneurial policy (see Figure 14.2).

Technology is the vehicle of opportunity exploration and exploitation. Technology-orientated firms invest in, and exploit, R&D with a view to obtaining competitive advantage (Chao and Teo 2004). Hung and Chu (2006)

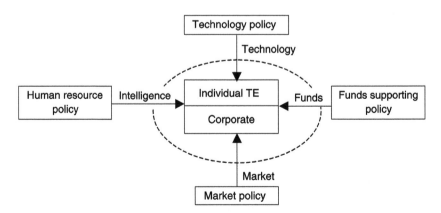

*Figure 14.2* Relationship between TE and entrepreneurship policy.

illustrate that emerging technologies are the prerequisite of new technology-based industry development and that the government holds an important role in shaping the development of emerging technology in new industries. In an increasingly open technological environment, there is evidence that firms are adopting an open innovation model so that they can acquire a significant proportion of technologies from external sources, while in the meantime exploiting the financial potential of their own R&D output through technology transfer (Chesbrough 2003). As a result, policies aiming to remove barriers to technology market development will undoubtedly facilitate technology transfer and motivate firms to engage in innovative activities. Eventually an increase in technology supply will enhance technological entrepreneurship. Accordingly, the following hypotheses are posited:

**Hypothesis 1** $H_{1a}$: *Developing the technology market will promote regional individual technological entrepreneurship.*

**Hypothesis 2** $H_{1b}$: *Developing the technology market will promote regional corporate technological entrepreneurship.*

Access to capital has been found to be a critical factor for new firms. Innovations, particularly radical innovations, are characterized by a huge demand for R&D investment and high uncertainty in relation to commercial prospects. There is plenty of evidence suggesting that, in the biotechnology and pharmaceutical industries, a successful new product breakthrough will take years to develop. Therefore, more conservative sources of funding like bank loans are inaccessible to these new technology firms. In response to this problem, many countries have launched various initiatives, such as increasing public input in basic research and launching public-supported venture capital programmes, encouraging the development of private venture capital funds, and providing seed funding for new business ventures. Empirical evidence from Cumming's (2006) research showed that the Australian innovation venture capital programme played a key role in the start-up stage of technological entrepreneurship, especially in high-technology entrepreneurship. Lerner (1999) found that companies supported by government were more entrepreneurial and grew more rapidly than otherwise. As in China, government investment will not only address the problem of inadequate investment in science and technology (S&T) resources, but also reduce concerns of investors and companies regarding investment in entrepreneurship, thereby promoting independent and corporate entrepreneurship. Hence we posit that:

**Hypothesis 3** $H_{2a}$: *More S&T fund investment by government will generate more independent technological entrepreneurship.*

**Hypothesis 4** $H_{2b}$: *More S&T fund investment by government will generate more corporate technological entrepreneurship.*

It was generally accepted that entrepreneurs' propensity for risk taking and managerial capability has a positive association with both independent and corporate entrepreneurship. Shea *et al.* (2005) report that high quality human resources and more venture capital will positively influence technology transfer from universities and the creation of new firms. Hayton (2005) also suggests that the stock and diversity of human capital in top management positively influences innovation and venturing in high-technology entrepreneurship. Entrepreneurial people, who shoulder the mission of making good use of funds and exploiting technology, are the main driving force of technological entrepreneurship. Evidence shows that many technological entrepreneurs come from a science and technology (S&T) background. Jones-Evans (1996) categories four types of technological entrepreneur on the basis of their occupational background: 'research entrepreneurs', 'product entrepreneurs', 'user entrepreneurs' and 'opportunistic entrepreneurs'. The profile of these entrepreneurs also indicates the importance of occupational experience and educational attainment. Although the stock of S&T human resources in a specific region is associated with factors such as the level of regional development, past history and culture, etc., local government policy in education, vocational training and the structure of incentives can positively influence the stock of human resources in a region. We thus posit that:

**Hypothesis 5** $H_{3a}$: *Positive human resource policy will generate more regional independent technological entrepreneurship.*

**Hypothesis 6** $H_{3b}$: *Positive human resource policy will generate more regional corporate technological entrepreneurship.*

The marketplace is where transactions of production factors are made and the values of entrepreneurship and innovation are materialized. Shane (2001) found that more new technology and more segmented markets lead to more technological entrepreneurship activity. Furthermore, there are more opportunities for technological entrepreneurship in a more open market. A supportive market, first, refers to a healthy market system that protects private property, and is seen as an important structure of incentives that motivates people to become entrepreneurs in the first place. Second, it also refers to the development of the production factor market that allows free flow of resources to more productive use in entrepreneurial activities. China is a transition economy, and government at all levels has responsibility for market development. On the one hand, less government interference in the market will improve the openness of that market; on the other hand, better services provided by the government to the market enablesthe market to develop healthily. Hence, the following hypotheses are posited:

**Hypothesis 7** $H_{4a}$: *Positive market policy of a local government will positively influence regional independent technological entrepreneurship.*

**Hypothesis 8** $H_{4b}$: *Positive market policy of a local government will positively influence regional corporate technological entrepreneurship.*

## Research methods

### Indicators of technological entrepreneurship

Operationalizing entrepreneurship for empirical measurement is a challenge because of the absence of a universally agreed definition of entrepreneurship and, consequently, a set of indicators to measure it (OECD 2001). Based on entrepreneurship dimensions exhibited in Table 14.1, we develop a set of indicators to measure technological entrepreneurship as in Table 14.2, with a combination of demographical statistics and firm statistics.

Indicators of both independent and corporate technological entrepreneurship can be constructed to measure four different aspects of entrepreneurship: scale of entrepreneurship (a measurement of the overall level of entrepreneurial activity), entrepreneurial vitality (a reflection of change in entrepreneurial activity in terms of business start-ups and exits), entrepreneurial intensity (a measurement of the degree and frequency of entrepreneurship occurring within the firm), and entrepreneurial proactiveness (a measurement of entrepreneurial alertness to opportunity). Taking into account data availability, we have employed a variety of proxies to measure these four aspects of entrepreneurship.

With regard to independent technological entrepreneurship, the scale of entrepreneurship is measured as the number of private technology firms; entrepreneurship vitality is measured as the change in the stock of private technology firms; entrepreneurship intensity is measured as the number of technology innovation fund programmes in S&T small and medium companies; and entrepreneurship proactiveness is measured as the number of patent applications per 10,000 population. As for corporate technological entrepreneurship, scale is measured as the total output of new products; vitality is measured as the total output of new products as a percentage of gross industrial product; intensity is measured as R&D investment as a percentage of sales revenue; and proactiveness is measured as number of invention patent applications in large industrial businesses (see Table 14.2).

### Indicators of entrepreneurship policy

Reynolds *et al.* (2001) measured policy of government interference with three proxy indicators, such as government employment as a percentage of total employment; taxes collected as a percentage of GDP; and collected income tax as a percentage of GDP. We use four indicators and seven measures to reflect financial support policy, human resource development policy, technology promotion policy and market support policy. Financial support policy is measured both as public R&D expenditure as a percentage of GDP and as

*Table 14.2* Indicators of level of technological activities

| Target | Dimensions | Perspective | Objective | Indicators |
|---|---|---|---|---|
| The level of TE Entrepreneurship | Independent TE | Output | Scale | $H_1$: number of private and technology firms |
| | | | Vitality | $H_2$: change in the stock of private and technology firms |
| | | Characteristics | Intensity | $H_3$: number of projects approved by the Innovation Fund for Technology-based Small and Medium Enterprises |
| | | | Proactiveness | $H_4$: number of individual patent applications per 10,000 population |
| | Corporate TE | Output | Scale | $H_5$: output of new products |
| | | | Vitality | $H_6$: output of new products as % of gross industrial product |
| | | Characteristics | Intensity | $H_7$: R&D as % of sales income |
| | | | Proactiveness | $H_8$: number of invention patent applications in large industrial corporation. |

regional R&D expenditure as a percentage of regional budget; human resource development policy is measured as regional number of S&T personnel as a percentage of total number of S&T personnel in China, regional R&D personnel as a percentage of total R&D personnel in China, and total number of full-time R&D personnel; technology promotion policy is measured as the value of technological transactions in the technology market; and market support policy is measured as private firms as a percentage of total number of industrial businesses (see Table 14.3).

## Data

Cross-sectional data in this study were obtained from secondary sources. In consideration of the time lag that occurs before policy takes effect, data in 2003 were used to measure entrepreneurial policy, and data in 2004 were used to measure technological entrepreneurship. Data concerning the number of private technology firms and change in stock of private technology firms were obtained from the website of the Beijing Science and Technology Commission (www.bjkw.gov.cn); the number of applications granted by the Innovation Fund for Technology-based Small and Medium Enterprises (IFTSME) was compiled with data from the IFTSME's website (www.innofund.gov.cn); the number of individual patent applications per 10,000 population was compiled based on data from the *Yearbook of Chinese*

*Table 14.3* Indicators of entrepreneurial policy

| Target | Dimension | Sub-dimension | Indicators |
|---|---|---|---|
| Entrepreneurial policy | Policy promoting either independent TE or corporate TE | Financial support policy | $P_1$: R&D as % of GDP <br> $P_2$: regional R&D appropriations as % of regionalsgovernment expenditure. |
| | | Human resource development policy | $P_3$: regional number of S&T personnel as % of total number of S&T personnel in China <br> $P_4$: regional R&D personnel as % of total R&D personnel in China <br> $P_5$: total number of full-timemR&D personnel |
| | | Technology promotion policy | $P_6$: transaction value in the technology market |
| | | Market support policy | $P_7$: private firm as % of total industrial enterprises |

*Statistics 2005*; data related to all indicators of corporate technological entrepreneurship as well as private firms as a percentage of total industrial enterprises were obtained from the First Bulletin of Key Economic Census Data by Regions. Data related to R&D as a percentage of GDP and regional R&D personnel as a percentage of total R&D personnel in China were obtained from the *Bulletin of National Science and Technology*, compiled by the Chinese Statistics Bureau; data for indicators of entrepreneurship policy were obtained from the *Yearbook of Chinese S&T Statistics 2004*. All data were standardized to eradicate the differences in the units of measurement. The calculating formula is as follows:

$$\chi_{ij} = (\chi_{ij} - \chi_j)/S_j \ I = 1,2, \ldots, 30, j \equiv 1, 2, \ldots, 12$$

## Results

### Factor analysis

Factor analysis was conducted to reduce instability due to too many indicators. The values of KMO and Bartlett's Test of Sphericity are 0.7017 and 0.565, respectively, and the significant level of $\times 2$ test is 0.000, suggesting it suits a factor analysis (see Table 14.4). Sums of squared loading of TE explained 83.992 per cent of total variance (see Table 14.5) and sums of squared loading of EP explained 89.811 per cent of total variance (see Table 14.6).

To reduce the synthesis of initial factors, the component matrix was rotated. The results of the rotated component matrix are shown in Tables 14.7 and Table 14.8. Taking into account only variables with a loading greater than 0.5, component 1 in Table 14.7 has the highest correlation with $H_4$, $H_5$ and $H_8$, and we name it the technological innovation factor ($TF_1$); component 2 has a range of higher order relationships with $H_1$, $H_2$ and $H_3$, and we name it the independent technological entrepreneurship factor ($TF_2$); and component 3 has the highest correlations with $H_6$ and $H_7$, and we name it the corporate technological entrepreneurship factor ($TF_3$).

*Table 14.4* KMO and Bartlett's test

| | |
|---|---|
| KMO measure of sampling adequacy | 0.718 |
| Bartlett's test of sphericity | |
| Approx. chi-square | 182.583 |
| df | 28 |
| Sig. | 0.000 |
| KMO measure of sampling adequacy | 0.698 |
| Bartlett's test of sphericity | |
| Approx. chi-square | 318.705 |
| df | 21 |
| Sig. | 0.000 |

*Table 14.5* Total variance in technological entrepreneurship explained

| Component | Initial Eigenvalues | | | Rotation sums of squared loadings | | |
|---|---|---|---|---|---|---|
| | Total | % of variance | Cumulative % | Total | % of variance | Cumulative % |
| 1 | 4.619 | 57.743 | 57.743 | 2.856 | 35.696 | 35.696 |
| 2 | 1.266 | 15.829 | 73.573 | 2.361 | 29.518 | 65.213 |
| 3 | 1.002 | 12.522 | 86.094 | 1.670 | 20.881 | 86.094 |
| 4 | 0.503 | 6.287 | 92.381 | | | |
| 5 | 0.267 | 3.342 | 95.722 | | | |
| 6 | 0.189 | 2.367 | 98.090 | | | |
| 7 | 0.102 | 1.270 | 99.359 | | | |
| 8 | 5.128E-02 | 0.641 | 100.000 | | | |

*Note:* Extraction method = principal component analysis.

*Table 14.6* Total variance in entrepreneurship policy explained

| Component | Initial Eigenvalues | | | Rotation sums of squared loadings | | |
|---|---|---|---|---|---|---|
| | Total | % of variance | Cumulative % | Total | % of variance | Cumulative % |
| 1 | 4.651 | 66.436 | 66.436 | 3.433 | 49.037 | 49.037 |
| 2 | 1.213 | 17.331 | 83.767 | 1.938 | 27.685 | 76.722 |
| 3 | 0.571 | 8.151 | 91.918 | 1.064 | 15.196 | 91.918 |
| 4 | 0.436 | 6.231 | 98.150 | | | |
| 5 | 0.117 | 1.667 | 99.816 | | | |
| 6 | 1.023E-02 | 0.146 | 99.963 | | | |
| 7 | 2.618E-03 | 3.7398E-02 | 100.000 | | | |

*Note:* Extraction method = principal component analysis.

*Table 14.7* Rotated component matrix of TE

| | Component | | |
|---|---|---|---|
| | 1 | 2 | 3 |
| $p_1$ | 0.304 | 0.910 | −0.189 |
| $p_2$ | 0.766 | 0.242 | −0.223 |
| $p_3$ | 0.914 | 0.363 | 4.945E-02 |
| $p_4$ | 0.891 | 0.405 | 4584E-02 |
| $p_5$ | 0.935 | 0.263 | 0.141 |
| $p_6$ | 0.500 | 0.816 | −7.22E-02 |
| $p_7$ | 2.810E-02 | −0.141 | 0.974 |

*Notes:* Extraction method = principal component analysis; rotation method = Varimax with Kaiser normalization; [a]rotation converged in three iterations.

*Table 14.8* Rotated component matrix of EP

|  | Component | | |
|  | *1* | *2* | *3* |
|---|---|---|---|
| H₁ | 0.309 | 0.899 | 0.140 |
| H₂ | 0.205 | 0.916 | 0.132 |
| H₃ | 0.442 | 0.586 | 0.458 |
| H₄ | 0.841 | 0.245 | 0.283 |
| H₅ | 0.870 | 0.333 | 0.129 |
| H₆ | 0.397 | −3.36E-02 | 0.791 |
| H₇ | −4.43E-02 | 0.407 | 0.834 |
| H₈ | 0.948 | 0.185 | 7.436E-02 |

*Notes:* Extraction method = principal component analysis; rotation method = Varimax with Kaiser normalization; [a]rotation converged in five iterations.

In Table 14.8, component 1 has a range of higher order relationships with $P_2$, $P_3$, $P_4$ and $P_5$, and we name it the human resource policy factor ($PF_1$); component 2 has the highest correlations with $P_1$ and $P_6$, and we name it the financial policy factor ($PF_2$); and component 3 has the highest correlation with $P_7$, and we name it the market policy factor ($PF_3$).

### Cluster analysis

In order to identify relatively homogeneous groups displaying technological entrepreneurship in different regions of China, cluster analysis of three components of technological entrepreneurship was conducted with SPSS11.0. The results of cluster analysis are shown in Table 14.9. The values in Table 14.9 are the average values of components in the same categories.

For further analysis, we construct a composite factor of technological entrepreneurship (CFT) and entrepreneurship policy (CFP), respectively, using values of initial factors multiplied by the sum of squared loadings. The calculating formulas are shown in the following:

$$CFT = \Sigma TF_i * a_i \quad CFP = \Sigma PF_i * \beta_i$$

where $a_i$ and $\beta_i$ are the sum of squared loadings of *TE* and *EP*, respectively.

We calculated the values of the composite components of different regions in terms of the aforementioned formula. The top ten provinces based on the scores of composite factors are shown in Table 14.10.

Based on the aforementioned analysis, 30 provinces and municipalities can be categorized into seven clusters, as seen in Table 14.9:

- *Category 1: Shanghai.* The components of $TF_1$ and $TF_2$ are relatively high, indicating a high level of independent technological entrepreneurship

Table 14.9 Cluster analysis of regional technological entrepreneurship

| Province | 1 | 2 | 3 | 4 | 5 | 6 | 7 |
|---|---|---|---|---|---|---|---|
| | Shanghai | Beijing | Guangdong Zhejiang Jiangsu Shangdong | Chongqing | Tianjin | Shaanxi Liaoning | Hebei, Shanxi, Henan, Heilongjiang, Jilin, Jiangxi, Anhui, Hubei, Hunan, Fujian, Hainan, Sichuang, Guanxi, Neimenggu, Xinjiang, Gansu, Qinghai, Ningxia, Guizhou, Yunnan |
| $TF_1$ | 0.934 | 0.276 | 1.893 | −.675 | 1.851 | −0.954 | −0.403 |
| $TF_2$ | 2.587 | 1.679 | 0.227 | −1.236 | −1.382 | 1.816 | −0.309 |
| $TF_3$ | 0.231 | 2.111 | −0.278 | 2.949 | .974 | 0.847 | −0.343 |

Table 14.10 Top ten provinces of composite components of TE

| Province | Guangdong | Zhejiang | Tianjin | Jiangsu | Shanghai | Beijing | Shangdong | Fujian | Hunan | Liaoning |
|---|---|---|---|---|---|---|---|---|---|---|
| Scores | 1.06 | 0.90 | 0.58 | 0.49 | 0.37 | 0.32 | 0.25 | −0.01 | −0.05 | −0.06 |
| Order | 1 | 2 | 3 | 4 | 5 | 6 | 7 | 8 | 9 | 10 |

and technological innovation. Surprisingly, Shanghai has a relatively low component of $TF_3$, implying that corporate technological entrepreneurship activity in Shanghai is relatively weak.

- *Category 2: Beijing.* The relatively high components of $TF_2$ and $TF_3$ indicate a high level of technological entrepreneurship activity, but a relatively low value of $TF_1$ (0.276) suggests low technological innovation.
- *Category 3: Guangdong, Zhejiang, Jiangsu and Shangdong.* These are the relatively developed regions in China, in particular with reference to the private economy. The relatively high scores of $TF_1$ in the four provinces (average 1.893) show the relatively high entrepreneurial proactiveness and capability of technological innovation in individuals and established firms. But they lag behind their rivals in technological entrepreneurship. Furthermore, these provinces have very low scores of $TF_3$, which may result from inadequate investment and support from central government since they have well-developed private enterprises and fewer state-owned enterprises (SOEs).
- *Category 4: Chongqing.* The highest score of $TF_3$ in all regions (2.949) may result from its core position within traditional industries and the large investment associated with the western development strategy adopted by China. However, the very low scores of $TF_1$ and $TF_2$ indicate the low intensity of technological innovation and low proactiveness of individual technological entrepreneurship. Chongqing relied on the nation too much, leading to its low performance of technological entrepreneurship (income of S&T business is ranked as twenty-first in all Chinese provinces and municipalities).
- *Category 5: Tianjin.* The city has a relatively high score of $TF_1$ (1.851) but low scores of $TF_2$ and $TF_3$. Significantly, its $TF_2$ component is the lowest in China (−1.382), suggesting that the advantage of technological innovation has not been transformed into market advantage through technological entrepreneurship, which partly explains the unsatisfactory performance of entrepreneurship.
- *Category 6: Liaoning and Shaanxi.* The two provinces have relatively high scores of $TF_2$ and low scores of $TF_1$ and $TF_3$. Specifically, they have the lowest score of $TF_1$ in all regions. They have some ability to commercialize innovations, but lack of innovation will restrict their further development ultimately.
- *Category 7: Other areas.* These areas have no obvious advantage in either technology innovation or technological entrepreneurship. All of their $TF_1$, $TF_2$ and $TF_3$ scores are lower than those of the other six clusters.

### Regression

To test the hypotheses proposed in the second section, hierarchical regression analysis was conducted. $TF_1$, $TF_2$ and $TF_3$ and $PF_1$, $PF_2$ and $PF_3$ were entered into the regression equations. The results are shown in Table 14.11. As can be

*Table 14.11* Standardized regression coefficients of TE on EP (standard errors in parentheses)

| Independent variables | Constant | $PF_1$ | $PF_2$ | $PF_3$ | $R^2$ | F |
|---|---|---|---|---|---|---|
| $TF_1$ | (0.000) | 0.729** (5.452) | −0.055 (−0.412) | 0.004 (0.030) | 0.535 | 9.964** |
| $TF_2$ | (0.000) | 0.373* (2.393) | 0.465** (2.981) | 0.101 (0.646) | 0.366 | 5.008** |
| $TF_3$ | (0.000) | 0.101 (0.611) | 0.521** (3.136) | −0.034 (−0.205) | 0.283 | 3.417* |

\* Correlation is significant at the 0.05 level (two-tailed); \*\*correlation is significant at the 0.01 level (two-tailed).

seen, $TF_2$ has significant correlation with $PF_1$ and $PF_2$, while $TF_3$ only correlates significantly with $PF_2$. Considering the meaning of these composite components, hypotheses $H_{1a}$, $H_{2a}$ and $H_{3a}$ were supported, while $H_{4a}$ cannot be supported. Hypotheses $H_{2b}$ and $H_{3b}$ were tested, while $H_{1b}$ and $H_{4b}$ cannot be supported. All the testing results are shown in Table 14.12.

Linear regression analysis was conducted by comparing a composite factor of TE on the composite of entrepreneurial policy. The results are shown in Table 14.13. As can be seen, technological entrepreneurship and entrepreneurial policy are significantly correlated, suggesting that integrated policies addressing technology, human resources, finance and the market will improve the level of regional technological entrepreneurship activity.

## Conclusions and discussion

From the results obtained from factor analysis, cluster analysis and hierarchical regression analysis, we drew a few tentative conclusions.

First, our analysis highlights considerable regional differences in activity of technological entrepreneurship in China, reflecting huge variations in the degree of commercialization and corporate innovation between regions. The pattern of regional differences shows, one the one hand, that regions in the coastal area perform much better than other regions, as indicated in the scores of composite factors. Particularly, seven coastal regions stand out from the crowd. This picture does not look surprising as it confirms, from the perspective of technological entrepreneurship, the persistent problem in regional development in China. On the other hand, the spatial pattern of technological entrepreneurship also displays interesting inter-regional differences among the leading regions. Generally speaking, these leading regions perform well in technological innovation but Shanghai, Beijing and Liaoning are doing better in individual technological entrepreneurship, and only Beijing distinguishes itself from others in corporate technological entrepreneurship.

Two policy implications emerge from this analysis. (a) technological

*Table 14.12* Tests of hypotheses

| Hypothesis | Results | Hypothesis | Results |
|---|---|---|---|
| $H_{1a}$ | Support | $H_{3a}$ | Support |
| $H_{1b}$ | Support | $H_{3b}$ | Partial support |
| $H_{2a}$ | Support | $H_{4a}$ | No support |
| $H_{2b}$ | Support | $H_{4b}$ | No support |

\* Correlation is significant at the 0.05 level (two-tailed); \*\*correlation is significant at the 0.01 level (two-tailed).

*Table 14.13* Standardized regression coefficient of composite TE on composite EP

| | Constant | Composite factor of entrepreneurship policy | $R^2$ | F |
|---|---|---|---|---|
| Composite factor of TE | (−0.30) | 0.644** (4.449) | 0.414 | 19.792** |

*Notes:* standard errors in parentheses; \*\*correlation is significant at the 0.01 level (two-tailed).

entrepreneurship correlates very strongly with levels of regional development, suggesting that policies aiming to promote technological entrepreneurship will have a wide-ranging impact on the way regional differences in development will change. Policy-makers therefore need to be aware of the likelihood that entrepreneurship policy for technological innovation, if it stands alone, may actually lead to a divergence rather than a convergence of regional development. Hence, entrepreneurship policy should be incorporated into a broader policy framework that addresses wider issues of growth and development. Bearing in mind the different infrastructures and different stocks of resources, policy-makers also need to take an evolutionary approach towards technological entrepreneurship, as the actors that drive changes in the rate of entrepreneurship are not to be manifest over short time periods (Gartner and Shane 1995). (b) As corporate entrepreneurship relating to technological innovation is rather weak in most regions, our research suggests that corporate entrepreneurship has to become a policy priority so that technological innovation and building of independent innovation capacity in established firms can be properly supported.

Second, regional entrepreneurship policy appears to have a significant impact on technological entrepreneurship. Financial support and technology promotion policies are found to have a positive effect on individual and corporate technological entrepreneurship. Our analysis has also found a positive relationship between policies relating to human resource development and individual technological entrepreneurship. However, this relationship cannot be confirmed with regard to corporate technological entrepreneurship. The reason may be that there is an internal labour market operating within larger corporations and that human resource management in these companies has a big influence on what incentive structures are in place and how organizational behaviour in favour of creativity and innovation is encouraged. Accordingly, the impact government policy has on larger businesses is not as straightforward as it can be on the supply of individual entrepreneurs in the region. Our research also cannot establish a correlation between market support policy and all forms of technological entrepreneurship. This may reflect the limitation in data availability that constrains the construction and measurement of market support policies relating to technological entrepreneurship. More aspects of market development will need to be taken into account, e.g. enhancing labour's flexibility, strengthening the financial sector, building the information infrastructure, and so on.

Third, our research confirms the correlation between the integrated factors of technological entrepreneurship and entrepreneurial policy, thus providing evidence to support the argument that local governments should employ a more integrated entrepreneurial policy approach (Lundström and Stevenson 2001b). The results of cluster analysis in this chapter also reinforce the point that a holistic, policy-orientated approach rather than a fragmented, programme-oriented approach should be pursued (Hindle and Rushworth 2002). A good entrepreneurship policy environment is the result of the joined-up implementation of all entrepreneurial policies (Bahrami and Evans 1995).

This chapter contains some limitations. The indicators of technological entrepreneurship and independent technological entrepreneurship are measured as existing private S&T businesses. But existing private businesses are not necessarily new firms. Furthermore, validity is measured as a change in stock of firms between 1999 and 2004 and does not consider the situation of simultaneous exit and entry. At the same time, the indicators of entrepreneurial policy only represent part of the entrepreneurship framework conditions. Further study on indicators of entrepreneurial policy and the impact of entrepreneurial policy on technological entrepreneurship are therefore needed.

## References

Atoncic, R.D. and Hisrich, B. (2003) Privatization, corporate entrepreneurship and performance: testing a normative model, *Journal of Developmental Entrepreneurship*, 8 (3): 197–218.

Audretsch, D. and Thurik, A.R. (2001) Linking entrepreneurship and growth, *STI Working Papers*, Directorate for Science, Technology and Industry, Paris: OECD.

Audretsch, D.B. (2003) *Entrepreneurship Policy and the Strategy Management of Places: The Emergence of Entrepreneurship Policy*, Cambridge: Cambridge University Press.

Bahrami, H. and Evans, S. (1995) Flexible recycling and high-technology entrepreneurship, *California Management Reviews*: 37(3): 62–89.

Bridge, S., ONeill, K. and Cromie, S. (2003) *Understanding Enterprise, Entrepreneurship and Small Business*, Basingstoke: Palgrave Macmillan.

Chao, C.J.T and Teo, T.H.Y. (2004) Corporate entrepreneurial behavior of late-comer technology firms, International Engineering Management Conference, 18–21 October 2004, Singapore pp. 689–693.

Chesbrough, H. (2003) *Open Innovation: The New Imperative for Creating and Profiting from Technology*, Boston, MA: Harvard Business School Press.

Corman, J., Perles, B. and Vancini, P. (1988) Motivation factors influencing high-technology entrepreneurship, *Journal of Small Business Management*, 26(1): 36–42.

Covin, J.G. and Slevin, D.P. (1991) A conceptual model of entrepreneurship as firm behavior, *Entrepreneurship Theory and Practice*, 16(1): 7–25.

Cumming, D. (2006) Government policy towards entrepreneurial finance: innovation investment funds, *Journal of Business Venturing*, 21: 1–43.

Gartner, W.B. and Shane, S.A. (1995) Measuring entrepreneurship over time, *Journal of Business Venturing*, (10): 283–301.

Gnynawali, D.R. and Fogel, D.S. (1994) Environment for entrepreneurship development: key dimensions and research implications, *Entrepreneurship Theory and Practice*, Summer: 43–62.

Gregorio, D.D. and Shane, S. (2003), Why do some universities generate more start-ups than others?, *Research Policy*, 32: 209–227.

Guth, W.D. and Ginsberg, A. (1990) Guest editor's introduction: Corporate entrepreneurship, *Strategic Management Journal*, 11: 5–15.

Hart, D.M. (2001) Entrepreneurship policy: what it is and where it came from, in D. M. Hart (ed.), *The Emergence of Entrepreneurship Policy*, Cambridge: Cambridge University Press.

Hayton, J.C. (2005) Competing in the new economy: the outcomes of intellectual capital on corporate entrepreneurship in high-technology new ventures, *R&D Management*, 35(2): 137–155.

Hébert, R.F. and Link, A.N. (1989) In search of the meaning of entrepreneurship, *Small Business Economics*, 1(1): 39–49.

Hindle, K. and Rushworth, S. (2002) *Entrepreneurship: A Policy Primer*, Melbourne: Swinburne University of Technology.

Hindle, K. and Yencken, J. (2004) Public research commercialization, entrepreneurship and new technology-based firms: an integrated model, *Technovation*, 24: 793–803.

Hung, S.C and Chu, Y.Y. (2006) Stimulating new industries from emerging technologies: challenges for the public sector, *Technovation*, 26: 104–110.

Jones-Evans, D. (1996) Experience and entrepreneurship: technology-based owner-managers in the UK, *New Technology, Work and Employment*, 11(1): 39–54.

Kenney, M. and Burg, V. (1999) Technology, entrepreneurship and path dependence: industrial clustering in Silicon Valley and Route 128, *Industrial and Corporate Change*, 8(1): 67–104.

Kirzner, I. (1973) *Competition and Entrepreneurship*, Chicago: University of Chicago Press.

Knight, F.H. (1921) *Risk, Uncertainty and Profit*, New York: Houghton Mifflin.

Lerner, J. (1999) The government as venture capitalist: the long-run impact of the SBIR Program, *Journal of Management*, 72(3): 285–318.

Lumpkin, G.T. and Dess, G.G. (1996) Clarifying the entrepreneurial orientation construct and linking it to firm performance, *Academy of Management Review*, 21(1): 135–172.

Lundström, A. and Stevenson, L. (eds) (2001a) *Entrepreneurship Policy for the Future*, Stockholm: Swedish Foundation for Small Business Research.

Lundström A. and Stevenson L. (eds) (2001b) *Patterns and Trends in Entrepreneurship: SME Policy and Practice in Ten Economies*, Stockholm: Swedish Foundation for Small Business Research.

Miller, D. and Friesen, P.H. (1982) Innovation in conservative and entrepreneurial firms: two models of strategic momentum, *Strategic Management Journal*, 3(1): 1–25.

OECD (2001) *Transition Economies Forum on Entrepreneurship and Enterprise Development Policy: Guidelines and Recommendations*, Paris: OECD.

Reynolds, P.D., Camp, S.M., Bygrave, W.D., Autio, E. and Hay, M. (2001) *Global Entrepreneurship Monitor 2001 Summary Report*, London: London Business School and Babson College.

Sahlman, W.A. and Stevenson, H.H. (1991) Introduction, in W. A. Sahlman and H. H. Stevenson (eds), *The Entrepreneurial Venture*, Boston, MA: McGraw-Hill.

Schumpeter, J.A. (1934) *The Theory of Economic Development*, Cambridge, MA: Harvard University Press.

Shane, S. (2001) Technology regimes and new firm formation, *Management Science*, 47(9): 1173–1190.

Shane, S. and Venkataraman, S. (2000) The promise of entrepreneurship as a field of research, *Academy of Management Review*, 25(1): 217–226.

Sharma, P. and Chrisman, J.J. (1999) Toward a reconciliation of the definitional issues in the field of corporate entrepreneurship, *Entrepreneurship Theory and Practice*, Spring: 11–27.

Shea, R.P., Allen, T.J., Chevalier, A. and Roche, F. (2005) Entrepreneurial orientation, technology transfer and spin-off performance of US universities, *Research Policy*, 34: 994–1009.

Smilor, R.W., Gibson, D.V. and Dietrich, G.B. (1999) University spin-out companies: technology start-ups from UT-Austin, *Journal of Business Venturing*, 5(1): 63–76.

Smilor, R.W., Gibson, D.V. and Kozmetsky, G. (1989) Creating the technolis: high-technology development in Austin, Texas, *Journal of Business Venturing*, 4(1): 49–67.

Spencer, J.W., Murtha, T.P. and Lenway, S.A. (2005) How governments matter to new industry creation, *Academy of Management Review*, 30(2): 321–337.

Venkataraman, S. (2004) Regional transformation through technological entrepreneurship, *Journal of Business Venturing*, 19(1): 153–167.

Verheul, I., Wennekers, S., Audretsch, D. and Thurik, R. (2001) An eclectic theory of entrepreneurship: policies, institutions and culture, Tinbergen Institute Discussion Paper, Tinbergen Institute.

Wennekers, S. and Thurik, R. (2001) Institutions, entrepreneurship and economic performance, in A. Lundström and L. Stevenson (eds), *Entrepreneurship Policy for the Future*, Stockholm: Swedish Foundation for Small Business Research.

Zahra, S.A. and Shaker, A. (1991) Predictors and financial outcomes of corporate entrepreneurship: an exploratory study, *Journal of Business Venturing*, 6(4): 259–286.

# 15 Efficient and equitable compensation for agricultural land conversion

## Theory and an application for China

*Xiuqing Zou and Arie J. Oskam*

### Introduction

The phenomenon of agricultural land conversion is very common all over the world. The process assumes (at least in theory) that the state has the power to acquire private land in the public interest, subject to the payment of compensation (Larbi *et al.* 2004). However, in practice the compensation standard in terms of property rights transfer is not the same in different countries. For example, in the US, farmers will be compensated according to an open market value at the time of taking (Chen 2004). In France, the taking arbitrage agency decides the compensation standard with reference to other agricultural lands' market value in the neighbourhood of the expropriated land or the enrolled value of owners when the properties are taxed (ibid.). In China, the revised Land Management Law 1998 states that compensation for state expropriation consists of compensation for the loss of land, resettlement subsidies and compensation for young crops and fixtures.[1] Standard compensation for the loss of land is set at six to ten times the value of the average annual output of the land calculated over the three years prior to expropriation; subsidies to assist the village collectively in relocating the agricultural population are four to six times the value of the average annual output of the land calculated over the three years prior to expropriation. The total amount of land compensation and resettlement subsidies is capped at 30 times the value of the average annual output for the three prior years. Provinces, autonomous regions and provincial-level municipalities stipulate compensation standards for surface fixtures and young crops.

However, how much compensation is efficient and equitable for agricultural land conversion?[2] This chapter attempts to deal with this question. An essential element in determining compensation is the difference in the market value of land before expropriation and the market value of land after creating the opportunities for a new development.[3] This difference plays an important role in this chapter.

## Literature review

The process of enforced transformation of agricultural land shows up in the literature under different names: compulsory purchase, compulsory acquisition, expropriation, eminent domain or (titular) taking (Larbi *et al.* 2004). This also depends on the various jurisdictions. The compensation paid for land takings is the central element of this short literature review.

Different conclusions about the compensation paid for land expropriation have been drawn as a result of different assumptions. Using standard neo-classical assumptions, Blume *et al.* (1984) conclude that zero compensation is optimal for government expropriation motivated by the maximization of social welfare. However, zero compensation is a controversial issue for the courts, who often prefer to use the market value at the time of land expropriation as the appropriate level of compensation (Giammarino and Nosal 2005).

Fischel and Shapiro (1988, 1989) consider a situation where the government's expropriation decision is determined by maximizing the welfare of the majority of voters, and conclude that the compensation schedule will be a fraction of the expropriated property's current market value.

Hermalin's (1995) model is motivated by informational asymmetries between the government and investors. He assumes that the government takes private property only if the benefit to society exceeds the price that the government must pay for the property. Hermalin's main conclusion is that efficiency requires compensating the citizen not based on what the citizen loses, but rather on what society gains from the expropriation.

Nosal (2001) observes that a citizen might take actions that are beneficial for himself but not for society. He proposes a very simple tax and compensation scheme that implements the socially optimal allocation when a government's expropriation decision might be privately motivated and not in that society's best interest. An implication of the tax and compensation policy is that an individual whose land is expropriated will receive its full market value at the time of expropriation as compensation.

Plantinga *et al.* (2002) decompose agricultural land values into components reflecting the discounted value of agricultural production and the discounted value of future land development. By identifying these price components, they can determine if landowners face strong economic incentives to convert agricultural land. They find that future development rents are a substantial share of agricultural land values in areas surrounding urban centres.

Giammarino and Nosal (2005) examine how the compensation rule adopted by a country affects both private investment decisions and expropriation decisions. The model provides strong support for current market value compensation for the taking of property rights.

Chinese scholars have carried out some analysis of the compensation of land expropriation in China. For example, based on the cost valuation approach, He *et al.* (2006) put forward a proposal that compensation for peasants should be equal to average land granting price minus the total of development cost, management profit, land tax and fee, and land ownership value of the collective. Liu and Peng (2006) conclude that the compensation standard should be determined by the actual loss of land property rights of farmers, the land remise price, and the payment capability of the government.

Further to the above-mentioned studies, some issues regarding compensation remain to be explored. First, full market value compensation is most popularly accepted in developed market economies, but it cannot be directly applied in many developing countries, especially for a country like China with no market price for agricultural land conversion. Second, for the compensation of a fraction of the expropriated property's current market value, how much should be compensated has not been specified. Therefore, this method cannot be implemented in practice. Third, most of the above mentioned studies agree that land value increments after agricultural land conversion should be distributed among landless owners, the developer and the government, but the way in which they should be redistributed to ensure a balance between efficiency and equity is still an unsolved problem.

## Purpose and structure

In market economies, agricultural land's market value at the time of its taking basically reflects both agricultural land value before expropriation and the value of transferable agricultural land's development right.[4] However, the compensation of its market value often leads to problems of 'holdout' and over-investment (Blume *et al.* 1984). Holdout occurs if at least one of the landowners is not prepared to sell the land in a voluntary exchange, when large contiguous parcels of land are required for development. In market-developing countries, market transactions rarely occur for agricultural land conversion in terms of property rights transfer. The compensation is often regulated by the law or informal arrangements and can be unbalanced (Guo 2001; Larbi *et al.* 2004). If regulated by law, the central question is: which compensation is both efficient and equitable? Should it be based on the 'pure' agricultural land rent or the commercial land rent or an amount in-between?

The basic idea of this chapter is to start from the highest price for which a willing developer would buy the land and the lowest price for which a willing farmer would sell the land. Assuming bargaining power is equal, an efficient and equitable compensation is obtained under the hypothesis of a perfect market. From the state-of-the-art view of land appraisal, a practical approximation of the theoretical 'optimal' compensation will be derived.

The remainder of the chapter is composed as follows. Based on some basic assumptions, the second section explores the agricultural land value development mechanism during the taking process, which divides the process of agricultural land conversion into four phases. On the basis of Ricardo's 'capitalization formula', $P = R/i$, where $R$ is the annual rent and $i$ the discount rate, we accordingly explore land value formation in different phases.

In the third section, we derive the theoretical efficient and equitable compensation price when taking takes place under perfect market conditions, keeping bargaining power equal. At the same time, the value of agricultural land's development rights is measured. Based on the First Welfare Theorem, the Second Welfare Theorem and the Coase Theorem, some conclusions are derived.

The fourth section illustrates practical implications. From the state-of-the-art view of land appraising, practical approximation of its theoretical optimal compensation price will be derived.

The fifth section provides an example for China, with different options for land development and the final section offers a number of conclusions.

## Agricultural land value development mechanism during the land-taking process

### *Some basic assumptions*

To explore the agricultural land value development mechanism during the land-taking process, we start with some assumptions. Figure 15.1 shows the location of village C. There are $N$ units of agricultural lands in Village C; their property rights belong to the farmers. The government represents the public interest and makes a decision according to public interest.

During the process of urbanization and industrialization, the government decides all the agricultural land in village C will be developed for commercial use according to land use planning. However, which parcels will be taken and in which round of the total development period is not clear and might depend on arrangements made between the developer and the government. In the first-round development period, $n_1$ units are chosen for taking, according to zoning. In the second-round development period, $n_2$ units are to be taken; ultimately, all the agricultural land in village C is to be taken in the near future.

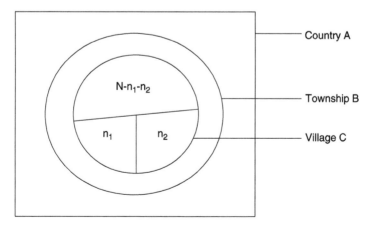

*Figure 15.1* The location of village C.

The farmers have no right to veto land use planning and the state taking their land. They can only bargain with the developer for reasonable compensation in terms of land ownership loss. The developer will pay the compensation and get land ownership for commercial use. After the land transaction, the government can tax part of the incremental land value according to specific circumstances.

### Process of agricultural land conversion to commercial development

Next, we introduce the process of agricultural land conversion. The process of the first-round agricultural land conversion to commercial development in village C is divided into four phases: planning process, investment negotiation, construction and commercial use (Figure 15.2):

- Phase 1 ($t_0$–$t_1$). N units of land in village C are used for agriculture. Government is planning land use but does not make a decision. Government's planning process has no special effects on farmers in village C. We denote the agricultural land value per unit in this phase as $P_N^1$. At time $t_1$, land use planning decision is made. All the agricultural land in village C will be developed for commercial use.
- Phase 2 ($t_1$–$t_2$). The government negotiates with the developer about the investment. The agricultural land value per unit in phase 2 is denoted as $P_N^2$. At time $t_2$, specific investment is decided. Only $n_1$ units of agricultural land in village C are chosen to be taken. The developer pays land price and farmers are compensated.
- Phase 3 ($t_2$–$t_3$). Construction is in progress. The value per unit of $n_1$ land under construction in phase 3 is denoted as $P_{n1}^3$. The value per unit of the other (N – $n_1$) agricultural lands that are not expropriated in phase 3 is denoted as $P_{N-n1}^3$. At time $t_3$, construction is completed. Developer begins to receive net rents from commercial use.
- Phase 4($t_3$ – ∞). The $n_1$ units of land are used for commercial purposes and developer gets continuous net land rents. We denote the value of $n_1$ commercial lands per unit in phase 4 as $P_{n1}^4$.

### The change of agricultural land value during the taking process

The change of agricultural land value during the taking process is illustrated in Figure 15.2.

Now we focus on the specific land value development in the first-round development period. The analysis of this section on land value formula combines the expressions used in previous studies about agricultural and developed land values (Cavailhes and Wavresky 2003; Plantinga and Miller 2001; Plantinga *et al.* 2002):

- Phase 1 ($t_0$–$t_1$). According to the Ricardo's 'capitalization formula', in a

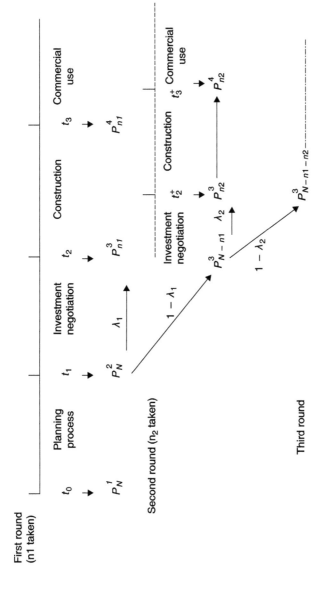

*Figure 15.2* Agricultural land value development mechanism during the taking process.

competitive land market the value of land equals the present discounted value of the stream of future rents. So in phase 1 agricultural land value equals the present discounted value of the stream of future agricultural net rents:

$$P_N^1 = \sum_{t=t_0+1}^{\infty} \frac{R_a}{(1 + i)^{t - t_0}} = \frac{R_a}{i} \tag{1}$$

where $R_a$ is future agricultural net rents (constant assumption) and $i$ is discount rate (constant assumption).

- Phase 2 $(t_1-t_2)$. At time $t_1$ the agricultural land value in village C is higher than in phase 1, as a result of potential capitalized rents from future commercial development due to the planning decision. However, because of uncertainty about the date of future development and future returns from development, the agricultural land value in phase 2 will lie between the value before the planning decision in phase 1 and the value at the time of taking in phase 3:

$$P_N^2 = E\left\{(1 - \lambda_1)\left[\sum_{t_1+1}^{t_2} \frac{R_a}{(1 + i)^{t - t_1}} + P_{N - n1}^3\right] + \lambda_1\left[\sum_{t_1+1}^{t_2} \frac{R_a}{(1 + i)^{t - t_1}} P_{N1}^3\right]\right\} \tag{2}$$

where $E$ is the expectation operator, $\lambda_1$ is expected probability of taking at time $t_2$, $P_{N - n1}^3$ is the value per unit of $N - n_1$ lands that are not taken in phase 3 and $P_{n1}^3$ is the value per unit of $n_1$ lands under construction in phase 3.

- Phase 3 $(t_2-t_3)$. The $n_1$ agricultural lands are chosen and taken for commercial development, but the other $(N - n_1)$ lands are not chosen in the first-round development period for commercial use. For the $n_1$ agricultural lands that are chosen and taken, their values in phase 3 are:

$$P_{n1}^3 = \sum_{t_3+1}^{\infty} \frac{R_m}{(1 + i)^{t - t_3}} - \sum_{t_2+1}^{t_3} \frac{C_m^t}{(1 + i)^{t - t_2}} \tag{3}$$

where $R_m$ is future commercial net rents (constant assumption) and $C_m^t$ is construction and development cost in year $t$ (from $t_2 + 1$ to $t_3$). For the other $(N - n_1)$ agricultural lands that are not chosen and taken in the first-round development period, their values in the first-round development period are:

$$P_{N - n1}^3 = E\left\{(1 - \lambda_2)\left[\sum_{t_2+1}^{t_2'} \frac{R_a}{(1 + i)^{t - t_2}} + P_{N - n1 - n2}^3\right]\right.$$

$$+ \lambda_2 \left[ \sum_{t_2^{*}}^{t_2^{*}} \frac{R_a}{(1 + i)^{t - t_2}} + P_{n2}^3 \right] \right\}$$   (4)

where $\lambda_2$ is expected probability of taking at time $t_2^{*}$ in the second-round development period, $t_2^{*}$ is expected taking time in second-round development period, $P_{N - n1 - n2}^3$ is the value per unit of $(N - n_1 - n_2)$ lands that are not taken in the second-round development period and $P_{n2}^3$ is the value per unit of $n_2$ lands under construction in second-round development period. Generally, due to higher expected taking probability over time, $P_{N - n1}^3 > P_N^2$. However, the other $(N - n_1)$ agricultural lands are still uncertain about the future development, so $P_{N - n1}^3 < P_{n1}^3$.

- Phase 4$(t_3 - \infty)$. Construction in the first-round development period is completed. Continuous commercial net rents are produced from $n_1$ taken lands.

$$P_{n1}^4 = \sum_{t_3^{*}}^{\infty} \frac{R_m}{(1 + i)^{t - t_3}}$$   (5)

where $R_m$ is future commercial net rents (constant assumption). Obviously, $P_{n1}^4 > P_{n1}^3$.

Summing up land value development of the above four phases in the first-round development period, we get

$$P_N^1 < P_N^2 < P_{N - n1}^3 < P_{n1}^3 < P_{n1}^4$$   (6)

### Deriving a land-taking price under equal bargaining power

Based on the above analysis, in this section we will derive a land-taking price under equal bargaining power. It is assumed that farmers and the developer are bargaining for a land transaction in a perfect market. Farmers know the highest price at which a willing developer will buy the land is $P_{n1}^3$ (If the price was higher, there would be no profit.) The developer knows the lowest price at which price a willing farmer will sell the land is $P_{N - n1}^3$ (because at phase 3, the other $(N - n_1)$ non-taken agricultural land value in the first-round development period amounts to $P_{N - n1}^3$. If the taken land price is lower than $P_{N - n1}^3$, farmers whose lands are taken will be considered to be in a disadvantage position compared to a farmer whose lands are not taken.)

As a result, we can imagine farmers and developer will share this part of incremental land value $(P_{n1}^3 - P_{N - n1}^3)$.

Keeping bargaining power equal, finally, the land transaction between farmers and developer will reach an equilibrium at the price $P_{n1}^e$, where $P_{n1}^e = \dfrac{P_{n1}^3 + P_{N - n1}^3}{2}$. In this situation the developer will get incremental land value $P_{n1}^d = \dfrac{P_{n1}^3 - P_{N-n1}^3}{2}$. Farmers will receive an incremental land value

$P_{n1}^f$, where $P_{n1}^f = \dfrac{P_{n1}^3 - P_{N-n1}^3}{2} + (P_{\overline{N-n1}}^3 - P_N^1) = \dfrac{P_{n1}^3 + P_{N-n1}^3 - 2\,P_N^1}{2}$, which is a

measure of the value of transferable agricultural land's development right for $n_1$ taken lands. If bargaining power is not equal, the incremental land value $(P_{n1}^3 - P_{N-n1}^3)$ will be distributed for a larger share to the more powerful party. Then the transacted price will not be $P_{n1}^e$.

Based on the First Welfare Theorem, there holds:
**Corollary 1** Keeping bargaining power equal, the compensation of $P_{n1}^e$, which farmers receive in terms of land ownership loss, will be Pareto-efficient and equitable under perfect market conditions.

Based on the Second Welfare Theorem, there holds:
**Corollary 2** If farmers receive the compensation of $P_{n1}^e$ in terms of land ownership loss, a Pareto-efficient and equitable allocation can be achieved.

Moreover, we assume that there is no transaction cost in this deal. Based on the Coase Theorem, there holds:
**Corollary 3** Regardless of who owns the agricultural land property rights initially, the efficient and equitable outcome $P_{n1}^e$ will occur under perfect market conditions, keeping bargaining power equal.

Combining Corollaries 1 and 2 with Corollary 3, we derive:
**Conclusion 1** If the individual farmer (the collective or state) owns the agricultural land property rights, under perfect market conditions the outcome $P_{n1}^e$ will occur during agricultural land conversion, keeping bargaining power equal; the compensation price $P_{n1}^e$ which the individual farmer (the collective or state) gets in terms of land ownership loss will be Pareto-efficient and equitable. The other way around, if the individual farmer (the collective or state) can get the compensation of $P_{n1}^e$ in terms of land ownership loss, a Pareto-efficient and equitable allocation can be achieved.

## Significant practical and policy implications

In this section, we try to derive a practical approximation of the theoretical optimal compensation price $P_{n1}^e$, which can be used as an alternative substitute for land market value in a market economy and can be used as a compensation standard for countries with no market transaction for agricultural land conversion in terms of property rights transfer.

From the state-of-the-art view of land appraisal, the appraiser can approximate the market values of $P_N^1$, $P_{n1}^3$ and $P_{n1}^4$ according to land appraisal method (the income approach, the cost approach or the comparable sales approach). The appraisal is to determine the market value of a property, utilizing all pertinent appraisal techniques.[5] The appraisal value is the market value of an asset that is derived from the appraisal process.[6] Accordingly, the appraisal values of $P_N^1$, $P_{n1}^3$ and $P_{n1}^4$ are denoted as $AP_N^1$, $AP_{n1}^3$ and $AP_{n1}^4$. Because

$$P_N^1 < P_N^2 < P_{N-n1}^3 < P_{n1}^3 < P_{n1}^4 \qquad (6)$$

there holds (because $P_{N-n1}^3 > P_N^1$):

$$P_{n1}^e > \frac{AP_{n1}^3 + AP_N^1}{2} \qquad (7)$$

$$P_{n1}^e \leq (\text{or} \geq) \frac{AP_{n1}^4 + AP_N^1}{2} \qquad (8)$$

That means, if $\dfrac{AP_{n1}^3 + AP_N^1}{2}$ is chosen to substitute the theoretical optimal price $P_{n1}^e$ in operational practice, farmers will get less than it, which reflects a balance in favour of the developer. If $\dfrac{AP_{n1}^4 + AP_N^1}{2}$ is chosen to substitute it, farmers may get less or more than it, or equal to it. In the latter situation, policy preference will be ambiguous.

In operational practice, the probability of $\dfrac{AP_{n1}^3 + AP_N^1}{2}$ chosen to substitute theoretical optimal price $P_{n1}^e$ is higher, considering implementation feasibility, for the developer usually has more economic and social power than the farmer.

Things bring us to:

**Conclusion 2** A practical approximation of the theoretical optimal price $P_{n1}^e$ in the first-round development period is $\dfrac{AP_{n1}^3 + AP_N^1}{2}$, considering implementation feasibility.

Based on conclusions 1 and 2, the following practical and policy implications hold:

- In reality, the actual compensation tends to be less than $P_{n1}^e$. First, due to lack of full information, farmers do not know the exact highest price $P_{n1}^3$ at which a willing developer will buy the land, and the developer does not know the lowest price $P_{N-n1}^3$ at which a willing farmer will sell his land. Second, usually the developer holds more bargaining power. Third, taking behaviour usually becomes compulsory expropriation in the name of public interest after land use planning and zoning. In land development practice, the relationship between the government and developer appears to be symbiotic, which usually leads to policy preferences for the developer during the taking process. As a result, judicial compensation according to taking arbitrage tends to be less than $P_{n1}^e$ when there is a conflict over compensation.

- For market economies, practical approximation $\dfrac{AP_{n1}^3 + AP_N^1}{2}$ of the actual market value provides an alternative effective solution with low transaction costs to the taking problems of 'holdout' and over-investment. The possibility of holdout can lead to an increase in the transaction cost for the purchase of contiguous parcels. Because $\dfrac{AP_{n1}^3 + AP_N^1}{2}$ is an approximate appraisal value of the efficient and equitable compensation, farmers can be directly compensated by means of the approximate appraisal value instead of a market price by a voluntary deal, when holdout occurs.

- For market-developing countries, especially for countries with no market transaction for agricultural land conversion, the practical approximation $\dfrac{AP_{n1}^3 + AP_N^1}{2}$ solves problems such as low compensation, government rent-seeking, potential social unrest, etc. to protect peasants' rights and obtain efficiency and equity through land value distribution (Guo 2001; Larbi *et al.* 2004).

- $\dfrac{AP_{n1}^3 - AP_N^1}{2}$ is an approximate practical measure of the value of $n_1$ transferable agricultural land's development rights $P_{n1}^f$ in the first-round development period.[7]

- After land transaction, the government can tax part of the incremental land value according to specific circumstances. There are three main elements to contribute to the incremental land value in agricultural land conversion: the farmer's land property transfer, the developer's investment, the government's planning decision and public infrastructure. According to the contribution rule of value formation, the government can gain part of the land value increments. However, if the government is directly engaged in the bargaining during the land transaction, the land market will tend to be largely distorted. The better method is to tax part of incremental land value after the transaction.

- In the *i*-th round development period, farmers can be compensated at the price of $\dfrac{AP_{ni}^3 + AP_N^3}{2}$ ($AP_{ni}^3$ is appraisal value for $P_{ni}^3$, and $P_{ni}^3$ is the market value per unit of $n_i$ lands under construction in the *i*-th round development period). $\dfrac{AP_{ni}^3 + AP_N^1}{2}$ can be regarded as a proximate practical measurement of the value of $n_i$ transferable agricultural land's development rights $P_{ni}^f$ in the *i*-th round development period (the specific reasoning is omitted due to chapter size constraints; further details are available upon request).

## A case for China: the application of the preceding compensation theory

### *Land value distribution during land expropriation and land development in China*

Land expropriation in China is known as a form of 'government behaviour', which is described as 'using coercive measures to acquire private land under compensatory arrangement by the government in the public interest' (Guo 2001). By law, the village collective has the right to use and supervise the use of the land, but it has no right to transfer land for commercial use. The state, on the other hand, 'may, in accordance with the law, expropriate land which is under collective ownership if it is in the public interest'. However, in practice collective-owned land is expropriated through nationalization for both public interest and commercial development because the collective has no land development rights and urban land belongs to the state. It is commonly claimed by local government that land development is to benefit the rural area and ultimately to achieve modernization, because it helps develop tertiary industry and provide business and employment opportunities for the rural population (ibid.). This is also called public interest by a number of local cadres during large-scale urbanization and industrialization in present-day China.

From the above analysis, it is not difficult to discover that local governments' land revenue is derived from the difference between the price paid for urban land use rights by developers and peasants' compensation. These land revenues belong directly to local government, that is, not in the form of tax. Obviously, local government becomes an economic agent, facing strong forces to maximize the land revenue behind the conversion of agricultural land to non-agricultural use.

However, in reality the actual land use right prices paid will be much lower than real land value, because the relationship between local governments and developers seems to be symbiotic (ibid. 2001). In present-day China, local economic development is the main political objective of local government. Urbanization and industrialization are the external embodiments of local leaders' performance. Sometimes the appointment of local cadres depends on their performance in attracting investment. Developers appear to be particularly distinguished guests of local government. Within this situation, local cadres' limitless demands for land development are far beyond the supply of normal investment. In order to attract developers to invest in their region, local governments' tend to negotiate on very friendly terms with developers regarding prices for land use rights. As a result, the actual land use rights will be paid for at discounted prices.

Concerning compensation, it tends to be as low as possible according to the law. First, according to the 1998 revised Land Management Law, the standard of compensation for land loss and resettlement subsidies can be between at least ten times and at most 30 times the value of the average annual output of the land calculated over the three years prior to expropriation. Second, the preceding analysis shows that, in fact, village leadership is the subordinate bureaucratic arrangement, although it is in the name of villagers' committees. Third, the present peasants' cooperative is a loose organization without close common interests. Peasants hardly have any political bargaining power during land expropriation. Fourth, the collective (in fact the village leadership) has the right to decide how to apportion compensation for land loss, and resettlement subsidies go to whoever is responsible for the resettlement.

Kung and Liu (1997) indicate that, although the amount of compensation paid to collective owners has increased substantially over time, peasants continue to receive extremely low levels of compensation, and in many cases no cash compensation whatsoever, in return for their land rights. Often, the collective retains all of the cash compensation under the pretext of expanding the collective economy, and simply spreads the burden of the land loss among all village peasants by conducting a large readjustment. Thus, those peasants who initially lose all or much of their land receive a somewhat smaller allocation at the expense of the land allocations for everybody else. This process has increasingly led to complaints by peasants. In some areas, serious unrest has resulted (Li 2003).

### An example for China: approximating optimal compensation

We suggest a practical approximation of the theoretical optimal compensation in China. Its advantages are: (1) income distribution from land value increments among peasants, developer and local government will be efficient and equitable; (2) appraisal values are easy to implement, and thus will provide low transaction costs; (3) systematic speculation in those areas waiting for development will be reduced; (4) corruption related to land development will be reduced; and (5) a temporary solution to central government's dilemma of present land institutional arrangement will be provided.

Now an example is given to calculate approximate optimal compensation.

**Assumption** In some locations, yearly net rent of agricultural land for rice is 1260 $/ha,[8] its commercial land ownership value under construction is 80$/m², its residential land ownership value under construction 60 $/m² and its industrial land ownership value under construction 40 $/m²; $i$ equals 6 per cent. It is assumed that 40 per cent of the total land area (one hectare) is developed for commercial (industrial or residential) use.

The specific calculation process is omitted due to chapter length constraints (further details are available upon request).[9] Results are summarized as follows (Table 15.1).

Table 15.1 shows that for one-hectare of agricultural land converted to 40-year commercial use, approximate optimal compensation is 154948$. The value of transferable agricultural land development rights is 133948$. The local government can tax the developer at 46882$. No matter which kind of usage agricultural land will be developed for, the theoretical distribution ratio of land value increments among peasants, developers and local government is 1: 0.65: 0.35.

According to present compensation standards described by the 1998 revised Land Management Law, the collective can gain the compensation for land loss and resettlement subsidies [10 × 1920, 30 × 1920] $/ha, which is (19200, 57600) $/ha, no matter what kind of usage agricultural land will be converted to. In fact peasants can only get their share depending on the how the collective apportions it. No statistics exist for public data relating to the price developers pay local governments for state-owned land use rights after expropriation.

Finally, we calculate the ratio of the present highest compensation standard by the law to the lowest 50-year theoretical compensation for industrial use, which is 57600/86156 = 67 per cent.

## Concluding remarks

How much compensation is efficient and equitable for agricultural land conversion? Essentially, this question is oriented towards the distribution of land value increments among farmers, the developer and the government, due to the difference in the market value of land before taking and the market value of land after creating the opportunity for a new development. Three main elements contribute to incremental land value: farmers' land property transfer, the developer's investment, and the government's planning decision and public infrastructure. Concerning compensation, this chapter not only pays attention to the efficiency point of view, but also to equity and income distribution effects.

*Table 15.1* Approximate optimal compensation in China

|  | *40-year commercial use* | *70-year residential use* | *50-year industrial use* |
|---|---|---|---|
| $P^e$ | 154948 | 138972 | 86156 |
| $P^f$ | 133948 | 107472 | 65156 |
| T | 46882 | 37615 | 22805 |

Theoretical distribution ratio of land value increments
  peasants: developer: local government = 1:0.65:0.35

*Notes:* $P^e$ – approximate optimal compensation; $P^f$ – the value of transferable agricultural land's development right; T – local tax.

This chapter has developed a method to analyse a compensation standard for state expropriation. The basic idea is to get the highest price for a willing developer to buy the land and the lowest price for willing farmers to sell the land, through exploring the land value development mechanism of agricultural land conversion during the land-taking process. Under perfect market conditions, efficient and equitable compensation is obtained, keeping bargaining power equal. After land transaction, the government can tax part of the incremental land value according to specific circumstances. From the state-of-the-art view of land appraisal, an approximation is substituted for a theoretical level of compensation. Under what circumstances would appraisers be likely to offer impartial and unbiased appraisal values? Whether such an approach works in practice depends, of course, on the professional standards of land appraisal. More effort is still needed to deal with this issue.

In the present China, property rights of agricultural land are ill specified and ambiguous. There is no market transaction for agricultural land conversion. There is no perfect market or equal bargaining power. So the present compensation is inefficient or inequitable, compared to the theoretical level of compensation. The difficulty of agricultural land's property rights arrangement in terms of agricultural land conversion is how to assign transferable agricultural land's development rights to peasants. The practical approximation of the theoretical level of compensation provides a solution to a number of problems. According to the compensation developed in this chapter, an example for China shows that peasants can obtain half of the land value increments, the developer 32 per cent and the local government 18 per cent. This income distribution is mainly oriented towards the one of the poorest groups in China with limited opportunities.

Theoretically, this chapter's conclusion enriches property rights theory. The central thesis of the property rights view is that the particular structure of the property rights in an economy influences the allocation and utilization of economic resources in specific and predictable ways. As a result, the value of traded assets depends on how the property rights over resources are defined (Furubotn and Pejovich 1972). Property rights have a value and a function only if they are specified, protected and enforceable. In this chapter, we start with the hypothesis of well-specified private land property rights, and reach an efficient and equitable compensation under perfect market conditions and with equal bargaining power. An example for China utilizes the theoretical optimal compensation (or its approximation) to obtain both efficiency and equity, maintaining the ambiguous collective-owned property rights structure. In this sense, essentially, peasants have here enjoyed the value of transferable agricultural land development rights through the price mechanism, even though law does not assign this type of property right to them. This illustrates that the value or price of traded assets is more essential than its nominal property rights structure. This point has a significant policy implication. That is, the government can simultaneously use a policy structuring institutional property rights and a price mechanism to obtain specific policy objectives.

In sum, for a market economy, the compensation for agricultural land conversion, developed in this chapter, provides an alternative solution, with low transaction costs, to the taking problems of holdout and over-investment. For countries with no market transaction for agricultural land conversion, it can be used as a compensation standard to solve problems such as low compensation, government rent-seeking and potential social unrest, to obtain efficiency and equity.

## Acknowledgements

An earlier version of this chapter was published by Wiley-Blackwell. Xiuqing Zou and Arie J. Oskam (2007) New compensation standard for land expropriation in China, *China and World Economy*, 15(5), 107–120. We are grateful to Wiley-Blackwell for their permission to use the material for this chapter.

## Notes

1 Fixtures are fixed capital goods connected with land, such as buildings, irrigation channels, etc.
2 In this chapter, we focus on agricultural land conversion for economic development, such as commercial, industrial and residential use. We do not consider the conversion to public parks, roads, etc.
3 Here, we do not calculate the total social cost or social benefit for economic development.
4 The value of a development right is the present value of the additional rents accruing to the landowner when the parcel is developed in the future (Plantinga and Miller 2001).
5 www.remax-western.ca/3001_glossary.html.
6 www.fhhlc.com/Glossary/Definition.asp?term=Appraisal+value.
7 We know that $P_{n1}^{f} = \dfrac{P_{n1}^{3} - P_{N-n1}^{3}}{2} + (P_{N-n1}^{3} - P_{N}^{l}) = \dfrac{P_{n1}^{3} + P_{N-n1}^{3} - 2P_{N}^{l}}{2} = \dfrac{P_{n1}^{3} + P_{N}^{l}}{2} +$

$\dfrac{P_{n1}^{3} - P_{N}^{l}}{2}$, for $P_{N-n1}^{3}$ is far less than $P_{n1}^{3}$, *and accurately evaluating* $P_{N-n1}^{3}$ from the state-of-the-art view of land appraisal is very difficult, so we can omit this part of $\dfrac{P_{N-n1}^{3} - P_{N}^{l}}{2}$ with $P_{n1}^{f}$ *is* measured.

8 Agricultural land is assumed to be used for rice production. Annual output 12000 kg/ha, with a price of 0.16$/kg, total yearly output value 1920$/ha. Economic costs are 660 $/ha, which include fertilizer, seed and pesticides. Yearly net rent is (1920 – 660) = 1260$/ha. Labour cost is not incorporated because it is considered a fixed cost of peasant households who often devote nearly 75 per cent of their working time to rice production.
9 According to the law in China, an individual can only have 40-year use rights of state-owned land for commercial development, or its 50-year use rights for industrial development, or its 70-year use rights for residential development. After that period, the government takes the land back. So, in this example we only calculate

40-year commercial land use rights value, 50-year industrial land use rights value, and 70-year residential land use rights value, but not ownership value.

## References

Blume, L., Rubinfeld, D. and Shapiro, P. 1984. The taking of land: when should compensation be paid?, *Quarterly Journal of Economics* 99, 71–92.

Cavailhes, J. and Wavresky P. 2003. Urban influences on periurban farmland prices, *European Review of Agricultural Economics* 30(3), 333–357.

Chen, H. 2004. Tu Di Zheng Yong Bu Chang Zhi Du De Guo Ji Bi Jiao Ji Jie Jian (International comparison of compensation system of land expropriation and its use for reference), *Shi Jie Nong Ye* (*World Agriculture*) 8, 13–15.

Fischel, W. and Shapiro, P. 1988. Takings, insurance, and Michelman: comments on economic interpretations of just compensation law, *Journal of Legal Studies* 17, 269–293.

Fischel, W. and Shapiro, P. 1989. A constitutional choice model of compensation for takings, *International Review of Law and Economics* 9, 115–128.

Furubotn, E.G. and Pejovich, S. 1972. Property rights and economic theory: a survey of recent literature, *Journal of Economic Literature* 10, 1137–1162.

Giammarino, R. and Nosal, E. 2005. Loggers vs. campers: compensation for the taking of property rights, *Journal of Law Economics and Organization* 21(1), 136–152.

Guo, X. 2001. Land expropriation and rural conflicts in China, *China Quarterly* 166, 422–439.

He, Xiaodan, Weidong Liu and Xiaoling Zhang 2006. Study on rational determination of the standard of compensatory payment for requisition of land in Zhejian Province, *Zhejiang Daxue Xuebao* (*Journal of Zhejiang University*) 32(2), 227–231.

Hermalin, B. 1995. An economic analysis of takings, *Journal of Law, Economics and Organization* 11, 64–86.

Kung, J. and Liu, S. 1997. Farmers' preferences regarding ownership and land tenure in post- Mao China: unexpected evidence from eight counties, *China Journal* 38(48), 33–63.

Larbi, W.O., Antwi, A. and Olomolaiye, P. 2004. Compulsory land acquisition in Ghana: policy and praxis, *Land Use Policy* 21(2), 115–127.

Li, P. 2003. Rural land tenure reforms in China: issues, regulations and prospects for additional reform, at: www.fao.org/docrep/006/y5026e/y5026e06.htm.

Liu, W. and Peng, J. 2006. Rational calculation of the compensation standard of land expropriation, *Zhongguo Tudi Kexue* (*China Land Science*) 2(1), 7–11.

Nosal, E. 2001. The taking of land: market value compensation should be paid, *Journal of Public Economics* 82(3), 431–443.

Plantinga, A.J. and Miller, D.J. 2001. Agricultural land values and the value of rights to future land development, *Land Economics* 77, 56–67.

Plantinga, A.J., Lubowski, R.N. and Stavins, R.N. 2002. Effects of potential land development on agricultural land prices, *Journal of Urban Economics* 52, 561–581.

# Index

Note: *italic* page numbers denote references to figures/tables.

For Product Safety Concerns and Information please contact our EU
representative  GPSR@taylorandfrancis.com
Taylor & Francis Verlag GmbH, Kaufingerstraße 24, 80331 München, Germany

www.ingramcontent.com/pod-product-compliance
Ingram Content Group UK Ltd.
Pitfield, Milton Keynes, MK11 3LW, UK
UKHW021116180425
457613UK00005B/111